Pfeiffer
& COMPANY

THE 1980 ANNUAL HANDBOOK FOR GROUP FACILITATORS

(The Ninth Annual)

Editors
J. WILLIAM PFEIFFER, Ph.D., J.D.
and
JOHN E. JONES, Ph.D.

Associate Editor
MARSHALL SASHKIN, Ph.D.

Managing Editor
MARION METTLER

Amsterdam • Johannesburg • London
San Diego • Sydney • Toronto

Looseleaf ISBN: 0-88390-096-3
Paperbound ISBN: 0-88390-097-1
ISSN: 1046-333X

Library of Congress Catalog Card Number 73-92841

Printed in the United States of America

Published by

Pfeiffer & Company
8517 Production Avenue
San Diego, California 92121
619-578-5900
FAX (619) 578-2042

Pfeiffer & Company
4190 Fairview Street
Burlington, Ontario L7L 4Y8
Canada
416-632-5832, FAX 416-333-5675

Pfeiffer & Company
Roggestraat 15
2153 GC Nieuw-Vennep
The Netherlands
31-2526-89840, FAX 31-2526-86885

Pfeiffer & Company
Ground Floor; 6-8 Thomas Street
Chatswood NSW 2067
Australia
61-2-415-1344, FAX 61-2-415-1051

PREFACE

The 1980 *Annual* signals a new decade of service for University Associates and of challenge for the field of human relations training. University Associates now has a European office as well as a Canadian subsidiary and a Canadian training center and has moved into new expanded offices in San Diego. At the same time that our operations have grown abroad to meet new needs, we are faced with an economic situation at home that may bode ill for those concerned with human relations training (including its various extensions and offshoots, such as organization development). In stressful times, it is the "soft," "support," and "service" areas that traditionally are cut first. Ironically, such savings are false, for they represent the liquidation of human resources, in the same way that the closing and sale of a factory represent the liquidation of physical assets. In both cases, the organization involved in such cutting back is in for more hard times when the economic situation improves, for human capacity is needed no less than physical capacity when full production returns.

Group facilitators can help prevent human-resource liquidation in two ways: first, by providing training that allows people to understand the danger involved and, second, by applying behavioral-science knowledge to deal with the problems produced by difficult economic conditions. In the broadest sense, this means improving individual and organizational problem solving. Users of this ninth *Annual* will find numerous resources that can be helpful in working through some of the economic problems we face as these problems impact people and organizations.

Our ultimate aim is effective application. To facilitate this, we continue our unusual policy that allows users to duplicate and modify University Associates *Annual* materials for educational and training purposes *only*. Although no special permission is required, users must identify the materials with the credit statement found on the copyright page of this *Annual*. However, *if University Associates materials are to be reproduced in publications for sale or are intended for large-scale distribution, prior written permission is required.*

Many people have been involved in creating this *Annual*, most of them practitioners of human relations training who share with us their original ideas and materials. We thank them for their patient cooperation in the face of the normal problems of putting together a publication. We also offer our appreciation to the University Associates staff members who have invested special energy, effort, and expertise in the making of this volume.

It is of interest to note that being published in the *Annual* is coming to be treated as worthy of "legitimate" academic credit. Although the *Annual* does not have a formal editorial board of Ph.D.-level behavioral scientists, most selections are made after consultation with professional peers and always involve both senior editors. Because we think there is an undiminished need for quality resources in the field, we want to encourage *Annual* users to continue to submit practical, useful materials suitable for applied behavioral science practitioners and trainers.

San Diego, California
December, 1979

J. William Pfeiffer
John E. Jones

About Pfeiffer & Company

Pfeiffer & Company (formerly University Associates, Inc.) is engaged in publishing, training, and consulting in the field of human resource development (HRD). The organization has earned an international reputation as the leading source of practical publications that are immediately useful to today's facilitators, trainers, consultants, and managers. A distinct advantage of these publications is that they are designed by practicing professionals who are continually experimenting with new techniques. Thus, readers benefit from the fresh but thoughtful approach that underlies Pfeiffer & Company's experientially based materials, resources, books, workbooks, instruments, and tape-assisted learning programs. These materials are designed for the HRD practitioner who wants access to a broad range of training and intervention technologies as well as background in the field.

The wide audience that Pfeiffer & Company serves includes training and development professionals, internal and external consultants, managers and supervisors, team leaders, and those in the helping professions. For its clients and customers, Pfeiffer & Company offers a practical approach aimed at increasing people's effectiveness on an individual, group, and organizational basis.

TABLE OF CONTENTS

*See Structured Experience Categories, p. 9, for an explanation of numbering.

GENERAL INTRODUCTION TO THE 1980 *ANNUAL*

This is the ninth *Annual Handbook for Group Facilitators*. Our primary aims continue to be gathering and sharing a variety of high-quality resource materials that will be of practical value for human relations trainers, organization development practitioners, educators, and others in the broad category of "group facilitators." The materials in this *Annual* are unique and do not duplicate the content of the eight previous *Annuals*.

Following the same basic format created for the 1972 *Annual*, this volume contains five sections: Structured Experiences, Instrumentation, Lecturettes, Theory and Practice, and Resources. Each section contains a specific type of resource materials.

Every *Annual* includes twelve structured experiences—each group activity, in one of eleven content categories, is described step-by-step to provide learning through direct experience. All 280 of the structured experiences published by University Associates in the *Annuals* and the *Handbook of Structured Experiences for Human Relations Training* (Vols. I-VII) are categorized in the list on pages 9 and 10.[1] Although the structured experiences in each *Annual* are selected for diversity, a frequent theme this year centers on power and conflict in a world of scarce resources, perhaps reflecting a major current concern. Among University Associates' published structured experiences, the facilitator should be able to find an experience relevant to a specific training concern. The value of any structured experience, however, is most critically dependent on the processing of the data generated, an issue discussed in detail in the introduction to the Structured Experiences section.

Four paper-and-pencil instruments are included in the second section, Instrumentation. One is directed to an individual's style of thinking and acting, while another concerns organizational diagnosis; the remaining two deal with individual-organizational interaction: roles and managers' attitudes toward job enrichment. As is true in earlier *Annuals*, these instruments are intended primarily for training and practice, rather than for research. It therefore becomes particularly important that the strengths and weaknesses of such instruments be recognized—a topic discussed in the introduction to the Instrumentation section, in the context of how instruments might be developed spontaneously within a training or consulting session.

Lecturettes are brief, focused conceptual presentations relating to practical issues in human relations training. Topics in this third section of the *Annual* deal with individual, group, and organizational concerns. Group facilitators can use these short discussions as the bases for more detailed presentations, as handouts, or as reference materials relating to structured experiences or other workshop training activities. The linkage between concepts and experiences is important if people are to apply what they learn; this concern is presented fully in the introduction to the Lecturettes section.

Papers in the Theory and Practice section are intended for the professional development of the facilitator rather than for participants. The intent of this fourth section of the *Annual* is to assist the facilitator by showing how theoretical issues relate to the practice of

---

[1] More detail on each structured experience category is provided in J. W. Pfeiffer & J. E. Jones, *Reference Guide to Handbooks and Annuals* (3rd ed.). San Diego, CA: University Associates, 1979.

human relations training and organization development. Each paper provides a sound statement of a significant topic or issue. The introduction to this section offers a pragmatic presentation of the theoretical issue of model building.

The final section of the *Annual*, Resources, contains four professionally relevant "tools" for the group facilitator—a bibliography, a glossary, and two directories. The introduction to the Resources section discusses the nature of such tools and their use.

An alphabetical list of the contributors to the *Annual* can be found at the end of the volume. Users will find the information useful if they wish to locate the authors of specific pieces for feedback, comments, or questions. Further information about contributors is presented in brief biographical sketches at the conclusion of articles.

The editors are pleased at what we believe is a continued increase in the quality of materials submitted to us for publication. As is to be expected with such a wide variety of materials, however, not all users will find everything in this *Annual* of equal value. We invite comments, ideas, materials, or suggestions that will help us make the next *Annual* as useful as possible to our users.

INTRODUCTION TO THE
STRUCTURED EXPERIENCES SECTION

In creating, adapting, and conducting structured experiences, the facilitator needs both a unifying theory and a practical translation of that thinking. This introduction will explore a variety of methods and design features that can be incorporated into a range of structured experiences. The facilitator can use these ideas both in developing structured experiences and in making sure that published ones fit the learning readiness of a particular group at a particular time.

FLESHING IN THE EXPERIENTIAL LEARNING CYCLE

Experiential learning occurs when a person engages in some activity, looks back at the activity critically, abstracts some useful insight from the analysis, and puts the result to work. Of course, this process is experienced spontaneously in everyone's ordinary living. We call it an *inductive* process: proceeding from observation rather than from a priori "truth" (as in the *deductive* process). Learning can be defined as a relatively stable change in behavior, and that is the usual purpose of training. A *structured* experience provides a framework in which the inductive process can be facilitated. The steps follow those of a theoretical cycle:

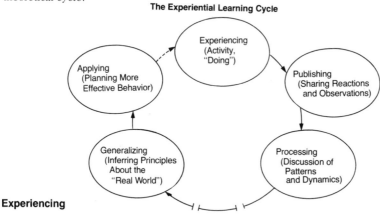

The Experiential Learning Cycle

Experiencing (Activity, "Doing")

Applying (Planning More Effective Behavior)

Publishing (Sharing Reactions and Observations)

Generalizing (Inferring Principles About the "Real World")

Processing (Discussion of Patterns and Dynamics)

Experiencing

The initial stage is the data-generating part of the structured experience. It is the step that is often associated with "games," or fun. Obviously, if the process stops after this stage, all learning is left to chance, and the facilitator has not completed the task. Almost any activity that involves either self-assessment or interpersonal interaction can be used as the "doing" part of experiential learning. The following are common individual and group activities:

- making products
- creating art objects
- writing skits

- role playing
- transactions
- problem solving
- feedback
- self-disclosure
- fantasy
- choosing
- nonverbal communication
- writing
- analysis of case material
- bargaining
- planning
- competing
- confronting

These activities can be carried out by individuals, dyads, triads, small groups, group-on-group arrangements, or large groups. Of course, the learning objectives would dictate both the activity and the appropriate groupings.

It is important to note that the objectives of structured experiences are necessarily general and are stated in terms such as "to explore. . . ," "to examine. . . ," "to study. . . ," "to identify. . . ," etc. Inductive learning means learning through discovery, and the exact things to be learned cannot be specified beforehand. All that is wanted in this stage of the learning cycle is to develop a common data base for the discussion that follows. This means that whatever happens in the activity, whether expected or not, becomes the basis for critical analysis; participants may learn serendipitously.

Sometimes facilitators spend an inordinate amount of energy planning the activity but leave the examination of it unplanned. As a consequence, learning may not be facilitated. It is axiomatic that the next four steps of the experiential learning cycle are even more important than the experiencing phase. Accordingly, the facilitator needs to be careful that the activity does not generate excess data or create an atmosphere that makes discussion of the results difficult. There can be a lot of excitement and "fun" as well as conflict in human interaction, but these are not synonymous with learning; they provide the common references for group inquiry.

Publishing

The second stage of the cycle is roughly analogous to inputting data, in data-processing terms. People have experienced an activity, and now they are presumably ready to share what they saw and/or how they felt during the event. The intent here is to make available to the group the experience of each individual. This step involves finding out what happened within individuals, at both cognitive and affective levels, while the activity was progressing. A number of methods help to facilitate the publishing, or declaring, of the reactions and observations of individual participants:

- Recording data during the experiencing stage (putting data "in the can" for later discussion)
  √ ratings of such things as productivity, satisfaction, confidence, leadership, communication, etc.
  √ adjectives capturing feelings at various points

4

- Whips
  √ quick free-association go-arounds on various topics concerning the activity
- Subgroup sharing
  √ generating lists such as the double-entry one "What we saw/how we felt"
- Posting/roundrobin listing
  √ total-group input recorded on newsprint
- Ratings
  √ developing ratings of relevant dimensions of the activity, tallying and averaging these measures
- Go-around
  √ systematic "interviewing" of individuals about their experience during the activity
- Nominations
  √ variation of "Guess Who?" technique, asking participants to nominate each other for roles they played during the experiencing stage
- Interviewing pairs
  √ asking each other "what" and "how" questions about the activity

Publishing can be carried out through free discussion, but this requires that the facilitator be absolutely clear about the differences in the steps of the learning cycle and distinguish sharply among interventions in the discussion. Group members' energy is often focused on staying inside the activity, and they need to be nudged into separating themselves from it in order to learn. (See, for example, the discussion of "de-roling" role players, on page 191 of the 1979 Annual.) Structured techniques such as those listed above make the transition from stage one to stage two cleaner and easier. That, after all, is the job of the facilitator—to create clarity with ease.

Processing

This stage can be thought of as the fulcrum, or the pivotal step in experiential learning. It is the systematic examination of commonly shared experience by those persons involved. This is the "group dynamics" phase of the cycle, in which participants essentially reconstruct the patterns and interactions of the activity from the published individual reports. This "talking-through" part of the cycle is critical, and it cannot be either ignored or designed spontaneously if useful learning is to be developed. The facilitator needs to plan carefully how the processing will be carried out and focused toward the next stage, generalizing. Unprocessed data can be experienced as "unfinished business" by participants and can distract them from further learning. Selected techniques that can be used in the processing stage are listed below:

- Process observers
  √ reports, panel discussions (observers are often unduly negative and need training in performing their functions)
- Thematic discussion
  √ looking for recurring topics from the reports of individuals
- Sentence completion
  √ writing individual responses to such items as "The leadership was. . . ," "Participation in this activity led to . . ."

- Questionnaires
  - √ writing individual responses to items developed for the particular structured-experience activity (for example, see "Motivation Feedback Opinionnaire" in the Structured Experiences section of the 1973 *Annual*)
- Data analysis
  - √ studying trends and correlations in ratings and adjectives elicited during the publishing stage
- Key terms
  - √ posting a list of dimensions to guide the discussion
- Interpersonal feedback
  - √ focusing attention on the effect of the role behaviors of significant members in the activity

This step should be thoroughly worked through before going on to the next. Participants should be led to look at what happened in terms of dynamics but not in terms of "meaning." What occurred was real, of course, but it was also somewhat artificially contrived by the structure of the activity. It is important to keep in mind that a consciousness of the dynamics of the activity is critical for learning about human relations outside of the laboratory setting. Participants often anticipate the next step of the learning cycle and make premature generalization statements. The facilitator needs to make certain that the processing has been adequate before moving on.

Generalizing

An inferential leap has to be made at this point in the structured experience, from the reality inside the activity to the reality of everyday life outside the training session. The key question here is "So what?" Participants are led to focus their awareness on situations in their personal or work lives that are similar to those in the activity that they experienced. Their task is to abstract from the processing some principles that could be applied "outside." This step is what makes structured experiences practical, and if it is omitted or glossed over the learning is likely to be superficial. Here are some strategies for developing generalizations from the processing stage:

- Fantasy
  - √ guiding participants to imagine realistic situations "back home" and determining what they have learned in the discussion that might be applicable there
- Truth with a little "t"
  - √ writing statements from the processing discussion about what is "true" about the "real world"
- Individual analysis
  - √ writing "What I learned," "What I'm beginning to learn," "What I re-learned"
- Key terms
  - √ posting topics for potential generalizations, such as leadership, communication, feelings, etc.
- Sentence completion
  - √ writing completions to items such as "The effectiveness of shared leadership depends on . . ."

6

It is useful in this stage for the group interaction to result in a series of products—generalizations that are presented not only orally but also visually. This strategy helps to facilitate vicarious learning among participants. The facilitator needs to remain nonevaluative about what is learned, drawing out the reactions of others to generalizations that appear incomplete, undivided, or controversial. Participants sometimes anticipate the final stage of the learning cycle also, and they need to be kept on the track of clarifying what was learned before discussing what changes are needed.

In the generalizing stage it is possible for the facilitator to bring in theoretical and research findings to augment the learning. This practice provides a framework for the learning that has been produced inductively and checks the reality orientation of the process. But the practice may encourage dependence on the facilitator as the source of defensible knowledge and may lessen commitment to the final stage of the cycle. The outside information is not "owned" by the participants—a common phenomenon of *deductive* processes.

Applying

The final stage of the experiential learning cycle is the purpose for which the whole structured experience is designed. The central question here is "Now what?" The facilitator helps participants apply generalizations to actual situations in which they are involved. Ignoring such discussion jeopardizes the probability that the learning will be useful. It is critical that attention be given to designing ways for individuals and/or groups to use the learning generated during the structured experience to plan more effective behavior. Several practices can be incorporated into this stage:

- Consulting dyads or triads
  - √ taking turns helping each other with back-home problem situations, applying generalizations
- Goal-setting
  - √ writing applications according to such goal criteria as specificity, performance, involvement, realism, and observability (see the 1972 *Annual*, pp. 133-134)
- Contracting
  - √ making explicit promises to each other about applications
- Subgrouping
  - √ in interest groups discussing specific generalizations in terms of what can be done more effectively
- Practice session
  - √ role playing back-home situations to attempt changed behavior

Individuals are more likely to implement their planned applications if they share them with others. Volunteers can be asked to report what they intend to do with what they learned, and this can encourage others to experiment with their behavior also.

It is important to note that on the diagram of the experiential learning cycle there is a dotted arrow from "applying" to "experiencing." This is meant to indicate that the actual application of the learning is a new experience for the participant, to be examined inductively also. What structured experiences "teach," then, is a way of using one's everyday experiences as data for learning about human relations. This is sometimes referred to as "re-learning how to learn." Actually, there are other ways to learn. For example, skills are best learned through practice toward an ideal model, knowledge of results, and positive reinforcement. Also, structured experiences do not readily facilitate the development of large-scale perspective; lecture-discussion methods are probably superior for such a purpose. What experiential learning does accomplish, though, is a sense of ownership over what is learned. This is most easily achieved by making certain that each stage of the learning cycle is developed adequately.

REFERENCE

Jones, J. E., & Pfeiffer, J. W. (Eds.). *The 1973 annual handbook for group facilitators.* San Diego, CA: University Associates, 1973.

STRUCTURED EXPERIENCE CATEGORIES

269. AUTOGRAPHS: AN ICE BREAKER

Goals

    I. To facilitate the getting-acquainted process in a large group.

    II. To alleviate anxiety experienced during the beginning of a training session.

Group Size

    Twenty or more participants.

Time Required

    Approximately one-half hour.

Materials

    I. One copy of the Autographs Work Sheet for each participant.

    II. A pencil for each participant.

Physical Setting

    A room large enough for participants to move around freely.

Process

    I. The facilitator briefly discusses the goals of the activity, establishing the expectation that the experience will be both useful and fun.

    II. The facilitator distributes one copy of the Autographs Work Sheet and a pencil to each participant and instructs the group members to follow the instructions on the form. He tells them that they have three minutes in which to select the ten autographs they want to solicit.

    III. The facilitator announces the beginning of the autograph-seeking period, which will last approximately twenty minutes.

    IV. When almost all participants have completed the task, the facilitator calls for everyone's attention and ends the activity. Any member who has an autograph missing can ask the entire group to find an appropriate person to sign.

    V. The facilitator leads the group in debriefing the activity.

Variations

    I. The list can be expanded or adapted to local conditions and issues.

    II. Participants can be instructed to obtain as many autographs as possible.

    III. Subgroups, based on some items, can be formed for discussion of the experience.

Similar Structured Experiences: *Vol. I:* Structured Experience **5**; *Vol. II:* **25**.

Submitted by John E. Jones.

John E. Jones, Ph.D., *is senior vice president for research and development, University Associates, Inc., San Diego, California. He is a co-editor of* Group & Organization Studies: The International Journal for Group Facilitators *and of the* Pfeiffer and Jones Series in Human Relations Training, *including* A Handbook of Structured Experiences for Human Relations Training *(Vols. I-VII) and the* Annual Handbook for Group Facilitators *(1972-1980). Dr. Jones's background is in teaching and counseling, education, and organization and community development consulting.*

AUTOGRAPHS WORK SHEET

Instructions: Select any ten of the following items by placing an X in front of each of your choices. During the autograph-seeking session you will be interviewing people to find one person who fits each of the ten categories or conditions that you have selected. You will then obtain that person's autograph in the appropriate space. You must have a different autograph for each of the ten items.

———— 1. Thinks the President is doing a good job _____

———— 2. Born under my astrological sign _____

———— 3. Prefers to work alone _____

———— 4. Likes liver _____

———— 5. Reads poetry _____

———— 6. Looks attractive to me _____

———— 7. Has a female boss _____

———— 8. Lives alone _____

———— 9. Might be intimidating to me _____

———— 10. Believes in magic _____

———— 11. Enjoys gardening _____

———— 12. Is new to his or her work _____

———— 13. Appears to be friendly _____

———— 14. Manages others _____

———— 15. Advocates openness _____

———— 16. Plays a musical instrument _____

———— 17. Works on weekends _____

———— 18. Enjoys competition _____

———— 19. Sleeps in a waterbed _____

———— 20. Drives a sports car _____

270. BASEBALL GAME: GROUP MEMBERSHIP FUNCTIONS

Goals

I. To gain insight into how one is perceived by others.

II. To study the variety of functions performed by group members.

III. To introduce a novel way of characterizing group-member roles.

Group Size

An unlimited number of groups of five to seven members each.

Time Required

Approximately three hours.

Materials

I. A copy of the Baseball Game Role Descriptions Sheet for each participant.

II. A copy of the Baseball Game Team Problem Sheet for each participant.

III. A copy of the Baseball Game Answer Sheet for each group.

IV. A copy of the Baseball Game Impressions Sheet for each participant.

V. Paper and a pencil for each participant.

Physical Setting

A room large enough to accommodate the groups comfortably and tables and chairs or circles of chairs for each group.

Process

I. The facilitator introduces the activity and explains the goals.

II. The facilitator gives a short lecture on the functions that members perform in groups, especially problem-solving groups (see Lecturette Sources), and discusses the various roles on the Baseball Game Role Descriptions Sheet. (Fifteen minutes.)

III. The facilitator divides the participants into groups of five to seven members each. The small groups are instructed to locate themselves comfortably around the room.

IV. The facilitator distributes copies of the Baseball Game Role Descriptions Sheet to each participant. Participants are instructed to familiarize themselves with the role descriptions and ask for clarification if necessary. (Ten minutes.)

V. The facilitator distributes copies of the Baseball Game Team Problem Sheet to each group and announces that the groups will have forty-five minutes in which to complete the problem-solving activity.

VI. At the end of forty-five minutes or when all groups have completed the task, the

University Associates

facilitator hands out copies of the Baseball Game Answer Sheet, and participants compare their answers with the correct answers. (Ten minutes.)

VII. The facilitator distributes copies of the Baseball Game Impressions Sheet and announces that observations are to reflect perceptions about members' behavior during the problem-solving activity. He says that members will have ten minutes in which to fill out the sheet.

VIII. Group members are instructed to predict which of the roles other members will assign to them. (Five minutes.)

IX. The groups are instructed to spend twenty minutes sharing their impressions. Members are then instructed to discuss how various roles were demonstrated during the problem-solving activity. (Thirty minutes.)

X. Group members discuss their predictions and reactions to the feedback they received about the roles that group members assigned to them. (Fifteen minutes.)

XI. The facilitator reconvenes the large group and leads a discussion of the importance of various group-member functions in the problem-solving process. (Twenty minutes.)

XII. The participants are directed to complete the following sentences:

1. Something I learned about myself is . . .
2. Something I learned about how people behave in groups is . . .

(Ten minutes.)

XIII. The small groups reconvene to share their learnings and discuss back-home applications. (Fifteen minutes.)

Variations

I. Participants can generate a list of group-member functions to describe each of the baseball positions.

II. The feedback aspect can be omitted by deleting goal I, the Baseball Game Impressions Sheet, and steps VIII through XI.

III. The fifteen items of information from the Baseball Game Problem Sheet can be written on separate cards and a set of cards can be distributed among each group's members.

IV. The activity can be shortened to two and one-half hours by cutting step V to thirty minutes and steps II and XI to ten minutes each.

Similar Structured Experiences: *Vol. I:* Structured Experience 12; *Vol. II:* 38; *Vol. IV:* 103.

Lecturette Sources: *'72 Annual:* "What to Look for in Groups"; *'76 Annual:* "Role Functions in a Group."

Submitted by Robert W. Rasberry.

Robert W. Rasberry, Ph.D., is director of the organizational communication program and assistant professor of organizational behavior and administration, Cox School of Business, Southern Methodist University, Dallas, Texas. He also is an instructor of the regularly scheduled public seminars "Power Talk–How to Win Your Audience," "Modern Techniques of Supervision," and "Clear Writing for Technical Professionals." Dr. Rasberry's background is in human relations, business ethics, corporate social responsibility, organizational communication, and family relationships and their effect on executive success.

BASEBALL GAME ROLE DESCRIPTIONS SHEET

Umpire

A good umpire helps an entire group work and participate peacefully. He often serves as both a mediator and an expeditor. As a mediator, he conciliates differences in points of view and seeks compromise solutions. As an expeditor, he keeps communication channels open by facilitating the comments of the two opposing sides.

If the umpire is a designated leader, he has the authority to administer all rules and to enforce penalties. Thus, he is cognizant of the procedures and rules by which the group functions.

Pitcher

The pitcher is the person who does the talking and often can determine the task outcome and direction of the group's movement. There are many different types of pitchers, and any member of the group can serve in this role. The pitcher's first job is to make sure that all other members are attentive and working on the task.

The pitcher also serves as a diagnoser and information or opinion giver. As a diagnoser, he determines the problem's source and both the supporting and resisting factors. In giving information or an opinion, he helps produce data that is pertinent to the group's problem-solving processes.

Catcher

The catcher listens to all members, solicits pertinent ideas, classifies the relationships between the ideas and suggestions, and draws together the efforts of members or sub-groups. In a task role he is a coordinator-integrator.

The catcher is in charge of maintenance and strategy. He also serves occasionally as an information or opinion seeker by asking other members for additional facts. Thus, he calls forth ideas and keeps the rest of the team informed about the group's progress.

Fielder

This player fields the ideas made by other team members, helps cover their positions, and supports their ideas. The fielder quickly assesses situations, pulls together all ideas and suggestions, and restates and clarifies these for the group. From a task standpoint he is an energizer. He is known for prodding the group to a higher quality of participation. He is alert and always ready to participate. He is also sensitive to the atmosphere and climate of the group, to the direction of the flow of ideas.

Batter

A good batter observes the group in process. He watches others and consciously determines how to influence the process in the most advantageous way.

The best batters have a sense for the flow of discussion. They have a good mental attitude, accurate timing on the question-answer sequence, and confidence that their statements will be instructional, correct, and accepted.

Coach

He expedites the group process by performing needed routine tasks such as the distribution of equipment and materials, the physical arrangement of seats and tables, and time keeping. He offers positive feedback and praise, and accepts each member's contribution. He serves as an advisor, not as an authority or disciplinarian. He attempts to create a feeling of trust and respect, and helps each person produce at his highest level of efficiency.

In a team-building and maintenance role the coach keeps the team focused on evaluating alternatives and reaching final decisions.

Scorekeeper

This member serves in a task role as a recorder. He takes minutes, writes down suggestions, and notes decisions.

Team Clown

The team clown serves a nonfunctional role. He is apt to joke, mimic, or engage in other disruptive acts at inopportune times. Some people resent his display of noninvolvement in the group's processes.

Hot Head

This player interferes with straight thinking and tends to throw fellow players off balance. He plays a nonfunctional role and becomes aggressive, criticizes or blames others, shows hostility against individuals or the group, is envious of the credit other members receive, and often deflates the ego of other members.

BASEBALL GAME TEAM PROBLEM SHEET

Instructions: Nine men: Duncan, Winters, Perry, Banks, Dixon, Billings, Woods, Johnson, and Lynch, play the several positions on a baseball team. As a group, determine from the following data the position played by each. Record your answers at the bottom of the page.

1. The second baseman beat Johnson, Duncan, Billings, and the catcher at golf.
2. Lynch and Duncan each won $50 playing cards with the pitcher.
3. Johnson has an apartment across the hall from the third baseman.
4. The outfielders bowl with Banks in their spare time.
5. Winters is taller than Billings; Woods is shorter than Billings. Each of them weighs more than the third baseman.
6. Duncan, Perry, and the shortstop lost $300 each betting on the horses.
7. The catcher has three daughters; the third baseman has two sons; Dixon is being sued for divorce.
8. Perry dislikes the catcher and lives in a house with his sister.
9. One of the outfield positions is played by either Perry or Woods.
10. The center fielder is taller than the right fielder.
11. The pitcher's wife is the third baseman's sister.
12. Dixon is taller than the infielders and the batter with the exception of Johnson, Lynch, and Perry.
13. Banks' sister is engaged to the second baseman.
14. The third baseman, the shortstop, and Billings made $150 speculating on commodities.
15. Four members of the team are married. Winters, Banks, Duncan, the right fielder, and the center fielder are bachelors.

Catcher ———————————————————

Pitcher ———————————————————

First Baseman ———————————————————

Second Baseman ———————————————————

Third Baseman ———————————————————

Shortstop ———————————————————

Left Fielder ———————————————————

Center Fielder ———————————————————

Right Fielder ———————————————————

BASEBALL GAME ANSWER SHEET

Catcher_____ **Lynch**

Pitcher _____ **Johnson**

First Baseman_____ **Duncan**

Second Baseman _____ **Winters**

Third Baseman_____ **Perry**

Shortstop _____ **Banks**

Left Fielder_____ **Dixon**

Center Fielder _____ **Billings**

Right Fielder_____ **Woods**

BASEBALL GAME IMPRESSIONS SHEET

Instructions: Write the names of the members of your group in the spaces that correspond to the roles you think they played in your group. Each group member can be listed in more than one position. You should also list yourself.

Umpire _____

Pitcher _____

Catcher _____

Fielder _____

Batter _____

Coach _____

Scorekeeper _____

Team Clown _____

Hot Head _____

271. VALUES FOR THE 1980s: CONSENSUS SEEKING

Goals

I. To provide an opportunity to explore differences between individual and group decision-making processes.

II. To practice consensus-seeking behavior in groups.

III. To explore group members' social values.

Group Size

Six to ten participants each.

Time Required

Approximately three hours.

Materials

I. A copy of the Values for the 1980s Work Sheet for each participant.

II. A copy of the Values for the 1980s Data Recording Sheet for each participant.

III. A copy of the Values for the 1980s Answer Key for the facilitator.

IV. A pencil for each participant.

V. Newsprint and a felt-tipped marker.

Physical Setting

A room that is large enough for each group to work without interfering with the other groups, and a writing surface for each participant.

Process

I. The facilitator introduces the activity as one that will explore social values while allowing the participants to examine their consensus-seeking skills.

II. The facilitator divides the participants into groups and gives each member a copy of the Values for the 1980s Work Sheet and a pencil.

III. The members are instructed to individually rank order the items on the work sheet according to the instructions provided. (Ten minutes.)

IV. The groups are then told that they have thirty minutes in which to try to arrive at a group consensus ranking. The facilitator gives a brief explanation of the consensus-seeking procedure: there must be substantial agreement among group members on the ranking assigned to each item; no averaging or "majority-rule" voting is allowed.

V. The facilitator calls time. On newsprint he lists the eight social changes and asks for each group's consensus rankings, which he posts in columns. He then writes the "correct" survey rankings and the percentage of population numbers (from the Values for the 1980s Answer Key) in the last column and directs the participants to copy these rankings onto their work sheets.

University Associates

VI. The facilitator gives a copy of the Values for the 1980s Data Recording Sheet[1] to each participant and instructs members to remain in their small groups and to compute an *average* from the individual members' rankings for each item. These averages are recorded in column A. The survey ("correct") ranking for each item is recorded in column B. The number of points of difference between the averaged individual rankings and the survey ("correct") rankings for that item is the "error score" for that item. These scores are recorded in column C. The group-consensus scores obtained for each item during the previous phase of the activity are now recorded in column D. Survey ("correct") scores are recorded in column E, and group-consensus error scores are computed in column F for each item. Comparisons are then possible between individual and group-consensus scores. One group member records these data on newsprint to facilitate discussion of the results.

VII. Members share their reactions and observations. Personal reactions to the content of the social-value changes may be discussed at this time.

VIII. The facilitator helps the groups to process the activity by focusing on one or more of the following points:

1. Identification of factors that influence decision making in groups;
2. Discussion of both positive and negative aspects of using consensus as a decision-making procedure when the situation involves value-based content;
3. Identification of appropriate situations in which to use the consensus procedure.

IX. The facilitator helps group members draw generalizations about the use of consensus seeking as a decision-making procedure. These learnings may be posted by the facilitator, who monitors them to ensure that they represent generalized statements.

X. Individuals reassemble in their small groups to formulate guidelines for the use of consensus seeking as a decision-making procedure.

Variations

I. A lecturette on consensus-seeking procedures can be given prior to the small-group task, and guidelines can be posted for reference during that phase of the activity.

II. One subgroup can engage in consensus seeking while other participants observe the interaction. Observers then give feedback on helping and hindering behaviors or other group-process variables.

III. The facilitator can include a comparison of results across groups before directing the groups to discuss the processing points in step VIII.

IV. A group profile can be generated to reflect the value rankings of the total group. A discussion of the implications of this profile or of changing social values can be conducted.

V. The time limit for the consensus-seeking phase of the experience can be modified or eliminated.

---

[1] This procedure differs somewhat from other consensus scoring procedures in that individuals do not compute error scores using their personal scores for each item. Instead, a score is obtained by averaging group members' individual scores for each item. These representative individual scores are then used in computing individual error scores for each item. Group-consensus scores are used in computing group-error scores for each item. This treatment of the data allows for comparisons between representative individual effort and possible synergistic effects of consensus procedures in problem solving. This treatment is thought to provide more useful comparisons since the "correct" rankings used to compute error scores represent averaged responses from all original survey participants. For a further discussion of the scoring procedure, see Dennis P. Slevin, "Observations on the Invalid Scoring Algorithm of 'NASA' and Similar Consensus Tasks," *Group & Organization Studies*, 3(4), 497-507.

VI. Helping or hindering behaviors can be identified as a part of step VIII.

VII. A feedback step can be added (step VII) in which each group member identifies the person who had the most influence on the member's decision making and gives feedback on that person's interpersonal style.

Similar Structured Experiences: *Vol. IV:* Structured Experience **115**; *Vol. VII:* **255**.

Suggested Instrument: *'75 Annual:* "Decision-Style Inventory."

Lecturette Sources: *'73 Annual:* "Synergy and Consensus-Seeking"; *'75 Annual:* "Humanistic Numbers."

Submitted by Leonard D. Goodstein, W. Warner Burke, and Phyliss Cooke.

Leonard D. Goodstein, Ph.D., is the president of University Associates, Inc., San Diego, California. He was previously professor and chairman of the Department of Psychology, Arizona State University, Phoenix, and was a senior consultant for University Associates. Dr. Goodstein has been the author or editor of several texts, including Organizational Change Sourcebook I *and* II *(1979). Dr. Goodstein has served as editor of* The Journal of Applied Behavioral Science *and has consulted with a variety of organizations.*

W. Warner Burke, Ph.D., is a professor of psychology and education at Teachers College, Columbia University, New York City. He is editor of Organizational Dynamics, *the quarterly journal for managers published by the American Management Association. Dr. Burke is the editor of* The Cutting Edge: Current Theory and Practice in Organization Development *(1978) and is co-editor of* Behavioral Science and the Manager's Role *(Second Edition) (1980). He was formerly chairman of the Department of Management at Clark University and has served as executive director of the O·D Network.*

Phyliss Cooke, Ph.D., is director of professional services for University Associates, Inc., San Diego, California, where she establishes and coordinates the schedules of public training events and serves as dean of the Laboratory Education Intern Program. She also serves as a dean of the UA Graduate School of Human Resource Development. Dr. Cooke's background is in clinical psychology, counselor education, school psychology, and graduate education.

VALUES FOR THE 1980s WORK SHEET

In April 1978 the Gallup Poll interviewed over 1,500 American adults, eighteen and older, in three hundred localities scientifically selected as representative of the country as a whole. Each person was asked whether or not he or she would welcome eight specific social changes that might occur in the coming years.

The percentage of persons welcoming each of these changes in the poll permit us to rank-order the eight items in terms of the degree to which the population as a whole welcomes these changes.

Instructions: Your task is to estimate the rankings that resulted from the survey for each item. In other words, place the number 1 beside the item you think people in the U.S. would welcome most as a social value, the number 2 for the second most welcomed change, and so on until you have ranked all eight social values, the number 8 representing the value people would welcome the least among these eight.

Social Change	Your Rank	Group Rank	Actual Rank	Percentage of Population
1. More emphasis on self-expression	_____	_____	_____	_____
2. Less emphasis on money	_____	_____	_____	_____
3. More acceptance of sexual freedom	_____	_____	_____	_____
4. More emphasis on technological improvements	_____	_____	_____	_____
5. More respect for authority	_____	_____	_____	_____
6. More respect for traditional family ties	_____	_____	_____	_____
7. Less emphasis on working hard	_____	_____	_____	_____
8. More acceptance of marijuana usage	_____	_____	_____	_____

VALUES FOR THE 1980s DATA RECORDING SHEET

A	±	B	=	C
Average of Group Members' Individual Rankings for Each Item	Plus or Minus	"Correct" Survey Ranking for Each Item	Equals	Individual Error Score
1. _____		_____		_____
2. _____		_____		_____
3. _____		_____		_____
4. _____		_____		_____
5. _____		_____		_____
6. _____		_____		_____
7. _____		_____		_____
8. _____		_____		_____

D	±	E	=	F
Average of Group Consensus Ranking for Each Item	Plus or Minus	"Correct" Survey Ranking for Each Item	Equals	Group Consensus Error Score
1. _____		_____		_____
2. _____		_____		_____
3. _____		_____		_____
4. _____		_____		_____
5. _____		_____		_____
6. _____		_____		_____
7. _____		_____		_____
8. _____		_____		_____

University Associates

VALUES FOR THE 1980s ANSWER KEY[2]

Social Change	National Survey Ranking	Percentage Welcoming Change
1. More emphasis on self-expression	4	74%
2. Less emphasis on money	5	70%
3. More acceptance of sexual freedom	8	5%
4. More emphasis on technological improvements	3	75%
5. More respect for authority	2	89%
6. More respect for traditional family ties	1	91%
7. Less emphasis on working hard	6	25%
8. More acceptance of marijuana usage	7	20%

---

[2] Source: *San Francisco Chronicle*, June 17, 1978.

272. SEXUAL ATTRACTION: A WRITTEN ROLE PLAY

Goals

I. To explore the dynamics of sexual attraction among co-workers.

II. To heighten awareness of the effect that assumptions can have on the shaping of an evolving relationship.

III. To provide an opportunity for participants to explore their personal interpretations of, assumptions about, and responses to issues regarding sexual attraction.

Group Size

Eight to twenty-four members in multiples of two.

Time Required

Approximately one hour and forty-five minutes.

Materials

I. A copy of the Sexual Attraction Situation and Reaction Sheet for each participant.

II. A copy of the Sexual Attraction Written Role-Play Sheet for each participant.

III. A pencil for each participant.

IV. Newsprint and a felt-tipped marker.

Physical Setting

Enough room so that participants can sit in a circle.

Process

I. The facilitator introduces the activity and describes its goals.

II. Each participant receives a copy of the Sexual Attraction Situation and Reaction Sheet and a pencil, and all group members are instructed to read the sheet and respond in writing to the questions that follow the description. (Ten minutes.)

III. Each participant receives a copy of the Sexual Attraction Written Role-Play Sheet and is directed to write in a response for the first character (the female team leader). Participants are told that they will have four minutes in which to complete the response and are given a "one-minute warning" at three minutes.

IV. Each participant is directed to pass the Sexual Attraction Written Role-Play Sheet to the person on the *right*. After everyone has received a sheet, each participant reads what was written by the first role player and formulates a response for the second character (the male systems analyst), using the second space. Participants are notified of the time at three minutes, and time is called after four minutes.

V. Each participant is directed to pass the Sexual Attraction Written Role-Play Sheet back to the person on the *left*. That person has four minutes in which to write the next response in the role of the female team leader. Then the sheets are passed to the *right*.

VI. The process is repeated in this manner with members alternating in the two roles and in passing the role-play sheets between right- and left-hand partners until each member has responded three times in the role of each character.

VII. Participants form dyads with one of the two people with whom the responses evolved. These dyads stay seated *within the circle* to discuss their feeling reactions to the activity. (Ten minutes.)

VIII. Participants are then instructed to switch partners by turning to the other person with whom they exchanged role sheets and to continue discussing the role-play activity for ten minutes.

IX. The facilitator asks the participants for their reactions to the experience and for applications of what they have learned. The following questions may be useful:

Were there differences in the two roles that you played? Why?

How did your assumptions affect the roles you played?

How have you handled similar situations in real life?

What coping mechanisms have you found useful in the past?

Variations

I. The "notes to myself" section on the situation sheet can be omitted.

II. The facilitator can conduct a brief discussion of the factors affecting sexual attraction between co-workers prior to the role play.

III. The situation can be rewritten to focus on sexual attraction in other settings or with other relationships between the characters, e.g., male boss with new female team member.

IV. Participants can be asked to identify the factors that affect them the most when working with attractive co-workers and to share effective coping strategies. The "notes to myself" section of the situation sheet can be expanded and/or a second round of note taking can be added following the activity.

V. The written-role-play technique could be used with boss-subordinate, teacher-student, or any other interpersonal situation which could benefit from a role play, using a situation created for that purpose.

Similar Structured Experiences: *Vol. VII:* Structured Experiences **249, 268.**

Submitted by Jeanne Bosson Driscoll and Rosemary A. Bova.

Jeanne Bosson Driscoll is an independent management and organization development consultant. She is also affiliated with Robert H. Schaffer & Associates, a management consulting firm based in Stamford, Connecticut. As an active member of the Organization Development Network for ten years, she has presented many workshops with Rosemary A. Bova. Her areas of expertise include management and productivity improvement, male/female collegial relationships, and consultant skill building.

Rosemary A. Bova is an organization development consultant at the Equitable Life Assurance Society of the United States, New York City. She holds a master's degree in group work from Columbia University, New York. Her background is in labor economics and social work. She is particularly interested in quality-of-work-life issues and human resource management.

SEXUAL ATTRACTION SITUATION AND REACTION SHEET

A two-person consulting team is led by a female organization development consultant. The other member is a male systems analyst. Their client, Bill, is manager of a sales division of a major company. The team has been working for several months on the redesign and evaluation of an existing system. A new consultant, Dave, has just been added to the team by the female team leader. The reasons she gave for adding him were his general competence and specialized expertise.

The next meeting was held with the original consultant team, the client, and the new team member, in the team leader's office. It went very slowly, and decisions were difficult to reach. Some debate occurred between team members. After the meeting, the client, Bill, lingered and was the last to leave the team leader's office. This was unusual behavior for him. He did not indicate to the others his reason for staying behind.

The next day, the female team leader and the systems analyst are discussing how the meeting went. He says, "I felt as if Bill (the client), you, and I were an established family. When Dave came in, I felt as if I were meeting my sister's new boy friend. I feel protective of you, especially because the guy is so attractive and high powered. I wouldn't be surprised if Bill feels a little jealous of the attention you paid to Dave. That is probably why he stayed in your office after the meeting. The three of us have worked together a long time, you know."

Answer the questions below using brief notes or key words.

1. Indicate any feeling responses you were aware of as you read the description of the situation (feelings and emotions, physical reactions).

2. Put yourself into the role of the male systems analyst. What do you imagine is the issue for him? What is he feeling? What does he want?

3. Imagine what the team leader might have been thinking and feeling as she listened to the systems analyst. What does she want?

When you have finished, wait for further instructions.

SEXUAL ATTRACTION WRITTEN ROLE-PLAY SHEET

Round

1. Female team-leader response:

2. Male systems-analyst response:

3. Female team-leader response:

4. Male systems-analyst response:

5. Female team-leader response:

6. Male systems-analyst response:

273. MANAGERIAL CHARACTERISTICS: EXPLORING STEREOTYPES

Goals

I. To increase awareness of the masculine and feminine characteristics typically associated with effective managerial performance.

II. To examine the male-manager stereotype and its implications for women in management.

III. To provide an opportunity to examine self-perceptions relating to the concept of masculinity/femininity.

Group Size

Ten to thirty-five participants.

Time Required

One and one-half to two hours.

Materials

I. A copy of the Managerial Characteristics Self-Description Check List for each participant.

II. A copy of the Managerial Characteristics Check List[1] for each participant.

III. A copy of the Managerial Characteristics Tally Sheet (to be prepared by the facilitator prior to the activity).

IV. A pencil for each participant.

V. Newsprint and a felt-tipped marker.

Physical Setting

Tables and chairs or other surfaces suitable for participants to write on.

Process

I. The facilitator briefly presents an overview of the activity without discussing the goals in depth.

II. The facilitator distributes a copy of the Managerial Characteristics Self-Description Check List to each participant, reads the accompanying instructions, answers any questions, and directs participants to mark their lists.

---

[1] The description check lists were developed from Inge K. Broverman, "Sex Role Stereotypes: A Current Appraisal," *Journal of Social Issues*, 1972, 28(2), 59-78. Used with permission.

III. After all participants have completed the list, the facilitator instructs them to turn it face down during the next step.

IV. The facilitator distributes a copy of the Managerial Characteristics Check List to each participant. He reads the instructions, answers any questions, and directs participants to mark their lists.

V. The facilitator describes the scoring procedure for the Managerial Characteristics Self-Description Check List. Participants are told to total the number of check marks they made next to odd-numbered items. This sum is their score for the number of male characteristics checked. They are instructed to record this sum somewhere on their check lists. Then the total number of even-numbered items checked is summed and recorded on the check lists as the score for the number of female characteristics.

VI. The participants repeat this procedure on the Managerial Characteristics Check List to obtain scores for the number of male and female characteristics checked.

VII. The facilitator polls the participants to see how many checked 10 male and 0 female characteristics, 9 male and 1 female, and so on for the participants' self-descriptions and for their effective-manager descriptions. A tally of the results of both lists is made on newsprint, using the Managerial Characteristics Tally Sheet.

VIII. The facilitator forms participants into small groups to discuss the results. The following points can serve as discussion guides:

1. Share with your subgroup members how you described yourself in terms of male-female characteristics. What reactions did you have to having male-female labels assigned to the descriptive characteristics you selected?

2. Did your group's effective-manager descriptions reflect more male or more female characteristics? What does this suggest in terms of a male-manager role stereotype?

3. What are the criticisms that are likely to be directed at a woman who manifests "masculine" behavior in a managerial role? "Feminine" behavior?

4. Would the same criticisms apply to a man in a managerial role?

5. Do managerial roles and situations require a combination of masculine and feminine traits and in what amounts?

6. What attitudes and specific stereotypes or myths about women as managers need to change if women are to move up in the managerial hierarchy?

IX. The facilitator asks for subgroup reports on the discussion items.

X. The facilitator leads a discussion focusing on the trends that emerged from the subgroup reports.

XI. The facilitator instructs the participants to formulate statements of their learnings.

XII. Generalizations about male-manager stereotypes are then formulated by the participants, and possible applications of these generalizations are discussed.

Variations

I. The responses of men and women in the group can be tallied separately and compared.

II. Teams of from five to seven members each can be formed to arrive at a group consensus for the Managerial Characteristics Check List.

III. In variation II, separate teams can be composed entirely of men or women and the results can be compared.

IV. At step VII, a group profile can be generated by computing a mean and a median score from the participants' responses. The facilitator can then direct participants to focus the processing of the activity on diagnoses of the participant groups' profile data and/or its implications for selected back-home business situations.

V. Participants can use the check-list items to describe themselves in terms of most *and* least descriptive. Processing would focus on personal growth and/or planning for desired change. With intact groups, these self-perceptions can be checked and a feedback session included in the processing step.

Similar Structured Experiences: *'76 Annual:* Structured Experience **184**; *Vol. VII:* **258**.

Suggested Instruments: *'73 Annual:* "Sex-Role Stereotyping Scale"; *'79 Annual:* "Women as Managers Scale (WAMS)."

Lecturette Source: *'77 Annual:* "Androgyny."

Submitted by Allen K. Gulezian, based on some materials developed by Marilyn Lockner and Allen K. Gulezian.

Allen K. Gulezian, Ph.D., is the coordinator of business administration programs and professor of business administration at Central Washington University, Ellensburg, Washington. Dr. Gulezian earned his doctorate in management and organization from the University of Oregon. He previously held positions in industrial relations and personnel management evaluations with the state of Oregon and has done management consulting and training with both private and public organizations.

MANAGERIAL CHARACTERISTICS SELF-DESCRIPTION CHECK LIST

Instructions: Using the list below, check ten characteristics that best describe you.

___ 1. aggressive

___ 2. talkative

___ 3. independent

___ 4. tactful

___ 5. unemotional

___ 6. gentle

___ 7. objective

___ 8. supportive

___ 9. dominant

___10. religious

___11. not easily influenced

___12. neat and orderly

___13. active

___14. submissive

___15. logical

___ 16. sensitive to the feelings of others

___ 17. competitive

___ 18. insecure

___ 19. worldly

___ 20. emotional

___ 21. ambitious

___ 22. subjective

___ 23. skilled in business

___ 24. dependent

___ 25. capable of making decisions easily

___ 26. interested in own appearance

___ 27. self-confident

___ 28. passive

___ 29. accustomed to behaving like a leader

___ 30. used to expressing tender feelings

University Associates

MANAGERIAL CHARACTERISTICS CHECK LIST

Instructions: Using the list below, check ten characteristics that best describe an effective manager.

___ 1. aggressive

___ 2. talkative

___ 3. independent

___ 4. tactful

___ 5. unemotional

___ 6. gentle

___ 7. objective

___ 8. supportive

___ 9. dominant

___ 10. religious

___ 11. not easily influenced

___ 12. neat and orderly

___ 13. active

___ 14. submissive

___ 15. logical

___ 16. sensitive to the feelings of others

___ 17. competitive

___ 18. insecure

___ 19. worldly

___ 20. emotional

___ 21. ambitious

___ 22. subjective

___ 23. skilled in business

___ 24. dependent

___ 25. capable of making decisions easily

___ 26. interested in own appearance

___ 27. self-confident

___ 28. passive

___ 29. accustomed to behaving like a leader

___ 30. used to expressing tender feelings

MANAGERIAL CHARACTERISTICS TALLY SHEET

Number of Characteristics Checked	Number of Participant Responses	
Male Female	Self-Description	Effective Manager
0 – 10		
1 – 9		
2 – 8		
3 – 7		
4 – 6		
5 – 5		
6 – 4		
7 – 3		
8 – 2		
9 – 1		
10 – 0		

University Associates

274. CHOOSING AN APARTMENT: AUTHORITY ISSUES IN GROUPS

Goals

    I. To experience the impact of authoritarian behavior during a competitive activity.

    II. To increase personal awareness of reactions to authoritarian behavior.

    III. To experience the effects of hidden agendas on decision-making processes.

Group Size

    An unlimited number of groups for four to six members each.

Time Required

    Two hours.

Materials

    I. A copy of the Choosing an Apartment Attribute List for each participant.

    II. A copy of the Choosing an Apartment Manager Instruction Sheet for each group's manager.

    III. A copy of the Choosing an Apartment Group Member Instruction Sheet for each group member.

    IV. A pencil for each participant.

Physical Setting

    A room large enough for all groups to work without distracting each other and a separate area for briefing the managers.

Process

    I. The facilitator introduces the activity as a small-group decision-making task but does not mention issues of authority.

    II. The facilitator forms subgroups of four to six members each and recruits a volunteer from each group to serve as its manager. The facilitator explains that each manager will be responsible for the completion of his group's task and that the managers will receive instructions about what their groups are to do.

    III. The managers are taken to a separate room to be briefed on their roles. Each manager is given a pencil, a copy of the Choosing an Apartment Attribute List, and a copy of the Choosing an Apartment Manager Instruction Sheet. The managers are told to look over these materials while the facilitator sets up the task for the work groups.

    IV. To each of the remaining participants the facilitator gives a pencil, a copy of the Choosing an Apartment Attribute List, and a copy of the Choosing an Apartment Group Member Instruction Sheet. The facilitator briefly summarizes the instructions and answers any questions. (If more than one staff member is available, steps III and IV can be conducted concurrently.)

V. The group members are instructed to spend fifteen minutes individually selecting apartment attributes that they prefer, keeping within the guidelines given on their instruction sheets.

VI. While group members are working, the facilitator returns to the managers and briefs them on the nature of their roles, encouraging them to act in a strong, authoritarian manner when they are participating in the negotiation phase of the task. The facilitator tells them that they are to convey the impression that they are hearing the preferences of their group members but that the manager's choices are clearly superior. It is important that the manager's selections are maintained throughout the negotiation phase, regardless of the reasoning or preferences of the group members.

VII. The managers make their final selections in preparation for the negotiation phase, while group members complete their individual preference lists. (Ten minutes.)

VIII. The managers then are recalled to join their groups to lead a negotiation to choose an apartment. The groups are told that they will have twenty minutes for this phase of the activity. They are to continue negotiation until each group has chosen an apartment. The facilitator monitors the groups, providing support for the managers if necessary.

IX. When all groups have chosen apartments, the individuals are directed to total their points to determine which member in each group "won" the bonus.

X. The facilitator calls time after twenty minutes and gives instructions for sharing reactions to the experience in the small groups. The following questions can help focus reactions:

Questions for group managers:

1. What were your feelings about behaving in an authoritarian manner?
2. Did you sense that you were in control of the situation? How did you feel about it?
3. How did you react to the demands of the members? Did they annoy you? Did you ignore them?
4. Were your feelings and reactions in this situation familiar ones?

Questions for group members:

1. How did you feel when the managers made the decisions for you?
2. Did you argue strongly for your choices? If you did not, what were your reasons?
3. How did you feel about the other members' conflicting preferences?
4. Do you usually react the way you did when you are in conflict with an authoritarian person?
5. How did the possibility of winning the bonus influence your behavior during the activity?

(Twenty minutes.)

XI. The facilitator instructs the small groups to take twenty minutes to complete the following tasks:

1. Generate a list of several typical dysfunctional reactions to authoritarian behavior.
2. Develop a strategy for dealing with each of these reactions to change them into more effective responses.

XII. The facilitator reconvenes all participants in the large group. Small-group reports are made to share lists and strategies. The facilitator looks for themes, identifies similarities across lists, and leads a general discussion of the implications of issues of authority and control in interpersonal relations. (Fifteen minutes.)

XIII. Participants are directed to complete the following statements individually:

  1. My typical response to authoritarian behavior is . . .

  2. A more effective response would be . . .

Variations

I. Managers can debrief their reactions to the experience in a group-on-group activity prior to meeting with their subgroups.

II. Role-play techniques can be used to help managers practice their roles.

III. The Choosing an Apartment Attribute List can be simplified. The number of categories can be reduced or points can be substituted for dollar amounts.

IV. Similar tasks such as buying an automobile or purchasing a house can be used.

V. The list in step XI can be generated in the large group.

VI. Specific real-life situations can be discussed during the application phase.

Similar Structured Experiences: *Vol. I:* Structured Experience 18; *Vol. V:* 154, 162; *'77 Annual:* 186; *Vol. VI:* 207.

Lecturette Sources: *'73 Annual:* "Win-Lose," "Dependency and Intimacy"; *'74 Annual:* "Hidden Agendas"; *'77 Annual:* "A Tavistock Primer."

Submitted by Julian J. Szucko, Richard L. Greenblatt, and Christopher B. Keys.

Julian J. Szucko is a doctoral candidate in the psychology department, University of Illinois at Chicago Circle. His interests are in the areas of clinical judgment and decision making. His background is in clinical psychology, research methodology, and measurement.

Richard L. Greenblatt is pursuing graduate studies in clinical psychology and methodology and measurement in the psychology department, University of Illinois at Chicago Circle. His interests are in the areas of clinical decision making and models of human judgment.

Christopher B. Keys, Ph.D., is an associate professor and chairman of the Division of Organizational Psychology, Psychology Department, University of Illinois at Chicago Circle. He is currently on sabbatical leave at the Center for Educational Policy and Management, University of Oregon. Dr. Keys is the author or co-author of over forty-five articles, presentations, and technical reports. He has served as a consultant to criminal justice, educational, religious, and mental health organizations.

CHOOSING AN APARTMENT ATTRIBUTE LIST

	A	B	C	D	E	Your Choice	Manager's Choice	Points
SIZE	Studio $100	2 rooms $150	3 rooms $200	4 rooms $250	5 rooms $300			
NUMBER OF BATHROOMS	One with shower only $10	One with tub and shower combination $15	One with separate tub and shower $20	1½ bath $25	2 full baths $30			
LOCATION	Near airport, 20 miles from client's offices $10	Suburban apartment complex, 15 miles from client's offices $15	Suburban apartment complex, 8 miles from client's offices $20	City residential, 2 miles from client's offices $25	Elegant downtown area near client's offices $30			
DISTANCE FROM SHOPPING AREA	5 miles $10	1 mile $15	¾ mile $20	½ mile $25	¼ mile $30			
PARKING	On street, few spaces $10	On street, many spaces $15	Off street $20	Garage $25	Garage with attendant $30			
PUBLIC TRANSPORTATION	None $10	Cab only $15	Cab & 1 mile from bus $20	Cab & bus at door $25	Near bus, rapid transit, and cab $30			
VIEW	Trash collection area for complex $10	Wall of next building $15	Other houses $20	Park $25	Park and lake $30			
CONDITION	Moldy oldie $10	Old but habitable $15	Renovated $20	Nearly new $25	Brand new $30			
APPLIANCES	None $10	Hotplate and cooler only $15	Old but functional appliances $20	New refrigerator and range $25	Fully modern including microwave and wok $30			
DECORATING	Stained carpet, weird paint $10	Carpet old but OK, paint old but OK $15	New carpet or new paint $20	New carpet and new paint $25	You choose carpet and paint $30			
FLOOR	Third-floor walk-up $10	Basement $15	Second story with balcony $20	First floor with enclosed patio $25	Top floor of high rise with elevator and garden patio $30			

40

CHOOSING AN APARTMENT MANAGER INSTRUCTION SHEET

Background: You are the manager of a group of professional consultants who frequently travel to a major city five hundred miles away from your home office to do business. To save on lodging expenses, the company has decided to lease an apartment to house the one, two, or three members of your division who will be in the city at any one time. Any of your group could be sent, including you, and could be required to stay for two or three months at a time.

You have been directed to announce that the members of your group will have input in selecting the type of apartment to be leased. The company is offering a $50 bonus to the employee who makes the best selection. You are not eligible for this bonus, but of course, since the final decision and responsibility are yours, you fully intend to select the apartment that *you* think is best.

Selection: You are to use the Choosing an Apartment Attribute List to make your selection. You can spend no more than $450 a month. This is $50 less than the group members have been instructed to spend, but you have recently been informed that the company is having some cash-flow problems. You do *not* want your work-group members to know about this, but you have definitely decided to spend no more than $450 a month in order to secure some leeway in your division's budget.

Negotiation: After you rejoin your group, the members will express their opinions about characteristics they prefer in an apartment. They will try to win points for themselves by convincing you to choose the characteristics they want most, but you, as the manager, have the *final say.* Be strong and authoritative. Go through each of the eleven characteristics, listening to what each individual has to say. If the person's choice differs from yours, offer a criticism so that the person will understand that you know best. Solicit each person's choice of features in each category, then reveal your own choices. Follow this procedure for each attribute until the apartment has been chosen. Be prepared to discuss the negotiation process and your role later in the large group.

CHOOSING AN APARTMENT GROUP MEMBER INSTRUCTION SHEET

Background: You belong to a group of professional consultants who frequently travel to a major city five hundred miles away from your home office to do business. To save on lodging expenses, the company has decided to lease an apartment to house the one, two, or three members of your division who will be in the city at any one time. Any of your group could be sent, and you could be required to stay for two or three months at a time.

The manager of your division has announced that the members of the group will have input in selecting the type of apartment to be leased. The company is offering a $50 bonus to the member whose choices of selection criteria are closest to those actually used.

Selection: You are to use the Choosing an Apartment Attribute List to select the kind of apartment in which *you* would most like to live. You have been told that you can spend $500 per month. You will have to make difficult decisions about the features you want and how much money you would be willing to spend for each feature. Pick your choice of features in each of the eleven categories and record it in the proper column. Remember that your total cannot exceed $500. Do not consult anyone else about your decision. You will have ten minutes to complete your list. After this time you will not be allowed to change what you have written.

Negotiation: Your group's manager has the final say over which characteristics will be included in your apartment since he or she is responsible for choosing *one* apartment for all individuals in your group.

After your manager rejoins the group, try to convince him or her to select an apartment that has as many of the characteristics that *you* chose as possible. Say whatever you think will be effective to convince the manager to accept your choices. Continue going through the characteristics until your manager selects an apartment within the monetary limit. You receive one point for each of the eleven categories for which the manager's choice matches yours. The group member with the most points will be the one who receives the bonus. Be prepared to discuss the negotiation process later in the large group.

275. MISSILES: SOURCES OF STRESS

Goals

    I. To identify sources of psychological stress.

    II. To demonstrate the effect that individual perceptions of situations have on behavior and decision making under stress.

    III. To experience the effects of various types of role power on persons in a decision-making situation.

Group Size

    Any number of groups of seven to nine members each.

Time Required

    Approximately two hours.

Materials

    I. A copy of the Missiles Situation Sheet for each participant.

    II. A copy of one of the Missiles Role Sheets for each participant. (If there are only seven members in a group, the guest roles are not used.)

    III. A copy of the Missiles Crisis Sheet for each group.

    IV. A copy of the Missiles Debriefing Sheet for each participant.

    V. A place card identifying each participant's role.

    VI. A pencil for each participant.

Physical Setting

    A separate room for each group or one large room with space enough for each group to deliberate without distraction.

Process

    I. The facilitator explains the objectives of the activity and creates a climate for the role-play situation. A copy of the Missiles Situation Sheet and a pencil are given to each participant. The participants are instructed to read the situation sheet thoroughly. (Ten minutes.)

    II. When the situation has been explained and is understood by all participants, the facilitator forms the participants into groups of seven to nine members each. Each participant in a group receives a Missiles Role Sheet that is different from the other members' and is told to read the role sheet but *not* to show it to other members of the group. (Ten minutes.) The facilitator checks to see that all role players are familiar with their roles and ready to proceed. The facilitator also puts a place card in front of each participant so that all members can see which roles have been assigned to the other group participants.

III. Members are directed to assume their assigned roles, and each group is told that it will have thirty minutes to decide on the best solution to the missile crisis situation.

IV. After twenty minutes of role playing, the facilitator announces that the President has suffered a heart attack and removes the President from each group. The facilitator then gives a copy of the Missiles Crisis Sheet to each group and tells them to continue role playing.

V. Upon completion of the thirty-minute role play, each participant receives a copy of the Missiles Debriefing Sheet and is directed to complete it. (Ten minutes.)

VI. Participants remain in the small groups and discuss the experience, including their answers to the questions on the Missiles Debriefing Sheet. Special attention is given to the need for participants to free themselves from the roles as part of the debriefing process. (Twenty minutes.)

VII. The facilitator leads a brief discussion comparing the effects of the experience across groups. (Ten minutes.)

VIII. The subgroups are then given the task of identifying three major sources of stress and an effective way to cope with each. (Twenty minutes.)

IX. The facilitator leads the total group through a sharing of subgroup reports. Patterns and similarities in these reports are noted. (Ten minutes.)

X. Generalized learnings from the experience are elicited from the participants, and participants are then encouraged to formulate their own ideas for personal application of their learnings. (Ten minutes.)

Variations

I. A single group can participate in the role play while other participants serve as observers. Following the role play, the observers identify factors that they believe contributed to the stress and/or solution.

II. The vice president can be removed from the group at the same time as the President. This often results in a leaderless group situation. During the debriefing the group can discuss who emerged as the leader and why.

III. Following the activity each member reads his role to the other participants. The discussion then focuses on how different aspects of role expectations can result in stress in work groups and how role-clarification activities can help to manage these stressors.

IV. During step VII the facilitator can give a lecturette on types of power, and the processing at step VIII of the activity can focus on members' reactions to various types of power in their work situations.

Similar Structured Experiences: *Vol. VII: Structured Experience* **266**; *'80 Annual:* **278.**

Suggested Instrument: *'75 Annual:* "Diagnosing Organizational Ideology."

Lecturette Sources: *'79 Annual:* "How to Maintain Your Personal Energy"; *'80 Annual:* "Dealing with Organizational Crises."

Submitted by Karl A. Seger.

Karl A. Seger is president of Corporate Consultants, an organization development consulting firm in Knoxville, Tennessee. Mr. Seger has consulted in the area of stress management for seven years. His clients include government agencies, utilities, police departments, and private corporations. His background is in organizational psychology, stress management at the individual and organizational levels, and interpersonal-skills training in management and supervisory-development programs.

MISSILES SITUATION SHEET

You are one of the foremost military or political leaders in the United States and have just been rushed to a bunker hidden deep in the hills near the capital. There are enough supplies in the bunker for the people present to remain here for three years.

The leaders of the second most powerful nation in the world, Country X, have just announced that they are going to launch a nuclear attack on the United States unless we immediately turn over to them all of our military bases and equipment outside the continental limits of the country. To demonstrate their sincerity in making this threat, they have designated five target cities—each with a population of over one million people—and have stated that they will launch nuclear missiles against these cities if their demands are not immediately answered.

In the past three months Country X has made similar threats to three smaller countries. On each of these occasions an emergency meeting of the U.N. Security Council has been called, but Country X holds a permanent seat on the Council and has vetoed all attempts for action against it. Two of the threatened countries relented to the demands of Country X; the third did not, and a city of 750,000 people was destroyed by an attack with nuclear weapons.

The threat against our country was delivered to the major television networks, and the entire nation knows about it. However, only the people in this bunker know the identities of the five target cities.

Country X also has stated that if one of your missiles is launched against it, it will unleash its entire arsenal against us, thereby insuring total annihilation of both countries. For us to give in means that Country X will have enough military power, strategic bases, and arms to effectively control the world. We do not know if Country X is bluffing.

It takes twenty-two minutes for a missile with a nuclear warhead to travel from Country X to the closest strategic location within our country.

The initial threat was issued at 12:39 p.m. It is now 1:45 p.m. Country X is waiting for our response.

Be sure that your group considers all the alternatives available to it and takes advantage of the time allocated to seek the best possible solution to the situation.

University Associates

MISSILES ROLE SHEET
President

You came from a poor family in Ohio and had to work your way through law school. Two years ago, when you were the junior senator from your state, your party asked you to run for the presidency. You agreed but did not expect to win. At forty-seven you are the youngest President in American history and are determined to do the best possible job while in office. You took office three months ago, and you know that all the people in this room feel that they are better qualified to deal with this crisis than you are. The vice president is especially difficult to deal with because he feels that he should have been the party's choice for the presidency. All the military officers know that you had a draft deferment and are considered a "dove," so it is likely that they consider you unqualified to serve as commander of the armed forces. But *you* are the President, and the responsibility for what happens today rests on your shoulders.

Your family has been moved to a safe area.

MISSILES ROLE SHEET

Vice President

You should be the President. You served twenty years in Congress, eight years as vice president during the previous administration, and expected your party to ask you to run for President in the last election. Instead they asked a young, unknown senator from Ohio, and you are again serving as the vice president. The new President is inexperienced and naive. He has never served in the armed forces and has been labeled a "dove." He took office just three months ago and is the youngest President in the history of the country. Now that the country is faced with a crisis the President is not capable of handling, it may be your opportunity to assert yourself and prove that you are the best man for the job. You know that the chief of staff and general of the Army are on your side and that the secretary of defense is on the President's side. You are not sure about the other people present. On your way to this meeting the President asked you to sit quietly and just nod your head to indicate "yes" when he says something to you.

Your entire family is in one of the target cities.

MISSILES ROLE SHEET

Secretary of Defense

You really wonder why you are here. You were recently nominated by the President but have not yet been confirmed by the Congress. You have not been briefed by the military and are meeting the generals present for the first time. The President, an old friend of yours, is forty-seven years old and assumed office just three months ago. His vice president is bitter because he expected to be asked to run for the presidency. All the military people present feel that you and the President are naive, and maybe they are right. You do not feel comfortable here and would like to check on your family since it is in one of the target cities.

MISSILES ROLE SHEET

Chief of Staff

You are the most experienced military officer in the world. All the generals at this meeting look up to you and know that you are the most important person in this room. The secretary of defense was just appointed and has not yet been approved by Congress. The vice president is a power-hungry has-been, who served eight years as the vice president under the last President and was not any better then. The new President is inexperienced and naive. He has never served in the military, has been labeled a "dove," and assumed office just three months ago. He is forty-seven years old.

The only way to survive this crisis is to call Country X's bluff. You have no family and believe that, if necessary, both countries should fire all their missiles, totally destroying the outside world. In three years the people in this bunker could emerge and begin a new, and much better, world.

MISSILES ROLE SHEET

General of the Army

There are a lot of stupid people at this table, especially the admiral of the Navy. For years he has been cutting into your budget, and now when you really need all the strategic weapons you have been asking for, they are not there. Let the Navy save the world if it is so damned important! The President is young, naive, and just took office three months ago. The chief of staff is becoming senile. Only the vice president may still have the capacity to assume leadership and resolve the crisis. The vice president is experienced, knowledgeable, and has been against the attacks on the Army's budget.

MISSILES ROLE SHEET

Admiral of the Navy

For years you have claimed that because of its mobility at sea the Navy would be the first line of defense in this type of crisis. Now that the crisis is here, it is up to you to solve it. The President is inexperienced and naive. He took office just three months ago. The vice president and chief of staff are ambitious and vengeful, sometimes even psychotic. The general of the army hates you for cutting into his budgets. He is waiting to prove that you were wrong and he was right. The pressure is on you to resolve this crisis.

Your family lives in one of the target cities.

MISSILES ROLE SHEET

General of the Air Force

Although you have been in the Air Force for twenty-seven years, your life recently underwent a dramatic change when you survived a serious airplane crash. You now believe that all things are planned somehow and will work out for the best. You wish you could transfer this faith to the new President, who is still naive, and the vice president and chief of staff, who are so hard and callous. If this crisis is meant to be, it must be for a reason. After all, history has shown that all events perform some function—even the great plagues reduced overpopulation and encouraged medical science. The way you see it, this situation is meant to teach mankind a great lesson.

MISSILES ROLE SHEET

Guest #1

All the other people at this table are maniacs! The President and the secretary of defense are young, naive, and inexperienced. Everyone else is a power monger. You may be the only rational person in this room, but none of these people know you. You are a military and political-science professor at a major university and are considered one of the world's greatest authorities on the potential threat of nuclear warfare. You had a briefing scheduled with the President for today, and when the crisis started you were asked to accompany his staff to this bunker. Actually you feel out of place because no one really wants you here. You would rather be with your family, which fortunately is not in one of the target cities.

MISSILES ROLE SHEET

Guest #2

You are the world's foremost authority on Country X and have been rushed here by the President's staff. You have never met any of the people at this table, and none of them know who you are or why you are here. The President was recently elected and is not ready for this type of crisis. You do not know if the other people here are capable of dealing with it either, but you are certain that Country X is not bluffing.

You are worried because your family lives in one of the target cities and you have three small children.

MISSILES CRISIS SHEET

Country X has just launched five missiles. We do not know if they are armed with nuclear warheads.

MISSILES DEBRIEFING SHEET

What was your group's solution to the crisis?

Did you agree with this solution? Did you state your disagreement?

Which of the following stressors did your group experience? What contributed to the presence of these stressors?

1. Interpersonal conflict

2. Intragroup competition

3. Role conflict

4. Role ambiguity

5. Overload

6. Conflicting demands

7. Responsibility for others

What other sources of stress were experienced within your group?

How did individuals respond to the stress that they experienced?

How did role power affect the decision making?

University Associates

276. SLOGANS: A GROUP-DEVELOPMENT ACTIVITY

Goals

I. To experience the processes and feelings that arise when a new member joins an ongoing group with defined tasks and roles.

II. To explore the coping mechanisms adopted by the individual and the group to deal with entry problems.

III. To examine functional and dysfunctional coping strategies of groups.

Group Size

One or more groups of ten to twelve members each.

Time Required

Approximately three hours.

Materials

I. Blank paper and a pencil for each participant.

II. Newsprint and a felt-tipped marker.

Physical Setting

A room large enough to accommodate all participants, a separate room for each group, and a place where the volunteers (one per group) can meet.

Process

I. The facilitator asks for several volunteers, who are told to go to a separate room to await their instructions. The facilitator then divides the remaining participants into subgroups of ten to twelve members each. (It is important that subgroups do not begin to form into cohesive units before volunteers are recruited.) The role of the volunteers and the purpose of the activity are not divulged at this time.

II. The facilitator gives the remaining participants the following information:

1. Each group is an advertising company engaged in the business of promotion.

2. Each company has two tasks to complete in the next thirty minutes:

   a. To organize the company, select a name, establish a hierarchy, assign roles, clarify tasks, and produce an organizational chart reflecting the members' decisions. This information will be collected by the facilitator at the end of ten minutes. If this task is completed before the allotted time, work may proceed on the second task.

   b. Prepare a set of twenty slogans or advertising themes for a potential client, the Fidelity Bank. The bank is interested in increasing deposits by means of an aggressive public relations campaign. (Twenty minutes.)

3. The work of each company will be evaluated as a whole. The bank will examine each company's submissions and will accept the one best complete *set* of slogans or themes.

III. After the facilitator has briefed the groups, they are directed to move to separate areas and to begin working.

IV. While the work groups are engaged in their tasks, the facilitator meets with the volunteers and briefs them on their task. They are told that each of them will be joining an advertising company in a managerial capacity. They are to spend the next ten minutes writing down some of their expectations for the job and listing contributions they think they can make to the company.

V. At the end of the first ten minutes of the activity the facilitator visits each work group, collects its organizational chart, and introduces one volunteer to the company members, announcing that the person is joining the company as a manager. No further details are given.

VI. While the work groups are completing the second task, the facilitator prepares a newsprint poster listing the criteria used to evaluate the slogans and adjusts the organizational charts to reflect the addition of the new managers.

VII. When the groups have been working on the second task for twenty minutes, the facilitator calls time and collects the materials prepared by each of the groups.

VIII. The participants are told to take a ten-minute break while the facilitator (as president of the Fidelity Bank) evaluates the slogans and decides on the winning company.

IX. The participants are reassembled in the large group to hear the Fidelity Bank's decision. The facilitator reads the winning set of slogans aloud.

X. The facilitator reassembles the work groups, distributes the adjusted organizational charts, and instructs the groups to discuss their reactions to the experience. He suggests that the following considerations can help to focus the group discussion:

1. Reactions to the results of the competition
2. Feelings experienced when the new member was introduced into the group
3. The new manager's feelings about joining an intact group and/or job expectations that were met or unmet
4. The ways in which the group assimilated the new member or reacted to the change in its hierarchy
5. The effect of the new member on the group's functioning.

(Fifteen minutes.)

XI. The facilitator leads the participants in the processing of their learnings. Groups are given the task of generating a short list of functional ways to cope with inclusion issues in intact task groups. (Twenty minutes.)

XII. Subgroups make their reports to the large group. The facilitator leads the participants in formulating generalizations about the effects of new members on group functioning. (Twenty minutes.)

XIII. The facilitator instructs individual members to state how they might apply the general principles learned from the experience to their own work situations. (Ten minutes.)

Variations

I. Each participant can be asked to contribute an amount of money sufficient to generate interest to a fund to be paid to the winning team.

II. One group can represent the Fidelity Bank and can be the judges of the slogans prepared by the advertising companies. While the companies work on their assigned tasks, this group can develop criteria for the evaluation.

III. During step VI the facilitator can ask each manager to appoint a representative to sit on a panel of judges to decide the winning slogans.

IV. The intergroup competition feature in the activity can be eliminated by modifying the instructions given in step II and omitting steps VI through IX and the "reaction" item in step X.

V. A group of process observers can be recruited at the start of the activity to give feedback on group processes during the task phases of the activity.

VI. The facilitator can follow this activity with a lecturette on group-process issues relating to new member inclusion at various stages such as pre-entry, entry, and post-entry.

VII. During step XIII the facilitator can instruct the participants to develop action steps that could be taken by organizations to reduce the dysfunctional effects of changes in work-group membership.

Similar Structured Experience: *Vol. IV:* Structured Experience **124.**

Lecturette Source: *'73 Annual:* "A Model of Group Development."

Submitted by Suresh M. Sant.

Suresh M. Sant is a faculty member with the State Bank Staff College, Hyberabad, India. His interests are organizational development, human relations training, and human resource development. He is a member of the Indian Society for Applied Behavioral Sciences.

277. POWER AND AFFILIATION: A ROLE PLAY

Goals

I. To become better acquainted with the positive and negative aspects of power and affiliation.

II. To explore the dynamics of power and affiliation in managerial situations.

Group Size

Eight to twelve members each.

Time Required

Approximately one hour and forty-five minutes.

Materials

I. A copy of the Power and Affiliation Role Sheet (Socialized Power, Unsocialized Power, Affiliative Interest, or Affiliative Assurance[1]) for each of the four managers in each group.

II. A copy of the Power and Affiliation Summary Sheet for each participant.

III. A sheet of newsprint and a pencil or felt-tipped marker for each subordinate.

IV. Newsprint and a felt-tipped marker for the facilitator.

Physical Setting

A room large enough to accommodate role playing and discussion, and a separate place where managers can wait so that they do not observe each others' role plays.

Process

I. The facilitator briefly discusses the goals of the activity and then forms groups of at least eight members each. He designates four members in each group to play the managers' roles.

II. The facilitator takes the managers out of the room, gives each of the four managers assigned to a group a copy of a different Power and Affiliation Role Sheet, and tells them that they have five minutes in which to study their roles and the tasks they have been assigned to do. The facilitator may want to coach the managers in their role-play preparations.

III. While the managers are studying their roles, the facilitator returns to the remaining participants and assigns at least one "subordinate" to each of the four managers selected from each group. Ideally, two or three subordinates enhance the role play.

---

[1]The two faces of power are from D. McClelland, "Two Faces of Power," in D. Kolb, I. M. Rubin, & J. M. McIntyre (Eds.), *Organizational Psychology: A Book of Readings* (2nd ed.). Englewood Cliffs, NJ: Prentice-Hall, 1974. The two faces of assurance are taken from R. Boyatzis, "The Need for Close Relationships in the Manager's Job," also in Kolb, Rubin, & McIntyre (1974).

University Associates

The facilitator gives each subordinate a sheet of newsprint and a pencil or felt-tipped marker.

IV. The facilitator directs the role-play process so that each manager comes into the group one at a time and enacts his or her role with the assigned subordinate(s). The other members of each subgroup observe. The facilitator should stop the role players after five minutes if they have not finished their task. (Twenty minutes.)

V. Following the completion of all the role plays, the facilitator aids the participants in reacting to the role plays. He may ask group members to discuss such questions as:

1. How did each manager feel about the role he or she played?

2. How did each subordinate feel about the way he or she was managed in the task?

3. What managerial behaviors were helpful and which ones hindered completion of the task?

(Ten minutes)

VI. The facilitator distributes a copy of the Power and Affiliation Summary Sheet to each participant. This information also may be posted on newsprint prepared in advance. The information is reviewed and the content is clarified if necessary. (Ten minutes.)

VII. The facilitator assembles the entire group and polls the members of each group about which manager played what role in that group. The results of the poll are posted on newsprint, using the following matrix for each group. (Ten minutes.)

Role Played (as Seen by Group Members)

Role Actually Played / Name of Role Player	Socialized Power	Unsocialized Power	Affiliative Interest	Affiliative Assurance

VIII. The facilitator directs each manager to read his or her assigned role. Even if a role player has not played the assigned role well, a discussion is held on the impact of the managerial behavior. The discussion then focuses on how accurately participants related role players to roles and the factors that contributed to correct matchings. (Ten minutes.)

IX. Subgroup members are instructed to identify both positive and negative aspects of each of the power and affiliative orientations discussed. Effective combinations for various work situations or tasks are considered. (Fifteen minutes.)

X. Group summary reports are given. (Five minutes.)

XI. The facilitator helps the participants formulate generalizations about the effects of power and affiliation needs on managerial style. (Five minutes.)

XII. Subgroups reassemble to discuss the application of these learnings to back-home work situations. (Five to ten minutes.)

Variations

I. One group of participants can conduct the role play in a group-on-group arrangement. Observers focus on the behavior of the role players to heighten their awareness of nonverbal reaction cues to interpersonal interactions. Observations are shared during step V.

II. Steps VI, VII, and X can be omitted.

III. When there is more than one subgroup, results from the tasks can be compared during step IV.

IV. Additional staff members can intervene as each manager's boss before or during each role play to create the desired climate. For example, the boss of the manager assigned to the unsocialized-power role could engage in negative power behaviors.

Similar Structured Experiences: *Vol. V:* Structured Experiences **154, 162;** *Vol. VI:* **207;** *Vol. VII:* **253.**

Suggested Instruments: *'76 Annual:* "Leader Effectiveness and Adaptability Description," "Organization Behavior Describer Survey."

Lecturette Sources: *'74 Annual:* "The Shouldist Manager"; *'76 Annual:* "Leadership as Persuasion and Adaptation."

Submitted by John F. Veiga and John N. Yanouzas.

John F. Veiga, D.B.A., is associate professor of organizational behavior, School of Business Administration, University of Connecticut, Storrs, Connecticut. He is co-author of The Dynamics of Organization Theory: Gaining a Macro Perspective *(1979), is associate editor of* Exchange: The Organization Behavior Teaching Journal, *and is chief financial officer of* The Organization Behavior Teaching Society. *Dr. Veiga's work has been in management education and career/life planning. He has consulted for several organizations in both the private and public sectors.*

John N. Yanouzas, Ph.D., is professor of management and head of the Management and Administrative Sciences Department, School of Business Administration, University of Connecticut, Storrs, Connecticut. He is co-author of Formal Organization: A Systems Approach *(1977) and* The Dynamics of Organization Theory: Gaining a Macro Perspective *(1979). Dr. Yanouzas is a member of the review board of* Exchange: The Organization Behavior Teaching Journal. *His background is in management education, group decision making, organization theory, and organization behavior.*

POWER AND AFFILIATION ROLE SHEET

Socialized Power

1. You believe that your subordinates will perform their best for you if you show *confidence in their ability* even if the task they are to do is difficult.
2. You are the boss but you tend to treat your people as adults and try to *help them recognize that they can do a fairly good job* even though they may not think so.
3. Your advice is minimal but constructive. You have a "can do" attitude and try to get your people to feel that way also.
4. You should try to recognize when your subordinates have done their best so as not to frustrate them. Just try to get their best efforts.
5. Show your keen sense of justice by reassuring them that those who have worked hard and made sacrifices will receive just rewards.
6. Try to develop a supervisor-subordinate relationship based on mutual goals and interests.

Task

Each subordinate must draw ten grids of identical size. The grids must be 3″ x 3″ (a square divided by horizontal and vertical lines into nine smaller but equal squares).

POWER AND AFFILIATION ROLE SHEET

Unsocialized Power

1. You are *confused* about how to do the job well but would *never admit this to your subordinates*. When they ask questions, tell them "I have given you all the information you need for the task; now do the best you can."
2. You tend to *scrutinize closely* what your subordinates do and *regularly criticize* their *lack of ability* by pointing out errors in their work. Show your low tolerance for mistakes.
3. You believe that people must make it on their own. Your job is to tell them whether or not they have accomplished it but not how to do it (since you are not certain yourself).
4. *Rules are rules* and *requirements are made to be adhered to*—to the letter. Your job is to police the rules.
5. Try to *develop a supervisor-subordinate* relationship based on your position as a manager. Confront your subordinates with your superiority.

Task

Each subordinate must draw fifteen parallel lines in a horizontal direction, two inches apart and three feet long.

POWER AND AFFILIATION ROLE SHEET

Affiliative Interest

1. You like to develop "we" feelings with your employees, i.e., "we are in this together," and you like *working toward a common goal* with your subordinates.
2. You *encourage* your subordinates to exert their *best effort* and you *show* them *regular support*.
3. You feel *comfortable in criticizing or praising* subordinates' efforts because you do not criticize the person. Your *feedback is constructive, helpful, and task related*.
4. You want them to do the best job they can do, given their abilities.
5. Try to develop a personal relationship with your subordinates based on mutual trust and friendship.

Task

Each subordinate must draw ten symmetrical five-point stars of equal size.

POWER AND AFFILIATION ROLE SHEET

Affiliative Assurance

1. You are *confused* about how to perform the task well and *show this* to your subordinates (in the hope that they will not blame you for any problems that might arise).
2. You *avoid* making any *negative comments* about how your subordinates are doing the task.
3. Above all you are agreeable. Anything your subordinates do is all right with you; that is better than creating hard feelings.
4. During the performance of the task, you try to get *assurances* regularly from your subordinates that *problems are not your fault* and that they *should not blame you* for having them do such a task.
5. Try to develop a personal relationship with your subordinates and avoid anything that may threaten the relationship. Avoid conflicts.

Task

Each subordinate must draw ten concentric rings.

POWER AND AFFILIATION SUMMARY SHEET

The manager with a high need for power can express it in two ways:

Socialized Power (Positive Face)	Unsocialized Power (Negative Face)
Uses persuasion	Uses physical threats or coercion.
Shows that he or she expects others to obey as long as it leads to the attainment of organizational goals	Expects subordinates to be blindly obedient and loyal
Uses control to make others feel strong and competent	Relies on dominance and submission
Defines goals, selects alternatives, and tries to reach goals by pushing others to use their strengths and capabilities	Uses "prestige supplies" to show power or uses rewards as a show of power over others
Expresses power through sports, politics, or holding office	Expresses power by drinking, fighting, or exploiting others

The manager with a high need for affiliation can express it in two ways:

Affiliative Interest (Positive Face)	Affiliative Assurance (Negative Face)
Strives for relationships based on personal concern and openness	Strives for close relationships based on a need for security
Does not allow feelings of closeness to be threatened or diminished by openness.	Looks for "proof" of others' commitment to him or her
Gives both negative and positive feedback	Avoids conflicts that may threaten a good relationship
Shows enthusiasm about the transfer or promotion of a subordinate and looks forward to establishing close relations with others	Equates a subordinate's happiness with acceptance of the manager as a person
Makes it clear that the subordinate's feelings and thoughts are important	Searches for communications that support closeness and approval by others

278. MOVE TO NEWTOWN: A COLLABORATION ACTIVITY

Goals

I. To increase awareness of the dynamics of competition and collaboration.

II. To experience the effects of the use of role power in negotiation situations.

III. To explore the effects of role expectations on behavior and reactions.

IV. To practice renegotiation of role responsibilities and expectations within a work unit.

Group Size

Six groups of two to twelve members each.

Time Required

A minimum of three hours.

Materials

I. A copy of one of the following Move to Newtown Role-Play Instructions for each group.
1. Top Management
2. Supervisory Personnel
3. Space Procurement: General Services Administration
4. Professional Personnel
5. Clerical Personnel
6. Union Representatives

II. A copy of the Move to Newtown Task and Instruction Booklet for each participant. (The booklet should be prepared in such a way that participants are presented with one page at a time.)

III. Blank paper and a pencil for each participant.

Physical Setting

A table and chairs for each group.

Process

I. The facilitator explains the activity and timing and sets the climate for the role play. He forms six groups, instructs each group to assemble around a separate table, and assigns each group one role from the Move to Newtown Role-Play Instructions.

II. The facilitator distributes a Move to Newtown Task and Instruction Booklet to each participant. He tells the groups to proceed, beginning with page 1.

III. The facilitator monitors the time and notifies the groups at the end of each round (round 1: twenty minutes; round 2: twenty minutes; round 3: twenty minutes; round 4: thirty minutes; round 5: twenty minutes).

IV. The facilitator calls time and polls the teams for their responses to items 4 and 5 on page 6 (reflections) of the Move to Newtown Task and Instruction Booklet.

V. The participants remain in their teams to complete the following tasks:

1. Identify two or more major factors that enhance dysfunctional competition (a) within groups and (b) between groups.

2. Identify two or more specific strategies for enhancing collaboration (a) within groups and (b) between groups.

(Fifteen minutes.)

VI. The facilitator leads the total group in a discussion of the team reports, emphasizing similarities. (Ten minutes.)

VII. Generalizations are drawn from the participants based on the data brought out in the summary reports. (Ten minutes.)

VIII. The facilitator instructs each participant to develop a list of action items for personal application of the learnings from the experience.

Variations

I. The situation and information can be adapted to suit the needs and background of the group. For example, the Space Procurement: General Services Administration team can be eliminated as a role designation and provided to each team as a given parameter in the decision-making process.

II. The facilitator can intervene after each round to present appropriate lecturettes on such subjects as self-disclosure, goal setting, planning change, risk taking, and power strategies.

III. Observers can be assigned to specific groups or can be directed to look for specific aspects of the group process. Observers are cautioned against participating in the group's discussion of the content.

IV. The facilitator can brief observers on how to be process consultants, telling them what to look for during the group process and instructing them to intervene as they deem necessary to help a group to clarify its process.

V. The facilitator can increase competition and frustration between groups by restructuring the time or using a kitchen timer with a bell. Another dynamic can be created by putting dominant personalities on one team and making this team larger than the others—for example, the management team can have eight members and the others only five or six.

VI. Guidelines for collaborative, negotiative, and coercive tactics can be eliminated from the instruction booklet.

VII. The role-play activity can be conducted following a lecturette on power tactics, and participants can be assigned one of the tactics to use during the activity.

VIII. Roles can be assigned to group members who then work in mixed planning teams.

Similar Structured Experiences: '75 *Annual:* Structured Experience 145; *Vol. V:* 171; *Vol. VI:* 217; '80 *Annual:* 275, 279, 280.

Suggested Instruments: '75 *Annual:* "Diagnosing Organization Ideology"; '80 *Annual:* "Role Efficacy Scale."

Lecturette Sources: '73 *Annual:* "Win-Lose Situations"; '80 *Annual:* "Dimensions of Role Efficacy."

Submitted by Richard Parker and Annette A. Hartenstein. This piece has been substantially revised from an earlier version developed by Richard Parker and several colleagues.

Richard Parker is a teacher of parapsychology at the Mansbridge Institute, Alexandria, Virginia, and an instructor/facilitator in team building, managerial development and career planning, and training systems consultation. He is the co-author of Ethics in the Public Sector (1977).

Annette A. Hartenstein is the associate director of the Washington Management Institute of the United States Office of Personnel Management, Washington, D.C. She conducts management training and consults with government organizations. She is currently completing her doctorate in public administration. Her background is in organization development and project management.

MOVE TO NEWTOWN ROLE-PLAY INSTRUCTIONS

(Roles should be printed separately on individual pages and distributed separately to appropriate teams.)

Top Management

You want to move to the Newtown facility as soon as possible so that your agency can really get underway in accomplishing its mission. You are interested in obtaining ideas about needs for the allocation and use of space. At this time you believe that the new facility is quite adequate. You have not decided whether the final decision on plans should be yours entirely or based on a joint group decision. You want employees to settle down to their regular work as soon as possible, so you want to get the move over with.

Supervisory Personnel

You have no strong objection to the move to Newtown, although it is farther from normal transportation routes than your present location. Among the things you want is a private office so that you can talk to workers privately. In addition you believe that a conference room is essential. You like the idea of having a bar in the building so that you can relax there from the strains of supervision—Newtown is rather isolated. You would definitely object to an open-space arrangement for supervisors.

Space Procurement: General Services Administration

The Newtown facility has been a problem from the beginning. Since you have been paying tight money for rent for the past few months, you are anxious for the agency to move in right away. You want to get the property off your books. Your views are that the open-space arrangement without permanent walls would be the most adaptable to the agency's needs and allow for growth and changes. It also is cheaper than permanent walls and would be a cost savings. You are strongly in favor of the agency using the open-space arrangement.

Professional Personnel

You are unhappy about the change to the Newtown location, since you will not be able to continue in your carpool. Because you live so far away from Newtown, your travel time will be increased. You are especially concerned that the new facility have a library, since you will be so far from any of the downtown resources. Because your work often requires intense concentration, you would like a private office, but you would be satisfied with sharing an office. You also would like a quiet lounge area for reading and meditation.

Clerical Personnel

You are extremely unhappy about the possibility of being located at Newtown. You are concerned about the problem of public transportation and the amount of time it will take to get to work; it is almost twice as far away from home as the agency's present location. You are willing to accept the location if space is made available for a day care center and lunch room. In addition you want things that will make a comfortable and attractive physical environment. You are also concerned because there are no stores nearby for convenient shopping.

Union Representatives

You are interested in seeing that the workers get a fair deal in this location, including the physical arrangements. You are not sure what the workers want, so you need to find out and help them get what they want. You are relatively new as union representatives and want to gain a good reputation with the workers. The previous union was voted out less than six months ago.

MOVE TO NEWTOWN TASK AND INSTRUCTION BOOKLET

(The facilitator should prepare a booklet for each participant. The booklet should be assembled so that only one page can be read at a time.)

1

Your agency was reorganized just a few months ago to deal with the problems of unemployment in this country. Your mandate is to develop regional (state) programs to lessen unemployment. Your agency will be limited to sixty people, to include the director and his or her staff of three, seven managers, twenty-five professionals, fifteen technicians, and clerical workers. The General Services Administration has informed your top management that sufficient space is available at the Newtown industrial park and that you should move there immediately. Your agency employees are presently housed in temporary facilities in the downtown area. The quarters are crowded and in scattered buildings without sufficient phones or equipment.

The Task

You are being given the opportunity as a member of the new central office staff to determine changes in management processes and administrative procedures. How the office will be organized, managed, and administered will affect your own ability to function and contribute to the agency's goals.

Round 1: Planning Period (Twenty minutes)

2

The purpose of this planning period is to determine the specific self-interests and needs of your group. Defining self-interests and needs is the first step in dealing with change. Having a goal and a focus can determine your satisfaction with your work life. During this task, assume that it is advisable to be self-concerned and to know what you want to happen—be assertive.

In this round complete the following tasks:

1. Discuss your reactions to the agency's move. What are the self-interests and needs of the members of your team in this situation?
2. Agree on the team's self-interests and priorities.
3. Develop a plan to gather the information you need.
4. Determine who can help you deal with the change.
5. Identify your resources for obtaining your goals.

(Stop here—Turn the page only when all members of the team have reached agreement on the task or the facilitator instructs the groups to begin round 2.)

Power is the ability to get what you want or to influence what you want to be done. In this basic sense we all use many different forms of power all the time, through work and by personal traits. Power, however, has a bad reputation; many people believe that power corrupts and destroys. This is true of only one type of power. A major aspect of power usage is to discover not only your own self-interests, but those of others, and to recognize them as valuable. Personal power is essential to self-esteem and a healthy, fully functioning personality.

In this round you are encouraged to get acquainted with other groups in order to assess their self-interests and resources.

(In twenty minutes the facilitator will stop this round and direct you to turn to the next page.)

Round 3: Strategy Period   (Twenty minutes)   4

Decide which strategy your group will undertake or what suggestions you will make in dealing with the change.

Choosing a Power Strategy

Whatever your goals, there are at least three possible strategies you can use:

1. Collaboration (mutual support)
2. Exchange-Bargaining (making deals)
3. Coercion (threats or punishment)

Power Strategy Analysis

Your group's planning will be improved by answering the questions below.

1. How do we now see our own self-interests?

2. What power do we now have?

3. How do we perceive the power of other groups/individuals that affect our self-interests?

4. Do others acknowledge our power? How?

5. With which groups are we in a situation calling for:
   Collaboration:
   Exchange-Bargaining:
   Coercion:

6. What strategic options do we have?

7. Which will work best?

8. What shall we do now and who specifically does what?

Strategic Procedures

A well-designed strategy gets the most results for the least effort. Any strategy entails a degree of risk. Nonaction generally is a losing choice.

Collaborative Strategy

To build a cohesive, united force (coalition) out of two or more groups, you will need to develop and use such skills as:

1. Risk taking, trust building, establishing credibility
2. Mutual support systems
3. Sharing and using member resources, consensus seeking
4. Sharing self-interests, openness
5. Listening and communicating skills
6. Joint goal setting, planning, organizing
7. Value clarification
8. Conflict-resolution skills.

Exchange-Bargaining Strategy

If your group is to be successful in negotiating, you will need to develop and use such skills as:

1. Bargaining without selling out
2. Assertively using group strengths
3. Demonstrating that you are supported by your group members
4. Authorized to make trades
5. Properly representing your team
6. Renegotiating/selling your own team members on the contract
7. Making the first demand as high as the facts will justify
8. Making binding contracts to establish interdependence of both groups
9. Seeking opportunities to turn a trade-off into a win-win situation.

Coercive Strategy

If your group is to be successful in using coercion, you will need to develop optimum skills consistent with your self-interest. These may include:

1. Overwhelming opponents with superior force and greater speed
2. Exploiting the weaknesses of other groups
3. Using good timing to shock or surprise
4. Making convincing threats
5. Using underhanded tactics, spying, hiring agents from other teams, sacrificing one individual, etc.
6. Confusing or goading opponents into acting irrationally
7. Passing incomplete or wrong information
8. Purposely using poor communications
9. Creating issues.

(After your team has reached strategy consensus—approximately twenty minutes—the facilitator will direct you to move into round 4.)

Round 4: Action Period (Thirty minutes)   5

Employ your chosen tactics to implement your strategy. For the remainder of the activity you are on your own. Hold strategy sessions in individual teams or with others as often as needed. Remember that what happens depends on how you react to the situation and/or handle the change.

(At the end of thirty minutes, the facilitator will stop all activity and direct you to turn the page.)

Round 5: Reflections (Twenty minutes)   6

In order to reflect adequately on your experience, discuss the following aspects of the role-play experience:

1. *Feelings:* What were the main feelings that team members shared during the activity? What helped or hindered this process of sharing? How did each member deal with these feelings?
2. *Self-Interest:* Were members' various self-interests met? How did these self-interests change, if at all?
3. *Information:* How did team members arrange for a flow of information? How well did your group obtain the necessary information? How well did the team use the information it had?
4. *Strategy:* What overall strategy did the team have (a) in collaboration? (b) in bargaining? (c) in coercion?
5. *Satisfaction:* Are team members generally satisfied with the task outcome? How many individual team members are dissatisfied? Why?
6. *Role:* What effect did the assigned role have on behavior during the activity?

279. CREATIVE PRODUCTS: INTERGROUP CONFLICT RESOLUTION

Goals

    I. To examine the effects of collaboration and competition in intergroup relationships.

    II. To demonstrate the effects of win-win and win-lose approaches to intergroup conflict.

    III. To practice intragroup planning and problem solving.

Group Size

    Any number of groups of eight to twelve members each.

Time Required

    Two and one-half to three hours.

Materials

    I. A copy of the Creative Products General Situation Sheet for each participant.

    II. A copy each of the Creative Products Personnel Information Sheet, the Creative Products Management Problem Sheet, and the Creative Products Management Salary Sheet for each member of a management team.

    III. A copy of the Creative Products Personnel Information Sheet and a copy of the Creative Products Employee Problem Sheet for each member of an employee team.

    IV. A copy of the Creative Products Team Perception Sheet for each participant.

    V. Name tags for each participant.

    VI. Blank paper and a pencil for each participant.

    VII. Newsprint, felt-tipped markers, and masking tape for each group.

Physical Setting

    A room large enough for all participants to meet comfortably as a total group, small work areas for each subgroup, and a table and four chairs for each management-employee grouping.

Process

    I. The facilitator divides the participants into groups of eight to twelve members each and divides each subgroup into two teams (management and employee). He directs each team to go to a separate location in the room.

    II. The facilitator distributes a copy of the Creative Products General Situation Sheet, blank paper, and a pencil to each participant.

III. The facilitator distributes a copy of the Creative Products Personnel Information Sheet and the appropriate Creative Products Problem Sheet (Management or Employee) to each participant according to team designation. He also gives each member of a management team a copy of the Creative Products Management Salary Sheet.

IV. Each team is informed by the facilitator that it has forty-five minutes in which to:

1. Read the appropriate background materials.

2. Agree on a role for each member from among those for the team (management or employee) on the Creative Products Personnel Information Sheet.

3. Decide as a team on a solution to the problem facing Creative Products and a strategy for gaining acceptance of the proposal from the other team (management/employee) in the subgroup.

V. The facilitator gives all members name tags and instructs them to fill in their role names and wear their name tags.

VI. The facilitator tells each management team and each employee team to select one or two representatives to meet with representatives of the other team in a setting with a table and four chairs. The two to four representatives from each grouping then conduct a meeting to determine a course of action for Creative Products while other group members observe the negotiation. Members of the management and employee teams should sit behind their respective representatives during the negotiation session. (Thirty to forty minutes.)

VII. The facilitator calls time and directs representatives to rejoin their teams. The facilitator then distributes a copy of the Creative Products Team Perception Sheet to each participant. He allows ten minutes for completion of the sheet (for "our team" and for "the other team").

VIII. The facilitator instructs each management-employee group to conduct a discussion to debrief the activity, including the following points:

1. How negotiating representatives felt during the negotiation.

2. The kind of relationship evidenced between managers and employees during their joint meeting: collaborative (win-win) or adversarial (win-lose).

3. Specific behaviors on the part of each representative team member that were indicative of this relationship.

4. The effectiveness of each team's original solution to the problem and strategy for gaining acceptance for that solution.

5. How observing members felt as the negotiation activity progressed.

(Fifteen minutes.)

IX. Group members then are directed to share their responses to the items on the Creative Products Group Perceptions Sheet. Differences in group members' perceptions of their own group are noted and discussed. Special attention also is paid to differences in perceptions of "our team" and perceptions of "the other team." (Fifteen minutes.)

X. The facilitator reconvenes the total group and leads a discussion of the effects of competition on intergroup problem solving. Participants are encouraged to identify factors that contribute to dysfunctional attitudes and to suggest specific strategies for creating a climate for collaboration. The facilitator records these strategies on newsprint. (Twenty to thirty minutes.)

XI. Participants are formed into triads to discuss learnings and back-home applications of the strategies developed. (Fifteen to twenty minutes.)

Variations

I. If participants have had prior experience with each other, they can be asked to explore the process of group perception formation and change. (Twenty to thirty minutes.)

II. The facilitator can have each participant complete the Creative Products Team Perception Sheet immediately after members are divided into subgroups and once again at the conclusion of the activity, preceding the discussion.

III. The facilitator can lead the group in a discussion of the following additional questions at the conclusion of the activity:

1. How did you initially rate the other team in comparison to your own team? Why?
2. What characteristics or factors did you use to form your impressions of the other team?
3. How would you rate the other team now?
4. Have you changed your views of your own team? Why?

IV. The activity can be extended to include intergroup team building. (One and one-half hours.)

1. At the end of the activity, each team can meet separately to prepare three perception sheets: "our team," "the other team," and "predictions of how the other team described us."
2. The groups come back together and a spokesperson for each team presents his or her team's lists. (Ten minutes.)
3. Group members ask each other questions to clarify points of view. (Ten minutes.)
4. Mixed subgroups composed of four to five management and employee representatives review the lists independently and propose actions for improving relationships. (Twenty minutes.)
5. The subgroups report back to the total group, which then formulates a list of action items that it commits itself to perform. (Thirty minutes.)

V. The role aspect of the activity can be omitted. Personnel information sheets and management/employee problem sheets can be eliminated. Groups can engage in the activity using only the information from the general situation sheet. Processing focuses on group members' stereotypic thinking as a dynamic in understanding their solution to the problem and strategy for the meeting.

VI. During the negotiation session, representatives of either team can call for a recess of not more than three minutes to allow representatives to caucus with their teams to develop new strategies.

VII. Team members can be allowed to pass notes to their representatives during the negotiation session.

VIII. The content focus can be rewritten to reflect the concerns of the participants.

Similar Structured Experiences: *'75 Annual:* Structured Experience **145**; *Vol. V:* **158**; *Vol. VI:* **217**; *'80 Annual:* **278, 280.**

Lecturette Sources: *'73 Annual:* "Win-Lose Situations"; *'74 Annual:* "Conflict Resolution Strategies"; *'76 Annual:* "Power"; *'77 Annual:* "Handling Group and Organizational Conflict."

Submitted by William J. Heisler and Robert W. Shively.

William J. Heisler, Ph.D., is associate professor of management and director of the M.B.A. Executive Program, Babcock Graduate School of Management, Wake Forest University, Winston-Salem, North Carolina. In addition to his teaching and administrative duties, Dr. Heisler is doing research on quality of work life, organization development, and personal causation. He is a former AACSB-Federal Faculty Fellow and is a co-editor of A Matter of Dignity: Inquiries into the Humanization of Work *(1977). His background is in organizational behavior, organization development, and human resource management.*

Robert W. Shively, Ph.D., is associate professor of management, Babcock Graduate School of Management, Wake Forest University, Winston-Salem, North Carolina. He served as an administrator at Cornell University prior to completing his graduate work there. Dr. Shively has taught and done research in Latin America and now combines teaching with a variety of organization development activities for businesses and nonprofit organizations.

CREATIVE PRODUCTS GENERAL SITUATION SHEET

Creative Products, Inc., founded in 1965, is a small, family-owned specialty product manufacturer.

The company got off to a fast start, mostly because of its creative and innovative approaches to designing and solving the manufacturing problems of a product line that was new to the whole nation when the company began and which is still subject to fast changes. Both managers and workers have put in many long hours, often sacrificing their personal time to get the company off the ground and keep it competitive.

A significant downturn in the national and local economies has been experienced recently and is expected by most experts to last for another three to five years. At Creative Products, it is becoming increasingly obvious that some adjustments will have to be made if the company is to survive.

Confronted with the current economic conditions, management is about to conduct an analysis of the entire situation. However, having recently attended an executive seminar on human relations at a nearby university, Creative's president is also asking employees of the company to consider the situation and to meet with management to present any ideas they have as to how to deal with the company's current difficulty. It appears that unless the company can achieve cost reductions of approximately $30,000 per year, it will not be able to remain financially viable.

CREATIVE PRODUCTS PERSONNEL INFORMATION SHEET

Management Staff

Name	Position	Age	Date of Employment	Comments
Claude Jones	President	58	January 1965	One of company's founders. Health questionable.
Marcel Jones	Executive Vice President & Manager of Manufacturing	32	June 1970	M.B.A., B.S. in engineering design. Son of Claude Jones.
Pat Sadowski	Marketing Manager	53	February 1973	Increased sales markedly in first two years with company.
Paul Jones	Managerial Trainee	24	March 1976	M.B.A., bright and creative but insensitive to others. Adopted son of Claude Jones' brother. Has already lost two jobs due to inability to relate to others.
Marcia Phelps	Controller	38	March 1965	One of the group who started with the company.
Alfonso Rodriguez	Accountant	32	October 1975	Still in training under Marcia Phelps.

University Associates

Hourly Work Force

Name	Position	Age	Date of Employment	Comments
Casper Michelson	Machinist	62	January 1965	Reputed to have solved original problems related to manufacturing of Creative's leading product. Visibly slowing down due to age and health.
Quentin Salter	Set-Up Man	35	November 1972	After a slow start has become one of hardest-working employees. Limited intelligence and imagination.
Mary Levine	Packaging	57	June 1967	Always a reliable worker. Has son in Hawaii. Has expressed concern about effect on her job of new packaging machinery considered last year.
Stella Marquand	Tool & Die Specialist	28	July 1976	Associate degree from Lamar Tech. Bright, creative. Has already brought about money-saving innovations.
Fred Chun	Maintenance	47	August 1968	Faithful if not overly intelligent. Some suspicion that his son's accidental death last year has resulted in beginning stages of alcoholism.
"Mugsy" Fredericks	Machinist	40	February 1966	Can really get the work out. Is as productive as two average machinists. Somewhat resented by other workers for pressure his performance places on them.
Alice McGovern	Mold Specialist	41	April 1974	Held in some disregard by other workers due to her fast-paced personal life outside of work. Possesses a skill crucial to the company's manufacturing process. Would be hard to replace.
Hal Banks	Electrician	55	December 1971	An average worker. Perceived as falling behind in technical knowledge required by his position. Becomes eligible next year to participate in the company's retirement plan, which is considered to be a very good one.

CREATIVE PRODUCTS MANAGEMENT PROBLEM SHEET

The preliminary analysis conducted by the company's management indicates that the company has no choice but to reduce its work force if it is to survive. The analysis has been a careful one, with other alternatives explored thoroughly. Accordingly, the problem facing management is to decide who must go. Its thinking is that the work force will have to be reduced to no more than five or six people.

In the time allotted, decide which employees are to be terminated and how and outline the strategy you will use to "sell" Creative's employees on this approach.

Representatives of Creative's employee group are scheduled to meet with Claude and Marcel Jones later in the day to discuss the company's situation and plans.

CREATIVE PRODUCTS EMPLOYEE PROBLEM SHEET

There has been general recognition among Creative's employees for the last few months that the company is in trouble and that something will have to be done. A particular concern among you is that management will decide to reduce the size of the work force, placing either you or some of your colleagues or friends out of work. You suspect that there is a great deal of slack in top management and that management salaries are highly inflated.

In the allotted time, consider how the problem facing the company might be resolved and outline the strategy you will use to "sell" management on this approach.

Claude Jones has asked for two representatives of your group to meet with him later in the day to discuss the situation facing the company.

CREATIVE PRODUCTS MANAGEMENT SALARY SHEET

Name of Manager	Annual Salary
Claude Jones	$52,000
Marcel Jones	$40,000
Pat Sadowski	$33,000
Paul Jones	$17,000
Marcia Phelps	$31,000
Alfonso Rodriguez	$19,000

CREATIVE PRODUCTS TEAM PERCEPTION SHEET

Team _____

Instructions: Below are two lists of several adjectives that might be used to describe your team and the other team. In each list, for each adjective, circle the number that indicates the degree to which you believe it is descriptive of your team or the other team (7=completely descriptive; 1=definitely not descriptive).

Own Team

Honest	1	2	3	4	5	6	7
Open minded	1	2	3	4	5	6	7
Self-serving	1	2	3	4	5	6	7
Intelligent	1	2	3	4	5	6	7
Irrational	1	2	3	4	5	6	7
Fair	1	2	3	4	5	6	7
Emotional	1	2	3	4	5	6	7
Conservative	1	2	3	4	5	6	7
Friendly	1	2	3	4	5	6	7
Reasonable	1	2	3	4	5	6	7
Inflexible	1	2	3	4	5	6	7
Cooperative	1	2	3	4	5	6	7
Defensive	1	2	3	4	5	6	7
Aggressive	1	2	3	4	5	6	7
Unrealistic	1	2	3	4	5	6	7

Other Team

Honest	1	2	3	4	5	6	7
Open minded	1	2	3	4	5	6	7
Self-serving	1	2	3	4	5	6	7
Intelligent	1	2	3	4	5	6	7
Irrational	1	2	3	4	5	6	7
Fair	1	2	3	4	5	6	7
Emotional	1	2	3	4	5	6	7
Conservative	1	2	3	4	5	6	7
Friendly	1	2	3	4	5	6	7
Reasonable	1	2	3	4	5	6	7
Inflexible	1	2	3	4	5	6	7
Cooperative	1	2	3	4	5	6	7
Defensive	1	2	3	4	5	6	7
Aggressive	1	2	3	4	5	6	7
Unrealistic	1	2	3	4	5	6	7

280. HIGH IRON: COLLABORATION AND COMPETITION

Goals

I. To examine the elements of negotiation and collaboration in achieving goals.

II. To experience the effects of collaboration and/or competition in problem solving.

Group Size

Any number of groups of four members each.

Time Required

Approximately two hours.

Materials

I. A copy of the High Iron Work Sheet for each participant.

II. A copy of the High Iron Reaction Sheet for each participant.

III. A copy of the High Iron Information Sheet for each participant.

IV. A pencil for each participant.

V. Newsprint and a felt-tipped marker.

Physical Setting

A room large enough to provide a work area for each group.

Process

I. The facilitator introduces the activity as one that will examine the effects of competition and collaboration in achieving goals.

II. The facilitator divides the participants into subgroups of four members each and instructs them to arrange themselves in separate locations around the room. Each subgroup then is told to divide into two teams of two members each to represent the traffic managers of the Appalachian Railroad and the Blue Ridge Rail Lines. If there are an uneven number of participants, extra persons may be assigned to subgroups as process observers or recorders.)

III. The facilitator distributes a copy of the High Iron Information Sheet, a copy of the High Iron Work Sheet, and a pencil to each participant and tells the participants to read their instructions. When all members understand the procedure, the facilitator reminds them that the length of each negotiation session is indicated on the work sheet and tells them that teams will have three minutes for planning between each negotiating session. The facilitator also tells them that the two members of a company's management team may caucus at any time to discuss their corporate strategy.

IV. The facilitator calls time at the end of each planning period and times each round of the negotiations. Results from each of the seven rounds are recorded on the High Iron Work Sheet. (Thirty minutes.)

V. At the end of the seven rounds the facilitator distributes a copy of the High Iron Reaction Sheet to each participant and allows time for the members to complete it.

VI. The facilitator leads the subgroups through a debriefing of the activity, covering the following points:

1. Personal reactions to the experience
2. Consideration of the practical effects (in profits) of their decisions during the activity
3. Sharing of data from the High Iron Reaction Sheet
4. Review of negotiating-team style with other company teams

(Twenty minutes.)

VII. Subgroup reports are made. The facilitator posts data from items 1 and 2 on the High Iron Reaction Sheet for each team and then discusses what these results show in terms of competition and collaboration. (Ten minutes.)

VIII. Subgroup members process the activity by:

1. Discussing factors that enhance collaboration between working teams;
2. Identifying elements of the negotiation process that affect the climate of collaboration.

(Twenty minutes.)

IX. The facilitator leads a total-group discussion of the nature of collaborative behavior based on subgroup learnings, and generalizations are drawn from the group. (Twenty minutes.)

X. Application to back-home problem-solving sessions can be formulated, or individuals can generate personal statements of intended behavioral applications. (Ten minutes.)

Variations

I. The facilitator can announce that during rounds 5 and 7 there will be a "bonus for early delivery" for one or both companies. The "profit" is multiplied by ten for early delivery if a company uses the main line.

II. An eighth round can be declared, with a "bonus for early delivery" offered to one or both companies. The bonus round should be preceded by a two-minute negotiating session.

III. After round 5, the facilitator may declare the route closed by snow or a rail strike. Participants may spend time discussing what is happening or planning strategy with other managers from their company.

IV. With small participant groups, one subgroup can engage in the activity while other participants act as coaches or other personnel in the companies.

Similar Structured Experiences: *Vol. II:* Structured Experiences **35, 36;** *Vol. III:* **54, 61;** *'80 Annual:* **278, 279.**

Lecturette Sources: *'73 Annual:* "Win/Lose Situations"; *'74 Annual:* "Conflict-Resolution Strategies"; *'77 Annual:* "Handling Group and Organizational Conflict."

Submitted by Donald T. Simpson. This experience was developed to complement the research of M. Deutsch and R. M. Krauss, "The Effect of Threat on Interpersonal Bargaining," *Journal of Abnormal and Social Psychology,* 1960, *61,* 183.

Donald T. Simpson *is an educational specialist on the staff for management and general education, Corporate Relations, Eastman Kodak Company, Rochester, New York. Mr. Simpson is active as a consultant and trainer in organizational behavior, management, and interpersonal relations in business and the community. His background is in military logistics management, industrial engineering, adult education, and management education.*

HIGH IRON INFORMATION SHEET

The Appalachian Railroad and the Blue Ridge Rail Lines both ship products between Happy Valley and Rocky Mountain. There are two rail lines available to each company to use, as shown on the map. One route is the main line, or "high iron," the other is the "scenic route" (usually reserved for weekend excursions).

Appalachian controls the switch at A; Blue Ridge controls the switch at B. Between points A and B, traffic on the main line, or "high iron," can proceed in only *one* direction—east *or* west—during any one day.

Both Appalachian and Blue Ridge handle high-priority cargo, although not in direct competition with each other. When cargo goes on the main line, a company makes a profit of $5 a ton. But when cargo has to go on the scenic route, the company makes only $2 a ton profit because of the delay.

Your objective, as a member of your company's management team, is to make as much profit as possible. Just prior to each day's operations, or "round," you may negotiate with the other company for use of the high-iron route. If you fail to reach an agreement before the negotiating time expires, the main line becomes unavailable (Nobody wants a head-on collision!)

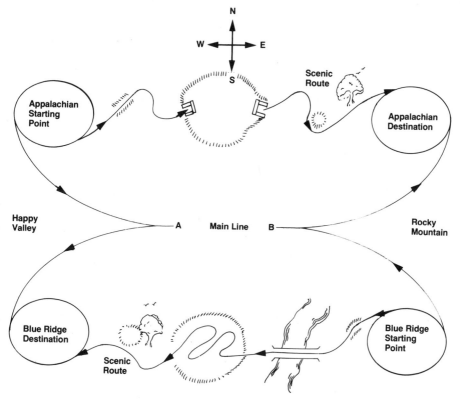

HIGH IRON WORK SHEET

Round (Day)	Negotiating Time	Decision: Main-Line Flow (East or West)	Appalachian's Profit	Blue Ridge's Profit
1	2 min.			
2	1 min.			
3	1 min.			
4	1 min.			
5	2 min.			
6	1 min.			
7	1 min.			

Total Profit _____   _____

HIGH IRON REACTION SHEET

Take twenty minutes to record your reactions to this activity.

1. Profit for my company   \$_____ per ton
   Profit for other company   \$_____ per ton

2. Generally, use of the main line was determined by:

   ( ) Threat of denial by other company (closing the switch at A or B)
   ( ) Threat of reprisal (if you do not let me use the main line, I will not let you use it next time)
   ( ) Reciprocal agreement (if you let me use it this time, I will let you use it next time)
   ( ) Negotiation and understanding (we will both come out with more profit if we cooperate)
   ( ) Other:

3. I felt that my team (was/was not) in competition with the other team.

4. Some problems we had in negotiating use of the main line were:

5. Some things we did to enhance cooperation were:

6. From this experience, I learned that:

INTRODUCTION TO THE
INSTRUMENTATION SECTION

One of the most serious problems that group facilitators encounter in using instruments in training and consulting is what is often referred to colloquially as "nitpicking," or challenging the validity of items and/or scales. This phenomenon is often interpreted as a defense mechanism, and facilitators need to avoid using instruments and methods that encourage this result.

DEVELOPING INSTRUMENTS SPONTANEOUSLY

There are a number of ways of responding productively to nitpicking, but it is important to avoid generating the reaction whenever possible. One good way is to develop instruments "on the spot," with participants actually writing the "items." An added advantage to this practice is that often the facilitator cannot locate (or did not anticipate the need for) an instrument that is appropriate to the situation.

We will explore five simple methods for involving participants in creating their own instruments. Of course, few scales evolved this way would stand up to statistical scrutiny. Spontaneously derived instruments are, however, helpful in exploring concepts, generating here-and-now data for discussion and/or processing, developing new models for exploring human interaction, and facilitating a sense of ownership about learning.

Adjective Check Lists

Adjectives are solicited by some appropriate procedure (for example, brainstorming, free association, critical incidents). These are alphabetized and then used for various purposes such as feedback, intergroup perception checking, and evaluating. One method is described in detail in Volume V of our *Handbook* series (Pfeiffer & Jones, 1975, pp. 114-115).

An example comes from a team-building session. The facilitator wants a way to focus an exchange of interpersonal perceptions about influence within the work group. Members are instructed (1) to recall an individual in their past (not present) who has influenced them both significantly and *positively* and (2) to write down two or three adjectives that describe how they experienced that person. Then the process is repeated for a person who influenced them both significantly and *negatively*. These two lists of adjectives are called out, alphabetized, and posted. This "instrument" is then used to guide the discussion of individuals in the team. There are no questions about reliability, validity, objectivity, or relevance.

Attitude Scales

The facilitator selects an appropriate topic (attitude object) such as overtime pay for managers, job enrichment, the MBO system, or consensus as a decision-making strategy. Each participant writes a "true" statement about the topic. These statements are posted and numbered, without discussion. (The facilitator needs to be careful not to edit the statements except to make them unidimensional. For example, the statement "Job enrichment is best done by imposing changes designed by management because workers do not have the proper perspective" is really two statements and should be posted as such.) The response scale is then introduced. Usually this is some variation of the familiar Likert scale:

SA = Strongly agree
A = Agree
U = Uncertain or undecided
D = Disagree
SD = Strongly disagree

Participants write down the number of each statement and their response to it. These responses are tallied by a show of hands, and the facilitator guides a discussion of the results.

In a recent company supervisory-skills session, the facilitator picked up a controversy among participants regarding the subject of women as managers. Since the group had resisted an earlier paper-and-pencil inventory that the facilitator had introduced, a spontaneously developed instrument might help to focus attention on both the subject and self-assessment. Participants were instructed to write down a completion of the following sentence: "As managers, women . . ." Members of the training group were reluctant to read their sentences aloud in order for the facilitator to post them, so small discussion groups were formed to explore the reasons why people were hesitant to reveal their attitudes. Reports indicated that this was a controversial topic in the company and that it was never addressed publicly. The facilitator then had participants write their sentences on cards and pass them in anonymously. These statements were then randomized and posted. Members used the five-point Likert scale to record their agreement or disagreement with each item. Individuals then asked for a group tally on any item of interest, and the facilitator directed the lively discussion that followed.

Semantic Differential Scales

Participants develop a list of bi-polar adjectives such as hot-cold, light-heavy, high-low, etc. These are posted as the ends of continua, with six or seven points in between, e.g.:

empty /————/————/————/————/————/————/————/ full
fast /————/————/————/————/————/————/————/ slow

Then a topic to be rated is announced. Each participant rates the topic according to his or her associations with it. These ratings are tallied and written on the posted instrument as the agenda for discussion. The group sees its profile of association for the topic rated. According to the research of Osgood, Suci, and Tannenbaum (1957), who developed this type of instrument, there should be three types of bi-polar adjectives included: those that are evaluative (sweet-sour, happy-sad, etc.), those that measure potency (large-small, strong-weak, etc.), and those that refer to activity (active-passive, fast-slow, etc.).

Public-school principals are discussing racial integration in their schools in a management-development seminar on conflict. The interchange is energetic, but the facilitator senses that participants are using familiar terms in ways that imply a variance of meaning. What "the neighborhood concept" means to one person is not what another associates with the phrase. The discussion is not building understanding, and emotions are running high. A set of semantic differential scales is constructed to clear up the connotative meanings of various emotionally loaded subtopics, such as forced busing, magnet schools, staff integration, ethnic studies, etc. This intervention helps to foster more effective self-expression and listening.

Behaviorally Anchored Rating Scales (BARS)

Participants write down individually important dimensions to be studied. These lists are melded on newsprint, and the group selects the most salient ones by some appropriate method (for example, voting for three, ranking, or rating). Subgroups are formed to correspond to the selected dimensions, and these groups construct behaviorally anchored rating scales. These scales are presented to and edited by the group. Then the BARS are used to perform ratings to generate data for discussion.

An example of this technique comes from team building. In sensing interviews members of the group had voiced dissatisfaction with their weekly staff meetings. In the beginning of the off-site session the group constructed BARS on six different aspects of effective staff meetings, such as cooperation, open communication, and attention to process. One of the scales was participation:

Participation 1 • • • 2 • • • 3 • • • 4 • • • 5 • • • 6 • • • 7 • • • 8 • • • 9

The meeting	People contribute	Everyone's
is dominated	when they have	input is solicited
by one or two	strong feelings	before decisions
members		are made

These scales were then used by individuals to rate their usual meetings and that particular meeting. A progress chart was constructed on which averages were posted. The BARS were used at the end of each three-hour segment of the team-building session and became the basis for team self-assessment at ensuing regular staff meetings.

Model-Based Questionnaires

The group is given the task of creating a model of the process to be studied. (See the introduction to the Theory and Practice section of this *Annual* for a step-by-step model-building process.) Subgroups are formed around the major aspects of the model, and they are instructed to develop one or two questionnaire items to measure the selected dimensions of the model. Each member of a subgroup makes a copy of the subgroup's item(s). As soon as all subgroups have completed this task, an "assessment circus" is held, in which everyone fans out from subgroups and "administers" items to each other. A participant approaches another, shows the item(s), records the response(s) on a separate sheet of paper (so as not to contaminate later responses by showing earlier ones), and then solicits a critique of the item(s). When all participants have been surveyed, the subgroups are reassembled to tally the data and to discuss the critiques of their item(s). Representatives are chosen to make brief reports to the total group. The facilitator leads a discussion of the aggregate data.

In a train-the-trainer workshop, the staff wanted to involve participants in exploring the norms of the "learning community" in order to increase commitment to shared responsibility. The group brainstormed community norms and selected a set of five that seemed particularly relevant to the workshop at that time. Members volunteered to work on a norm area of interest, and subgroups each wrote one or two items. After all the data were collected and collated, subgroup representatives had a confrontation meeting with the workshop staff to present the findings. (All the other participants were observers.) The staff members had their own meeting at that time to explore methods to deal with dysfunctional norms and to reinforce facilitative ones. Subgroups reassembled to rewrite their items, based on the critiques; these items formed the basis for a later diagnosis of community functioning.

Developing instruments spontaneously not only serves as a highly effective training and consulting intervention, but it also forms the basis for scales that can later be refined into publishable form.

This section contains four instruments which we believe to be widely useful to group facilitators. One is personal, one role-oriented, one management focused, and one organizational based. A great deal of attention has been given to the measurement of Jung's typology over the years, and the "Personal Style Inventory" is a simple, inexpensive way of introducing these concepts in training and development. Pareek has devoted much of his professional attention to organizational roles, and his "Role Efficacy Scale" is beneficial in training, team building, and coaching individual managers. The subject of Harvey's instrument is controversial, and opening up discussion and self-assessment on the issues is a good use of "Increasing Employee Self-Control." The final instrument in this set, "Organizational Diagnosis Questionnaire," was selected to meet facilitators' need for easy-to-use assessment devices.

REFERENCES

Osgood, C. T., Suci, G. J., & Tannenbaum, P. H. *The measurement of meaning.* Urbana, IL: University of Illinois Press, 1957.

Pfeiffer, J. W., & Jones, J. E. (Eds.). *A handbook of structured experiences for human relations training*(Vols. I-VII).San Diego, CA: University Associates, 1973-1979.

PERSONAL STYLE INVENTORY

R. Craig Hogan and David W. Champagne

Everyone brings to interactions a headful of assumptions, values, and needs that engender either congenial, comfortable, productive discussion or frustrating, conflicting, unproductive argument (or, worse, silent uncooperation) that reflects the prejudices and needs of the participants rather than the real issues.

When people who interact daily understand their own values and assumptions that affect their thinking and interaction, they will more likely be tentative about the ideas and suggestions they advance, seeing them as ideas they value rather than as commandments carved in stone. They also will be more able to accept the ideas or actions of others that differ from their own, realizing that these, too, are the result of the values and assumptions of others.

THE INSTRUMENT

The 32-item Personal Style Inventory is designed to measure a person's Jungian typology, a construct first described by Jung (1921) and then later elucidated by Myers (1962). Hogan (1979) has recently completed a manual to accompany the inventory, explain the typology, and suggest uses for it in various human organizations.

The purpose of the Personal Style Inventory is to enable training participants to identify their personality typologies so that they can learn to understand better the influence of personality style on their thoughts and actions and on the thoughts and actions of those with whom they interact. The inventory will also help them identify strengths and weaknesses in their own styles of thinking and acting as reflected in their personality typologies.

THE TYPOLOGY

There are four pairs of dimensions in the typology. Every person exhibits both dimensions of each pair in thought and action, but for each person one dimension of each is used more often, is more comfortable, and has given rise to a greater number of beliefs, values, and cognitive skills congruent with it than has the other member of the pair. The stronger dimension consequently characterizes the person's outlook, personality, and thought processes. As a result, a person's typology of preference for four of these dimensions (one from each of the four pairs) can be determined, and predictions about values, beliefs, and behavior can be made based on the resulting typology.

When participants understand how profoundly the dimensions in the typology affect their values, choices, assumptions, beliefs, decisions, thoughts, and behavior and those of their spouses, colleagues, superiors, subordinates, students, and instructors, then they can begin to realize that the statements and actions that they and those around them live by are the result of different views of the world, not right or wrong thinking. The points of view of other people, and the people themselves, can be more easily understood and accepted.

(The four pairs of dimensions as well as their strengths and weaknesses and some generalizations and implications based on the typology are further described on the Personal Style Inventory Interpretation Sheet following the instrument.)

DEVELOPMENT OF THE INSTRUMENT AND VALIDITY DATA

The ideal method of determining validity would be to have a Jungian therapist interview and assign types to a sample of subjects, have the subjects fill out the inventory, and then compare resulting typologies. Instead, the authors elected to gather enough data to indicate that the inventory has reasonable accuracy through an analogous procedure in which higher-education faculty members judged their own typologies.

Higher-education faculty members in small groups filled out the inventory without scoring it and then were taught the characteristics of the dimensions in the Jungian typology. After instruction about each pair of dimensions, the individuals were asked to assign a score to each member of the pair to indicate the strength of each in their Jungian typology. When estimates had been made for all four pairs of dimensions, the inventories were scored, and the scores were compared with the faculty members' estimated scores. It was assumed that if the correlations were high, the inventory was a reasonably valid measure of Jungian typology that could be used in workshops for which research accuracy is not necessary. This procedure was repeated a number of times with small groups of faculty members as the inventory was revised and refined.

Pearson correlations comparing inventory scores and participant estimate scores for the last groups of faculty involved in workshops (n=20) were .60, .74, .66, and .61 for the four areas measured by the typology. Phi correlations comparing resulting dimensions of the typology estimated by the faculty members and obtained from the inventory (either one dimension or the other of each pair) resulted in correlations of .78, .55, .90, and .71.

The authors decided that these validity correlations, obtained in the situation of having to train people to discriminate personality styles in themselves in a short period of time, were sufficiently high to suggest that the survey can be used with confidence when participants also learn about the dimensions so that they can assess the accuracy of the instrument's indications of typology. Actual results were that 60 percent estimated all four dimensions of the typology the same as the inventory indicated, 90 percent indicated three of the four the same, 95 percent indicated two of the four the same, and 100 percent indicated at least one of the dimensions the same as did the inventory.

SUGGESTED USES

The inventory is best used with groups in which participants have the opportunity to discuss with others their differences in styles and preferences. The Jungian typology has gained acceptance in a wide variety of fields, including business, education, counseling, criminal justice, health, engineering, and religion. Interactions among people in any setting will benefit when those interacting understand the style differences that result in conflict or in weak, ineffective decisions.

A Helpful Workshop Procedure

The following sequence may be useful for the facilitator.

1. Introduce the need to understand and consider values that are based on personality styles.
2. Give out the inventory and have participants fill it out.

3. Explain each pair of dimensions in turn and ask participants to estimate whether they feel themselves to be more like one dimension or the other.
4. Have participants score the survey.
5. Then have participants examine the descriptions of the typology dimensions that are different from their own and discuss the results of the inventory with people who have the same and different typologies.
6. Discuss the implications for interaction in the participants' own settings.

ADMINISTRATION

The inventory is self-administering and self-scoring. It takes about ten minutes to fill out and five minutes to score. The facilitator needs to remind participants of the following points:

1. Fractions are not permitted.
2. Scores for each pair must add up to 5.
3. Participants should mark items to indicate the way they actually are rather than the way they would like to be and the way they are when not under duress rather than when pressured to act in a particular way.
4. Participants should check their scores after writing them down.

It is important, also, to explain to participants that the inventory is only an indication of typology and that the final determination of personal style and values must be made by each individual.

REFERENCES

Jung, C. G. Personality types. *Collected works* (Vol. VI). NJ: Bollingen Press, 1921.
Myers, I. B. *The Myers-Briggs type indicator manual.* Palo Alto, CA: Consulting Psychologists Press, 1962.
Hogan, R. C. *Learning to love our differences.* Unpublished manuscript, 1979.

R. Craig Hogan, Ph.D., is an assistant professor and curriculum specialist at the University of Health Sciences, the Chicago Medical School, Chicago, Illinois. He was previously an educational development consultant, McMaster University, Hamilton, Ontario, Canada, and curriculum coordinator at the University of Pittsburgh. Dr. Hogan's interests are higher education curriculum and instruction, self-instruction, applications of Jungian typology to interactions, clinical supervision of instructors in health education, and training of supervisors of instructors.

David W. Champagne, Ed.D., is an associate professor of curriculum and supervision, School of Education, University of Pittsburgh, Pittsburgh, Pennsylvania. He regularly serves as a consultant to school districts and other organizations in the United States and Canada in the areas of supervision, organization development, curriculum development, in-service education, and staff development. He is the author of several books on parent education, individualization of instruction, and supervision and management.

PERSONAL STYLE INVENTORY
R. Craig Hogan and David W. Champagne

Just as every person has differently shaped feet and toes from every other person, so we all have differently "shaped" personalities. Just as no person's foot shape is "right" or "wrong," so no person's personality shape is right or wrong. The purpose of this inventory is to give you a picture of the shape of your preferences, but that shape, while different from the shapes of other persons' personalities, has nothing to do with mental health or mental problems.

The following items are arranged in pairs (a and b), and each member of the pair represents a preference you may or may not hold. Rate your preference for each item by giving it a score of 0 to 5 (0 meaning you *really* feel negative about it or strongly about the other member of the pair, 5 meaning you *strongly* prefer it or do not prefer the other member of the pair). The scores for a and b MUST ADD UP TO 5 (0 and 5, 1 and 4, 2 and 3, etc.). *Do not use fractions such as 2½.*

I prefer:

1a.＿＿ making decisions after finding out what others think.

1b.＿＿ making decisions without consulting others.

2a.＿＿ being called imaginative or intuitive.

2b.＿＿ being called factual and accurate.

3a.＿＿ making decisions about people in organizations based on available data and systematic analysis of situations.

3b.＿＿ making decisions about people in organizations based on empathy, feelings, and understanding of their needs and values.

4a.＿＿ allowing commitments to occur if others want to make them.

4b.＿＿ pushing for definite commitments to ensure that they are made.

5a.＿＿ quiet, thoughtful time alone.

5b.＿＿ active, energetic time with people.

6a.＿＿ using methods I know well that are effective to get the job done.

6b.＿＿ trying to think of new methods of doing tasks when confronted with them.

7a.＿＿ drawing conclusions based on unemotional logic and careful step-by-step analysis.

7b.＿＿ drawing conclusions based on what I feel and believe about life and people from past experiences.

8a. _____ avoiding making deadlines.

8b. _____ setting a schedule and sticking to it.

9a. _____ talking awhile and then thinking to myself about the subject.

9b. _____ talking freely for an extended period and thinking to myself at a later time.

10a. _____ thinking about possibilities.

10b. _____ dealing with actualities.

11a. _____ being thought of as a thinking person.

11b. _____ being thought of as a feeling person.

12a. _____ considering every possible angle for a long time before and after making a decision.

12b. _____ getting the information I need, considering it for a while, and then making a fairly quick, firm decision.

13a. _____ inner thoughts and feelings others cannot see.

13b. _____ activities and occurrences in which others join.

14a. _____ the abstract or theoretical.

14b. _____ the concrete or real.

15a. _____ helping others explore their feelings.

15b. _____ helping others make logical decisions.

16a. _____ change and keeping options open.

16b. _____ predictability and knowing in advance.

17a. _____ communicating little of my inner thinking and feelings.

17b. _____ communicating freely my inner thinking and feelings.

18a. _____ possible views of the whole.

18b. _____ the factual details available.

19a. _____ using common sense and conviction to make decisions.

19b. _____ using data, analysis, and reason to make decisions.

20a. _____ planning ahead based on projections.

20b. _____ planning as necessities arise, just before carrying out the plans.

21a. _____ meeting new people.

21b. _____ being alone or with one person I know well.

22a. _____ ideas.

22b. _____ facts.

23a. _____ convictions.

23b. _____ verifiable conclusions.

24a. _____ keeping appointments and notes about commitments in notebooks or in appointment books as much as possible.

24b. _____ using appointment books and notebooks as minimally as possible (although I may use them).

25a. _____ discussing a new, unconsidered issue at length in a group.

25b. _____ puzzling out issues in my mind, then sharing the results with another person.

26a. _____ carrying out carefully laid, detailed plans with precision.

26b. _____ designing plans and structures without necessarily carrying them out.

27a. _____ logical people.

27b. _____ feeling people.

28a. _____ being free to do things on the spur of the moment.

28b. _____ knowing well in advance what I am expected to do.

29a. _____ being the center of attention.

29b. _____ being reserved.

30a. _____ imagining the nonexistent.

30b. _____ examining details of the actual.

31a. _____ experiencing emotional situations, discussions, movies.

31b. _____ using my ability to analyze situations.

32a. _____ starting meetings at a prearranged time.

32b. _____ starting meetings when all are comfortable or ready.

PERSONAL STYLE INVENTORY SCORING SHEET

Instructions: Transfer your scores for each item of each pair to the appropriate blanks. Be careful to check the a and b letters to be sure you are recording scores in the right blank spaces. Then total the scores for each dimension.

	Dimension			Dimension	

I	**E**	**N**	**S**
Item	*Item*	*Item*	*Item*
1b._____	1a._____	2a._____	2b._____
5a._____	5b._____	6b._____	6a._____
9a._____	9b._____	10a._____	10b._____
13a._____	13b._____	14a._____	14b._____
17a._____	17b._____	18a._____	18b._____
21b._____	21a._____	22a._____	22b._____
25b._____	25a._____	26b._____	26a._____
29b._____	29a._____	30a._____	30b._____
Total I_____	**Total E**_____	**Total N**_____	**Total S**_____

	Dimension			Dimension	

T	**F**	**P**	**J**
Item	*Item*	*Item*	*Item*
3a._____	3b._____	4a._____	4b._____
7a._____	7b._____	8a._____	8b._____
11a._____	11b._____	12a._____	12b._____
15b._____	15a._____	16a._____	16b._____
19b._____	19a._____	20b._____	20a._____
23b._____	23a._____	24b._____	24a._____
27a._____	27b._____	28a._____	28b._____
31b._____	31a._____	32b._____	32a._____
Total T_____	**Total F**_____	**Total P**_____	**Total J**_____

PERSONAL STYLE INVENTORY INTERPRETATION SHEET

Letters on the score sheet stand for:

I—introversion	E—extroversion
N—intuition	S—sensing
T—thinking	F—feeling
P—perceiving	J—judging

If your score is: the likely interpretation is:

20-21   balance in the strengths of the dimensions

22-24   some strength in the dimension; some weakness in the other member of the pair

25-29   definite strength in the dimension; definite weakness in the other member of the pair

30-40   considerable strength in the dimension; considerable weakness in the other member of the pair

Your typology is those four dimensions for which you had scores of 22 or more, although the relative strengths of all the dimensions actually constitute your typology. Scores of 20 or 21 show relative balance in a pair so that either member could be part of the typology.

DIMENSIONS OF THE TYPOLOGY

The following four pairs of dimensions are present to some degree in all people. It is the extremes that are described here. The strength of a dimension is indicated by the score for that dimension and will determine how closely the strengths and weaknesses described fit the participant's personality.

Introversion—Extroversion

Persons more introverted than extroverted tend to make decisions somewhat independently of constraints and prodding from the situation, culture, people, or things around them. They are quiet, diligent at working alone, and socially reserved. They may dislike being interrupted while working and may tend to forget names and faces.

Extroverted persons are attuned to the culture, people, and things around them, endeavoring to make decisions congruent with demands and expectations. The extrovert is outgoing, socially free, interested in variety and in working with people. The extrovert may become impatient with long, slow tasks and does not mind being interrupted by people.

Intuition—Sensing

The intuitive person prefers possibilities, theories, gestalts, the overall, invention, and the new and becomes bored with nitty-gritty details, the concrete and actual, and facts unrelated to concepts. The intuitive person thinks and discusses in spontaneous leaps of intuition that may leave out or neglect details. Problem solving comes easily for this individual, although there may be a tendency to make errors of fact.

96   *University Associates*

The sensing type prefers the concrete, real, factual, structured, tangible here-and-now, becoming impatient with theory and the abstract, mistrusting intuition. The sensing type thinks in careful, detail-by-detail accuracy, remembering real facts, making few errors of fact, but possibly missing a conception of the overall.

Feeling—Thinking

The feeler makes judgments about life, people, occurrences, and things based on empathy, warmth, and personal values. As a consequence, feelers are more interested in people and feelings than in impersonal logic, analysis, and things, and in conciliation and harmony more than in being on top or achieving impersonal goals. The feeler gets along well with people in general.

The thinker makes judgments about life, people, occurrences, and things based on logic, analysis, and evidence, avoiding the irrationality of making decisions based on feelings and values. As a result, the thinker is more interested in logic, analysis, and verifiable conclusions than in empathy, values, and personal warmth. The thinker may step on others' feelings and needs without realizing it, neglecting to take into consideration the values of others.

Perceiving—Judging

The perceiver is a gatherer, always wanting to know more before deciding, holding off decisions and judgments. As a consequence, the perceiver is open, flexible, adaptive, nonjudgmental, able to see and appreciate all sides of issues, always welcoming new perspectives and new information about issues. However, perceivers are also difficult to pin down and may be indecisive and noncommittal, becoming involved in so many tasks that do not reach closure that they may become frustrated at times. Even when they finish tasks, perceivers will tend to look back at them and wonder whether they are satisfactory or could have been done another way. The perceiver wishes to roll with life rather than change it.

The judger is decisive, firm, and sure, setting goals and sticking to them. The judger wants to close books, make decisions, and get on to the next project. When a project does not yet have closure, judgers will leave it behind and go on to new tasks and not look back.

STRENGTHS AND WEAKNESSES OF THE TYPES

Each person has strengths and weaknesses as a result of these dimensions. Committees and organizations with a preponderance of one type will have the same strengths and weaknesses.

Possible Strengths	Possible Weaknesses
Introvert	
independent	misunderstands the external
works alone	avoids others
is diligent	is secretive
reflects	loses opportunities to act
works with ideas	is misunderstood by others
is careful of generalizations	needs quiet to work
is careful before acting	dislikes being interrupted

Extrovert

understands the external
interacts with others
is open
acts, does
is well understood

has less independence
does not work without people
needs change, variety
is impulsive
is impatient with routine

Intuitor

sees possibilities
sees gestalts
imagines, intuits
works out new ideas
works with the complicated
solves novel problems

is inattentive to detail, precision
is inattentive to the actual and practical
is impatient with the tedious
leaves things out in leaps of logic
loses sight of the here-and-now
jumps to conclusions

Senser

attends to detail
is practical
has memory for detail, fact
works with tedious detail
is patient
is careful, systematic

does not see possibilities
loses the overall in details
mistrusts intuition
does not work out the new
is frustrated with the complicated
prefers not to imagine future

Feeler

considers others' feelings
understands needs, values
is interested in conciliation
demonstrates feeling
persuades, arouses

is not guided by logic
is not objective
is less organized
is uncritical, overly accepting
bases justice on feelings

Thinker

is logical, analytical
is objective
is organized
has critical ability
is just
stands firm

does not notice people's feelings
misunderstands others' values
is uninterested in conciliation
does not show feelings
shows less mercy
is uninterested in persuading

Perceiver

compromises
sees all sides of issues
is flexible, adaptable
remains open for changes
decides based on all data
is not judgmental

is indecisive
does not plan
has no order
does not control circumstances
is easily distracted from tasks
does not finish projects

University Associates

Judger

decides	is unyielding, stubborn
plans	is inflexible, unadaptable
orders	decides with insufficient data
controls	is judgmental
makes quick decisions	is controlled by task or plans
remains with a task	wishes not to interrupt work

GENERALIZATIONS

The following generalizations can be helpful in applying this inventory to individual settings.

1. People who have the same strengths in the dimensions will seem to "click," to arrive at decisions more quickly, to be on the same wave length. Their decisions, however, may suffer because of their weaknesses, exhibiting blind spots and holes that correspond to the list of weaknesses for that type.

2. People who have different strengths in the dimensions will not see eye-to-eye on many things and will have difficulty accepting some views, opinions, and actions of the other. The more dimensions in which the two differ, the greater the conflict and misunderstanding of each other. However, decisions resulting from their interaction will benefit from the differing points of view and strengths of each.

3. People may be sensitive about criticisms in their areas of weakness and likely will prefer not to use these dimensions. As a result, conflict may occur when they must do so or when others point out deficiencies in these areas.

4. People will normally gravitate toward others who have similar strengths and weaknesses, although people of differing types are often drawn to one another because the strengths of one are admired and needed by the other.

5. People's values, beliefs, decisions, and actions will be profoundly influenced by all four of the stronger dimensions in their typology.

6. While a person's typology cannot be changed to its opposite, each person can learn to strengthen the weaker dimensions to some extent and to develop personal life strategies to overcome problems that result from the weaknesses.

IMPLICATIONS

The Personal Style Inventory raises several implications to consider.

1. Individuals, groups, and organizations with a preponderance of members whose strengths are in one type should seek out and listen to people of the opposite types when making decisions. Task-oriented groups would often benefit from a mixture of types.

2. People should realize that many differences in beliefs, values, and actions are the result of differences in style rather than of being right or wrong. Rather than be concerned over the differences, we need to understand and accept them and value the perspective they give.

3. When people must, of necessity, interact often with the same people (in teaching, business, marriage, etc.), interactions can be more congenial, satisfying, and productive if those involved, especially those with the greater power, understand the needs of others based on typology differences and adjust to them.

4. When interacting to accomplish tasks, people should be careful to label their values as values and then proceed to examine the facts and forces involved without defending the value position.

ROLE EFFICACY SCALE

Udai Pareek

The performance of people working in an organization depends on their own potential effectiveness, their technical competence, their managerial skills and experience, and the design of the roles they perform in the organization. It is the integration of individuals and their roles that ensures their effectiveness in the organization. Unless people have the requisite knowledge, technical competence, and skills required for their roles, they cannot be effective. But if the role does not allow a person to use his or her competence, and if the individual constantly feels frustrated in the role, effectiveness is likely to be low. The closer that role *taking* (responding to the expectations of various other people) moves to role *making* (taking the initiative in designing the role creatively so that the expectations of others as well as of the role occupant are integrated), the more the role is likely to be effective. This potential effectiveness can be called efficacy. Role efficacy can be seen as the psychological factor underlying role effectiveness.

DIMENSIONS OF ROLE EFFICACY

Role efficacy has ten dimensions, and the more these dimensions are present in a role, the higher the efficacy of that role is likely to be.[1]

1. Centrality vs. Peripherality
   The dimension of centrality measures the role occupant's perception of the significance of his or her role. The more central that people feel their roles are in the organization, the higher will be their role efficacy. For example, "I am a production manager, and my role is very important."

2. Integration vs. Distance
   Integration between the self and the role contributes to role efficacy, and self-role distance diminishes efficacy. "I am able to use my knowledge very well here."

3. Proactivity vs. Reactivity
   When a role occupant takes initiative and does something independently, that person is exhibiting *pro*active behavior. On the other hand, if he or she merely responds to what others expect, the behavior is *re*active. For example, "I prepare the budget for discussion" versus "I prepare the budget according to the guidance given by my boss."

4. Creativity vs. Routinism
   When role occupants perceive that they do something new or unique in their roles, their efficacy is high. The perception that they do only routine tasks lowers role efficacy.

5. Linkage vs. Isolation
   Interrole linkage contributes to role efficacy. If role occupants perceive interdependence with others, their efficacy will be high. Isolation of the role reduces efficacy. Example of linkage: "I work in close liaison with the production manager."

---

[1] See "Dimensions of Role Efficacy" in the Lecturettes section of this *Annual*.

University Associates

6. Helping vs. Hostility

One important aspect of efficacy is the individual's perception that he or she gives and receives help. A perception of hostility decreases efficacy. "Whenever I have a problem, others help me," instead of "People here are indifferent to others."

7. Superordination vs. Deprivation

One dimension of role efficacy is the perception that the role occupant contributes to some "larger" entity. Example: "What I do is likely to benefit other organizations also."

8. Influence vs. Powerlessness

Role occupants' feeling that they are able to exercise influence in their roles increases their role efficacy. The influence may be in terms of decision making, implementation, advice, or problem solving. "My advice on industrial relations is accepted by top management." "I am able to influence the general policy of marketing."

9. Growth vs. Stagnation

When a role occupant has opportunities—and perceives them as such—to develop in his or her role through learning new things, role efficacy is likely to be high. Similarly, if the individual perceives his role as lacking in opportunities for growth, his role efficacy will be low.

10. Confrontation vs. Avoidance

When problems arise, either they can be confronted and attempts made to find solutions for them, or they can be avoided. Confronting problems to find solutions contributes to efficacy, and avoidance reduces efficacy. An example of confrontation: "If a subordinate brings a problem to me, I help to work out the solution." "I dislike being bothered with interpersonal conflict" is a statement indicating avoidance.

USING THE DATA GENERATED

Measurement of role efficacy is not done for its own sake; it should lead to a program of improvement in efficacy. Since factors concerned both with the individual (the role occupant) and with the design of the role contribute to efficacy, two approaches can be adopted for increasing role efficacy.

Role Redefinition

After the dimensions in which role efficacy is low have been diagnosed, the problem can be approached from the perspective of the role. The diagnosis may show that some dimensions are missing from the role and may suggest various ways of building in those missing dimensions. For example, if centrality is missing from the role, ways can be worked out to enrich the role. However, there are no standard solutions to build various dimensions into the role; the solutions will differ from situation to situation. In redefining roles, various ways of developing the missing dimensions can be prepared first by individuals involved in the situation (the role occupant and significant persons who work with him or her). Then these individual suggestions can be discussed in detail to discover to what extent they are feasible and likely to increase role efficacy.

Action Planning

It is equally important to work on role efficacy from the point of view of the role occupant. Role efficacy may be low because the role occupant is not able to perceive certain dimensions in the role, or the individual may not be able to use his or her own power to build those dimensions into the role. Counseling and coaching may be necessary. For example, if the person perceives that linkages with other roles are weak, he can be worked with to build stronger linkages with other roles. Or if she feels that her role does not provide opportunities to learn new things and grow, she can be helped to perceive other dimensions of the role. The purpose of action planning is to help the individual take necessary steps without waiting for redesign of the role.

USES OF THE ROLE EFFICACY SCALE

The Role Efficacy Scale is useful in a number of different situations. It can be used for role clarification in team building, for coaching key managers, for problem identification within a work team, and for training managers and supervisors about the concept of role efficacy.

Udai Pareek, Ph.D., is Larsen & Toubro professor of organizational behavior at the Indian Institute of Management, Ahmedabad, Gujarat, India. Dr. Pareek's background is in organization development, human resource development, organizational designing, and change in persons and systems. He has consulted with industrial and nonindustrial systems in various countries and with many international organizations.

ROLE EFFICACY SCALE
Udai Pareek

Your name _____   Your role _____

In each of the following sets of three statements, check the one (a, b, or c) that most accurately describes your own experience in your organizational role. You must choose only *one* statement in each set.

1. _____ a. My role is very important in this organization; I feel central here.

_____ b. I am doing useful and fairly important work.

_____ c. Very little importance is given to my role in this organization; I feel peripheral here.

2. _____ a. My training and expertise are not fully utilized in my present role.

_____ b. My training and knowledge are not used in my present role.

_____ c. I am able to use my knowledge and training very well here.

3. _____ a. I have little freedom in my role; I am only an errand boy.

_____ b. I operate according to the directions given to me.

_____ c. I can take initiative and act on my own in my role.

4. _____ a. I am doing usual, routine work in my role.

_____ b. In my role I am able to use my creativity and do something new.

_____ c. I have no time for creative work in my role.

5. _____ a. No one in the organization responds to my ideas and suggestions.

_____ b. I work in close collaboration with some other colleagues.

_____ c. I am alone and have almost no one to consult in my role.

6. _____ a. When I need some help none is available.

_____ b. Whenever I have a problem, others help me.

_____ c. I get very hostile responses when I ask for help.

7. _____ a. I regret that I do not have the opportunity to contribute to society in my role.

_____ b. What I am doing in my role is likely to help other organizations or society.

_____ c. I have the opportunity to have some effect on the larger society in my role.

8. _____ a. I contribute to some decisions.

_____ b. I have no power here.

_____ c. My advice is accepted by my seniors.

9. _____ a. Some of what I do contributes to my learning.

_____ b. I am slowly forgetting all that I learned (my professional knowledge).

_____ c. I have tremendous opportunities for professional growth in my role.

10. _____ a. I dislike being bothered with problems.

_____ b. When a subordinate brings a problem to me, I help to find a solution.

_____ c. I refer the problem to my boss or to some other person.

11. _____ a. I feel quite central in the organization.

_____ b. I think I am doing fairly important work.

_____ c. I feel I am peripheral in this organization.

12. _____ a. I do not enjoy my role.

_____ b. I enjoy my role very much.

_____ c. I enjoy some parts of my role and not others.

13. _____ a. I have little freedom in my role.

_____ b. I have a great deal of freedom in my role.

_____ c. I have enough freedom in my role.

14. _____ a. I do a good job according to a schedule already decided.

_____ b. I am able to be innovative in my role.

_____ c. I have no opportunity to be innovative and do something creative.

15. _____ a. Others in the organization see my role as significant to their work.

_____ b. I am a member of a task force or a committee.

_____ c. I do not work in any committees.

16. _____ a. Hostility rather than cooperation is evident here.

_____ b. I experience enough mutual help here.

_____ c. People operate more in isolation here.

17. _____ a. I am able to contribute to the company in my role.

_____ b. I am able to serve the larger parts of the society in my role.

_____ c. I wish I could do some useful work in my role.

18. _____ a. I am able to influence relevant decisions.

_____ b. I am sometimes consulted on important matters.

_____ c. I cannot make any independent decisions.

19. _____ a. I learn a great deal in my role.

_____ b. I learn a few new things in my role.

_____ c. I am involved in routine or unrelated activities and have learned nothing.

20. _____ a. When people bring problems to me, I tend to ask them to work them out themselves.

_____ b. I dislike being bothered with interpersonal conflict.

_____ c. I enjoy solving problems related to my work.

ROLE EFFICACY SCALE SCORING AND INTERPRETATION SHEET

Instructions: Circle the number corresponding to your response to each of the twenty items. Total these numbers and enter this sum in the box just below the key. Then compute your Role Efficacy Index according to the formula given.

Dimension	Item	a	b	c	Item	a	b	c
Centrality	1.	+2	+1	−1	11.	+2	+1	−1
Integration	2.	+1	−1	+2	12.	−1	+2	+1
Proactivity	3.	−1	+1	+2	13.	−1	+2	+1
Creativity	4.	+1	+2	−1	14.	+1	+2	−1
Interrole Linkage	5.	−1	+2	+1	15.	+2	+1	−1
Helping Relationship	6.	+1	+2	−1	16.	−1	+2	+1
Superordination	7.	−1	+2	+1	17.	+1	+2	−1
Influence	8.	+1	−1	+2	18.	+2	+1	−1
Growth	9.	+1	−1	+2	19.	+2	+1	−1
Confrontation	10.	−1	+2	+1	20.	+1	−1	+2

Your total [ ]

Role Efficacy Index

$$\frac{\text{Total score} + 20}{60} \times 100 = \boxed{\quad \% \quad}$$

Example: $\dfrac{36 + 20}{60} \times 100 = 93\%$

Interpretation

Note that the scale (−1, +1, +2) allows a maximum score of +40 and a minimum score of −20. Your Role Efficacy Index represents a percentage of your potential effectiveness in your organizational role. A high percentage indicates that you perceive that in your role you have a great deal of opportunity to be effective.

The ten dimensions of role efficacy are each measured by two items. Look at each dimension to determine in what areas you perceive yourself as having less than what you think you need to be effective. Look for pairs of items for which you have low scores and compare these dimensions. You may want to discuss your findings with your colleagues and your supervisor.

INCREASING EMPLOYEE SELF-CONTROL (IESC)

Barron H. Harvey

As a topic in the area of management training, motivation has received enormous attention. Many theorists have come forth with motivational theories that attempt to explain and predict behavior from the point of view of motivation. The concept of self-control is an important element in most motivational theories, even those that are built on the principle of hedonism. Organization-wide attempts to improve motivation have as their goal increasing employee self-control within organizational constraints.

The Increasing Employee Self-Control (IESC) questionnaire was developed to assess managers' receptiveness toward increasing employees' self-control in organizations. Many techniques today are built on this concept: e.g., management by objectives (MBO), participative decision making, flexitime, job enrichment, goal setting, motivation training, personal time bank, and staggered work hours. Because the success or failure of these techniques may rest on management's reactions, it is important for the organization to determine how these suggestions will be received by managers. The IESC responses will indicate if respondents are in favor of, indifferent to, or not in favor of conveying more control to subordinate employees.

DEVELOPMENT

The IESC questionnaire was developed using Likert's method of summated ratings. Originally, twenty-four statements were composed based on four definitions of employee self-control:

Definition 1. Employees (especially lower level personnel) manage their own organizational contingencies and consequences (on an individual basis whenever possible).

Definition 2. Employees participate in decision making.

Definition 3. Employees in organizations have more responsibility.

Definition 4. Employees determine their contingencies.

After a factor analysis, the original statements were reduced to sixteen. The questionnaire contains items that are assumed to be approximately equal in attitude loading. Half of the items are negative and half are positive.

The reliability of IESC was estimated using the internal consistency method. The technique used was Behrnstedt's (1969) method of determining the reliability of multiple-item scales (which utilizes a covariance matrix) from data generated during the pretest. The reliability estimate for IESC was .76.

SCORING AND INTERPRETATION

The questionnaire consists of an equal number of positive and of negative statements. The responses available are Strongly Agree (SA), Agree (A), Undecided (U), Disagree (D), and Strongly Disagree (SD). These responses are scored in reverse numerical order for positive and negative statements: for positive statements, (SA)=5, (A)=4, (U)=3, (D)=2, and (SD)=1; for negative statements, (SA)=1, (A)=2, (U)=3, (D)=4, and (SD)=5. The total score may range from sixteen to eighty. The letter responses are translated to numerical scores with the aid of the IESC Scoring and Interpretation Sheet.

The final numerical score on the IESC questionnaire is designed to indicate the manager/respondent's attitude or receptiveness toward increasing subordinate employees' self-control. A score of 16-23 indicates that the manager is definitely not in favor of the items assessed; a score of 24-29 indicates that the manager is not in favor of the items assessed; a score of 40-55 indicates that the manager is undecided; a score of 56-71 indicates that the manager is in favor of increasing employee self-control; a score of 72-80 indicates that the manager is strongly in favor of increasing employee self-control. Based on these interpretations, initial or additional training may be necessary before a particular technique is implemented.

ADMINISTRATION AND USES

Approximately ten to twenty minutes is required to complete the questionnaire. The following are suggested uses for IESC:

1. This questionnaire can be administered prior to training (in areas such as motivation, goal setting, participative decision making, job enrichment, delegation, etc.) and again at the end of training. By comparing the two sets of scores, participants have an indication of how much new knowledge and/or attitude change has occurred.

2. The IESC questionnaire can be administered before an organization implements a technique that seeks to increase employee self-control. Scores will indicate whether management training on the technique is necessary prior to implementation in order to increase the chance of success.

3. IESC can be used to assess training needs when organizational morale/satisfaction is low. The results may indicate which techniques employees desire most.

4. The questionnaire can be administered to management personnel and to subordinate personnel and the results from the two groups compared. Such comparison serves as excellent feedback and workshop discussion, especially in team-development activities.

5. IESC can be used effectively to assess Theory X ("definitely not in favor," "not in favor") managers and Theory Y ("strongly in favor," "in favor") managers.

6. A trainer will find that various items in the IESC questionnaire can also serve as excellent discussion items in training sessions.[1]

REFERENCES

Behrnstedt, G. W. A quick method for determining the reliability and validity of multiple-item scales. *American Sociological Review*, August 1969, *34*(4), 542-548.

Harvey, B. H. Exploring the effects of increasing employee self-control/determination. Unpublished dissertation, University of Nebraska, Lincoln, Nebraska, 1977.

Barron H. Harvey, Ph.D., is an assistant professor of organizational behavior and accounting at the School of Business Administration, Georgetown University, Washington, D.C., and president of Barron H. Harvey and Associates, a management training and development consulting firm in Herndon, Virginia. Dr. Harvey has published and presented papers in the areas of affirmative action, problems of the federal manager, self-control, and flexitime. His background is in management training and assessment, affirmative action, managerial accounting, organizational behavior modification, tax accounting, and organizational behavior and development.

[1]The Increasing Employee Self-Control (IESC) workshop and facilitator's *Guide* may be obtained from Barron H. Harvey & Associates, 1003 Trinity Gate Street, Herndon, Virginia 22070.

INCREASING EMPLOYEE SELF-CONTROL (IESC)
Barron H. Harvey

Your Name _____

Date _____

Instructions: For each statement below circle your response:

Strongly Agree (SA)
Agree (A)
Undecided (U)
Disagree (D)
Strongly Disagree (SD)

1. When opportunities exist for employees to work independently (without supervision), there will be an increase in efficiency.   SA   A   U   D   SD

2. Although attempts are made at giving employees more responsibility, they will seldom utilize these opportunities.   SA   A   U   D   SD

3. Employees, on their own, will in most cases do what is required of them.   SA   A   U   D   SD

4. Employees should be given more opportunities to determine their tasks to be accomplished.   SA   A   U   D   SD

5. Strict controls in organizations are required for efficient operation.   SA   A   U   D   SD

6. Subordinate participation in decision making produces greater harmony between superior and subordinate.   SA   A   U   D   SD

7. More responsibility given to subordinates will result in benefits to the individual employee and organization.   SA   A   U   D   SD

8. Allowing employees to manage their own personal leave time (sick, vacation, personal business, and holiday time) will result in abuse.   SA   A   U   D   SD

9. Allowing more employee initiative in the work place would cause much confusion.   SA   A   U   D   SD

10. Participative decision making is of little value because most subordinates do not understand the overall objectives of the organization.   SA   A   U   D   SD

11. When employees are given more responsibility in the work environment, they will be more committed to organizational goals and objectives.   SA   A   U   D   SD

12. Allowing employees to start work anytime they desire (within a two-hour flexible range) will result in confusion and inefficiency.   SA   A   U   D   SD

University Associates

13. When left on their own, most subordinates will not do the work that is required of them.   SA   A   U   D   SD

14. Employees who are committed to organizational goals and objectives require little supervision.   SA   A   U   D   SD

15. Given the opportunity, most employees will make decisions that benefit the organization and the employees.   SA   A   U   D   SD

16. Most employees are unable to identify with the organization or its objectives.   SA   A   U   D   SD

IESC SCORING AND INTERPRETATION SHEET

Instructions: Circle the response you gave to each item; sum all circled numbers under each column (SA, A, U, D, and SD), and then sum across all columns for an overall total score.

	SA	A	U	D	SD
1	5	4	3	2	1
2	1	2	3	4	5
3	5	4	3	2	1
4	5	4	3	2	1
5	1	2	3	4	5
6	5	4	3	2	1
7	5	4	3	2	1
8	1	2	3	4	5
9	1	2	3	4	5
10	1	2	3	4	5
11	5	4	3	2	1
12	1	2	3	4	5
13	1	2	3	4	5
14	5	4	3	2	1
15	5	4	3	2	1
16	1	2	3	4	5
Subtotals		+	+	+	+	=

Total

University Associates

Interpretation

Place an "X" on the continuum below to indicate the degree to which you are in favor of increasing employee self-control and self-determination. For example, scores of 16-24 indicate that you are definitely *not* in favor of having employees manage their own organizational contingencies, have more responsibility, and participate more in decision making.

A Continuum of Attitudes Toward Increasing
Employee Self-Control

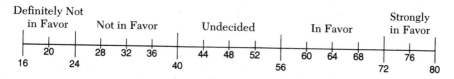

ORGANIZATIONAL DIAGNOSIS QUESTIONNAIRE (ODQ)

Robert C. Preziosi

Both internal and external organization development (OD) consultants at some point in the consulting process must address the question of diagnosis. Recently the need for two levels of diagnosis, preliminary and intensive, was addressed (Lippitt & Lippitt, 1978). The purpose of the Organizational Diagnosis Questionnaire (ODQ) is to provide survey-feedback data for intensive diagnostic efforts. Use of the questionnaire either by itself or in conjunction with other information-collecting techniques (such as direct observation or interviewing) will provide the data needed for identifying strengths and weaknesses in the functioning of an organization and/or its subparts. The questionnaire produces data relative to informal activity.

A meaningful diagnostic effort must be based on a theory or model of organizational functioning. This makes action research possible as it facilitates problem identification, which is essential to organization development. One of the more significant models in existence is Weisbord's (1976) Six-Box Organizational Model (Figure 1). Weisbord's model establishes a systematic approach for analyzing relationships among variables that influence how an organization is managed. It provides for assessment in six areas of formal and informal activity: purposes, structure, relationships, rewards, leadership, and helpful mechanisms. The outer circle in Figure 1 determines an organizational boundary for diagnosis. This boundary clarifies the functioning of the internal environment, which is to be analyzed to the exclusion of the external environment.

THE INSTRUMENT

The Organizational Diagnosis Questionnaire (ODQ) is based on Weisbord's practitioner-oriented theory. The ODQ generates data in each of Weisbord's suggested six areas as well as in a seventh, attitude toward change. This item was added as a helpful mechanism for the person involved in organizational diagnosis. In attempting any planned-change effort in an organization it is wise to know how changeable an organization is. Such knowledge helps the change agent understand how to direct his efforts.

Thirty-five items compose the ODQ, five in each of the seven variables. Respondents are asked to indicate their current views of their organization on a scale of 1 to 7, with a score of 4 representing a neutral point.

USES OF THE ODQ

The ODQ can be administered to a work unit, an entire organization, or a random sample of each. It might also be used to analyze staff or line functioning as well as to assess the thinking of different levels of management or supervision. It should be administered by the consultant or process facilitator in order to insure that an adequate explanation of the questionnaire and its use will be given. The consultant could also train others to administer the questionnaire.

Administration and Scoring

The administrator of the questionnaire must emphasize to the respondents that they be open and honest. If they are not, data that yield an inaccurate assessment of the organization on any or all of the seven variables may be produced. All ODQ statements are positive and can easily be discerned as such, which may influence the manner in which the respondents react to the questionnaire.

Scoring the questionnaire may be done in more than one way. Aggregate data will be most useful; an individual's set of responses is not significant. A self-scoring sheet is provided for each individual. Individual scoring sheets could then be tabulated by the consultant, an assistant, or, for large-scale studies, a computer.

Processing the Data

Once aggregate data have been collected, they must be processed. The first task is to prepare a bar or line graph (or any similar technique) to present the data so that they can be readily understood. The consultant/facilitator should present the data first to the organization's president or the work unit's supervisor (whichever is applicable) to establish understanding, commitment, and support.

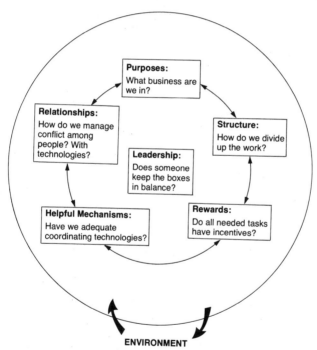

Figure 1. The Six-Box Organizational Model[1]

---

[1] Reproduced from M. R. Weisbord, Organizational diagnosis: Six places to look for trouble with or without a theory, *Group & Organization Studies*, 1976, *1*(4), 430-447, by permission of the publisher and the author.

Next, a meeting with the work group is essential. During this meeting the consultant/ facilitator must weave a delicate balance between task and maintenance issues in order to be productive. During this meeting a number of things take place: information is presented (feedback); information is objectively discussed; group problem solving is encouraged; brainstorming for solutions is facilitated; alternative solutions are evaluated against criteria; a solution is chosen; an action plan is developed; and a plan for future evaluation is determined. This process is presented in detail in Hausser, Pecorella, and Wissler (1977).

The ODQ produces information about the informal system. As Weisbord suggested, the formal system must be considered also. A consultant/facilitator may review an organization's charter, operations manual, personnel policies, etc. Gaps between the two systems lead to a diagnosis of what is not happening that should be happening, or vice versa.

In sum, the ODQ is useful for diagnostic efforts insofar as it provides data about people's perceptions of their organization. It is an instrument that may be used separate from or in addition to other information-collecting techniques.

REFERENCES

Hausser, D. L., Pecorella, P. A., & Wissler, A. L. *Survey-guided development: A manual for consultants.* San Diego, CA: University Associates, 1977.

Lippitt, G., & Lippitt, R. *The consulting process in action.* San Diego, CA: University Associates, 1978.

Weisbord, M. R. Organizational diagnosis: Six places to look for trouble with or without a theory. *Group & Organization Studies,* 1976, *1*(4), 430-447.

Robert C. Preziosi, D.P.A., is a consulting associate with Organization Renewal, Inc., and an instructor in the behavioral science and management areas for Nova University's master's program in management and public service, Miami, Florida. He has conducted many leadership and human relations training programs for local, state, and national groups and published a series of case studies on human relations training. Dr. Preziosi's special interests are management training, organization development, and internal change agentry.

ORGANIZATIONAL DIAGNOSIS QUESTIONNAIRE
Robert C. Preziosi

From time to time organizations consider it important to analyze themselves. It is necessary to find out from the people who work in the organization what they think if the analysis is going to be of value. This questionnaire will help the organization that you work for analyze itself.

Directions: Do not put your name anywhere on this questionnaire. Please answer all thirty-five questions. *Be open and honest.* For each of the thirty-five statements circle only *one (1)* number to indicate your thinking.

1—Agree Strongly
2—Agree
3—Agree Slightly
4—Neutral
5—Disagree Slightly
6—Disagree
7—Disagree Strongly

1. The goals of this organization are clearly stated.   1 2 3 4 5 6 7

2. The division of labor of this organization is flexible.   1 2 3 4 5 6 7

3. My immediate supervisor is supportive of my efforts.   1 2 3 4 5 6 7

4. My relationship with my supervisor is a harmonious one.   1 2 3 4 5 6 7

5. My job offers me the opportunity to grow as a person.   1 2 3 4 5 6 7

6. My immediate supervisor has ideas that are helpful to me and my work group.   1 2 3 4 5 6 7

7. This organization is not resistant to change.   1 2 3 4 5 6 7

8. I am personally in agreement with the stated goals of my work unit.   1 2 3 4 5 6 7

9. The division of labor of this organization is conducive to reaching its goals.   1 2 3 4 5 6 7

10. The leadership norms of this organization help its progress.   1 2 3 4 5 6 7

11. I can always talk with someone at work if I have a work-related problem.   1 2 3 4 5 6 7

12. The pay scale and benefits of this organization treat each employee equitably.   1 2 3 4 5 6 7

13. I have the information that I need to do a good job.   1 2 3 4 5 6 7

	Agree Strongly	Agree	Agree Slightly	Neutral	Disagree Slightly	Disagree	Disagree Strongly

14. This organization is not introducing enough new policies and procedures.   1 2 3 4 5 6 7

15. I understand the purpose of this organization.   1 2 3 4 5 6 7

16. The manner in which work tasks are divided is a logical one.   1 2 3 4 5 6 7

17. This organization's leadership efforts result in the organization's fulfillment of its purposes.   1 2 3 4 5 6 7

18. My relationships with members of my work group are friendly as well as professional.   1 2 3 4 5 6 7

19. The opportunity for promotion exists in this organization.   1 2 3 4 5 6 7

20. This organization has adequate mechanisms for binding itself together.   1 2 3 4 5 6 7

21. This organization favors change.   1 2 3 4 5 6 7

22. The priorities of this organization are understood by its employees.   1 2 3 4 5 6 7

23. The structure of my work unit is well designed.   1 2 3 4 5 6 7

24. It is clear to me whenever my boss is attempting to guide my work efforts.   1 2 3 4 5 6 7

25. I have established the relationships that I need to do my job properly.   1 2 3 4 5 6 7

26. The salary that I receive is commensurate with the job that I perform.   1 2 3 4 5 6 7

27. Other work units are helpful to my work unit whenever assistance is requested.   1 2 3 4 5 6 7

28. Occasionally I like to change things about my job.   1 2 3 4 5 6 7

29. I desire less input in deciding my work-unit goals.   1 2 3 4 5 6 7

30. The division of labor of this organization helps its efforts to reach its goals.   1 2 3 4 5 6 7

31. I understand my boss's efforts to influence me and the other members of the work unit.   1 2 3 4 5 6 7

	Agree Strongly	Agree	Agree Slightly	Neutral	Disagree Slightly	Disagree	Disagree Strongly
32. There is no evidence of unresolved conflict in this organization.	1	2	3	4	5	6	7
33. All tasks to be accomplished are associated with incentives.	1	2	3	4	5	6	7
34. This organization's planning and control efforts are helpful to its growth and development.	1	2	3	4	5	6	7
35. This organization has the ability to change.	1	2	3	4	5	6	7

ODQ SCORING SHEET

Instructions: Transfer the numbers you circled on the questionnaire to the blanks below, add each column, and divide each sum by five. This will give you comparable scores for each of the seven areas.

Purposes	Structure	Leadership	Relationships
1 _____	2 _____	3 _____	4 _____
8 _____	9 _____	10 _____	11 _____
15 _____	16 _____	17 _____	18 _____
22 _____	23 _____	24 _____	25 _____
29 _____	30 _____	31 _____	32 _____
Total _____	Total _____	Total _____	Total _____
Average _____	Average _____	Average _____	Average _____

Rewards	Helpful Mechanisms	Attitude Toward Change
5 _____	6 _____	7 _____
12 _____	13 _____	14 _____
19 _____	20 _____	21 _____
26 _____	27 _____	28 _____
33 _____	34 _____	35 _____
Total _____	Total _____	Total _____
Average _____	Average _____	Average _____

ODQ PROFILE AND INTERPRETATION SHEET

Instructions: Transfer your average scores from the ODQ Scoring Sheet to the appropriate boxes in the figure below. Then study the background information and interpretation suggestions that follow.

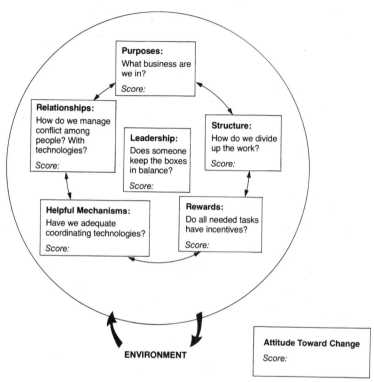

BACKGROUND

The ODQ is a survey-feedback instrument designed to collect data on organizational functioning. It measures the perceptions of persons in an organization or work unit to determine areas of activity that would benefit from an organization development effort. It can be used as the sole data-collection technique or in conjunction with other techniques (interview, observation, etc.).

Weisbord's Six-Box Organizational Model (1976) is the basis for the questionnaire, which measures seven variables: purposes, structure, relationships, rewards, leadership, helpful mechanisms, and attitude toward change. The first six areas are from Weisbord's model, while the last one was added to provide the consultant/facilitator with input on readiness for change.

The instrument and the model reflect a systematic approach for analyzing relationships among variables that influence how an organization is managed. The ODQ measures the informal aspects of the system. It may be necessary for the consultant/facilitator also to gather information on the formal aspects and to examine the gaps between the two.

Using the ODQ is the first step in determining appropriate interventions for organizational change efforts. Its use as a diagnostic tool can be the first step in improving an organization's or work unit's capability to serve its clientele.

INTERPRETATION AND DIAGNOSIS

A crucial consideration is the diagnosis based upon data interpretation. The simplest diagnosis would be to assess the amount of variance for each of the seven variables in relation to a score of 4, which is the neutral point. Scores above 4 would indicate a problem with organizational functioning. The closer the score is to 7 the more severe the problem would be. Scores below 4 indicate the lack of a problem, with a score of 1 indicating optimum functioning.

Another diagnostic approach follows the same guidelines of assessment in relation to the neutral point (score) of 4. The score of each of the thirty-five items on the questionnaire can be reviewed to produce more exacting information on problematic areas. Thus diagnosis would be more precise. For example, let us suppose that the average score on item number 8 is 6.4. This would indicate not only a problem in organizational purpose, but also a more specific problem in that there is a gap between organizational and individual goals. This more precise diagnostic effort is likely to lead to a more appropriate intervention in the organization than the generalized diagnostic approach described in the preceding paragraph.

Appropriate diagnosis must address the relationships between the boxes to determine the interconnectedness of problems. For example, if there is a problem with relationships, could it be that the reward system does not reward relationship behavior? This might be the case if the average score on item 33 was well above 4 (5.5 or higher) and all the items on relationships (4, 11, 18, 25, 32) averaged above 5.5.

INTRODUCTION TO THE
LECTURETTES SECTION

The lecture method is often criticized as dull, lifeless, boring, and inefficient, but this does not need to be true. Presenting theoretical models and research findings to groups can be enlivened by incorporating dialogs and other interactions into the experience. The facilitator can build into the input some pauses for experiential interchange. We have published three experiential lectures in past *Annuals:*

"Communication Modes," 1972 *Annual* (pp. 173-177);

"Don't You Think That. . . ?", 1974 *Annual* (pp. 203-208);

"Individual Needs and Organizational Goals," 1974 *Annual* (pp. 215-219).

In addition, there are suggested activities included in many of the lecturettes published in this section of the *Annual* over the years.

MAKING CONCEPTUAL INPUTS EXPERIENTIAL

With a little imagination the facilitator can make almost any conceptual input experiential. The advantages for doing so are primarily as follows:

- *Involvement.* In general it is important to design any training or consulting activity in such a way as to avoid putting participants in a passive posture because commitment can result only from a sense of ownership through meaningful involvement.

- *Relevance.* It is difficult to anticipate what will be significant to each member of a group. When participants are engaged in activities correlated with conceptual input, they make the content immediately credible for themselves.

- *Expanding the data base.* Using experiential techniques in conjunction with lecturettes capitalizes on the experience pool (both "here and now" and "there and then") that exists within the participant group.

- *Two-way communication.* The facilitator models effective communication when the content is continuously clear, and two-way exchanges are much more likely to meet this criterion than one-way telling.

- *Checking understanding.* Since considerable screening of information occurs as participants listen to a lecturette, it is important for the facilitator to determine the accuracy of the communication and to clear up any misconceptions. Experiential exchanges help to isolate misunderstandings of concepts.

- *Maintaining rapport.* Presenting conceptual inputs can create a sense of distance between the facilitator and the group. The group may come to depend on the facilitator to explain everything, rather than to look within itself for conceptual models.

- *Excitement.* Participants are more likely to be receptive to input that they experience in a lively manner.

One potential disadvantage needs to be pointed out. Participants may become overly involved in the experiential components of the event and may not gain a sense of perspective or overall understanding of the information being disseminated. The facilitator needs to fit each segment of input and activity into an overall framework and reinforce that overview throughout the experience.

Numerous methods for making conceptual inputs experiential are available for experimentation. In the sections that follow several representative ideas are presented to be used before, during, and after lecturettes.

Preparing for Conceptual Inputs

It is usually advisable to engage in some activity to promote readiness for learning a model. These methods are best carried out quickly, leading directly into the facilitator's presentation.

- *Energizers.* These activities usually are fun, and they entail physical movement. Although they are almost content-free, they prepare participants for a period of seated work. Several designs are included in Volume V of our *Handbook* series (pp. 3-4).

- *Associations.* Participants call out their associations with the topic of the conceptual input. This gives the facilitator a sense of the "audience," and it promotes a feeling of connectedness to the topic. A simple method is to put a heading on a sheet of newsprint (for example, "OD is . . .") and record spontaneous responses of participants.

- *T-charts.* On a sheet of newsprint the facilitator makes two columns, headed "Good News" and "Bad News" and posts reactions to the topic from participants.

- *Plus-minus-question mark.* The facilitator instructs participants to make three columns on note paper, headed with the symbols, "+," "−," and "?." Individuals make notes about their predispositions toward the theory topic. These are called out and may be posted.

- *Fantasy.* A guided fantasy can be conducted by the facilitator to establish a mental and emotional set for the input. Several examples are included in Volume I of the *Handbook* (pp. 75-77). The theory and technique of using fantasy in training and consulting are discussed in the 1976 *Annual* (pp. 191-201).

- *Assigned listening.* The audience is divided into thirds, with each segment instructed to listen in a particular way. One group listens for points with which it agrees, another for points with which it disagrees, and the third for points that need clarification and/or amplification. Reports can be solicited from these groups midway through the lecturette, and assignments can be changed for the second half.

- *Spontaneous lecture.* The group brainstorms ideas around the planned topic. Then individuals stand and talk briefly and extemporaneously on various aspects of the topic. This technique is described in more detail in Volume III of the *Handbook* (pp. 31-32). For large groups the "Quaker Meeting" design is an alternative. (See the 1972 *Annual*, pp. 11-12.)

- *Self-assessment.* Participants are instructed to apply the conceptual input to themselves. From time to time personal statements are solicited by the facilitator.

These methods can be used together, of course, but the facilitator needs to be careful not to make the preparation so involved as to detract from the input to follow. The data generated by these activities can give clues about how to begin the lecturette.

Linking Input with Participation

During the presentation of the lecturette the facilitator needs to maintain effective contact with participants and to break up the input with interspersed activities that will give points added meaning. The following methods can aid in keeping participants at work during the event:

- *Soliciting examples.* Instead of giving examples related to the cognitive input, the facilitator can ask participants to offer their own. The request to "think of an incident in your experience that illustrates this point" can provoke both task-relevant thinking and productive sharing.
- *Current events.* The facilitator asks for examples from the news to illustrate points in the lecturette.
- *Dyadic interviews.* Participants sit in pairs and are instructed to interview each other at selected points when the lecturette is interrupted. A good practice is to encourage interviewers to avoid "yes-no" and "why" questions and to experiment with "what" and "how" ones.
- *Right-left comparisons.* At appropriate points during the lecturette the facilitator stops giving input and instructs participants to compare their reactions with the persons on their right and on their left. Similarities and differences are reported to the total group.
- *Synonyms and euphemisms.* Participants devise an alternate terminology for any technical language or jargon in the conceptual input. This task can be carried out in subgroups.
- *Checking understanding.* The facilitator stops from time to time and asks the simple question "What do you hear me saying?" Distortions, misinterpretations, and omissions can then be dealt with before continuing the conceptual input.
- *Interviewing the facilitator.* Participants act as reporters at a news conference and pose questions to the facilitator on the points just raised in the lecturette.
- *"Right now I . . ."* At appropriate points in the presentation the facilitator solicits statements from the participants. These statements begin with the phrase "Right now I . . ." Variations include "Right now I'm thinking. . . ," "Right now I'm feeling. . . ," and "Right now I'm imagining . . ."

It is important to repeat that using these techniques in excess can work against cognitive integration. The significant considerations are to keep participants actively involved with the content and to make certain that they see the "big picture."

Integrating Cognitive Inputs

After the lecturette there should be some activity that builds on the conceptual learning. Otherwise, the retention of the content will be lessened. Lecturettes should be sequenced in such a way that they link the previous activities with later ones. (See "Design Considerations in Laboratory Education," 1973 *Annual*, pp. 177-194.) Several methods can be employed to "nail down" the conceptual learning:

- *Question/answer period.* This traditional teaching method helps to clarify points in the lecturette. A good practice is to have participants rehearse their questions with each other before asking them of the facilitator.
- *Quiz.* The facilitator administers a test based on the concepts in the lecturette. The presentation may be oral, posted, or printed. Individuals respond to the items, compare their answers with each other, and discuss any disagreements with the facilitator. It is important not to establish a traditional classroom-like atmosphere with adult learners. The use of this method should not result in anxiety about learning.

- *Statements.* The facilitator explains that most questions posed after a lecturette imply points of view, and participants are invited to make declarative statements to the facilitator and to the group. The facilitator directs a discussion of the points raised. This method requires some patience on the part of the facilitator since many participants have been heavily conditioned to ask "expert" questions rather than to look within themselves for meaningful reactions. Many participant questions are statements in disguise, however, and need to be turned around before the facilitator responds. (See "Don't You Think That. . . ?" in the 1974 *Annual*, pp. 203-208.)
- *Handouts.* Conceptual learning can be reinforced by giving participants the essential content in print form after the lecturette has been presented. If this is done before or during the presentation, participants can distract themselves through reading instead of listening. The facilitator needs to announce beforehand that a handout will be provided after the lecturette because some participants will resent having taken notes unnecessarily. A significant proportion of participants, however, will listen better if taking notes at the same time and will do so even if handouts are going to be distributed. A rule of thumb is to provide a handout for any lecturette in which participants are likely to feel anxious that they will not be able to write everything down. Having numerous pre-prepared posters on the wall prior to presenting conceptual input can make many participants tense. Some persons copy posters rather than listen, and they can often be behind or ahead of the point the facilitator is discussing. Lecturettes in the *Annual* can be photoduplicated as handouts.
- *Applications planning and goal setting.* Participants are instructed to work individually or in pairs to apply the concepts presented in the lecturette to actual situations "back home." In pairs some goal-setting criteria can be applied. (See "Criteria of Effective Goal Setting: The SPIRO Model," in the 1972 *Annual*, pp. 133-134.)
- *Role playing.* Subgroups are formed to create role plays to illustrate various points in the conceptual input. These skits are presented to and discussed by the total group. For additional variations on this method see "Role Playing" in the 1979 *Annual* (pp. 182-193).
- *Skill practice.* The facilitator demonstrates the application of one or more concepts from the lecturette and structures situations to provide opportunities to act out effective behaviors in practice activities. For example, after a lecturette on assertion theory, participants practice saying "no" to unwarranted requests in various situations.
- *Linking with other experiential methods.* A lecturette can lead into a structured experience, or it can augment the generalizing stage of the experiential learning cycle. (See the introduction to the Structured Experiences section of this *Annual*.) In addition, lecturettes are incorporated into using instruments in training. The theory input step in using an inventory is, in effect, a lecturette. (These steps are illustrated in detail in Pfeiffer, Heslin, and Jones, 1976.) Participants can create their own instrument spontaneously, based on the conceptual input. (See the introduction to the Instrumentation section in this *Annual*.)

The major concerns of the facilitator after presenting a lecturette are to ensure that the input has been understood clearly and that it has practical usefulness for participants. The "so what?" and "now what?" stages of the experiential learning cycle need to be applied to conceptual inputs as well as to structured experiences.

In a sense all learning is experiential in that there must be some experience on which to base one's behavioral changes. What these methods can do is to increase the likelihood that the learner will have meaningful contact with concepts and that talking through this experience will result in self-directed change toward more effective behavior. The purpose of the lecturette in human relations work is not to enlighten so much as to provide the basis for choice. Making conceptual inputs experiential is an effort to facilitate change in model-based ways.

REFERENCES

Pfeiffer, J. W., & Jones, J. E. (Eds.). *The annual handbook for group facilitators* (1972-1980). San Diego, CA: University Associates, 1972-1980.

Pfeiffer, J. W., & Jones, J. E. (Eds.). *A handbook of structured experiences for human relations training* (Vols. I-VII). San Diego, CA: University Associates, 1973-1979.

Pfeiffer, J. W., Heslin, R., & Jones, J. E. *Instrumentation in human relations training* (2nd ed.). San Diego, CA: University Associates, 1976.

THE FOUR-COMMUNICATION-STYLES APPROACH

Tom Carney

Communication at cross purposes is all too unhappily common in everyday life. Mary tries to persuade Bill to adopt a certain way of doing things, arguing logically for the efficiency of her way. Bill responds with counterarguments about its human costs. Mary reacts with a yet more telling cost-benefit analysis. Bill counters with examples of likely inconveniences for specific clients. By now the metamessages have taken over: each person is bent on defending her or his approach, and emotional misperceptions of the other person distort all further communication.

One frequent cause of crossed communication is the common tendency to favor one particular style of communication, often at the cost of being insensitive to other styles—in others as well as in oneself. Ideally, one should be:

- conscious of one's own stylistic preferences and dislikes;
- able quickly to detect such preferences and dislikes in another person;
- able to adjust one's own style to that of another person. If one attempts to achieve this ideal, a surprising number of payoffs result, both in personal insights and in interpersonal skills.

COMMONLY PREFERRED STYLES OF COMMUNICATION

Jung (see Jacobi, 1968) identified two major dimensions in our modes of relating to events: a thinking-feeling polarity and, at right angles to it, a sensing-intuiting one. These polarities are familiar in everyday life:

- *Thinking:* the logical, rational, sequential analysis that has been associated with left-brain hemisphere (Ornstein, 1978) dominance—or with "convergent" or "vertical" thinking (DeBono, 1970; Hudson, 1970). If this is one's preferred mode of relating to "reality," one will probably use a precise, analytical form of communication.
- *Intuiting:* the making of associations; having insights that yield a novel "big picture" of a situation; the free flow of creative ideas. Currently associated with openness to right-brain hemisphere (Ornstein, 1978) functioning, this dimension is also termed "divergent" or "lateral" thinking (DeBono, 1970; Hudson, 1970).
- *Feeling Group Maintenance:* empathy with others' feelings, leading to a stress on human relationships when communicating about how things get done.
- *Doing/Task Orientation* (Jung's knowing by experiencing/sensing): a tendency to sense reality by doing and to emphasize practicality in communicating about that reality.

Credit for originating this approach should go to P. P. Mok of Drake Beam Associates. Jay Nisberg further developed the approach, along with his associates Ed Reimer and Brian Trump.

These continua can be illustrated graphically as follows:

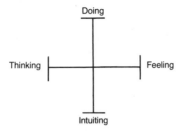

Use of the Styles

Suppose you had a television set with four channels on which you could regularly get programs. Suppose, further, that reception was excellent on the first channel, good on the second, indifferent on the third, and poor on the fourth. In time, you would probably find yourself using the first and second channels and avoiding the third and especially the fourth. People's use of the four modes of relating to, and communicating about, reality is somewhat similar.

We each have a mix of all four styles.[1] There is our "strong-suit" style, which we use easily and skillfully, and our "back-up" style, which we use fairly easily and skillfully. Then there is generally a style that we use only with effort and rather clumsily. Finally there is a style that always gives us trouble, that does not "work" when we have to use it. Generally we are fairly conscious of our use of our stronger styles, but we often put the weaker ones out of mind. We tend not to dwell on how little we practice them or how much we avoid having to use them. As a result, we tend to have blind spots—not being aware of how much we overuse our strong-suit style and underuse our weakest one.

Shifting Styles Under Stress

Our society tends to overtrain and overuse the thinking style and underpromote and underuse the feeling one. Likewise, the doing style is much appreciated and used, the intuiting style-somewhat less so. Usually we are not very conscious of these preferences. If we think about these things at all, we are most conscious of the style that is dominant when we are "really" ourselves—when we are under nonstress conditions. Usually, however, our strong-suit style drops back when we come under stress; and often our nonstress back-up style comes to the fore. Generally, under stress, our doing and feeling styles seem to come to the fore, and our thinking and especially intuiting styles tend to recede. This shift can make us seem, to associates, a "different person" under extreme stress.

Some people are much more self-aware than others in these matters. The thinker—that is, the person for whom thinking constitutes the dominant style in the foursome—tends to be most aware of his or her communication styles. But the thinker does not necessarily handle stress best. Knowing about one's inner tendencies and being able to handle those tendencies are two different things. It is the feeler who seems to handle stress best. Feelers are more at home with their emotions—even though feelers sometimes do not appear very conscious of their dominant styles. Because doers generally cannot be bothered with introspection, they are not overly aware of their style mixes and can shift a great deal under

---

[1] See Parr (1979) for a self-inventory to determine one's own style mix. Also see R. C. Hogan & D. W. Champagne, "Personal Style Inventory," in the Instrumentation section of this *Annual* for an instrument based on Jungian typology.

University Associates

stress, precisely because they tend to undervalue feelings. Intuitors, who are often surprisingly unaware of their style mix, seem to be the least stable under stress of all the dominant modes.

Figure 1 diagrams some examples of the style shifts that can result from stress, showing how extensive these shifts can sometimes be. A style's position (or several styles' positions) in an individual's order of preference can change—and the emphasis given to a style can change too.

Style Blind Spots

The bigger one's blind spot, the more one tends to overuse one's strong suit style and to be oblivious to the need to match styles with someone else on a markedly different wavelength. People get along best with others who are on their wavelength: like attracts like. Thus thinkers will tend to gravitate together, producing a group with tremendous ability to handle analytical problems; as all group members have strongly developed thinking skills, they enhance one another's effectiveness. While such a group builds an enviable record for its success in coping with analytical problems, sooner or later it will be handed a problem that calls for skills in intuition or empathy—and then disaster can very well result. It is not just that the group's skills do not match the skills the problem calls for; worse, "groupthink" (Janis, 1972) can result, as the group's mutually shared blind spots *increase* its members' tendency *not* to use their—in this case, more appropriate—weak styles.

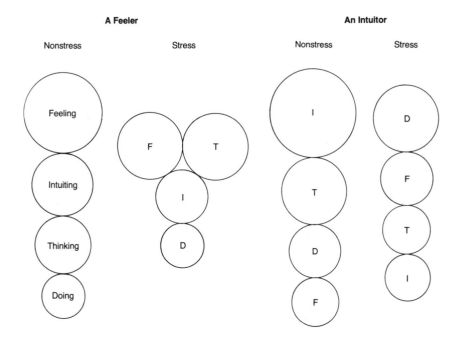

Figure 1. Style Shifts Under Stress

APPLICATIONS OF THE FOUR-COMMUNICATION-STYLES APPROACH

Knowledge about stylistic preferences has been used to hamstring juries. If, by questioning, it is possible to eliminate all the "feelers" from a jury, the group that results will not be able to achieve consensus on any issue that is at all emotional or controversial.

Style Flexing

The most frequent use of expertise in these four communication styles is "style flexing." This involves:

- Knowing your own most and least favored styles, in stress and nonstress situations alike;
- Knowing how you come across to others in either situation;
- Learning how to identify the dominant style of any person(s) to whom you may be talking;
- Learning how to switch your style so as to get on the same wavelength as your conversational partner(s).

Team Building

The next most frequent use of expertise in this approach is in team building. It is quite unusual to be a "team in one" (equally strong in all four styles both under stress and nonstress conditions). Most of us have overdeveloped some styles and underdeveloped others, but there are some different strong-suit styles that seem to go well together—feelers and thinkers in growth groups, for instance. The thinkers can dispassionately analyze a complex interpersonal issue, while they envy the feelers their ability to express their emotions and bring interpersonal issues to a head (Eisenstadt, 1969).

By and large, however, naturally formed teams in organizations usually turn out to have the same *one* strong-suit style dominant in each member. Yet it is known that a heterogeneous group will outperform a homogeneous one, if only in-fighting can be prevented. Here, a team-building consultant can help to bring a well-rounded team together and use its members' range of skills to keep it together without conflicting viewpoints degenerating into in-fighting.

Teaching

Application of this approach to teaching (not yet common) holds great promise. Most teachers tend to have one, or at most two, strong communication styles. But they face classes in which all four dominant styles are represented, and the consequences are all too familiar. A teacher who has a dominant hard-line, analytical thinking style will simply make any student who is a feeler curl up inside as a result of what the feeler perceives to be a cold, calculating, impersonal presentation.

Furthermore, the overrepresentation of certain styles of teaching is reinforced by the teaching technology and by the examination system. Any given teaching approach or instrument may be effective with a student whose dominant style is thinking and ineffective with another student with a dominant feeling style (DeNike, 1976). For example, seminars suit thinkers/analysts, practica suit doers, and instructional simulations suit feelers with a thinker back-up style. Basically, the school system is particularly suited to the thinker, whose activities—mathematical or linguistic—it can quantify and certificate. The other strong-suit styles, especially that of the feeler, find a much less supportive atmosphere in the school sytem (Bolles, 1978; Torrance, 1971).

A teacher needs to know his or her least and most favored styles. He or she should be able to communicate on *any* of the four wavelengths and should be equipped with teaching instruments that represent *all* of those four styles. School curriculums should be expressly designed to accommodate all styles.

Position Papers

Writers of position papers, or of any submission to a multimember board, can be trained to present their material in such a way that readers of each of the four dominant styles can easily understand communications conveyed in "their" respective styles. A reader who is a doer will want a *brief* expression of basic findings and recommendations: that person will go straight for the "bottom line." The feeler will look for an assessment of the implications, in human relations, for the company team. The intuitor will expect a "big picture," a "look down the road" (futurist orientation), and an impact assessment. The thinker will search for appendices in which details have been marshalled in sequence, options stated, and trends extrapolated and reviewed. A report has to speak to its reader in the *reader's* own dominant communication style if it is to be seen as "realistic."

VALIDATION AND SUMMATION

The four-communication-styles approach is so obviously and immediately useful that most practitioners' energies have been directed toward evolving new and more powerful ways of teaching or using it (see Carney, 1976; Parr, 1979). Little energy has been put into validation and reports (see Slocum, 1978). Some observations, however, can be made. First, breaking mental sets does not necessarily mean innovative thinking. With thinker-analysts, it may involve criticism or mere negativeness. Second, fluency of ideas does not necessarily mean novelty in thinking. Doers prove amazingly fertile in ideas for ways of coping, but these ideas are remarkably commonplace or simply variations on one theme: doers are concerned with effectiveness rather than originality. Originality is the predominant characteristic of the intuitors, as a group.

Third, feelers are not emotional in their thinking. They tend to ask, "How is this going to affect *people?*" It is the intuitors who, if they become blocked (that is, if they cannot produce their usual spate of novel ideas), evidence most emotion. If they are producing well, they are very genial. The thinkers, too, if they cannot offer constructive suggestions and begin to produce spates of negative criticism, soon become emotional in the way they express their ideas.

Fourth, the most outstanding performance comes from a participant whose unique balance of *two* strong suits is ideally suited to the twin demands—criticism and originality—of the problem. This concept of balance may well be one of the most important ideas involved in the four-communication-styles approach.

SUGGESTED ACTIVITIES

The following activities can be used to encourage participants to examine their own styles of communication.

1. Workshop participants break up into helping groups of five or six. Each person rates himself or herself as a "doer," "feeler," "intuitor," or "thinker" in each of the following characteristics: body language, dress, social "props" (office decor), tidyness, use of time, phone mannerisms, memo-writing habits. Then each participant rates each of the other members on the same dimensions. Group members compare ratings to see to what extent self-images correspond with others' images.

2. A role play is set up in which a player is required to persuade a committee to adopt a controversial project or policy of the role player's choosing. This role play compels the persuader to "style flex" repeatedly, as the individual responds to the questions and criticisms of the members of the committee. The role player's performance is evaluated, with each group member indicating how the persuader was perceived by that member. The role player discusses what he or she learned about his or her use of a dominant and a back-up style.

REFERENCES

Bolles, R. N. *The three boxes of life*. Berkeley, CA: Ten Speed Press, 1978.

Carney, T. F. *No limits to growth: Mind-expanding techniques*. Winnipeg, Manitoba: Harbeck, 1976.

De Bono, E. *Lateral thinking: A textbook of creativity*. London: Ward Lock Educational, 1970.

De Nike, L. An exploratory study of the relationship of educational cognitive style to learning from simulation games. *Simulation & Games*, 1976, 7(1), 72-73.

Eisenstadt, J. W. *Personality style and sociometric choice*. Washington, DC: NTL Institute, 1969.

Hudson, L. *Frames of mind: Ability, perception and self perception in the arts and sciences*. Harmondsworth, Middlesex: Penguin, 1970.

Jacobi, J. *The psychology of C. G. Jung*. London: Routledge & Kegan Paul, 1968.

Janis, J. L. *Victims of groupthink*. Boston: Houghton Mifflin, 1972.

Ornstein, R. The split and the whole brain. *Human Nature*, 1978, *1*(5), 76-83.

Parr, B. P. *Organizational communications: Working papers*. Windsor, Ontario: Department of Communication Studies, University of Windsor, 1979.

Slocum, J. W., Jr. Does cognitive style affect diagnosis and intervention strategies of change agents? *Group & Organization Studies*, 1978, 3(2), 199-210.

Torrance, E. P. Four types of gifted adolescents. In W. M. Cruickshank (Ed.), *Psychology of exceptional children and youth*. Englewood Cliffs, NJ: Prentice-Hall, 1971.

Tom Carney, Ph.D., is a professor of communication studies at the University of Windsor, Ontario, where he teaches undergraduate and graduate courses in organizational communication. He has consulted with business and government as well as educational and religious groups and has published seventeen books and over a hundred articles and reviews on a variety of subjects. His current interests are career management, futurism, and psychosynthesis.

INTERACTION PROCESS ANALYSIS

Beverly Byrum-Gaw

"If you want an opposing opinion, look to Fred."
"Anne talks more than anyone else in the group."
"Leave it to Toby to crack a joke."
"David has kept this group together."
"This group has an issue with conflict."
We make observations and draw conclusions about the members of our groups and the group process. A helpful tool for making sense of what happens in a group is Bales' interaction process analysis categories (Bales, 1950). This approach provides a focus for descriptive reports from which inferences can then be drawn.

Interaction process analysis is designed to analyze two basic types of group behavior: that oriented toward accomplishing the *task* and that oriented toward maintaining the group's *socioemotional* atmosphere. The socioemotional dimension is further subdivided into *positive* and *negative* answers and questions, while the task dimension is considered neutral. Twelve categories of behavior (verbal and nonverbal) exist under these two dimensions (Figure 1).

A tally is made for each member's acts occurring in any of the twelve categories during a specified time period. A *verbal* act is a simple sentence. A *nonverbal* act is any vocal or bodily movement that appears to have meaning in the categories given. A message can be composed of a number of different acts. If an act indicates an emotional reaction as well as a task-related question or answer, it is tallied under each of the appropriate categories.

USES OF INTERACTION PROCESS ANALYSIS

An observer can use this basic method of analysis in a number of ways to increase the participants' awareness of their individual interaction styles and the group's awareness of its process.

Individual Participation

By analyzing the tally sheet, a participant can discover his level of participation. Additionally, since each category of action corresponds to a role within the group, the participant can identify his typical role behaviors.

Interpersonal Interaction

The richest use of interaction process analysis is at this level. Leadership and subgrouping can be identified. While these two phenomena obviously have meaning for the individual participant, they involve interaction and are therefore nonexistent without other group members.

		1. Shows solidarity; raises others' status; gives help, reward
Socioemotional Dimension (Positive)	A	2. Shows tension release; jokes, laughs; shows satisfaction
		3. Agrees; shows passive acceptance; understands; concurs; complies
		4. Gives suggestions, direction (implying autonomy for others)
	B	5. Gives opinions, evaluation, analysis; expresses feelings, wishes
		6. Gives orientation, information; repeats; clarifies; confirms
Task Dimension (Neutral)		7. Asks for orientation, information, repetition, confirmation
	C	8. Asks for opinions, evaluation, analysis, expression of feeling
		9. Asks for suggestions, directions, possible ways of action
		10. Disagrees; shows passive rejection, formality; withholds help
Socioemotional Dimension (Negative)	D	11. Shows tension; asks for help; withdraws out of field
		12. Shows antagonism; deflates others' status; defends or asserts self

Figure 1. Bales' Interaction Process Analysis Categories[1]

Leadership

An accurate but involved method of determining leadership is to record the originator and the target of each act rather than simply to put a check on the tally sheet. For example, Fran (Member 1) comments to Mike (Member 2), "I appreciate your work"; this act would be recorded in category 1 as 1-2. Her direction to the group ("Okay, let's get down to business") would be recorded as 1-0 (0 indicating group-directed remarks). Tallying each act in this way yields a clear picture of who initiates, who receives, and who offers the most group-directed statements. This participant will be the leader, a finding consistent with research on leadership behavior.

A tension exists between the often opposing forces toward task and toward socioemotional maintenance. Because task achievement and member satisfaction are both important outcomes of group work, these forces must be balanced. Since one person will find it difficult to focus on task and on maintenance simultaneously, both a task leader (the one who is seen as contributing most to directing task accomplishment) and a socioemotional leader (the one who is best liked) will emerge. Leadership, then, becomes differentiated into two specific functions. The task leader will initiate and receive more acts from the task and negative socioemotional dimensions, while the maintenance leader will initiate and

134

receive more acts in the positive socioemotional category. The tally sheet can be utilized to identify the two members most often performing these necessary leadership behaviors.

Once the leaders have been identified, a closer look at frequently used categories can reveal information about the leaders' styles. An autocratic leader tends to give more verbal directions and commands (4), answers and opinions (5), and expressed concern for productivity (5 and 9), while appearing nonverbally dominant (12). A democratic leader tends to lead the group to come to its own conclusions by giving suggestions (4), asking questions (7, 8, 9), and encouraging suggestions and participation (1, 7, 8, 9). Nonverbally the democratic leader appears animated, attentive, and friendly (1, 2, 3). A laissez-faire leader does little other than extend the group's knowledge by giving information (6) while nonverbally exhibiting attentive and friendly behavior (1, 3).

Subgrouping

Subgrouping can be analyzed in two ways. The first way is to determine which members initiate and receive reciprocally with each other in both verbal and nonverbal modes. While one member of the subgroup may talk more than another, reciprocity can also be exhibited through nonverbal emotional reactions (1, 2, 3). The second method is based on the fact that members of a subgroup will have positive supportive responses to one another. Subgroups that support the leader(s) by validating the leader(s) and one another can be differentiated from subgroups that oppose the leader(s) by disconfirming him or her (them) while supporting one another.

Group Phenomena

Building on information from the personal and interpersonal levels, interaction process analysis can be further used to look at whole-group phenomena. Because a group progresses through phases of development that are related to the twelve categories, the group's history can be recorded using this method of analysis.

Phases of Development

The first phase of development is *orientation*. During this phase, members struggle with ambiguity to define their problem or situation to everyone's agreement. This phase is characterized by acts in categories 6 and 7. The second phase of development is *evaluation*, during which members cooperate to establish the norms and standards that the group will follow in completing its task. In this phase, individual value differences must be transcended; acts in categories 5 and 8 are characteristic. The last phase of development is *control*. During this phase of concern about internal influence and external environment, the pressure to finish the task shifts the focus to determining leadership for solving the problem. This phase is characterized by acts in categories 4 and 9.

Maintenance Problems

Throughout the phases of development, problems of maintenance can be noted concurrently. *Decision-making* is characterized by agreement and/or disagreement (3 and 10); *tension management* by being involved or withdrawing (2 and 11); group *integration* by a show of solidarity or antagonism (1 and 12). As the group moves from the orientation to the control phase, both positive and negative reactions increase as members become more involved and closer to their goal.

Explanation of Task Achievement/Nonachievement

In order to accomplish the group's task, as has been noted, an equilibrium between task and maintenance must be maintained. This dynamic homeostasis can exist only if positive acts occur more frequently than negative acts. Thus, at the group's termination, the tally sheet can be used as a tool to explain the achievement or nonachievement of the task. During the group's progress, interaction process analysis can be used as a predictive tool. If positive acts predominate, there is evidence of solidarity and cohesiveness, and the group is likely to achieve its goal. If negative acts predominate, there is evidence of dysfunctional strain and discord; the group is unlikely to achieve its goal.

Group Generalizations

At a more abstract level, some generalizations about group behavior can be based on this model.

Sequence of Acts. Questions seem to be followed by answers, and agreement or disagreement then ensues.

Percentage of Acts. More answers and opinions are offered than questions asked (56 percent to 7 percent). Positive acts occur twice as frequently as negative ones (25 percent to 12 percent).

Group Size and Balance. As group size increases, so does the release of tension (2), the giving of suggestions and information (4 and 6), and the showing of solidarity (1), while decreases occur in the showing of tension (11), agreement (3), the asking for opinions (8), and the giving of opinions (5). Groups with an even number of members show frequent disagreement (10) and antagonism (12) with infrequent requests for suggestions (9).

Role and Status. Status (as determined by the number of acts received) increases as the importance of a member's role (as determined by the category used most frequently) and/or the member's control of the group's direction increases. Role differentiation (as determined by members performing acts in some categories significantly more than in others) and status differentiation increase as problems increase (as determined by negative acts). Control (as determined by positive acts received in response to task direction) and rewards (as determined by positive acts) increase as role differentiation increases. Strain (as determined by negative acts) increases as status differences increase.

Solidarity. As determined by reciprocal positive acts, solidarity between members of unequal status increases the strain to equalize status (as determined by the leveling out of acts received). As status becomes equalized and solidarity increases, the exercise of control, task emphasis, and therefore the achievement of goals decrease.

SUMMARY

Bales' method of interaction process analysis provides an explanatory tool to increase personal, interpersonal, and group awareness, thus facilitating the exercise of intelligent choice. Furthermore, its predictive potential allows a group and its members more control over their existence—the course they will follow and whether that course leads to the satisfaction of group members and the accomplishment of the group's goals.

SUGGESTED ACTIVITY

The following activity will help a group to experience interaction process analysis.

I. The facilitator instructs the participants to read the behaviors listed in Figure 1 and asks each participant to choose one behavior/role that he/she will exhibit exclusively during this activity. At no time are participants to share or discuss with each other which role they are taking.

II. The facilitator then asks for groups to generate a list, arrived at by consensus, of ten behaviors that *inhibit* effective group functioning. An observer is designated for each group.

III. At the end of the established time limit, the groups are stopped, whether their task is completed or not, and the observer joins the group and shares his observations.

IV. The facilitator leads all group participants in a discussion of the following points:

1. Feelings generated when one is required to perform one behavior exclusively.

2. The effect of each participant's behavior on group atmosphere and task accomplishment.

3. The appropriateness and functionality of each behavior at each stage of task accomplishment.

4. Thoughts and feelings experienced when participants were aware that a role needed for task accomplishment was not being performed.

5. Reasons for participants choosing their particular roles/behavior.

6. The relationship of functional role taking to leadership theory.

7. The correlation between the list of hindering behaviors generated and the group's behavior.

BRIEF BIBLIOGRAPHY

Bales, R. F. *Interaction process analysis: A method for the study of small groups.* Reading, MA: Addison-Wesley, 1950.

Bales, R. F. Adaptive and integrative changes as sources of strain in social systems. In A. P. Hare, E. F. Borgatta, & R. F. Bales (Eds.), *Small groups: Studies in social interaction.* New York: Alfred A. Knopf, 1955. (a)

Bales, R. F. The equilibrium problem in small groups. In A. P. Hare, E. F. Borgatta, & R. F. Bales (Eds.), *Small groups: Studies in social interaction.* New York: Alfred A. Knopf, 1955. (b)

Bales, R. F. Task status and likeability as a function of talking and listening in decision-making groups. In L. D. White (Ed.), *The state of the social sciences.* Chicago: University of Chicago Press, 1956.

Bales, R. F. Task roles and social roles in problem solving groups. In E. E. Maccoby, T. M. Newcomb, & E. L. Hartley (Eds.), *Readings in social psychology.* New York: Holt, Rinehart & Winston, 1958.

Bales, R. F., & Borgatta, E. F. Size of group as a factor in the interaction profile. In A. P. Hare, E. F. Borgatta, & R. F. Bales (Eds.), *Small groups: Studies in social interaction.* New York: Alfred A. Knopf, 1962.

Bales, R. F., & Slater, P. E. Role differentiation in small decision-making groups. In T. Parson & R. F. Bales (Eds.), *The family, socialization, and interaction process.* Glencoe, IL: Free Press, 1955.

Bales, R. F., & Strodtbeck, F. L. Phases in group problem-solving. *Journal of Abnormal and Social Psychology,* 1951, *46,* 485-495. (b)

Bales, R. F., Strodtbeck, F. L., Mills, T. M., & Roseborough, M. E. Channels of communication in small groups. *American Sociological Review,* 1951, *16,* 461-468. (a)

Bradley, P. H., & Baird, J. E. Management and communication style: A correlational analysis. *Central States Speech Journal,* 1977, *28,* 194-203.

Burgoon, M., Heston, J. K., & McCroskey, J. *Small group communication: A functional approach.* New York: Holt, Rinehart, & Winston, 1974.

Johnson, D. W., & Johnson, F. P. *Joining together: Group theory and group skills.* Englewood Cliffs, NJ: Prentice-Hall, 1975.

Rosenfeld, L. B. *Human interaction in the small group setting.* Columbus, OH: Charles E. Merrill, 1973.

Shaw, M. E. *Group dynamics: The psychology of small group behavior.* New York: McGraw-Hill, 1976.

Beverly Byrum-Gaw, Ph.D., is an associate professor in the Department of Communication at Wright State University, Dayton, Ohio. She is the director of the basic interpersonal communication course, teaches courses in small-group and organizational communication, and directs workshops on communication skills. Dr. Byrum-Gaw is co-author of Personal and Interpersonal Communication *(1975) and* May I Join You? *(1979).*

JEALOUSY: A PROACTIVE APPROACH

Colleen Kelley

An increasing number of self-actualizing people are re-examining their views of and personal styles of reacting to the "difficult" emotions such as anger, shyness, depression, and jealousy. Their aim is to expand both their understanding of how these emotions develop and their means of dealing with these emotions within themselves.

Jealousy is one of the least studied emotions. It has long been a key element in novels but has made few appearances in journals, scientific studies, or even popular psychology books (see Clanton & Smith, 1977, for exceptions). Jealousy has generally been viewed as an unwelcome emotion to which people have strong negative reactions; yet, when treated proactively, jealousy can be a very helpful and useful emotion. A closer look at some characteristics, targets, and causes of jealousy; some personal styles of reacting to this unwieldy emotion; and a theoretical model for constructively facing jealousy should help us gain a greater understanding of and more effective ways of dealing with the "green-eyed monster."

CHARACTERISTICS

Jealousy is the *fear of losing* to a third party something to which one feels one has a right and which one finds desirable. Thus jealousy involves (1) a valued thing and (2) a perceived threat of loss of this valued thing (3) to a usurper.

Jealousy vs. Envy

Often confused are the two emotions of jealousy and envy; both stem from wanting something that we perceive someone else to have that we consider to be important to our personal well-being, but they are created by somewhat different stimuli. Jealousy is based on wanting to keep something to which we feel we have a right or which we have already experienced as our own. Envy is a desire for something that another has but of which we have not experienced ownership.

This feeling of ownership inherent in jealousy usually derives from a psychological contract, either real or imagined, between the person experiencing jealousy and the person who is the target of the jealousy. Just as people generally do not envy a *person* but rather such *things* as that person's money, position, or characteristics, so with jealousy one does not generally feel ownership over another *person*, but only over those *things* that one believes to be part of one's psychological contract with that person. For example, I may not need my partner in a primary relationship to be by my side constantly, but I may become jealous if my partner is not available when I need him or her for substantial emotional support and I feel this support is being given elsewhere.

Perceived Threat of Loss

Generally, the jealousy that most of us have difficulty handling involves the perceived threat of loss of a relationship that is important to us because we depend on it to meet

University Associates

certain of our needs—to be who we are in the world. Thus jealousy is a reaction to a threat to our self-esteem and feeling of security. Many times we have become so dependent on the thing we fear to lose, have come to identify ourselves so clearly with it, have made ourselves so vulnerable through the trust we have placed or investment we have made in it, that our own feelings of identity, adequacy, and self-confidence may be shaken by the threat of its loss. Conversely, when we have less self-esteem or feel less secure, we are more vulnerable to jealousy.

In many ways, jealousy is based on a belief in scarcity rather than abundance. I choose to believe that something important to me is scarce and necessary to my well being, I invest myself in the psychological contract and trust that the other person will remain faithful to it. The more I have invested or trusted or valued, the greater the potential threat of loss and the stronger the potential jealousy.

TARGETS AND CAUSES OF JEALOUSY

Jealousy takes many forms; both the target person and the cause of jealousy can vary widely. Romantic jealousy, especially between husband and wife, is the type of jealousy most commonly understood. However, many people, even as adults, wrestle with the jealousy they feel over the parental attention or approval that their siblings receive; some people are jealous of the attention and affection their friends give to others; others are jealous of their child's affection for their spouse.

Just as the most common type and target of jealousy is usually thought to be romantic jealousy directed toward a spouse, the most commonly presumed cause of jealousy is sexual infidelity. Yet many people who are jealous of their spouses are far less concerned about exclusivity in sexual relations than they are about the spouse's time, attention, or companionship. Jobs or avocations can as easily be the "other woman" or the "other man." The potential targets and causes of jealousy are as numerous as the number of people one has relationships with and the number of things one feels one has a right to and wants to keep.

PERSONAL STYLES OF COPING WITH JEALOUSY

Reactions to jealousy are unique to the person experiencing it. Most people have developed a definite personal style of coping with jealousy and are reinforced in that style by certain outcomes or payoffs of which they may not even be aware. Some air their feelings immediately by attacking angrily and asking questions later. Others withdraw into themselves and their misery until the other person feels guilty and comes to their aid. Whatever our styles of coping, it is important for us to become aware of them and the positive outcomes we receive from them. Even if our present style is destructive, we receive some payoffs from it. Before we can adopt a more constructive style, we must be willing to give up the payoffs we are receiving from our present style.

Another variable in coping styles is one's philosophy or view of jealousy. Some people see jealousy as a proof of another's real love, others think it shows that the other person does not believe in their love for that person. The former group tends to react tolerantly and even encouragingly to jealousy, the latter in a violent or depressed manner. How each of us perceives or understands jealousy will have a great impact on our particular response to it.

A PROACTIVE PHILOSOPHY OF JEALOUSY

Inherently, jealousy is neither helpful nor harmful. It is our view of it and our reaction to it that determines its impact and import. If examined in this light, some constructive ways of dealing with jealousy emerge—ways that can be very beneficial.

Making Psychological Contracts Clear

Most people have certain assumptions and expectations about their psychological contracts or relationships with friends, lovers, children, parents, co-workers, etc. These assumptions and expectations are largely colored by personal values and past experiences. Two people who believe they both share the same relationship are often unpleasantly surprised to find that something one partner has become fearful of losing the other never saw as part of the contract in the first place. Thus probably the most proactive step two people can take to avoid jealousy is to be clear and specific about the assumptions and expectations each holds regarding the behavior of each member of the relationship.

A MODEL FOR CONSTRUCTIVELY DEALING WITH JEALOUSY

Viewing jealousy as an alarm system—a valuable signal designed to protect our own needs and emotional life—is the basis of the Proactive Jealousy model. Jealousy is a warning to us that someone on whom we depend for certain things may be giving those things to someone else at our expense. Through this model, jealousy can be seen as a way of looking after our own welfare.

In the three-stage (alert, alarm, affect) Proactive Jealousy model (Figure 1), jealousy is seen in its preliminary stage as an alert system by which we perceive a threat of loss. Since

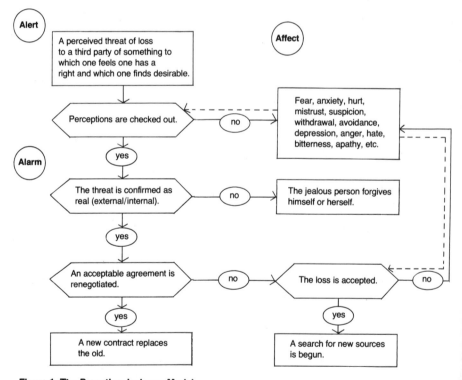

Figure 1: The Proactive Jealousy Model

at this point there is only a *perceived* threat, the constructive step is to check out the perception to see if it is based on reality. We might share our feelings with the person involved and ask whether these fears have any basis in fact. We might also check within ourselves to determine whether the fear springs from our own feelings of insecurity or inadequacy.

For example: Phil has been Yvonne's boss for some time. Yvonne has worked hard to do a good job and has earned Phil's respect and support. New staff members were added recently, and the boss has been spending a great deal of his time on Tad, a new male colleague of Yvonne's. Yvonne fears she is losing the attention she deserves to Tad. She decides to discuss her feelings with Phil; she also asks herself if her fear is based on her own feelings of inadequacy.

If perceptions are not verified at this stage, one moves to the affect stage of the model—a pool of emotions generally associated with jealousy. The combination of emotions can change at any given time, but the cycle feeds on itself and does not allow for a great deal of rational thinking. The affect stage of the model is primarily a feeling state and is ultimately destructive to the individual choosing to remain there.

At any stage in the Proactive Jealousy model, a person has two choices: to take a constructive path or to wallow around in the affective pool of emotions. The constructive choice is not always free of these emotions, but they are not the *principal* means of dealing with the situation.

If the constructive path is taken at the Alert stage—the perceived threat is checked out—and we find our fear has no basis in reality, we can forgive ourselves for feeling jealousy and let go of our fear. Upon talking to Phil, Yvonne finds that he is training Tad to help Yvonne so that Yvonne can be promoted to work on a special project with Phil. Rather than blame herself for having felt jealous in such a situation, she can congratulate herself for recognizing the feeling of a threat and proactively investigating it.

If, however, the perceived threat is found to be based on reality, either internal (Yvonne realizes that her fear is based on her insecurity about being a female in a male-dominated division) or external (Phil confirms that he has been considering Tad for a position that Yvonne has been working toward), the alarm stage has been reached, and the constructive step is to try to renegotiate an acceptable agreement. In the case of an internal threat, Yvonne can work on some new ways of increasing her self-esteem or self-confidence, or, in the case of an external threat, she can discuss with Phil a more acceptable way of handling the situation.

If renegotiation occurs, the constructive outcome is a new contract—a mutually agreed-upon way of approaching the situation or redefining the relationship. If renegotiation is not possible, either because no acceptable agreement can be found or because the other person involved is not willing to renegotiate, the constructive step is to accept the loss and to begin a search for new sources or relationships to replace the old. If the loss is not accepted, however, we find ourselves in the affect stage.

SUMMARY

Jealousy is based on the fear of loss and will probably be with human beings as long as we have needs. It has many targets and causes, and we all have our own individual ways of reacting to and coping with this emotion. Proactive methods based on a view of jealousy as a protective signal can be used both to prevent the emotion and to deal with its effects. Perhaps jealousy is most usefully viewed as a very special friend, sometimes prone to sending out false alarms but always watching out for some of our most precious "possessions."

SUGGESTED ACTIVITIES

The following activities may be useful in learning to deal with jealousy.

1. Group members draw colored pictures of jealousy and share what their drawings symbolize for them.

2. Group members together explore which targets and causes typically produce jealousy for them as well as their characteristic coping style and its payoffs.

3. The Proactive Jealousy model can be used by individuals to chart their normal responses to jealousy and the route they would prefer to take and to do some problem solving about changing their behavior.

4. Group members can share some ways they have found useful to deal with jealousy from their own experiences.

OTHER READINGS

Clanton, C., & Smith, L. G. *Jealousy.* Englewood Cliffs, NJ: Prentice-Hall, 1977.

Jones, J. E., & Banet, A. G., Jr. Dealing with anger. In J. W. Pfeiffer & J. E. Jones (Eds.), *The 1976 annual handbook for group facilitators.* San Diego, CA: University Associates, 1976.

Kelley, C. *Assertion training: A facilitator's guide.* San Diego, CA: University Associates, 1979.

Sherwood, J. J., & Glidewell, J. C. Planned renegotiation: A norm-setting OD intervention. In J. E. Jones & J. W. Pfeiffer (Eds.), *The 1973 annual handbook for group facilitators.* San Diego, CA: University Associates, 1973.

Colleen Kelley is a human relations consultant in La Jolla, California, and an instructor for the master's degree program in human resources management for Pepperdine University, Los Angeles, California. Her consulting experience in the human relations field includes workshops, labs, and projects conducted in various foreign countries as well as in the United States. Her background is in educational psychology, social psychology, and languages. She is the author of Assertion Training: A Facilitator's Guide *(1979). Ms. Kelley has conducted jealousy workshops based on her Proactive Jealousy model since May, 1976.*

DIMENSIONS OF ROLE EFFICACY

Udai Pareek

Role efficacy can be thought of as the potential effectiveness of a role occupied by an individual in an organization. The higher the individual's role efficacy, the more likely that the role and the individual are effectively integrated.[1] Individuals must have the appropriate skills for their roles, but the roles must also be designed to use these skills. Ten dimensions of role efficacy are explored here.

1. Centrality

If persons occupying a particular role in the organization generally feel that the role they occupy is central to the organization, role efficacy is likely to be high. If persons occupying a particular role feel that their role is peripheral, i.e., not very important, their potential effectiveness will be low. This is true not only of persons at a highlevel in the organization, but also of people at the lowest levels.

In a large hospital, ward boys and attendants had very high motivation when they joined the hospital. They would proudly bring their friends and relatives to show them the place where they were working. However, within a few months, they began to neglect their work and were rated very low in their effectiveness. An investigation showed that their perception about the perceived importance of their role had changed: they felt that their role was not important at all. Their low motivation stemmed from the perceived lack of importance of their roles.

2. Integration

Every person has a particular strength—experience, technical training, special skills, some unique contribution. The more that the role a person occupies provides an opportunity for the use of such special strengths, the higher the role efficacy is likely to be. This is called self-role integration. The self and the role become integrated through the person's use of special strengths in the role. In one organization, a person was promoted to a responsible position that was seen as a coveted prize and was at first quite happy. However, he soon discovered that in the new position he occupied he was not able to use his training, counseling, and diagnostic skills. In spite of the fact that he worked very well in the new role, his efficacy was not as high as it had been in the previous job. When the role was redesigned to enable him to use his skills, his efficacy went up. Because all of us want our special strengths to be used so that we can demonstrate how effective we can be, integration contributes to high role efficacy.

3. Proactivity

A person who occupies a role responds to various expectations that people in the organization have of that role. This gives the individual a certain satisfaction, and it also satisfies others in the organization. However, if a person is able to take some initiative in his or her

---

[1] See "Role Efficacy Scale" in the Instrumentation section of this *Annual*.

role, efficacy will be higher. Reactive behavior (responding to the expectations of others) helps a person to be effective to some extent, but proactivity (taking initiative) contributes much more to efficacy. If a person would like to take initiative but has no opportunity to do so in the role, his or her efficacy will be low.

4. Creativity

Not only initiative is important for efficacy. An opportunity to try new and unconventional ways of solving problems or to be creative is equally important. In one state government department, as a part of a reorganization experiment, people performing clerical roles met to discuss suggestions of individuals for cutting processing time. The results were amazing. Not only did the satisfaction of the people in that department go up, but delays were considerably reduced and some innovative systems emerged. The opportunity people had to be creative and to try innovative ideas increased their role efficacy and their performance.

5. Interrole Linkage

Linkage of one's role with other roles in the organization increases efficacy. If there is a joint effort to understand problems, find solutions, etc., the efficacy of the various roles involved is likely to be high. Similarly, if a person is a member of a task group set up for a specific purpose, his efficacy, other factors being the same, is likely to be high. The feeling of isolation if a person works without any linkage with other roles reduces role efficacy.

6. Helping Relationship

In addition to interrole linkages, the opportunity for people to receive and give help also increases role efficacy. If persons performing a particular role feel that they can get help from some source in the organization whenever they have such a need, they are likely to have higher role efficacy. On the other hand, if no help is given when asked for, or if respondents are hostile, role efficacy will be low. A helping relationship requires both the expectation that help will be available when it is needed and the willingness to respond to the needs of others.

7. Superordination

When a person performing a particular role feels that the role he or she carries out is likely to be of value to a larger group, that person's efficacy is likely to be high. The roles that give role occupants opportunities to work for superordinate goals have the highest role efficacy. Superordinate goals serve large groups and cannot be achieved without some collaborative efforts. Many people have voluntarily accepted reduced salaries to move from the top level of the private sector to the public sector mainly because the new role would give them an opportunity to serve a larger interest. Thus, roles in which people feel that what they are doing is helpful to the organization in general usually have some role efficacy.

8. Influence

Related to superordination is the influence a person is able to exercise in his or her organizational role. The more influence a person is able to exercise in the role, the higher the role efficacy is likely to be. One factor that may make roles in the public sector or civil service more efficacious is the opportunity to influence a larger sector of society.

9. Personal Growth

One factor that contributes greatly to role efficacy is the perception that the role provides the individual with an opportunity to grow and develop. There are many examples of people switching roles primarily because of the opportunity to grow. One head of a training institute accepted a big cut in her salary when she took a new position because she felt that she had nothing more to learn in her previous role. The factor of self-development is very important for role efficacy. Institutions that are able to plan for the growth of people in their roles have higher role efficacy and gain a great deal of contribution from role occupants.

10. Confrontation

In general, if people in an organization avoid problems or shift them to someone else to solve, their role efficacy will be low. Confronting problems to find relevant solutions contributes to efficacy. When people face interpersonal problems and search for solutions their efficacy is likely to be higher than if they either deny such problems or refer them to their superiors.

SUMMARY

In summary, the performance of people working in an organization depends on their own potential effectiveness, their technical competence, their managerial skills and experience, and the design of the roles they perform in the organization. Integration of individuals and their roles ensures effectiveness.

SUGGESTED ACTIVITIES

This lecturette may be used in conjunction with the "Role Efficacy Scale" in the Instrumentation section of this *Annual* or Structured Experience 171 in Volume V of the *Handbook* (Pfeiffer & Jones, 1975).

REFERENCE

Pfeiffer, J. W., & Jones, J. E. (Eds.). *A handbook of structured experiences for human relations training* (Vol. V). San Diego, CA: University Associates, 1975.

Udai Pareek, Ph.D., is Larsen & Toubro professor of organizational behavior at the Indian Institute of Management, Ahmedabad, Gujarat, India. Dr. Pareek's background is in organization development, human resource development, organizational designing, and change in persons and systems. He has consulted with industrial and nonindustrial systems in various countries and with many international organizations.

A NINE-STEP PROBLEM-SOLVING MODEL

Leigh C. Earley and Pearl B. Rutledge

As individuals, we are confronted with problems—some serious, many not so serious—and somehow most of them are resolved. However, when several individuals become a group and a serious problem surfaces that the group must deal with, otherwise capable and functioning individuals can become immobilized. Often a feeling of helplessness results, and the most immediate concern for group members and leaders is likely to be overcoming the feeling of impotence. Some will suggest a digression to other matters (which is really a method of avoiding the problem): "I know this is important, but it can wait until after we deal with. . . ." Others will seek to place blame for the problem, preferably on something outside the group: "The real problem is inflation, which makes our dollars worth less." And still others will, for a time, withdraw from the group, if not physically at least emotionally.

If, indeed, individuals solve group problems that arise in their own lives, why cannot these same individuals solve group problems? There seem to be three basic reasons why the natural problem-solving ability of individuals cannot be easily transferred to working in a group.

1. Because there are several people involved, individuals frequently assume the problem is bigger than their ability.

2. Many individuals are unaware of their problem-solving skill because they have never thought of it in those terms.

3. Groups tend to reject tentative solutions before giving them a thorough hearing, consequently reducing the desire of individuals to contribute more solutions.

A NINE-STEP PROBLEM-SOLVING MODEL

This problem-solving model (Figure 1) is designed for individuals and small groups and may be applied to any problem regardless of its size or intensity. For more complex problems the model may be used in successive rounds on different aspects of the problem through step V; then the various choices can be integrated into a single or coordinated plan of action.

The problem-solving model is designed to be used by following the steps or arrows as indicated. At several points it is necessary to make choices; those choices will have significant effects on the overall problem-solving effort.

Counterproductive Steps

As indicated, these steps are unnecessary although they frequently delude us into a false sense of security about the problem. They do nothing to resolve it, while in many cases allowing the situation to become worse. Denying or ignoring the problem (a form of withdrawal) frequently takes a great deal of energy away from more productive activities, and, even if blame can be placed or self-blame is justified, these approaches do nothing to remedy the situation.

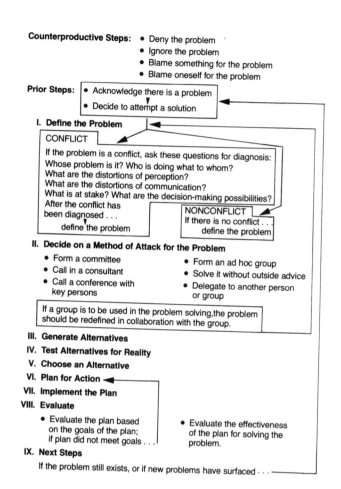

Counterproductive Steps:
- Deny the problem
- Ignore the problem
- Blame something for the problem
- Blame oneself for the problem

Prior Steps:
- Acknowledge there is a problem
- Decide to attempt a solution

I. Define the Problem

CONFLICT

If the problem is a conflict, ask these questions for diagnosis:
Whose problem is it? Who is doing what to whom?
What are the distortions of perception?
What are the distortions of communication?
What is at stake? What are the decision-making possibilities?
After the conflict has been diagnosed . . . define the problem

NONCONFLICT
If there is no conflict . . . define the problem

II. Decide on a Method of Attack for the Problem
- Form a committee
- Call in a consultant
- Call a conference with key persons
- Form an ad hoc group
- Solve it without outside advice
- Delegate to another person or group

If a group is to be used in the problem solving, the problem should be redefined in collaboration with the group.

III. Generate Alternatives
IV. Test Alternatives for Reality
V. Choose an Alternative
VI. Plan for Action
VII. Implement the Plan
VIII. Evaluate
- Evaluate the plan based on the goals of the plan; if plan did not meet goals . . .
- Evaluate the effectiveness of the plan for solving the problem.

IX. Next Steps
If the problem still exists, or if new problems have surfaced . . .

Figure 1. The Nine-Step Problem-Solving Model

Prior Steps

Before any action can be taken to resolve a problem we must recognize that it exists. But acknowledging the problem is not enough; deciding to do something about it is also essential. Many of us know people who admit that smoking is bad for their health but continue to light up regularly: what is lacking is the decision to do something about the problem.

Acknowledging that there is a problem does not necessitate having a clear understanding of the whole problem or all its possible effects; deciding to attempt a solution does not imply that there must be a clear idea of what that solution might be or even of how to best approach finding a solution.

I. Define the Problem: Conflict or Nonconflict

Many problems present themselves as conflicts. The six diagnostic questions included in the problem-solving model may help get below the conflict. The purpose of the diagnosis is to define the problem, but occasionally diagnosis reveals some clues about possible alternative solutions or possible methods of attacking the problem.

If the problem is not a conflict, it is still essential to come to a definition of the problem. If several people (as a group or independently) are working on the problem, it is especially important to have a common definition, preferably in writing. A definition provides clarity, understanding, and a commonality of purpose. How a problem is defined will either expand or limit the possible solutions, and it is desirable to define a problem in such a way as to maximize the possible solutions.

II. Decide on a Method of Attack for the Problem

The scope, intensity, and urgency of the problem should be considered when deciding which method to apply. There may be additional methods that can be considered. If a group method is used, it is best to include, if possible, representatives from any organized group or program that will be affected by the problem or potential solutions. The best group size for problem solving seems to be five to seven persons.

III. Generate Alternatives

The method known as brainstorming is frequently used for this step. In brainstorming, everyone is encouraged to suggest possible solutions, and *no* ideas are rejected or evaluated until all ideas have been noted. Even seemingly ridiculous alternatives should be shared and listed; they may be the spark needed to produce a really creative solution. The most important aspect of this step is to generate many possible solutions before selecting one.

IV. Test Alternatives for Reality

The most important thing to keep in mind during this step is not to eliminate possibilities too quickly. The "itemized response," which requires three positive statements to be given before a negative statement can be voiced about an alternative, is a good device for reality testing. The itemized response reduces the tendency of a group to discard an idea before seeing the positive values it may have.

If there are many possible solutions, it may be necessary to place them in some order of priority before testing. One method is to allow each participant to choose a specified number of alternatives that must be considered before any are eliminated. When time permits, it is wise to apply the itemized response to all the alternatives suggested, even those that do not receive a priority rating.

V. Choose an Alternative

Force-field analysis (see Spier, 1973) is a good device for making final choices. Simply stated, force-field analysis involves listing those forces that attract one to the use of a particular alternative and those forces that repel one from the same alternative. The two lists can be placed side by side for easy comparison.

Some problems require multiple solutions. The process does not always result in the choice of a single alternative. But caution should be taken not to choose more solutions than the available resources can implement.

VI. Plan for Action

There are many usable planning processes, including several designed for use with groups. In problem solving it is necessary to choose a planning process appropriate to the potential solution chosen. The most difficult part of planning is to keep the problem and potential solution in view at all times. It is possible to become so involved in planning that what results is a program that has no effect on the problem or that ignores the previous alternative selection.

VII. Implement the Plan

Part of planning is to determine who is responsible for carrying out the various parts of the plan. This step is simply stated: *Get on with it.*

VIII. Evaluate

Evaluation occurs at two levels. The first level is an evaluation of the action plan itself. How well did the plan meet the goals and objectives set for the plan? If it is discovered that the basic goals and objectives of the plan were not met, it may be desirable to go back to step VII and develop a new method of implementation for the plan or return to step VI to develop a new plan.

The second level of evaluation rates the effectiveness of the overall problem-solving effort. How well did the plan contribute to the solving of the problem? The results of this evaluation may lead to the next steps.

IX. Next Steps

Adequate follow-up on evaluation is important. If the problem still exists or some new problems have been uncovered, the individuals or group involved may need to take some action. That action could include a continued commitment to work on the problem or a return to the point of redefining the problem.

Even when the problem has been resolved, follow-up is helpful to participants and the organization. At the very least, a word of appreciation is required for those who helped make the solution work. In some cases the plan may need to become a part of the regular processes of the organization or stored as a resource for the future. It is also good for the individuals and the organization to summarize what was learned about problem solving.

SKILLS AND ATTITUDES

The basic skills and positive attitudes of a problem solver will increase as the person gains experience, particularly in successful problem solving. A problem-solving venture is successful when the problem is eliminated or reduced or when the persons affected are more able to cope. People are not problems; people are either resources or blocks in problem solving.

A goal of the Nine-Step Problem-Solving model is to enable people to become resources rather than blocks in problem solving. To accomplish this, the problem solvers need to cultivate certain attitudes:

1. A healthy *self-respect* accompanied by a self-image that accepts the consequences of one's own personal worth and contributions.
2. A *respect for others* that is sufficient to cause one to doubt malice or ineptitude in one's enemies and to encourage one to use listening and clarifying skills at all times.

3. An *optimism* that says that any problem can be solved if the parties are willing to work long enough to find a mutually acceptable solution.
4. A *respect* for, but not fear of, conflict as a potentially creative process.
5. A *willingness* to invest energy and take risks in an effort to reduce or resolve problems.

Some essential skills are needed throughout the process of problem solving. These include *active listening, clarifying, paraphrasing, self-disclosure, team building,* and facilitating the development of *group process.*

Other skills are needed at specific points in the process: *diagnostic* skills in steps I and II; *decision-making* skills in steps II through V; *data-collecting* skills in steps V and VI; *design* and *planning* skills in steps V through VIII; *organizing* and *administrative* skills in step VII; *evaluation* and *analysis* skills in step VIII.

It is good to have these special skills available to the group through at least one of its members. If that is not possible, then the group should seek skilled help from some other resource person or consider using a consultant.

Leadership Style

Extremely important is the leadership style of the person initiating the problem-solving effort. If that person's style is radically different from the style of others in the problem-solving effort, attention needs to be given to the differences and to the varied expectations that those differences may imply. The more democratic and collaborative the style of the leaders, the easier it will be for them to use the Nine-Step Problem-Solving model.

GROUP OR INDIVIDUAL SOLUTIONS

Serious problems deserve serious problem-solving efforts. The more wide-ranging the problem or the higher the stakes if it is not solved, the more important it is that groups dedicate time and energy to the task of problem solving.

There are, however, many problems that do not need the efforts of a group. The situation may involve only a few individuals, or in many cases the problem can be solved by an individual alone. These are times when it is appropriate, as a method of attack to consider conferring with key persons, delegating to another, using a consultant, or deriving a solution without outside advice.

A nongroup method of attack would also be appropriate on an occasion when the problem is so critical that there is no time to convene a group or when all the people involved have a radically different style of leadership from one's preferred leadership style. If one desires to move toward a more collaborative and democratic style of leadership and decision making, it may well be that a collaborative problem-solving effort is a good time to demonstrate the value of such a style. One must, however, be prepared to take the risks and invest the energy.

The Nine-Step Problem-Solving model is not dependent on a group to be effective. It can be used by individuals, consultants, or with key leaders to work through a problem.

SUGGESTED ACTIVITIES

The following activities may enhance the use of this lecturette in a learning group.

1. The facilitator asks participants to recall a successful problem-solving experience. Using the model, each participant individually analyzes his or her experience to discover what made it work. After ten minutes, the participants form into groups of three or four to share what they have learned.

2. The above process can be repeated using an unsuccessful or incomplete problem-solving experience, with particular attention paid to those steps that were left out or the places at which the process broke down.

3. A real problem or conflict that exists in the group can be explored. This allows for testing the model while a real task is accomplished.

REFERENCE

Spier, M. S. Kurt Lewin's "force-field analysis." In J. E. Jones & J. W. Pfeiffer (Eds.), *The 1973 annual handbook for group facilitators*. San Diego, CA: University Associates, 1973.

Leigh C. Earley is a pastor at First Christian Church, Vandalia, Illinois. He is recognized as a trainer for denominationally sponsored human relations training programs, serves as a consultant and trainer for the Whole Church Project, Institute for Advanced Pastoral Studies, Bloomfield Hills, Michigan, and is chairman of the Leader Development Commission of the Christian Church in Illinois and Wisconsin. His background is in group and organization development, planning, evaluation, human relations training, and consulting.

Pearl B. Rutledge, Ph.D., is the director of R&R Human Resource Development, a management consulting firm in Bloomfield, New Jersey; a trainer with the American Management Association's Executive Effectiveness Course; and a senior trainer with Mid-Atlantic Training and with Consultants and Laboratory Trainers and Consultants. She is also in private practice as a Gestalt therapist in Kentucky. She was previously on the faculty at Pace University, New York City, and Centre College of Kentucky, Danville, Kentucky.

JOB-RELATED ADAPTIVE SKILLS: TOWARD PERSONAL GROWTH

John J. Scherer

The term "skills" is often used rather loosely. There are various levels and kinds of skills, and this discussion is an attempt to classify and to detail in some depth the job-related adaptive skills that lead one toward personal growth.

Three different levels of job-related skills can be identified (see Figure 1).[1] At the top of the pyramid are *work-content skills*. These are competencies required to perform a particular job. They frequently include theories, concepts, or procedures that are highly specific and not transferable. A dentist, for instance, needs to know how to do a crown preparation or an extraction, and a lawyer must be knowledgeable about the rulings and precedents in a certain kind of case. These skills are applicable only to the particular kind of work content in which the person is involved and will not be useful in any other job.

Functional skills, the second level, are transferable. These skills, learned in order to perform one job, have applicability or usefulness in a wide variety of other situations. There are approximately one hundred or more transferable skills that are required of a minister, for example, to prepare and preach a sermon, including the ability to speak to a large group of people, the ability to persuade through verbal interaction, the ability to take abstract ideas and translate them into more concrete illustrations, and so on. The human relations field requires many such skills, for example, leading a meeting, communicating well with others, supervising others, listening to employees' needs.

The bottom level is called *adaptive skills*. These are the competencies developed when a child is very young that center around how that person interacts with his or her

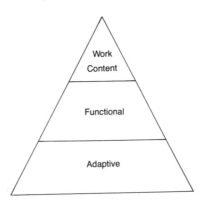

Figure 1. Three Levels of Job-Related Skills

---

[1] This concept is based on the work of Bolles (1972) and Fine (1967).

University Associates

world. How the *child* adapts to his or her environment has a great deal to do with how the *adult* gets along with authority, how high one's self-esteem is, how fluctuations in self-esteem are handled, how available a person's feelings are, how defensive or receptive a person is to criticism.

The skills that can cause a person trouble in many jobs and professions—particularly people-oriented professions—are not the work-content skills or the functional skills, but the adaptive skills. These are the skills that apply to individuals themselves and to their personal growth. People find themselves in unhappy conflicts with work colleagues and, because of poor adaptive skills, are not able to work their problems through even though their views may be "correct" from the point of view of work-content skills or functional skills. The way people behave at the adaptive-skill level seems to affect greatly their performance no matter how competent they are at the other two levels. For this reason, it is especially important to consider the adaptive skills from a job-related perspective.

A LIST OF ADAPTIVE SKILLS

Participation in Learning Experiences

If job performance were based purely on competence, all a person would need to do would be to pass a test indicating the possession of certain knowledge, and there would be no further problem. But people are part of groups, work in one-to-one relationships with colleagues, subordinates, and supervisors, and are members of larger organizations. Contact with others is inevitable. People who refuse to expose themselves to new learning experiences may fear that they are inadequate or believe that "if people discover who I am, they will see through my facade and will not like or respect what they find." Even though many of us are anxious when we take risks with others, an essential adaptive skill involves confronting that anxiety and developing a growing capacity to deal with it. If nothing else, learning to articulate one's anxiety is a step in the right direction.

Relationship to Authority

Dealing with authority is one of the most significant job-adaptive skills. No matter what supervisors do, employees project their own stance toward authority into the relationships they have with their bosses. Attitudes range from dependent to counterdependent to independent to interdependent.

Each person has his or her own particular areas of expertise and abilities that others may not possess, but each can be influenced by and influence other people. The best way for a person to begin that process is to develop the ability to discern what one's own authority relationship is like and to articulate it, if only to oneself, so that eventually one will be able to tell at a particular moment when one is in a dependent or counterdependent stance toward a person of authority.

Availability of Affect

A basic adaptive skill is the ability to be aware of an emotional state and to do something appropriate with it. There is no list of "right" or "wrong" feelings. Our feelings have a will of their own and come and go as they please without any influence from us. The goal is to be able to track our feelings and utilize them creatively and constructively in our relationships with other people. Our feelings are built-in protective and expressive phenomena, designed to serve us under stress or pleasure. They are a source that needs to be available to us in such situations.

The only clues others have about a person's feelings are what show on the outside. Are feelings expressed occasionally, frequently, never? Are there certain emotional states that a person will allow to be seen and certain others that will be hidden? The goal is to allow most of the four major feelings (mad, sad, glad, scared) to show.

The other part of this skill is to be able to describe our own emotional states, not being controlled by the feeling but simply describing it to another person. This is an essential skill in a conflict when problem solving becomes necessary.

Receiving Feedback

We all receive feedback, on or off the job, every day. How we receive it, however, is an extremely important adaptive skill; our success at this skill seems to be linked to our experience of receiving feedback when we were young. If such experience was painful or humiliating for us, we are likely, as adults, to resent receiving feedback. If we sensed a large measure of acceptance along with our early criticism, we will tend to be less anxious and defensive today about the feedback process.

We need to develop the ability to receive feedback "cleanly," watching our feelings of defensiveness or argumentation as they develop. The goal is not to receive feedback nondefensively; that seems almost impossible, given the nature and the depth of the feedback that a person is likely to encounter in his or her job or professional life. But one must begin to develop the capacity to *be aware of defensiveness* and to describe it in such a way that one can get enough distance from it to be more receptive to the feedback. A simple rule of thumb is to ask, "How 'costly' is it for others to give me feedback?"

Giving Feedback

Giving feedback is obviously important, too. If we view *getting* feedback as a learning experience, then *giving* it will cause us less anxiety. In most segments of our lives it is hard to get helpful information about ourselves because people either do not want to, or do not know how to, give good feedback. It is usually loaded with inferences, judgments, and projections of the person's own issues and values and feelings about the other. A manager or supervisor must be able to give feedback cleanly, which means noting his or her own issues as they invade the feedback being given to the other person.

In most places the dictum "If you don't have anything nice to say, don't say anything at all" is the norm. This means that it is precisely those things that an individual needs most to hear that he or she never hears. People are "protected" from what they need by well-meaning friends, co-workers, and colleagues. There are, of course, those colleagues who "hit and run," tossing off a criticism like a hand grenade and disappearing safely out of reach of the explosion. Obviously, that approach is at the other end of the scale.

Capacity for Self-Correction

The basic question is what to do with the feedback we receive. Some people deflect it, deny it, explain it away, or in some other way try to protect themselves from the potential impact of the feedback they receive. One's personal goal ought to be to be able to develop the capacity to *stay open* to the feedback at precisely those moments when it is easier to become defensive, to be able to report the defensiveness, but to *stay with the process* until the individual has discovered what is happening. When someone feels about to shut down and get defensive, it can mean that the feedback is getting close to the point where that person can learn something very important about himself or herself.

A person who is highly practiced in this skill will frequently solicit feedback from supervisors and work colleagues as a way to learn from mistakes and to make changes.

154

Self-Esteem: The Accuracy of One's Self-Image

There is a Biblical notion called "humility" that has been widely misunderstood in this context. It is often interpreted as the "worm syndrome"—people are supposed to make themselves as low as possible and have the lowest possible opinion of themselves. But the word "humble" does not mean this at all; it simply means "to have an accurate self-image": to think neither more highly nor less highly of oneself than is warranted. We should be able to recognize where we are strong and where we are weak and to accept our strengths and weaknesses.

Some people have an extremely inflated self-concept, and other people seem to have a much lower self-image than would be appropriate. The goal with this skill is for individuals to develop the ability to see themselves accurately, knowing what they are capable of, what they are not capable of, and what they are learning to be more competent at. There is an implicit assumption that this skill also includes the capacity for self-acceptance. Any place along the line in a person's development is an acceptable place for that person to be.

Self-Esteem: Adapting to Fluctuations

All of us experience fluctuations in self-esteem; there are three classic kinds of patterns. In the first one, the person has fairly high feelings of self-esteem punctuated by moments of feeling "down." In the second, the person feels down most of the time with pleasantly surprising moments of feeling "up" or acceptable. The third is a kind of middle ground where the fluctuations are extremely minute.

The people in each of these patterns will adapt to the fluctuations in their self-esteem in different ways. A person in the first pattern may feel like a failure during those moments of being down and may in fact be out of touch with significant weaknesses while he or she is feeling high. The second pattern may cause a person to be totally paralyzed by feelings of inadequacy, when in fact he or she is quite capable of performing at a high level of proficiency but does not know it. A person in the third pattern may be out of touch with feeling either high or low and has learned to protect himself or herself from fluctuations by denying changes in those feelings.

The important ability in this adaptive skill is to develop a way not to believe totally either extreme of feelings. We should be aware of them, notice them and experience them, but not use them to make a final judgment on ourselves. A person's *actual* worth or competence is not connected with his or her *feelings* of competence. It is essential that one develop the ability to step back from those feelings and to watch oneself having those feelings, but to try, through the highs and lows, to determine the *actual* value of one's efforts. Competent individuals know that their feelings of self-esteem are not valid indicators of their own value in the world. However, even though large fluctuations in a person's self-esteem may not be connected with actual competence, they may be useful to examine, since they may reveal other important factors in the situation that led the individual to feel inadequate.

Awareness of Impact on Others

Some people seem to be able to go through life totally unaware of the impact their behavior has on other people. This is an impossible luxury for anyone in a supervisory or managerial position. It is essential that a person be able to assess what his or her impact on others is. It is not enough to know that one is having a general impact on other people; it is necessary to be able to describe in very specific, concrete terms the *kind* of impact one is having on others and to be able to connect it to personal behavior. In that way, an individual can correct or guide his or her personal behavior with some idea of its effects on others.

Congruence

One attribute that is difficult to describe is congruence, or naturalness. Yet we all know when it is present or absent. Some people, in an effort to become competent in their role, spend much of their energy "role playing" their idea of a competent person in that role. They try hard to be someone that they may not be or may not be ready to be, and it is apparent to their colleagues that there is a gap between the self they are trying to project and other pieces of themselves that peek out from behind the projection. For example, they may try to appear 100 percent in control of everything, but the stress of holding it all together may show in their voice, facial expressions, and other nonverbal behaviors.

The important adaptive skill here is the ability to know when we are pretending, when we are trying to be something we are not, and to be able to describe the fears or other feelings that are prompting us to pretend. As soon as we have described those fears, we are once again natural and congruent.

When people continually deny that they are pretending or role playing in the face of frequent feedback to the contrary from their colleagues, it may be that they are in a "blind spot" and need to do some intensive work in a one-to-one relationship in order to discover what is stopping them from accepting the possibility that there may be a gap between who they are and the image they are trying to project. This is difficult to work on because people will frequently become irritated when they are told that they are not trusted. A climate of open mutual inquiry is absolutely essential for any progress to be made.

Confronting Conflict

Since we are constantly encountering differences around us—in our jobs, in our personal relationships—we need to be able to confront those conflicts and to work through them. Again, we learned what conflict meant when we were young and how to react to it, and now we may respond in one set way to whatever conflict we encounter: we may fight, or run away, or demand help. What we need to develop is our ability to respond in a flexible way, according to the situation.

The competent human needs first to recognize that conflict is a normal, inevitable phenomenon of life. Developing our repertoire of reactions to conflict so as to include all response patterns is an adaptive skill that will lead us toward our own personal growth.

SUMMARY

The competent human being is not necessarily the one who has all these skills perfected, but one who is open to exploration and insight in each of these dimensions, is struggling to learn what he or she can about himself or herself, and allows those gifts, strengths, and forces that lie within to be released in a slow but perceptible movement toward wholeness as a person.

REFERENCES

Bolles, R. *What color is your parachute?* Berkeley, CA: Ten Speed Press, 1972.

Vine, S. *Guidelines for the development of new careers.* Kalamazoo, MI: Upjohn Institute, 1967.

John J. Scherer is the associate director of the Whitworth/LIOS Graduate Center for Applied Studies at Whitworth College, Spokane, Washington, where he is a core faculty member for the Master of Arts in Applied Behavioral Science program. He is also executive vice president of Concern for Corporate Fitness. He is a member of NTL, IAASS, ACC, ASTD, OD Network, and AHP.

TEAM BUILDING FROM A GESTALT PERSPECTIVE

H. B. Karp

Working together productively has been a concern of mankind for so long and in such varied contexts that it has become one of our identifying characteristics as a species. From the time the first mastodon was killed in a group hunt, we have been looking for more effective ways of combining individual human efforts in order to meet both organizational and individual needs.

WHAT IS A TEAM?

A team is a group of individuals who must work interdependently in order to attain their individual and organizational objectives. Teams can be differentiated from other types of groups by certain definable characteristics. According to Reilly and Jones (1974), there are four essential elements:

> (1) The group must have a charter or reason for working together; (2) members of the group must be interdependent—they need each other's experience, ability, and commitment in order to arrive at mutual goals; (3) group members must be committed to the idea that working together as a group leads to more effective decisions than working in isolation; (4) the group must be accountable as a functioning unit within a larger organizational context. (p. 227)

The most obvious example of a team is an athletic team. The members have a purpose, which gives them an identity. Each player has a unique function (position) that must be integrated with that of the other members. The players are aware and supportive of the need for interdependent interaction, and the team usually operates within the framework of a larger organization (a league).

Not all working groups, however, are teams, nor should they necessarily be. The faculty of a department in a university is a good contrast to an athletic team. Although there is a reason to work together, and departmental faculty members do function as part of a larger organization, there is very little need for interdependent action, since normally each member is totally responsible for the design, execution, and evaluation of his own work, i.e., his teaching and/or research. In this case, team building would have little or no relevance. (Recently, a professor jokingly described her department as "a bunch of screaming anarchists held together by a common parking lot.")

Other examples of work groups that are not teams are committees, in which the purpose is representation, rather than interdependence; training groups, for which no charter exists; and "love puddles," in which the emphasis is on getting along well rather than on working together effectively.

From a Gestalt point of view, there are several necessary assumptions concerning the nature of teams. The first assumption is that all the talent necessary to allow the team to be anything it wishes is already present within the group. The second is that everyone already knows what he or she wants to do; the prime focus is on how the members are stopping themselves from doing what they want. Third, the team's maximum potential for strength and effectiveness is limited only by the limitations each individual member sets on his or her potential. And, fourth, the work itself is potentially exciting.

TEAM EFFECTIVENESS

Two perspectives can be applied to the question of how team effectiveness is achieved: vertical (through leadership) and horizontal (through group dynamics).

Leadership

Much has been written and spoken advocating the participative leadership approach as the one best way to manage team development; currently, the participative approach is highly favored in the business setting. Nevertheless, autocracy or any other particular leadership style is not precluded from being effective: one has only to look at the sports team to see that this is true. It is highly unlikely that either the Green Bay Packers or a high school football team would vote as a team, prior to each game, on what plays will be run.

More important than the particular leadership style is the team leader's ability to combine individual efforts into group output, provide the necessary liaison between the team and the total organization, and accomplish this in a manner consistent with the values of the team leader and other members.

Group Dynamics

The very nature of teamwork depends on the effectiveness of the interaction among team members. The concepts of contact, role, and values are elements of effective team interaction.

Contact

Good contact is based on authenticity among team members. It implies that each individual is aware of his or her individuality and is willing to state views and ideas clearly and to support the principles of *awareness* and *conscious choice.*

Effective work teams are also characterized by relationships that are fairly relaxed but not necessarily warm; i.e., members get along well enough to attain organizational objectives. The norm can be stated: "You are free to be who you are, and I am free not to like you, as long as this does not detract from team effectiveness."

An environment that encourages the open expression of disagreement as well as agreement accepts the reality that an individual may like some people more than others. This is legitimate as long as openly stated preferences do not result in discriminatory, unfair, or task-destructive behavior.

Role

Two elements, function and relationship, are combined in the concept of role. Function is the specific task each member is there to perform; relationship relates to the interaction necessary to get the task completed—with whom each member must interact and how the interaction occurs.

In the well-functioning team, role clarity is evident. The team's objectives are clear and agreed upon, and each team member knows each member's *unique* contribution to those objectives, thus eliminating any duplication of effort. Usually, the effective team is comprised of individuals who have complementary, rather than similar, talents and approaches.

Values

All decisions, whether made by individuals or by groups, are based on values. Three specific values seem to identify good working teams: task effectiveness, dealing in the present, and conflict viewed as an asset.

- *Task Effectiveness.* The well-functioning group places a high value on task effectiveness, with greater emphasis on doing the right things, rather than on doing things right. This value implies that the team also focuses on the objective, or end result, rather than only on the team's ongoing activity.
- *Dealing in the Present.* The effective team focuses on "right here, right now," an emphasis that allows a flexible response to changing conditions within the team itself and within the larger organization. The team can make more appropriate decisions when it is concentrating on *what* is happening rather than *why* it is happening.
- *Conflict Viewed as an Asset.* Conflict provides two very necessary elements to the effective work group. First, it is the prime source of energy in systems, and, second, it is the major source of creativity. Since conflict is absolutely unavoidable, in any case, an effective team's approach to dealing with it is to use it rather than to try to resolve, avoid, or suppress it. More potential for ineffectiveness and marginal performance exists in avoiding conflict than in conflict itself. When conflict is seen as an asset, the preferred approach is to deal with it through collaboration, although competition or even compromise is not precluded, when called for by the situation (Karp, 1976).

WHY TEAMS?

Although establishing teams frequently involves much hard work, the effort provides three important factors to group effectiveness: synergy, interdependence, and a support base.

Synergy

What energy is to the individual, synergy is to groups. The synergy of a group is always potentially greater than the sum of the combined energies of its members. Thus, it is not infrequent in laboratory exercises that a group effort results in a better performance than that achieved by the group's most competent member (Nemiroff & Pasmore, 1975). When team concepts are applied to group formation, the result is not only the effective use of energy, but also the creation of new energy.

Interdependence

Effective teams are made up of highly independent individuals who must combine their separate efforts in order to produce an organizational result. The focus of the team effort is on *combining*, rather than on *coordinating*, resources. Interdependence in today's organizations is a simple reality. Most products and services are too complex, and their respective technologies too specialized, for any one individual to accomplish alone. The team concept provides the necessary link to approach organizational objectives from a position of strength and creativity.

Support Base

It is no overstatement that the average adult spends most of his waking hours in a work setting. It is also a reality that the individual carries all his or her needs with him or her at all times, regardless of the location or situation. From this perspective, the quality of life must be attended to in the work setting as much as in the home setting.

The team constructed along authentic lines has the potential to provide social and emotional support for its members, producing a more satisfying and work-productive environment. It is important to note that, in order for a group truly to function as a support base, the group norms that emerge for any specific team *must* originate from within the team itself and not represent a set of "shoulds" from the behavioral sciences, social institutions, or other external sources. Sometimes, also, it is simply more fun to work with someone else than to work alone.

CONCLUSION

Team construction is one of many viable organizational approaches and structures. It is a situational alternative and not a matter of organizational dogma and clearly needs to be based on conscious choice. Some questions can help determine whether teams are appropriate in a particular organizational situation: Is there a need for interdependent work in order to meet organizational objectives and, if so, to what extent? Can individual satisfaction or higher and better output be better attained through the combination of individual efforts? If the responses to these questions are positive, team building would seem to be a good choice.

REFERENCES

Karp, H. B. Gestalt approach to collaboration in organizations. In J. W. Pfeiffer & J. E. Jones (Eds.), *The 1976 annual handbook for group facilitators.* San Diego, CA: University Associates, 1976.

Nemiroff, P. M., & Pasmore, W. A. Lost at sea (structured experience 140). In J. W. Pfeiffer & J. E. Jones (Eds.), *The 1975 annual handbook for group facilitators.* San Diego, CA: University Associates, 1975.

Reilly, A. J., & Jones, J. E. Team building. In J. W. Pfeiffer & J. E. Jones (Eds.), *The 1974 annual handbook for group facilitators.* San Diego, CA: University Associates, 1974.

H. B. Karp, Ph.D., is an associate professor in the Department of Business Management, Old Dominion University, Norfolk, Virginia. He conducts public and in-house workshops and serves as a consultant through his own organization, Personal Growth Systems, Norfolk, Virginia. Dr. Karp's background is in organizational psychology, organization development, human motivation, and Gestalt applications to individual and organizational growth.

DEALING WITH DISRUPTIVE INDIVIDUALS IN MEETINGS

John E. Jones

Persons who conduct meetings often are troubled by the behavior of a person in attendance who is disrupting the proceedings. It is important for leaders to have a repertoire of responses in such situations in order to maintain control and to accomplish the objectives of the meeting. This discussion will enumerate several methods that can be used to prevent, and to respond effectively to, attempts by individuals to dominate meetings at the expense of the leader. The basic theme in this approach is that the leader should take initiatives to minimize disruptions and to maintain control over meetings when dominating behavior occurs.

Individuals can initiate many forms of disruptive behavior in meetings. Some of the more common ones are:

- Interrupting, cutting people off while they are talking;
- Speechmaking, especially repetitious discourse;
- Sidetracking, topic-jumping, changing issues, multiplying concerns;
- Polarizing, pushing people to take sides, attempting to co-opt people into agreement with one point of view;
- Emotionalizing issues, expressing fear or anxiety about probable outcomes;
- Challenging the leader and others with regard to data sources, rights, legalities;
- Expressing sarcasm, claiming that "the sky is falling," or "they won't let us do what you propose";
- Complaining about the system, meeting, leader, agenda;
- Threatening to withhold support, resign, deny responsibility, seek retribution;
- Accusing the leader of being political, impugning motives;
- Pouting, withdrawing from active participation or controversial topics;
- Saying "Yes, but . . ." a lot, discounting the contributions of others;
- Throwing a "wet blanket" over the proceedings by pointing out all possible failures;
- Personalizing issues and agenda topics, taking all remarks as directed toward persons rather than ideas.

Many of these disruptive behaviors constitute attempts to take over or subvert the leadership of the meeting. Whenever possible the leader needs to anticipate these dominating postures and prevent their occurrence. In addition the leader needs to be able to respond to disruptions when they occur within a meeting, whether they were anticipated or not, and there are some situations in which the leader needs to resort to drastic methods.

It is assumed in this treatment that the leader establishes the agenda, designs the meeting, and facilitates the meeting process. All of these prerogatives are sources of authority and power for the leader, and it is critical for the leader to have a broad power base from which to deal with disruptive behavior. Of course, that includes maintaining high rapport with the majority of those in attendance at the meeting. It is a good rule not to have meetings for which specific goals cannot be articulated and to avoid having meetings that are highly likely to produce negative results. The leader, then, has objectives; what are needed are strategies, tactics, and techniques to ensure that those objectives are not jeopardized by the disruptive behavior of a dominating individual.

Preventing Disruptions

A number of political moves can be made prior to the meeting to attempt to preclude an individual's domination of the event. These tactics are meant to keep intact the leader's ability to conduct a productive interchange among members. They are "power plays" in the sense that they are designed to erode the other person's base of support and courage and make it possible to carry out leadership functions. These methods are not necessarily "nice," but neither is the disruption of an honest meeting. Eight tactics can be considered by the leader in advance of the meeting.

1. Get the dominator's cooperation for this one meeting. Ask the person to agree not to argue from a fixed (and often familiar) position.
2. Give the person a special task or role in the meeting, such as posting the viewpoints of others.
3. Work out your differences before the meeting (possibly with a third-party facilitator) to present a united front to all other members.
4. Structure the meeting to include frequent discussion of the process of the meeting itself.
5. Take all of the dominator's items off the agenda.
6. Set the person up to be concerned about what might be the consequences of disruption. For example, "It has come to my attention that a number of people are angry with you, and I am thinking about opening up their discussion in the meeting."
7. Set up other persons who will attend the meeting to support you in dealing with the disruptive behavior of the individual. For example, they can be asked to refuse to argue with the person, give feeling reactions to the dominating behavior, and confront the dysfunctional behavior directly.
8. Make the person's behavior a published agendum.

Obviously, these methods are manipulative in that they involve deliberate attempts to influence the behavior of another person or persons. People who attempt to dominate meetings have energy that can sometimes be channeled productively, and the best outcome of these preventive postures would be that the person who is often disruptive becomes an effective meeting participant. If these methods are not feasible, the leader needs to have options for keeping control during the meeting itself.

During the Meeting

The leader has two major methods for dealing with disruptive individuals during the course of the meeting: to work with that person "head-on," that is, to confront and otherwise attempt to change behavior, and to use the group of people present to work with the domination. The important consideration is that the leader has to maintain control over what is done and must initiate change. Nine tactics can be used in a direct exchange with the disruptive individual:

1. Interview the person, modeling effective listening. The leader may learn something that is significant to the goals of the meeting by developing the dominating individ-

ual's perspective, and that person may learn how to contribute to the exchange in a productive manner.

2. Turn all of the dominator's questions into statements. This forces the person to take responsibility for expressing a point of view rather than blocking the process through questions.

3. Point out the win-lose character of debates and refuse to argue.

4. Suggest a role reversal. The person can chair the meeting while you attempt to dominate. The person may also be invited to argue the other side of the issue for a time or may be asked to be silent for ten minutes and report the gist of the interchange.

5. Reflect the dominator's feelings and ignore the person's content input. "You seem particularly upset today, especially when I disagree with you. How are you feeling about my interaction with you right now?"

6. Give emotional responses to the dominator. "I feel powerless to accomplish anything here with you, and I get angry when you try to take over by attempting to ramrod through your procedural suggestions."

7. Reduce the person's position to absurdity by interviewing the dominator to the logical extremes of the argument.

8. Agree with all of the person's presentation that is not directly germane to the issue or problem. Agree with the individual's need to be heard and supported.

9. Draw out the motives of the dominator and respond to these aims rather than to the content of the presentation.

The leader must be careful to remember that the "audience" for such exchanges can be made anxious by these techniques. The leader can inadvertently put the dominator in an "underdog" position, gaining sympathy from other meeting participants. There is a good chance that others in the meeting are just as annoyed as the leader is about the disruptive behavior, and there are ways to use that situation to maintain control. Five interventions can be considered to that end:

1. Have the meeting participants establish ground rules to avoid polarization. For example, the word "issue" can be made illegal; people have to couch their discussions in terms of problem solving rather than right-wrong, either-or dichotomies.

2. Post all points raised on a given topic, without names. This makes the information available to all and can lessen repetition.

3. Post all contributions made by the dominator and set the expectation that everyone has a responsibility to avoid "axe-grinding."

4. Create small audiences. Give the dominator only one or two persons to influence. Instruct subgroups to generate statements by consensus. Pair persons with differing points of view, instruct them to interview each other, and have individuals report to the entire meeting.

5. Structure an agreement between the dominator and a major opponent. Pick the person whose position is most dissimilar to the dominator's (or ask the dominator to do this). Have this pair discuss the topic for three to five minutes and come to an agreement about one piece of the problem. Other participants sit in a circle around the pair, observe their process, and give them feedback afterwards.

Leaders can use the "audience" to control disruptive behavior by encouraging others to be open about their responses to the domination. Sometimes, however, these strategies do not succeed completely, and the leader needs more drastic approaches to consider.

When All Else Fails

When the leader feels that the meeting's purposes are being sucessfully thwarted by the dominator, it is important to be able to intervene in such a way as to protect the objectives. Three options are available:

1. Create a chaotic condition in the meeting, exaggerating if necessary, and show the group a way out. This often-used political ploy capitalizes on people's need for closure and order, and the dominator's position can often be lost in the process.
2. Adjourn the meeting when the dominator takes over.
3. Leave the meeting when the dominator takes over, disavowing responsibility for what is done.

These three methods are, of course, bold, and they should not be chosen unless the situation is clearly dangerous for the leader. The final one, sometimes called the "Gromyko Intervention," because of that leader's penchant for walking out of United Nations sessions, requires follow-through in order to maintain the leader's power.

Caveats

All of these methods require that the leader adopt a cool, unruffled posture. Becoming angry means giving away power, and the leader of a meeting needs to focus detached attention on managing the situation in the light of the purposes established for the event. Using many of these techniques in rapid succession can result in "overkill," and the leader needs to make certain that the motive is not to punish an individual but to promote functional behavior.

Leaders who use these tactics as a matter of routine style even when they are inappropriate become sources of disruption themselves in that they prevent meeting participants from having the opportunity to influence the discussion. Too frequent use of these methods can intimidate meeting participants who are less bold than dominators, and the result can be that they contribute less to the meeting out of fear of being confronted.

Disruptive behavior in meetings is almost always a symptom of some defect in the organizational system that the meeting is designed to support. Leaders need to consider that every meeting is, in reality, an organization development session, and they should facilitate it in ways that isolate problems for remedial action.

SUGGESTED ACTIVITIES

Several activities are possible for participants to work on the issue of domination.

1. Prior to the lecturette participants can be instructed to discuss with each other examples of meetings they have attended in which individuals have disrupted the proceedings. The focus should be on how the leader handled the situation.

2. Participants can add to the twenty-five tactics from their own experiences.

3. The group can make a list of behaviors that the leader should *avoid* in responding to disruptions, such as "putdowns," arguing, etc.

4. The facilitator can ask that participants imagine being in all of the twenty-five situations and record their probable emotional responses as (a) leaders, (b) dominators, and/or (c) other meeting participants.

5. The Mach V Attitude Inventory (Christie, 1978) can be used in conjunction with this lecturette to give participants a way of exploring their reactions to the use of these tactics.

6. Various meeting situations can be role played to attain skill in using these methods.

REFERENCE

Christie, R. Mach V attitude inventory. In J. W. Pfeiffer & J. E. Jones (Eds.), *The 1978 annual handbook for group facilitators.* San Diego, CA: University Associates, 1978.

John E. Jones, Ph.D., is senior vice president for research and development, University Associates, Inc., San Diego, California. He is a co-editor of Group & Organization Studies: The International Journal for Group Facilitators *and of the Pfeiffer and Jones Series in Human Relations Training, including* A Handbook of Structured Experiences for Human Relations Training *(Vols. I-VII) and the* Annual Handbook for Group Facilitators *(1972-1980). Dr. Jones's background is in teaching and counseling, education, and organization and community development consulting.*

DEALING WITH ORGANIZATIONAL CRISES

Marshall Sashkin and John E. Jones

The term "management by exception" is not so common as it once was, but it is not totally unheard of today. It describes an approach by which managers are cued into action when a situation is identified as being outside the normal limits of tolerance. A manager becomes a sort of quality-control inspector, moving into high gear and taking direct action only when the product (or process) is unacceptable. (Of course, the manager does many other things as well, designed to prevent just such exceptions from occurring.)

A crisis is a particular, unusual type of exception. In our definition, *a crisis situation will lead to lasting negative consequences unless some immediate corrective action is taken.* One of the open-system principles defined by Katz and Kahn (1978) is "homeostasis," the built-in tendency of all systems (people as well as organizations) to maintain a certain equilibrium state, which does not, however, exclude change. Thus, as children grow larger in a relatively standard way, conforming to a growth curve, so do organizations (see Greiner, 1972; Starbuck, 1965). For various reasons—illness, nutritional deficiencies, hormonal problems, etc.—a child's growth may depart significantly from the norm, being either too slow or too fast. If the deviation becomes too great, correction is impossible, the system suffers irremediable damage, and the child becomes a midget or a giant. This can be called a crisis situation only if we refer to the condition during that brief period of time just before it is "too late."

At such times, whether the crisis is medical or organizational, most people involved experience considerable stress, anxiety, and discomfort. The normal human response to such conditions is automatic physical preparation for "fight or flight" (Selye, 1974)—the adrenal glands go to work, blood pressure rises, and these and other more subtle physiological changes have a major psychological impact on the people in the crisis situation. A calm and rational approach is not typical, although such a reaction is the single most important means for effectively dealing with crisis.

In an organizational crisis situation, when the situational impact on the body as well as on the thought processes of the manager is usually negative, two forms of action will prove helpful: controlling the physiological stress effects, and carefully following a problem-solving process. A variety of relaxation/stress management approaches and techniques are easily accessible to anyone (see Adams, in press; Benson, 1976; Mulry, 1976). Perhaps the simplest is the relaxation response (Benson, 1976), which is similar to the effect of meditation. More sophisticated techniques involve deep breathing and muscle relaxation. Most complex are the biofeedback approaches, which allow one to control more directly the previously automatic stress responses and to modify these responses. Only by counteracting the negative physical effects of stress can one proceed with effective problem solving.

TEN STEPS FOR EFFECTIVE CRISIS MANAGEMENT

Special attention should be given to the problem-solving process. The combination of human-relations process skills and good procedures is the best bet for effective crisis

166   *University Associates*

management. A helpful procedure, showing where skills are particularly important, is outlined here.

1. *Become calm.* As noted earlier, a person who is primarily under the influence of his or her own physiological stress mechanisms is in no condition to solve crisis problems. Thus, the very first step is to gain control over one's own functioning. For most of us this means consciously applying any of the common physiological stress-management techniques mentioned above. Doing this is relatively easy; the difficulty is becoming aware of the need to do it.

2. *Acknowledge the crisis.* Defense mechanisms, typically low in effectiveness, are particularly prone to lead to disaster in crisis situations. Denial and procrastination are especially dangerous. It is important to make public as early as possible the true extent of the crisis, in as much descriptive (nonjudgmental and nonanalytical) detail as is needed to give people a clear understanding of the situation. Those directly affected and those responsible for action should be informed. Panic is worse than loss of confidence, and because rumors spur panic, they should be squelched by clear, factual information. At the same time it is not useful to publish unnecessary details that would fuel a panic or to dispense information that reduces the ability to make action decisions by those persons responsible for dealing with the crisis.

Waffling (Chicken Little and the Tortoise) is one excellent way to create panic. By alternatively shouting warnings ("The sky is falling!") and withdrawing (into one's shell) and pretending nothing is wrong, the crisis can be made to appear at least twice as bad as it really is, with more than twice the negative effect.

3. *Accept ownership of the crisis problem.* This does not mean accepting the "blame," but rather the responsibility for corrective action. It is especially important that as many as possible of the people having a role in solving the problem actually recognize the problem as theirs. "My" problems are always higher on anyone's priority list than "your" problems. Thus, the more people accepting problem ownership, the faster, more powerful, and generally more effective will be the solutions. This is not to imply that the party or parties responsible for causing the crisis should go unnoted; those who cause a problem should be held responsible for their actions. However, judgment, justice, and blame are often not relevant for resolving a crisis. Blaming is another defense mechanism, at its worst called scapegoating (when innocent parties are blamed and efforts are directed against them instead of toward solving the problem). Aircraft pilots blame controllers and mechanical problems for a crash, controllers blame the pilots' "human errors" and mechanical failures, and mechanics blame both the controllers and the pilots. None of this activity answers the question of what happened to cause the crash and how to prevent future crashes like it.

4. *Generate innovative solutions.* A crisis situation is, by definition, a "rare event." It may well take an equally rare type of solution to counteract the crisis. A variety of techniques can be used to raise the level of creativity (see Ulschak, 1979), including brainstorming, synectics, and other more formal techniques. Spending a lot of time considering conservative solutions is not useful; they are obvious and are not likely to be overlooked in any case.

5. *Assess costs and benefits of solution ideas.* This is a standard problem-solving step that is often omitted—even more dangerously in a crisis situation than in a normal problem situation. Grasping at straws may cause one to miss the floating timber. Naturally, time pressures are likely to make an extensive, comprehensive cost/benefit analysis impossible, but a "rough" idea of the cost/benefit ratio for each solution or action possibility should still be a necessity.

6. *Take risks.* Once some rough comparative cost/benefit data are available, a rational choice can be made among action alternatives. At this point one must be careful not to be too cautious or conservative. In a crisis situation a risky action that could have great success

is probably better than a low-risk course of action that would also be unlikely to have great positive impact. Although a less risky course may seem a natural choice, there are good reasons for choosing risk, especially when its extent is known and can be taken into account.

7. *Take actions designed to produce quick, visible results.* It is not reasonable to expect a crisis to be fully resolved very quickly, but it is necessary that some positive results be rapidly evident. This creates a cycle of optimism, a positive "self-fulfilling prophecy." Organization members gain faith by knowing that something positive is being done, even if it is only a relatively small part of the long-range solution. Thus one criterion for selecting a course of action is the likelihood that it will have immediate, visible impact.

8. *Plan for contingencies.* Some people are bound to say, "It won't work." This may "cover" them, should the action not work ("I was against it all along"), but it is also part of a vicious cycle of creating and then, purposefully or not, helping fulfill negative expectations. To avoid this effect as much as possible, unrealistic expectations must not be created by touting the solution as the answer to all human/organizational problems. It must also be expected that there will be some problems in implementing actions and generating the desired effects, and minor and major contingency plans should be prepared. Minor contingency planning involves setting up correction plans for the problems—some known and expectable, others unpredictable—that will inevitably arise. If there is a corrective process that can be "turned on" as needed (such as a monitoring team, an automatic data report to certain people, etc.), then minor problems can be easily eliminated. A major contingency plan would be an alternate action that could be implemented if and when the first plan is determined to be unsatisfactory. Contingency planning is the primary way to reduce the risk of the action solution.

9. *Develop a commitment to long-range development.* A crisis implies a basic rather than a superficial problem. Therefore, while immediate action and correction are the focus, it is also of great importance that a long-range problem-solving approach be seen as a commitment. Crisis solutions may treat only symptoms, an approach that is not necessarily bad unless deeper causes remain ignored. Since people are often willing to promise a great deal in an emergency situation but renege on such promises when the immediate emergency is over, it is wise to have long-range commitments, including at least an outline of the development plan, made public, put into writing, and widely understood.

10. *Seek out learnings.* Learnings from dealing with a crisis occur on two levels. First, one can learn to prevent similar crises or can, at least, have excellent action plans ready should similar situations occur. It is possible, also, to generalize these learnings in a variety of ways to other problem situations that are related to the crisis. A second and more difficult—but also more useful—type of learning concerns the crisis-management process. Crises are rare but inevitable, and a small reduction in pain and difficulty when the next one comes can mean a large increase in organizational adaptability and a significant decrease in costs. Unless someone purposely attends to this second type of learning *during* (not after) the crisis, it will not occur. This is a difficult task, but the payoff is high, whether the immediate crisis is effectively resolved or not.

PREVENTIVE OPTIONS

Few specific crises are predictable, yet there are some preventive actions that can be taken to reduce the probability of crisis or to increase the probability of effective crisis management.

- Clarify organizational objectives in terms of major products and processes (ongoing activities); develop a picture (chart, graph, etc.) of desired goal attainment and analyze what range of deviations from the desired "track" the organization can tolerate or can deal with more or less automatically.

- Identify "key communicators," people who always know what is happening, who are part of or control crucial information flows in the organization; use these people to develop an early-warning system for crises "over the horizon."
- Define the five most likely crisis events and develop detailed contingency plans. Police departments have plans for riot control; hospitals develop similar plans for floods, fires, earthquakes, etc.

  √ Identify key resource people for potential crisis situations; negotiate roles and responsibilities in advance.

  √ Hold a "dress rehearsal" of crisis-response procedures for all parties likely to be involved in the crisis and its management.

- Develop techniques and skills needed for effective crisis management and practice these in low-risk, noncrisis situations:

  √ relaxation techniques

  √ confrontation skills

  √ problem-solving procedures

- Develop a support system (Kirschenbaum & Glaser, 1978) for coping emotionally with ongoing crisis situations.

SUMMARY

A crisis situation calls for rapid comprehension of the problem and for quick, accurate communication. The following summary statements may be helpful.

- Crises require immediate action to prevent highly probable, lasting negative effects.
- Crises are normal and characteristic of organizational functioning.
- Crises are dangerous not only because of the obvious problems they involve but because of the complex physical and psychological dynamics they provoke in human participants.
- There are preventive and preparatory actions one can take to reduce the likelihood of crises and to minimize potential negative effects.
- There are specific, learnable actions that can be taken to manage and resolve crises effectively.
- Crises can be productively considered as sources of energy for organization development.
- Coping is not developing.
- "You can't cook without heat."

SUGGESTED ACTIVITIES

The following activities may help the facilitator discuss the topic of organizational crises.

1. The facilitator asks group members to think of the most recent organizational crisis they faced and to suggest adjectives that could be used to describe or characterize the crisis. These are posted on newsprint as they are called out. The list generated can be sorted into groups of similar terms until a set of "basic" characteristics is left. The facilitator then relates these to this lecturette as the consequences of crisis—stress, anxiety, etc.—and uses them to lead into a discussion of solutions.

2. Group members are asked to think of the last organizational crisis situation they were personally involved in that was resolved effectively and to make some notes to themselves if they wish. The members then form small subgroups (perhaps triads) with the task of identifying characteristics common to effective crisis management. The facilitator might suggest that group members first spend three minutes each giving a brief outline of their crisis situation to their subgroup. The subgroups then take ten to twenty minutes to discuss the details of their cases, extracting common characteristics. Each subgroup posts its list on newsprint and reports to the reassembled full group. The facilitator then forms one merged list, which can serve as the point of departure for the ten steps elaborated in this lecturette.

REFERENCES

Adams, J. *Stress management workbook.* San Diego, CA: University Associates, in press.

Benson, H. *The relaxation response.* New York: Morrow, 1976.

Greiner, L. E. Evolution and revolution as organizations grow. *Harvard Business Review,* 1972, 50(4), 37-46.

Katz, D., & Kahn, R. L. *The social psychology of organizations* (2nd ed.) New York: Wiley, 1978.

Kirschenbaum, H., & Glaser, B. *Developing support groups: A manual for facilitators and participants.* San Diego, CA: University Associates, 1978.

Mulry, R. *Tension management and relaxation.* San Diego, CA: Author, 1976. (Available from Learning Resources Corporation, 8517 Production Ave., San Diego, CA 92121.)

Selye, H. *Stress without distress.* New York: Lippincott, 1974.

Starbuck, W. H. Organizational growth and development. In J. G. March (Ed.), *Handbook of organizations.* Chicago: Rand McNally, 1965.

Ulshack, F. L. Finishing unfinished business: Creative problem solving. In J. E. Jones & J. W. Pfeiffer (Eds.), *The 1979 annual handbook for group facilitators.* San Diego, CA: University Associates, 1979.

Marshall Sashkin, Ph.D., is a professor of industrial and organizational psychology at the University of Maryland, University College, College Park, Maryland. He is also senior editorial associate with University Associates, San Diego, California. He is a co-author of Organization Behavior in Action *(1976) and* Resourcebook for Planned Change *(1978) and has published numerous articles in scholarly journals. Dr. Sashkin's background is in group dynamics, including leadership and problem solving, human relations training, and organization development consulting with a wide variety of organizations.*

John E. Jones, Ph.D., is senior vice president for research and development, University Associates, Inc., San Diego, California. He is a co-editor of Group & Organization Studies: The International Journal for Group Facilitators *and of the* Pfeiffer and Jones Series in Human Relations Training, *including* A Handbook of Structured Experiences for Human Relations Training *(Vols. I-VII) and the* Annual Handbook for Group Facilitators *(1972-1980). Dr. Jones's background is in teaching and counseling, education, and organization and community development consulting.*

INTRODUCTION TO THE
THEORY AND PRACTICE SECTION

DEVELOPING THEORETICAL MODELS

In this section in past *Annuals* we have included two basic types of content. A number of papers have been concerned with models or theories, and many have focused primarily on applications of theory in professional practice. Still others have been largely atheoretical discussions of effective methods and strategies in training and development. Since this field has often been accused of engaging in practice without a unified theory, we have been encouraging users of this publication to look at their work systematically and to develop models to guide their professional behavior. Accordingly, we felt that it would be appropriate to explicate in this introduction a step-by-step method for model building that can be useful for group facilitators.

Models have many functions. Applied behavioral scientists develop models primarily to:

- *explain* various aspects of human behavior and interaction
- *integrate* what is known through research and observation
- *simplify* complex human processes
- *guide observation* in such dynamics situations as group interaction
- *teach* relationships among concepts
- *predict* human behavior in various situations
- *control* human relations for experimental purposes
- *evaluate* effects of various treatments of people
- *invent* new ideas and processes
- *plan interventions* into human systems

As practitioners we are usually most interested in the teachability of ideas of training and in using models to guide organization development interventions.

How does a model come to be? Obviously people create models, but there seems to be a lack of practical guidance for doing so. The purpose of a model is to communicate, in an effective and simplified way, complex information that generally includes statements about the causal relationships between and among specific variables or concepts. Thus, a model facilitates understanding, prediction, and control over real-world phenomena.

Types of Models

There are at least two basic types of models, and it is important to be aware which of these one is building or using. The first, more common, type involves an analogy (analog model). Thus, one could develop a "switchboard" model of the human brain, to communicate more clearly certain important neurological concepts and processes. Of course, everyone is aware that the brain is not a telephone switchboard, with plugs being connected and disconnected, even though, in certain limited ways, the brain functions *like* a switchboard.

The second, less common, type of model is intended to express, depict, or simulate how something actually works. For example, scientists engaged in research that will someday lead to working nuclear *fusion* reactors have developed mathematical models that describe precisely the actual operation of such a device. We will not be concerned with this second kind of model here.

PHASES AND STEPS IN MODEL BUILDING

The dimensions of our model-building model are "steps" and "phases." (See Figure 1.) There are ten steps and four phases; each phase has two or three steps in it. Steps are, then, subparts of phases. The steps and the phases exist in a specific sequence, which describes how they are interrelated. The first two steps in model building are (1) to *observe* the phenomena involved in the model and (2) to *identify* aspects important to the model. The third step is to *specify* only those variables to be included. In creating a model-building model, we are limiting ourselves to analog models (as identified previously). We are, furthermore, interested specifically in models that are concerned with human behavior.

Phases	Steps
I. Delimiting	1. *Observe* phenomena 2. *Identify* areas of interest 3. *Specify* which areas are to be covered
II. Defining	4. *Develop* salient dimensions 5. *Define* interactions among dimensions
III. Describing	6. *Describe* model in writing 7. *Depict* model visually
IV. Demonstrating	8. *Test* model in a new situation 9. *Refine* model based on results 10. *Review* relationships and graphic presentation

Figure 1. A Model-Building Model

These three steps—*observing* the phenomena of interest, *identifying* important aspects, *specifying* those aspects to be included in the model—comprise the first model-building phase, *delimiting*. In this phase one examines, narrows, and selects the phenomena to be included in the model.

The second phase of model building is *defining* the specific variables (or phenomena) that the model deals with and their interrelations. Within this phase, step four is to *develop dimensions*, to create labels, to define and redefine the specific phenomena selected in the first phase. A number of concepts are useful in determining the aspects of the phenomena to be taken into account by a model. Some key ways of thinking during step four are taken from various academic disciplines:

- dimensions
- factors
- components
- forces
- resources
- variables (dependent, independent, intervening)
- elements
- functions
- routines

- effects
- contingencies
- constructs
- systems, subsystems, suprasystems
- parameters
- boundaries
- roles

Step five in our model-building model consists of defining the relationships among the dimensions one has chosen. This involves accounting for the observed phenomena in terms of the interplay among the various aspects of the situation deemed important. A number of concepts are useful in this process. One can think along several lines:

- Randomness—What part does pure chance play in the situation?
- Cause and effect—Is there evidence that serial linkages can be found that would lead to inferences or causations?
- Association—What effects seem to be correlated with each other (temporal or geographical associations, for example)?
- Parallelism—What behavioral phenomena seem to track together?
- Dependence—What dimensions seem to depend on, be independent of, or be interdependent with other dimensions?
- Complexity—How do I balance the demands for simplicity in the ultimate model (for the function it is supposed to perform) with the actualities of the behavioral phenomena?
- Intervening processes—What conditions/factors/contingencies seem to mediate the responses to the stimuli in the situation?

The important consideration here is to find appropriate ways of thinking about relationships among the selected dimensions. Appropriateness is dictated by the purposes for which the model is intended to be used.

We have now partly and very roughly defined the model-building model. Phases three and four (steps six through ten) are presented in the following discussion as we continue to illustrate the model-building process by using it.

Phase three is *describing* the model. Step six is to *describe* the entire model in writing. Thus, this entire discussion, from beginning to end, is an example of step six. Step seven is to *depict* the model visually, as in Figure 1. Numerous graphic representations can be considered. These depictions vary, of course, from very simple to highly complex. The tabulation below includes the most common:

- list
- table
- ranking
- continuum
- categorization
- taxonomy
- morphology
- facet design
- whirlpool
- concentric circles
- grid

- cube
- triangle
- PERT diagram
- flow chart
- diagram
- "black box"
- linear/curvilinear/nonlinear graph
- cyclical representation

The choice of graphic design depends on the hypothesized interrelationships among the defined dimensions.

The fourth and last phase is *demonstrating* that the model works. Step eight involves *testing* the model by applying it to a situation, case, example, or problem situation other than the one that was used in developing the model. Thus, to carry out this step we could (as an example) use our model-building model to develop a model of experiential learning, of facilitator intervention style, etc. This would provide experience in using the model-building model and feedback on it, which are necessary for step nine, *refining* the model. This could mean adding important elements that were left out in the first version, simplifying concepts, or revising the written or visual descriptions for clarity. Finally, step ten is *reviewing* the entire model, in detail, to incorporate all of the refinements and to make any further changes that are necessary because of these refinements.

In our presentation of the model-building model, we did not carry out phase four (steps eight through ten) since that would have taken the discussion beyond the scope of this introduction. We shall leave it to the reader to attempt an application of the model-building model. Of course, we are interested in the results of such efforts and would consider publishable models for this section of the *Annual*.

In the Theory and Practice section this year we have selected pieces heavily weighted toward practice. We have always striven for a practical, "how-to" bias in choosing and editing pieces for this part of the *Annual*, and the contents of this volume strongly reflect that position. We have attempted to fill a gap by publishing two treatments of evaluation strategies, and we have included treatments of various effective training methods.

METHODS OF CENTERING

Anthony G. Banet, Jr.

Centering is a term that "refers to a series of processes that strive simultaneously to increase an awareness of the body center and to promote the discovery of the true self that is beyond the mask of ego. Centering is the integration of body, mind, and spirit into a harmonious whole" (Banet, 1977, p. 99).

When we are centered, we are maximally effective. The virtues of centeredness can be explained through the following characteristics: a focus on the present; the efficient use of human energy; a unity of inner calm and outward action; an awareness of fit between one's self and the universe; a simplicity of movement and behavior; a willingness to transcend apparent dichotomies; and a belief in inner control and responsibility.

The work of centering, the attainment of these characteristics, is by no means easy. It involves integrating difficult philosophical concepts with the physical aspects of the person. Many methods and techniques (many derived from or part of Eastern religious or philosophical systems of thought and practice) have been developed to assist one in becoming centered. These methods are ancient and yet new. A particular method may, for uncertain reasons, become popular and be adapted to Western needs, achieving a popular following, only to slip away after a few years into the realm of the esoteric, of interest only to a "chosen few" devotees. Several of the methods currently most popular are reviewed here.

T'AI CHI CHUAN

T'ai Chi Chuan (literally, the "supreme ultimate") is a series of slow-motion body movements that appear to be a form of dance, ritual choreography, or "shadow boxing." Its history is obscure; in some texts, the origins of T'ai Chi are attributed to an observer watching a fight between a serpent and a crane; in others, T'ai Chi is regarded as the earliest martial art whereby combat techniques and self-defense were taught under the guise of poetic imagery. The number of movements varies, but generally it ranges from twenty-five to one hundred, with many repetitions. T'ai Chi movements are very slow and graceful; about half an hour is required for an experienced practitioner to complete the series.

In T'ai Chi, breath is chi, the energy we use to move. The *tant'ien*—the center of gravity in the body—is both the reservoir for chi energy and the source from which all body movement originates. T'ai Chi involves a flowing circular breathing pattern, constant but nearly imperceptible movement, and an absorption into the form, as one movement blends into and becomes another. "Repulsing the Monkey" gives way to "Waving Hands Like Clouds," which in turn becomes "Embrace Tiger, Return to Mountain" as the practitioner symbolically mimics the body positions required for these activities. As Huang (1973), a noted T'ai Chi master, describes it

> you move very slowly. By moving very slowly you have time to be aware of all the subtle details of your movement and your relationship to your surroundings. It's so slow that you really have no way of saying this is slower than that or faster than that. You reach a level of speed that is like slow motion, in which

everything is just happening. You slow it to the point that you are fully involved in the process of each moment as it happens. You transcend the form and any concern you might have to achieve some particular motif. (p. 19)[1]

T'ai Chi can be viewed as an exercise, a meditation or a self-defense martial art. For many people, it is centering *par excellence*, for it incorporates breathing with attention to the *tant'ien*, and it combines inner calm with exterior action. The grace and power of the T'ai Chi movements can be appreciated by practitioner and observer alike, but, like most centering activities, T'ai Chi must be experienced and practiced under the guidance of a qualified teacher. T'ai Chi at its best appears to be an effortless dance—a willow confluent with the gentle breeze—but discipline and concentration are required for proper execution. Sources that describe T'ai Chi include Huang (1973) and Kauz (1974).

AIKIDO

In Japanese, the center is *hara* (belly), or the one point in the lower abdomen *(seika-no-itten)*, the seat of *ki*, or "intrinsic energy," the strength and spirit possessed by everyone but developed consciously by only a few. *Ki* is a somewhat alien concept to Westerners; "soul" and "spirit" approximate its meaning. The *hara*, from the viewpoint of the Japanese, is "the place where the spirit should be concentrated. It is a joint spot for both body and spirit. Once you have mastered it correctly, you will for the first time be able to unify your body and your spirit, and by always maintaining the single spot, you will be able to move with a unified spirit and body" (Tohei, 1966, pp. 63-64).

Aikido (literally, the way to the harmony or coordination of energy) is a martial art that provides the discipline to develop an awareness of *hara* and to use that awareness to develop inner calmness, relaxation, and a harmonious integration of self. Aikido is, secondarily, a method of self-defense that emphasizes neutralization of an opponent's aggression rather than attack. It is the least aggressive and most philosophical of the martial arts; judo, karate, sumo wrestling, although they also use centering exercises, are more concerned with the development of combat prowess. This unification of inner calm and coordinated activity is the goal of aikido discipline and practice. Four principles are taught in the aikido regimen: *centralization, extension, leading control,* and *sphericity.*

In aikido, centralization—developing awareness of *hara* or the "one point"—is a technique, a discipline, and not an end in itself. Centralization enables the aikido practitioner to unify and coordinate mental, physical, and functional powers through abdominal breathing, correct posture, and balance. Practice of the discipline leads to "relaxed suppleness" and an attitude of gentleness toward opponents.

The principle of extension refers to the way in which *ki* (centralized energy) is channeled and applied in combat situations. Many aikido exercises involve the extension of *ki* through body parts. In aikido folklore, extending *ki* is often compared to a bubbling spring, constantly pouring out crystal clear water. As long as the spring continues to bubble, it keeps itself pure and clear; when it ceases, the polluted *ki* from the external environment enters and disrupts the flow.

Leading control refers to the way in which *ki* emanating from the one point is applied to thwart an aggressor. In aikido, the intent is to neutralize, not overcome, the opponent. Anyone who transgresses the space of another is, by definition, off-center; the attack is thwarted by deflection—by "leading" the control of the opponent so that it misses its target. The fierce shouts and kicks of karate have no place in the aikido *dojo* (gymnasium).

---

[1] Reprinted from A. C. Huang, *Embrace Tiger, Return to Mountain.* Copyright © 1973, Real People Press. Used with permission of the publisher.

Instead, the aikido expert moves adroitly to avoid the attack, to remove himself from possible contact with the opponent's uncentralized *ki* while leading it away from its target.

A final principle in aikido concerns sphericity. All body movement is seen as describing a circle, with the *hara* or one point at the center. By learning a variety of circular hand, leg, and body movements, the aikidist creates a sphere or "energy body" (Leonard, 1974) around himself.

Aikido is seen by its teachers as a gentle way to achieve harmony—inside the body, in relationships, with the universe. Morihei Uyeshiba, who originated the aikido system, viewed aikido—and all the martial arts—as based on love and the laws of nature.

ARICA

There are three centers in the human animal: the intellectual, the emotional, and the vital, or as we call them, the path, the oth and the kath. Ideally the kath is the master of life; it is the center which directs vital movement and allows us to relate to the world with instinctual immediacy. We sense our basic unity with all life in our guts. (Ichazo, quoted by Keen, 1973, p. 68)[2]

Arica is a body of theory, doctrine, and method that synthesizes the wisdom of the past and applies that wisdom to contemporary human problems. Named for a city in Chile and developed by Oscar Ichazo, the Arica system applies teachings from Sufism, Gurdjieff, Zen, and humanistic psychology to develop an awareness of the *kath* and to reduce the hold that the ego has over the body. Lilly (1975) has commented to the effect that the sum of human evolutionary development and intrinsic responses to the environment is stored in the *kath*. And, since it is through the *kath* that life is experienced, Arica training has the aim of centering one's consciousness in one's *kath*. In this way, suggests Lilly (1975), one can respond to life experiences directly, without having to go through a separate cognitive process.

Arica training takes place usually in groups, the belief being that the combined energy present in the group accelerates the spiritual development of the individual.

The techniques of Arica are many and varied, but all involve centering and a *kath* awareness. A representative method is the Mentations, a guided relaxation-meditation that aims at infusing all body parts with consciousness. The body is divided into twelve parts, each of which has a physiological and a parallel psychological function:

Ears perceive the *substance* of things, their inner meaning, their very nature.

Eyes give us knowledge of the outward *form*, what a thing looks like.

Nose smells out *possibilities*. It is a hunter.

Mouth and stomach tell us what our *needs* are, not only food but nourishment for the whole person.

Heart is the source of our *impulses* toward something or away from something. Love is centered here.

Liver is the organ of *assimilation;* through it we make food, experiences, and ideas part of ourselves.

Colon, bladder, and kidneys *eliminate* anything that we cannot assimilate, whether it be food, experiences, memories, ideas.

Genitals indicate our *orientation* toward life, whether we love it or fear it.

Thighs and upper arms are indications of our strength and *capacity*. Nor is this strength merely physical; it also includes strength of character.

Knees and elbows are used to make one's way through a crowd, so they indicate one's *charisma* or the effect one generally has upon others.

Calves and forearms are the necessary *means* for our actions. With them we move about and perform our duties.

Feet and hands take us toward our *goals* and help us to grasp them.

(Ichazo, quoted by Keen, 1973, p. 68)[2]

[2] Reprinted from *Psychology Today*, 1973, 7(2), 68. Copyright © 1973, Ziff Davis Publishing Co. Used with permission of the publisher.

Another centering activity involving a dyad is *trespasso,* in which two people sit opposite each other and focus their gaze on the left eye of the person across from them. Each individual concentrates on the *kath* and allows divine energy,(*Baraka*) to be transmitted one to another. This exercise may continue for fifteen minutes or half an hour and is useful in promoting feelings of inner peace and caring for the other.

A hallmark of the Arica training is its exceptional catholicity: T'ai Chi, Sufi stories, the *I Ching,* the enneograms of Gurdjieff, fantasy, Christian theology, meditation, movement, dance, diet, massage, alchemy, yoga, cleansing and purifying exercises, and physical fitness are combined to enhance the centering capacity and the spiritual development of individuals. Arica, in fact, is more than a system of centering. It aspires to be a religiously toned worldwide social movement aimed at creating "family" harmony among all peoples.

ZEN

One day a man of the people said to the Zen master Ikkyu: "Master, will you please write for me some maxims of the highest wisdom?"

Ikkyu immediately took his brush and wrote the word "Attention."

"Is that all?" asked the man. "Will you not add something more?"

Ikkyu then wrote twice running: "Attention. Attention."

"Well," remarked the man rather irritably, "I really don't see much depth or subtlety in what you have just written."

Then Ikkyu wrote the same word three times running: "Attention. Attention. Attention."

Half-angered, the man demanded: "What does that word, 'Attention' mean anyway?"

And Ikkyu answered, gently: "Attention means attention."[3]

To write about Zen is senseless, because it refers to an experience, an attitude, a posture toward reality. "If one clings to what others have said about Zen," reads an old commentary, "he is like a dunce who thinks he can beat the moon with a pole." And yet, Zen is *here,* written about, described, categorized, analyzed. What is Zen? "True Zen shows itself in everyday living, *consciousness* in action. More than any limited awareness, it opens every inner door to our infinite nature" (Reps, undated, p. 175).

Zen as a form of centering is known to the West in at least two expressions: Soto Zen, which emphasizes Zazen, or "just sitting," and Rinzoi, which utilizes scripture parables and the *Koan,* the unanswerable riddle that leads to the experience of *satori,* or enlightenment.

Zazen involves many initial exercises, such as deep abdominal breathing, focus on the body center, and emptying of the mind. In Zazen practice, one sits without motion, without thought, to practice these exercises. The uniqueness of Zazen, as Kapleau (1973, p. 239) describes it, lies in this: "that the mind is freed from bondage to *all* thought-forms, visions, objects and imaginings, however sacred and elevating, and brought to a state of absolute emptiness, from which alone it may one day perceive its own true nature, or the nature of the universe." The goal of practice is to keep our "beginner's mind," the fresh appreciation of what is. Zazen strives for nothing, attains nothing—it is simply a way of being alive and making direct contact with reality. Other forms of Zen may employ stories, riddles, or focus on everyday activities as a way to keep the "beginner's mind." Flower arrangement, the Japanese tea ceremony, kite-flying—all can become ways to center our attention, to focus on what is actually present, rather than on what we want to be present. Perhaps Zen's

---

[3] Reprinted from D. Kapleau (Ed.), *The Three Pillars of Zen: Teaching, Practice and Enlightenment.* Copyright © 1965, Beacon Press. Used with permission of the publisher and the author.

greatest contribution to the serious, striving person who works to *"get it all together"* is its sense of humor, play, and absurdity. Nothing is all that important—even enlightenment.

It has been said that if you have Zen in your life, you have no fear, no doubt, no unnecessary craving, no extreme emotion. Neither illiberal attitudes nor egotistical actions trouble you. You serve humanity humbly, fulfilling your presence in this world with loving-kindness and observing your passing as a petal falling from a flower. Serene, you enjoy life in blissful tranquillity. Such is the spirit of Zen. (Reps, undated, p. 4)[4]

ATHLETICS

For most Westerners, athletics is synonymous with sport and competition. Only recently have physical exercise and athletic endeavor been rediscovered as methods of centering and inner calm. The danger that sport presents as an aggressive, competitive challenge is well-expressed in the *Way of Chuang Tzu:*

> When an archer is shooting for nothing
> He has all his skill.
> If he shoots for a brass buckle
> He is already nervous.
> If he shoots for a prize of gold
> He goes blind
> Or sees two targets—
> He is out of his mind!
> His skill has not changed. But the prize
> Divides him. He cares.
> He thinks more of winning
> Than of shooting—
> And the need to win
> Drains him of power.

(Merton, 1965, p. 107)[5]

Solitary sport, especially, lends itself to centering through increased body awareness and attention to what is happening in the present moment. Running, swimming, hiking, or golfing allow individuals to experience what Leonard (1975) calls the "energy body" in which the physical body is seen as one with the total energy of the universe.

Running or jogging illustrates clearly the centering potential of athletics. Once the run has started, it becomes impossible to focus on anything except the pounding heart, the breathing process, the pain and power of muscles, lungs and movement cohesively becoming one. Many runners report the purifying, clarifying effect of their activity. The challenge of reaching beyond limitations is ever present; by becoming absorbed with self, the self escapes the confines of body, time, and space. The running becomes, in Leonard's term, the "dance of existence." The more tangible gains of running—weight loss, conditioning, physical fitness—become secondary to the sense of inner peace, energy, and well-being that comes with repeated practice.

MEDITATION

The term meditation encompasses a series of diverse practices that involve focused attention and enriched awareness. As Naranjo and Ornstein (1971) describe it, meditation is "concerned with the development of a *presence*, a modality of being, which may be expressed or developed in whatever situation the individual may be involved . . . all

---

[4] Reprinted from P. Reps, *Zen Flesh, Zen Bones*. Copyright © Charles E. Tuttle Company, Inc., Tokyo, Japan. Used with permission of the publisher.

[5] Reprinted from Thomas Merton, *The Way of Chuang Tzu*. Copyright © 1965 by the Abbey of Gethsemani. Used by permission of New Directions, New York, and George Allen & Unwin Ltd., London.

meditation is a *dwelling upon* something" (pp. 8, 10). These authors discuss meditation as *directive*, in which an individual places himself under the influence of an external symbol; as *nondirective*, in which a person lets himself be guided by interior fantasy; or as *negative*, in which the person empties himself of all inferior and exterior forms.

Directive meditation is common in many religious practices. Reflection on the Torah or a scriptural passage; repetition of prayers, such as the Jesus prayer or the rosary; a sensory focus on chanting, a mandala, an image or a symbol of God are all ways to quell the "chatter" of hectic living and to become centered.

Nondirective meditation may include guided fantasy to "get in touch with" patterns of thought and feelings that may be below the level of conscious awareness and yet may profoundly affect behavior. By following one's "random" or fantasy thought, one may be led to these deeper areas which must be brought into the center of awareness so that they can be integrated within the self. Whereas directive meditation is a means for centering by focusing all of one's self on an object of attention, nondirective meditation seeks to identify the various unknown parts of the self and, by a more active process, develop and unify one's center.

Negative meditation, a focus on nothingness, is probably best known as a Zazen technique, which has already been described in some detail. It is through nothingness that one may read a total understanding and integration of one's self and the universe. In this way one may become centered not only within one's self but in the context of the universe, although when this occurs this distinction is of course meaningless.

These three approaches are not exhaustive of all meditation techniques, nor is the three-type set defined by Naranjo and Ornstein (1971) the only categorization of such techniques. It is a reasonably comprehensive way to look at meditation, and it does highlight two important facts. First, the aim of most meditation techniques is the manipulation of attention or consciousness in order to identify a focus, integration, or center of self-awareness. Second, it is clear that these techniques vary greatly in degree of difficulty of practice, with the directive methods the easiest and the negative approach the hardest. While all three categories have attained popularity in the United States at various times during the past decade, only the simpler directive techniques, such as used in transcendental meditation or to produce the "relaxation reflex" seem to have developed a large stable following.

CONCLUSION

To close this brief review of centering, it is imperative to say that none of the methods described here can make us centered; we cannot make it happen, because it already is — we are already centered. The methods and techniques do not create the center; they are means for directing and exercising our attention and can increase our awareness and appreciation of what is already there. Centering is always a beginning, a start on a journey that is never completed. What makes it worthwhile is that it is all we have, a mystery, says Richards (1964), that

> sucks at our breath like a wind tunnel. . . . Centering is a severe and thrilling discipline, often acutely unpleasant . . . I become weak, discouraged, exhausted, angry, frustrated, unhappy, and confused. But someone within me is resolute, and I try again. Within us lives a merciful being who helps us to our feet however many times we fall. (p. 8)

REFERENCES

Banet, A. G., Jr. Centering. In J. E. Jones & J. W. Pfeiffer (Eds.), *The 1977 annual handbook for group facilitators*. San Diego, CA: University Associates, 1977.

Huang, A. C. *Embrace tiger, return to mountain*. Moab, UT: Real People Press, 1973.

Kapleau, P. Zen meditation. In R. E. Ornstein (Ed.), *The nature of human consciousness: A book of readings*. New York: The Viking Press, 1973.

Kauz, H. *T'ai chi handbook*. Garden City, NY: Doubleday, 1974.

Keen, S. "We have no desire to strengthen the ego or make it happy": A conversation about ego destruction with Oscar Ichazo. *Psychology Today*, 1973, 7(2), 64-72.

Leonard, G. *The ultimate athlete*. New York: The Viking Press, 1975.

Lilly, J. C. *Simulations of God: The science of belief*. New York: Simon & Schuster, 1975.

Merton, T. *The way of Chuang Tzu*. New York: New Directions, 1965.

Naranjo, C., & Ornstein, R. E. *On the psychology of meditation*. New York: The Viking Press, 1971.

Reps, P. *Zen flesh, zen bones*. Garden City, NY: Doubleday, undated.

Richards, M. C. *Centering in pottery, poetry, and the person*. Middletown, CT: Wesleyan University Press, 1964.

Tohei, K. *Aikido in daily life*. Tokyo: Rikugei Publishing House, 1966.

Anthony G. Banet, Jr., Ph.D., *former senior consultant, University Associates, San Diego, California, holds a master's degree in psychology and a doctorate in clinical psychology. He is the author of many articles and has had extensive clinical training. His work experience includes positions as chief of psychological services and director of mental health consultation and education at a community mental health center and as associate professor of psychology in the Department of Psychiatry at the School of Medicine, Indiana University, Bloomington, Indiana.*

ACCELERATING THE STAGES OF GROUP DEVELOPMENT

John J. Scherer

The ten-day group-development laboratory experience is hard to find nowadays. Only a few training organizations can still get people for a long-term event. It is clear that such events have certain benefits over short-term groups:

1. There are more chances for participants to focus again and again on their dysfunctional and functional behaviors and to receive feedback.
2. More opportunity exists for a participant to "digest" the experience.
3. Members can watch the trainer at work for a longer period of time, making it more possible for them to discern key factors in group leadership skills.
4. There is an increased likelihood that the group will make more progress through its stages of development and that more time can be spent making these shifts clearer to participants.
5. More opportunities for lecturettes and other plenary sessions exist without reducing group time significantly, thus keeping the theory and experience balanced.
6. With more time to devote to it, transfer of learning to back-home arenas and closure are much easier.

Most of us, however, have to settle for a weekend-length experience with client groups. This shortening of the critical group time available can seriously jeopardize these optimum learning goals, thus offering trainers a significant challenge: how to have a high-quality, high-impact group learning experience in three to four days.

Discussed here are eight design features that have come together over the past six years of seeking ways to retain the vivid learning impact of longer events while compacting the time to a long weekend (Thursday evening through Sunday noon).

There are certain factors, however, that might limit the applicability of these concepts to other client groups. The participants implied in this discussion are, for the most part, mid-career professionals from a wide variety of fields, male and female, about thirty-five years old, with all participants enrolled in either an eighteen-to-twenty-month or a two-summer, six-week residency master of arts program in applied behavioral science. These participants have had limited experience in the laboratory method of learning, including exposure to staff members who will conduct the event, and have had prior contact with their fellow participants. In other words, the concepts discussed here have not been applied to a typical residential laboratory group of strangers.

Some or all of these design factors, however, taken singly or in combination, *can* have application in different settings and may prompt similar kinds of positive results in accelerating group development while retaining impact and quality. Hoylman (1979) reports

Colleagues collaborating in the development of these concepts were Ron Short, Bob Crosby, Barbara Scherer, and Brenda Kerr, all faculty members for the Whitworth College/LIOS MA-ABS Program, Spokane, Washington. Thanks to Jack Sherwood and Dick Schmuck for their suggestions on earlier drafts.

successfully using several of these design features with an NTL laboratory group of strangers.

THE GOALS OF THE LABORATORY GROUP EXPERIENCE

Historically there have been several different goals and names for group learning experiences. The prototype, the classic Bethel "sensitivity training group" of the late forties,[1] had as a major focus sensitizing participants *not* to their feelings (a later development more accurately called an "encounter group") but to social processes, primarily racial prejudice, being acted out in the group (Bradford, 1974, pp. 4f) Later trainers realized the powerful individual impact of the group experience and began using the sensitivity training groups (by then shortened to "T-groups") as settings to promote personal growth, with a de-emphasis on group dynamics learning goals (Schutz, 1967, p. 22). (Also see Burton, 1969.) Organization development consultants saw in the T-group a vehicle for softening rigid work team norms that were inhibiting trust, for working through interpersonal tangles, and for learning communication skills (Fordyce & Weil, 1971; Jacobs & Spradlin, 1974; Schein & Bennis, 1965). Innovative educators began to capitalize on the remarkable capacity of the T-group to open learners to receive new concepts; they believed that the group's subtle democratization process would also reduce the authority dilemmas so often faced by teachers in dependent/counterdependent students (Schmuck & Schmuck, 1974). Church workers, pastors, youth leaders, and educators have adapted the T-group to utilize the group's powerful, life-changing, and "peak experience" capability, as well as employing it as an arena for caring and learning to share more deeply (see Casteel, 1968, for one example).

These various uses and goals for the T-group tend to overlap in actual practice. All the group phenomena—personal growth, awareness of group processes, learning, norm changing, trust formation, communication-skills development, feedback growing out of here-and-now experiences—will likely happen in almost *any* T-group because of the anxious ambiguity of the situation and the basic needs of the participants to move toward competence (Hampden-Turner, 1972). Trainers can, however, deflect or support certain aspects of the group's life, setting norms that ultimately help shape the outcomes of the group. This paradox—that these phenomena can happen on their own but that they can also be influenced by both participants and the trainer—makes the goal orientation of the leader and the participants a significant factor in influencing the outcomes of the group experience.

The design factors described here are aimed at accelerating the development of the group experience as a laboratory in which the primary goal is learning to "see" group phenomena in action and the way individual behaviors affect the group's development. As a colleague, Bob Crosby (1971), says it, "A T-group has a *curriculum*: group dynamics." The goal is transferring the learning so that participants will be able to discern the same dynamics at work in back-home groups and attempt more effective interventions there. If the participant has a powerful life-changing experience (as many do) of an existential or therapeutic nature, it is a serendipitous happenstance, but not a primary goal. Training practitioners in the applied behavioral sciences is the major aim, and the group experience is designed primarily for learning about group processes.

---

[1]See "Sensitivity Training (T-Groups)" in M. Sashkin, "A Brief Glossary of Frequently Used Terms in Organization Development and Planned Change," in the Resources section of this *Annual.*

DESIGN FEATURES FOR ACCELERATING GROUP DEVELOPMENT

Preparation Before the Event

Two important factors enable participants to enter the group in an increased state of readiness for learning:

1. *Knowledge about and basic skill practice in communication.* The concepts of behavior description, paraphrasing, description of feelings, perception checking, the interpersonal gap (Wallen, 1968), and distinctions between personalness and openness (Crosby, 1971) are taught, and participants practice these skills. One way to view the group experience is as an arena to integrate these skills.

2. *Developing a context in which to place the group experience.* Learnings about group processes and basic communications are a core for understanding many other practitioner skills, such as how task groups function, the consulting process, and organizational dynamics. A larger context is the history of the T-group and the contrasts between the T-group, encounter group, and therapy group (Cohen & Smith, 1976).

Starting with a Group-on-Group Activity

The group-on-group activity has been a stock item in many a trainer's repertoire. One consultant (Porter, 1978) recently reported that in a week-long group he co-facilitated some years ago, groups were kept in a group-on-group process for the whole seven days, with what he believed were very positive results. Many others have used shorter versions of the group-on-group activity to teach observation and feedback skills. (See examples in Pfeiffer & Jones, 1972-1980.)

A suggested design is to *begin* the weekend experience by pairing groups for a group-on-group arrangement at the *first* session. A brief introduction of how this process can help participants and groups get started usually leads into some variation of the following basic design:

Group A inside	15 minutes
Reflect with partner/observer from the other group	5 minutes
Group A back inside	15 minutes
Rotate	
Group B inside	15 minutes
Reflect with partner/observer	5 minutes
Group B back inside	15 minutes
Rotate	
Group A in	10-15 minutes
Rotate	
Group B in	10-15 minutes
Partners meet to discuss the groups and clarify their personal plans for the next group session	10 minutes

Groups meet separately after that except for primary theory sessions and another group-on-group session in the middle of the weekend.

During the reflection time, participants are paired with a person from the other group. During the group-on-group experience the observing partner watches both the group's interaction and his or her partner, looking for specific things each time to share with the partner later, such as:

- Moments when it seemed that the partner had a strong feeling about what was happening but did not say anything;
- Whether or not and to what degree the partner seemed to feel included in the group's activities and why it seemed so;
- What the observer or the partner wishes were happening in the group and what could be done the next time the group meets to help that happen.

Being "in" and then "out" *spatially* introduces the participant/observer role split in such a way that participants begin to *feel* it. Based on the Gestalt principle of contact-withdrawal (Perls, 1973), this in-out sequence also gives the participants an opportunity for closer, cleaner contact while *in* the group by legitimizing their *withdrawal* during their observing period.

The group-on-group beginning also raises the agenda item of group cohesion, with members usually leaving for their own group session with a judgment of some kind about the two groups. "I wish I were in that group" or "Boy, *they* sure can't handle inclusion, can they?" or "I liked the way their trainer helped them . . ." These judgments are extremely important data for the group, and, when surfaced, they set early norms about the acceptability of having judgments about the trainer, group members, and the group itself. These are the kinds of feelings and evaluations that are present under the surface in any group experience right from the start, but the group-on-group experience seems to legitimize them and make it more likely that they will be shared earlier in the group's life. Norms supporting criticism of one's own or another group are usually later in developing. This beginning, instead, tends to bring things to the surface sooner, where they can be confronted.

In short, the group-on-group design gets things rolling very quickly, without reducing the predictable anxiety people bring with them as they face the ambiguity of the group's beginning. In fact, they may get a stronger sense of their anxiety level when they are able to contrast how they felt *observing* and how they felt *participating*.

Repeating the Group-on-Group Design

A repetition of the group-on-group activity in the middle of the event, sometimes with the same groups paired, has several important functions:

1. It can help trainers when they talk to their trainer partners about what they saw, e.g., participants' recurring or unresolved issues.
2. It can give group members a clearer sense of their progression through the stages of group development. (They will have had a lecturette beforehand.)
3. It increases awareness of group cohesion or lack of it.
4. It can provide participants (if they are paired with the same observer) with useful feedback about how their predictions or intentions are unfolding. "I still see you doing . . ." or "You seem to have that problem with Mary worked out."
5. Getting exposure to different trainer styles heightens the awareness of trainer functions and alternatives.

While participants frequently complain beforehand about "losing valuable time with our own group," there is a predictable shift in the group after the group-on-group experience toward more confrontation of perceived shortcomings about "the way we're doing things here," thus sparking intragroup criticism.

Staff members are also able to monitor each other, which is especially important with trainers of varying experience. The second group-on-group activity is a valuable time for trainers to give each other feedback about their behavior and the interventions they made. In a short group experience, working through difficult issues with participants fairly soon after they develop helps keep the group moving toward developing mature norms, and it can protect participants and/or trainers from being scapegoated without being aware of it. The mid-event group-on-group experience is made more critical by the next concept, using participants as trainers-in-training.

Rotating Participants as Trainers-in-Training

Starting with the first session, participants are chosen, one for each session, to be trainers-in-training and to work with the staff trainer or trainers and "function as best they can as a facilitator." (Although the participants here are trainee practitioners, this approach has been used with relatively naive participants with positive results.)

Trainers-in-training are briefed and debriefed publicly before and after each session and, when not designated as trainers-in-training, they simply revert to being group members. This design feature tends to have these kinds of consequences:

1. Group members begin to see how they relate to people in authority when they become aware of how their attitude toward someone changes when that person becomes a "trainer."

2. Trainers-in-training get a sense of what it is like to feel responsible for the facilitation of a group's learning (their own authority issues) and what that does to their way of participating in the group.

3. The interventions of the trainer-in-training provide material for the debriefing process (as do the staff trainer's), giving participants more clarity about the intentions behind trainer interventions.

4. In a smaller group (eight to twelve) or in longer events (three to four days), people have a chance to be a trainer twice, giving them a practice-feedback-repractice sequence, which is reported frequently to be a successful experience.

Staff Trainer Behaviors: A Note

It would seem that the staff trainer's style would have a powerful impact on the effectiveness of trainers-in-training, but this is apparently not true, if the debriefing addresses the impact of the staff trainer's behavior on the trainers-in-training and the group. In any case, the staff trainer, the trainer-in-training, and the group can learn something from what happens.

The shifts in communication patterns and decision making that occur as people take on and then leave the role of "leader" is striking and frequently clear to both the group and those involved. It tends to raise very sharply the issues of group leadership, power, authority, and role-bound behavior. The person acting as trainer-in-training gets an experience of moving into and out of the authority role and a chance to see what that did to his or her participation, raising personal issues around "feeling responsible."

Another interesting thing occurs for the person who is the next designated trainer-in-training: the rehearsal phenomenon. Anxiety rises, stress affects usual communication patterns, he or she begins to get ready a long time before actually being "on." Again, these things will surface in a group given time and circumstances, but the design features suggested here set up conditions that accelerate their development.

University Associates

Placing participants in the challenging situation of trainer-in-training might actually increase member anxiety dysfunctionally rather than accelerate group development, if it were not for the following design feature.

Switching Staff Trainers

Once during the weekend event each staff trainer moves to another group for an hour or so, usually at the beginning of a block of time (e.g., from 9:00 a.m. to 10:15 a.m. on Saturday). The switch is announced beforehand, even noted on the schedule, so that participants know it is going to happen. The trainers just "drop in," as it were, for an hour and then leave. Their interventions frequently have an "unfreezing" effect on the group and can also produce some benefits to the group's process.

- If the "new" trainer picks up on the same kinds of things the other trainer did, it can "confirm the diagnosis" more profoundly to the group. "I guess we *were* avoiding the competitiveness issue—both trainers picked up on it."
- The drop-in trainer can be more active, press on issues, and in other ways be more precipitative. This can loosen up issues, model new norms, challenge old ones, and provide a new authority person to deal with.
- This design feature models the existential validity of training. One does not have to know a great deal about the *history* of a group to intervene effectively in a T-group.
- Trainers can act as checks and balances on each other. If one trainer is being unduly influenced by a member of the group, a new trainer can sometimes work on that concern more clearly.
- Trainers usually meet in a *public* debriefing of the switching experience, discussing each other's groups. A fruitful way to do this is to complete the following statement: "One thing I experienced in your group which does not surprise me about a group *you* would lead is . . ."
- Switching also helps trainers get free from any content seductions they may have fallen prey to. The familiar plaint "Oh, I don't want to switch right now—I'm really needed to help with this issue!" is probably a good indication that it *is* a good time to switch.

The switching of trainers for a one-hour session frequently breaks groups into new, deeper levels of work and allows trainer and participant relationships to move into more mature encounters.

Public Debriefing of Group Sessions

At the end of each group meeting, the trainer spends twenty to thirty minutes publicly debriefing the experience with the outgoing and incoming co-trainer. The three people sit in the center of the group with an open chair and openly discuss what happened in the last session. The conversation frequently addresses these kinds of issues:

1. (With the outgoing trainer-in-training): "What did you see going on?" "What were your intentions when you did X and what effect did it seem to have?" "How did you feel when X happened; what effect did that have on your participation?" The staff trainer responds to these questions also.
2. (With the incoming trainer-in-training): "What are you nervous about in the next session?" "What are we going to do about that?" "Who are some people here you're anxious about?" "Plans?" "What would you like me to do or not do as staff trainer when one of these things happens?"

3. (With the group): "What is happening now in this group?" "What seem to be the major issues we are facing and how are we dealing with them?" "What does this group need now from its trainer(s)?"

This debriefing is often the most powerful part of the experience for many participants. They report that the debriefing helps them to:

- Obtain some emotional distance;
- Begin to see what trainers are doing and why;
- Understand the unfolding process of group development as they see it explained and illustrated during the debriefing;
- Raise and address their own authority issues;
- Learn to be present in the group as both a participant and an observer;
- Stimulate transfer of learning applications to their back-home arenas.

Because of the openness and vulnerability this design models, it is powerful and accelerates the group's process. The "authorities" are sharing their fears and observations in a safe environment and in such a way that more timid participants are encouraged to enter the life of the group.

Since the comments about group phenomena occur very close to the actual events being talked about, learning becomes extremely easy. The debriefing can help develop an understanding of what happened. Important data can be shared with clarity and gentleness, sensitizing members to their own and others' behaviors and their impact on the group.

Integration (I) Groups

Early in the weekend event participants are put into integration (I) groups, composed of people from different groups. This session is introduced as an "integrative opportunity in which people basically can talk about their group, their trainer, and their experience in order to help digest the experience." This notion runs counter to the traditional group norm of not talking about anything that happens *in* the group *outside* the group. The rationale for the older norm makes sense: if people's feelings and affective energy are allowed to be turned elsewhere, that emotional energy will not be available to the group.

However, when lightly structured I-groups are used to help people discuss their experience, they come away from the conversation clearer, more confident, and more ready to confront issue(s) or person(s) in their own group. As they share experiences with each other they also discover samenesses and differences between groups, getting a perspective on their own group life and their involvement in it. When they help someone else clarify an issue, they may even work through their own version of the same issue.

I-groups also do not seem to diminish the affective agendas generated in the group. Instead, they seem to spring loose a lot of that stored-up energy in the group. The experience of sharing still evokes anxiety and defensiveness, but the hurdle has frequently been cleared about whether or not to deal with a particular issue in the group. The I-group helps people make that decision and strategize how to begin.

By legitimizing such personal discussion, the I-group also builds accountability: "I have to go back to those people after our next group session and report what happened." Participants will frequently preface an intervention in the T-group with, "My I-group members helped me see what was happening and now I want to deal with it." In a short group experience, without the discussion in the I-group, that might not have happened.

Transfer Role Plays or "Coming-Home Skits"

Throughout the event, several of the other suggested features give people a chance to reflect on back-home applications:

- The *pre-event* work begins with that focus;
- The *public debriefings* can be guided to talk about back-home phenomena;
- The *I-groups* are structured so as to begin discussion of transfer issues toward the end of the event.

But as for many group events, a block of time, usually three hours or more, is set aside toward the end of the experience for working on twin concerns—closure and transfer—at the same time. One particular design feature, transfer role plays, consistently demonstrates a high potential for helping people with both these needs.

Participants are asked to form into groups of three to eight people and then to create a humorous skit that shows some kind of coming-home encounter with people from either their primary (close family or friends) or secondary (work) arena. In the process of producing the skit they are forced to step back and take a look at the broad range of group experiences they have had. Poking fun at their experience helps them avoid the tendency to become either "true believers" or "irrational critics" of the group experience. The skit helps participants laugh at the "other-world" qualities of the group and start the process of re-entry on a more balanced note.

At first glance these skits may seem to be a trivial design feature that lacks the heavy impact of the group-on-group experience or the usefulness of a powerful lecturette, but it serves several crucial functions for participants and has a subtle but profound effect on their re-entry:

1. It lets them begin to say "good-bye" to the other group members and to the experience.
2. It encourages them to think about their back-home environment and the major differences in norms and behaviors between it and the group environment.
3. It begins the process of sifting through the very heavy affective and cognitive data generated in the group for usable and acceptable applications.
4. Laughing at a profound experience helps to integrate it.
5. Humor transcends the pressure to convert or warn others and transforms that urge into acceptance.

SUMMARY

The eight design features described in this article have proven themselves as expediters of the process of a group's development and of participants' ability to learn from that development. Participants can continue to have their usual peak experiences resulting from successful encounters with themselves and others and to learn about who they are, based on who they have been during this unique event. With these design features, many of the benefits of the longer group experience can be retained at the same time that the pace of group development is stepped up, thereby condensing the same process into a shorter time period.

REFERENCES

Bradford, L. *The laboratory method of changing and learning.* Palo Alto, CA: Science & Behavior Books, 1975.

Burton, A. (Ed.). *Encounter.* San Francisco: Jossey-Bass, 1969.

Casteel, J. L. *The creative role of interpersonal groups in the church today.* New York: Association Press, 1968.

Cohen, A., & Smith, D. *The critical incident in growth groups.* San Diego, CA: University Associates, 1976.

Crosby, R. P. *Touch and tell, or....* Unpublished manuscript, Whitworth/LIOS Graduate Center for Applied Studies, Whitworth College, Spokane, Washington, 1971.

Fordyce, J. K., & Weil, R. *Managing with people.* Reading, MA: Addison-Wesley, 1971.

Hampden-Turner, C. *Radical man.* Garden City, NY: Doubleday, 1970.

Hoylman, F. Private communication, 1979.

Jacobs, A., & Spradlin, W. *The group as agent of change.* New York: Behavioral Publications, 1974.

Perls, F. *The Gestalt approach—Eyewitness to therapy.* Palo Alto, CA: Science & Behavior Books, 1973.

Pfeiffer, J. W., & Jones, J. E. (Eds.). *The annual handbook for group facilitators.* (1972-1980). San Diego, CA: University Associates, 1972-1980.

Porter, L. Private communication, 1978.

Schein, E., & Bennis, W. *Personal and organizational change through group methods.* New York: John Wiley, 1965.

Schmuck, R., & Schmuck, P. *Humanistic psychology of education.* Palo Alto, CA: National Press Books, 1974.

Schutz, W. *Joy.* New York: Grove Press, 1967.

Wallen, J. *The interpersonal gap.* Unpublished manuscript, Northwest Regional Laboratories, Portland, Oregon, 1968.

John J. Scherer is the associate director of the Whitworth/LIOS Graduate Center for Applied Studies at Whitworth College, Spokane, Washington, where he is a core faculty member for the Master of Arts in Applied Behavioral Science program. He is also executive vice president of Concern for Corporate Fitness. He is a member of NTL, IAASS, ACC, ASTD, OD Network, and AHP.

190

ORGANIZING AND CONDUCTING MICROLABS FOR TRAINING

T. Venkateswara Rao and Udai Pareek

The technique of the "microlab" emerged historically as an introductory exercise for the sensitivity training laboratory. In place of verbal statements to introduce the training program, a microlab enables participants to live through an epitome of a laboratory program by being exposed to a variety of experiences in a brief period. The T-group culture is based on experiential learning, self-presentation, interpersonal feedback, experimentation, identification of feelings, etc., in a climate of trust and openness, using the method of learning by discovery.

A microlab represents the nature and the variety of the experiences and processes the participants are going to have. If it is designed and used properly, the microlab technique is a very useful activity in many training programs.

For a training program to be effective, it is necessary that participants be prepared for the changes that are to occur. To use the terminology of Lewin (1958), this may be called "unfreezing." Without such an initial input, the benefit from the various training inputs may not be maximized. The microlab technique, with its emphasis on unfreezing the participants and enhancing their motivation to benefit from the training program, is one way of approaching this problem. A microlab can be compared to an abstract preceding an article in a journal: it gives a preview of what is to follow.

CONDUCTING A MICROLAB

In a typical microlab situation the participants and the trainers assemble in a large room with enough open space to move about freely. The trainer makes no attempt to introduce the training program; instead he begins the microlab. He states that the first session will start with one trainer announcing an event, to which the participants may respond in any way they like. The trainer then requests the group to mill around the room. The participants may show surprise and hesitancy. The trainer repeats his request to "move around." After a minute or so, the trainer may instruct the participants to form pairs, triads, or small groups. The trainer then announces the task and indicates the time limit. At the end of the period allotted (often only a few minutes), the trainer requests the participants to move away from their partners and mill again. He then restructures the group, announces the next event, and the microlab continues.

Different tasks are given for brief periods of time, between which there are short periods of physical activity. These physical activities start with milling about and include things like blind walking, slow walking, fast walking, silent walking, crawling, walking while greeting others nonverbally, paired walking, or back walking. Other innovative physical activities of short duration (usually about a minute or less) can also be used.

The structure of the group generally changes with each change in activity. Sometimes the activities may be in pairs, sometimes in triads or foursomes, and sometimes small subgroups.

PURPOSES OF A MICROLAB

A microlab serves as a mechanism to *unfreeze* or *open up* the participants. It is an excellent and quick warm-up mechanism that puts participants immediately into the program. Generally, participants come with certain expectations or fears. They may be expecting some lectures, they may be thinking that the program will be another routine set of activities, they may be feeling anxious and uncertain and afraid to ask questions. By going through several quickly changing activities, their preconceived notions and inhibitions are broken down. They begin to ask questions and get an opportunity to talk and to explore freely, which helps them unfreeze and sets the stage for learning.

Another purpose served by the microlab is to *introduce the participants to the experience* that they are going to have in the total program. In the microlab various items used or questions shared deal with the different dimensions, concepts, or aspects that are likely to be discussed during the program. For example, in a microlab used to start a motivation program, several questions dealing with motivation are utilized. However, the particular methodology that is going to be used in the program need not be simulated in the microlab. For example, if some psychological tests are being used to provide feedback to the participants, it may not be feasible to use a micro-instrument in a microlab. Instead, the dimension of feedback could be simulated by asking participants to point out good or bad points in one another.

A microlab serves as *an instrument* to tune the participants to the program by arousing their curiosity about what is happening. It also helps to communicate to the participant that the program is *unconventional* and *different*, requires active participation, and gives participants freedom to discuss their ideas.

One of the *usual expectations* that participants have about a training program—that it involves passively receiving instructions—*can be broken* by the microlab technique. A microlab helps to *raise new expectations* and establish new norms of behavior, such as expressing feelings to one another, feeling free to seek help, and experimenting in behavior.

A microlab also *helps to maximize interaction* among participants and allow them to know one another on levels at which they usually do not get acquainted or interact.

DESIGNING A MICROLAB

A microlab is generally introduced only at the beginning of a laboratory program. However, it can be used in various other situations and forms. For example, a microlab can be used to begin a lecture-based program in which no methodology is used. Here the microlab may not communicate the unconventionality of the program, but it may prepare the participants for free transactions. On such occasions it is advisable to announce that the microlab is being used only to provide an opportunity for multiple interactions among participants in a short period and for generating a free atmosphere.

A microlab can be used for various lengths of time. In short-term programs the microlab may be for an hour, while in longer programs it may take a full day. In such cases it could appropriately be called "microprogram," "microcourse," "microlecture," "microsession," etc., rather than microlab. However, as long as the micro-event offers people opportunities to experiment, it is still a micro*lab*.

The following points may be kept in mind when planning a microlab:

1. It is not intended that the items introduced in a microlab be completely discussed in that time frame. A microlab should function as a stimulation for participants.
2. There should be a high level of activity in the microlab. The success of the microlab depends on the pace with which the various activities are done.

3. There should be a variety of items in the microlab.
4. The microlab should be designed well in advance, including sequencing of the various items. For example, one microlab could move from items relating to the self to those relating to individual roles and then to the total organization. Items should be well prepared and written down in detail.
5. There should be some unconventional ways of stimulating people, such as fantasies, drawings, skits, blind walking, group-on-group, crawling, role plays, etc.
6. If more than one trainer is involved in the microlab, it may be useful to take turns in conducting the items. Those who are not directing a particular activity may participate.

MICROLABS IN DIFFERENT GROUPS

This section presents some sample activities that could be included in microlabs for different groups. These activities could be carried out in pairs, triads, or small groups. Generally it is useful to start with pairs and go on to groups as people become acquainted with one another.

Cross-Cultural Groups

A microlab can be a very valuable tool to warm up and bring closer together cross-cultural groups that are meeting for a brief period of time in a conference or a training program. The following activities are suggested for such groups (not necessarily in this sequence).

- Explain the significance your name has in your country.
- Share one significant aspect of the role you perform in your organization.
- Mention a significant role your organization has played in the past in your country.
- Use three adjectives to describe some positive aspects of your culture.
- Use three adjectives to describe some aspects of your culture that you do not like or that you think need improvement.
- Share the image you have of your partner's culture by using three adjectives.
- Tell your partner three things you like about his or her country.
- Share with the others in your group the image you have of the host country.
- Share with your partner the places of interest you are planning to visit in this country during your stay here.
- Share with your partner one problem you have recognized about yourself in programs of this kind in the past and how you plan to overcome it.
- Share with your partner one of your strong points and one of your weak points.
- Tell your partner something you like in him or her.
- Tell your partner something about yourself that you are proud of and something you would like to change.
- Mill around and greet the other members of the group nonverbally or through symbols.
- Form pairs and tell each other (nonverbally) something about the place at which you are working.
- Share with each other something that has particularly struck you in this country since the time of your arrival here.
- State what impresses you most about people in this place.
- Use three adjectives to describe the people with whom you work.

- Share in your triad your image of the people who perform similar roles in those countries represented by the other two members.
- Share one thing your country can give to other countries.
- Tell the other persons in your triad one thing that you need to be effective in your work.
- Share with the others a small prayer or a proverb you like. You may recite in your own language and then explain.
- Share with others how you feel about being in this country and in this group.
- Divide into groups of four and suggest different ways of overcoming the language barrier during the time of the conference. Share your thoughts in the total group.
- Break into triads representing different countries. Share with the others a pressing problem in your country. One person makes a statement, a listener repeats the statement, and the third person comments on how well the first individual narrated and how well the second one understood and communicated back. This activity allows every member of the triad an opportunity to comment on the statements of the other two.

Because in cross-cultural groups there are likely to be communication barriers, the use of nonverbal activities is suggested. If self-oriented sessions are not a part of the program, self-oriented items should be kept to a minimum in the microlab. If language is a barrier, it is necessary to give participants enough time after every item. Abrupt interruptions in such cases may cause frustration. It is also necessary to ensure that the instructions are understood properly.

Motivation Laboratories

Motivation development laboratories, particularly those dealing with achievement and power motivation, have been growing rapidly in the last few years. These are becoming popular for developing entrepreneurs, builders of institutions, and managers. The following are some items that could be used in such motivation laboratories. Additional items could be devised, depending on whether the participants are drawn from the same organization or different organizations.

- Describe one thing that you like most in your job and one thing that you like least in your job.
- Share with your partner a driving force prompting you to do your job in your organization.
- Think of a successful person you know and describe his or her behavior anonymously to your partner.
- Share with your partner his or her weak points.
- Describe the climate of your organization nonverbally to your partner.
- Think of a significant incident in your life and describe it to your partner, telling how you felt and why it was significant to you.
- Use three adjectives to describe the strong points of your subordinates and three to describe their weak points.
- Use three adjectives each to describe the strengths and weaknesses of your superiors.
- Recall a situation in which you felt very powerful and describe it to others in your triad or group.

- Share with your partner an important goal of your life.
- Share with your partner a strength that you think helps you achieve your goal.
- Share with your partner a weak point that you fear might block you from achieving your goal.
- Ask your partner about what outside help you can get to overcome something that prevents you from achieving an important goal.
- Share with your partner something you consider significant about your role.
- Share with your partner one of your strong points and one of your weak points.
- Share with your partner one of your dreams.
- Imagine yourself ten years from now and describe your fantasy to your partner.
- Tell a story you like.
- Share with your partner your ideas about how children should be treated in school.
- Share with others in your group your motivation for attending this event and describe how you feel being here.
- Share with others something about this place that has struck you.
- Tell your partner something you like about him or her and something you do not like.
- Think of a situation in your life or your work when you failed and share with your partner how you reacted and felt in that situation.
- Describe your style of reacting to strangers and ask your partner to do the same.
- Share with your partner one complaint/criticism from your wife/husband, one from your children, one from a teacher when you were young, one from your subordinates, and one from your superiors.
- Share, similarly, one compliment from your wife, one from your children, one from your teachers, one from your subordinates and superiors.

Programs for Change Agents

Laboratory and other experiential programs are held for developing change agents in different areas, e.g., health, education, population, or community development. Depending on the nature of the program planned, microlabs could be designed. Some examples are presented here.

Change Agents in Population Control and Family Planning

In such programs, motivating the participant and providing him or her the necessary skills to be a change agent are integral. A sample of items useful for developing such change agents:

- Share with your partner how you spend your leisure time and the hobbies you have.
- Describe to your partner some things about which you are happy and some things about which you are unhappy.
- Imagine that you have achieved everything you want. Share with your partner what your life would be like.
- Share with your partner your future ambitions and dreams about your own career or the careers of your children.
- Tell your partner about some of the comforts you have at present about which you are happy.

- Imagine that your country has developed very well economically twenty years from now. Technology, industry, education, and health have progressed. Discuss what your home, its surroundings, and this city would look like. Present a tourist's description of this city and a foreign visitor's description of your home. Take fifteen minutes to write these descriptions as imaginatively as you can.
- Imagine now that in twenty years the population has grown at its predicted rate. Unemployment has increased, resources are depleted, and there are many other problems because population growth could not be controlled. Write an essay describing how your city looks, what your home is like, what educational facilities are available, the comforts that are possible. Share your description in the total group.
- Think of three adjectives to describe family planning methods and share them in your group.
- Share with your partner two of your views about family planning: one positive and one negative.
- Describe to your partner a couple you know who has a small family and another couple who has a large family and contrast their lives.
- Imagine your group to be a group of workers in a mill. Give them a two-minute lecture on family planning.
- Share with your partner any family planning practices in which you engage.
- Identify one thing that you can do in your role to contribute to the cause of family planning and discuss it with your partner. Invite your partner to raise questions.
- Think of a situation in which you influenced another person or group of persons because of your abilities rather than because of your role. Describe that situation to your partner and tell him or her how effective that influence has been.
- Narrate one of your success experiences in life and one of your failure experiences and the lessons you have learned from each of them.

This microlab focused mainly on inducing participants' fantasies about family planning and also attempted to cover some dimensions likely to be faced in the following training program.

Internal Change Agents in Education and Health

The following items could be used for programs to develop change agents in education and health.

- Introduce yourself by telling the other person something about you other than your name, age, role, and title.
- Describe to the other person, through the use of adjectives, the organizational climate in your institution.
- Share with your partner one thing that you like most in your job and one thing that you like least in your job. Think of your own personal strengths and the weak points that could block your efforts as a change agent and share these with your partner.
- Think of a situation in which you were instrumental in bringing about a change in any place you worked. Share it with your partner.
- Describe to your partner the image you have of your style as a change agent.
- Identify one thing in your institution that you find difficult to change.
- Share with your partner something about yourself that you would like to improve.
- Share with your partner something of which you are proud.

- Think of a person whom you consider a good change agent in your area of work. Describe his or her qualities and how he or she manages change.
- Find an issue on which your opinions or beliefs are different from those of your partner. Work out a strategy to change your partner's views and try to implement it.
- Identify three different resources you see in the place where your organization is located.
- Identify one area in which improvement can be made in the curriculum you teach to your students. Share with your partner your thoughts on how such improvements could be made.

Creativity Labs

The following are some of the items that could be used to introduce a program in creativity and problem solving. These items deal with various dimensions of creativity and serve the purpose of introducing the laboratory and its methodology.

- Introduce yourself nonverbally to your partner.
- Select one object in the room and describe the various uses of that object in two minutes. Your partner will time you and count the number of uses you cite. Then your partner will repeat the activity.
- List (in three minutes) ten more uses of the object your partner has chosen.
- List the various attributes of a pen in your pocket.
- Share your image of and attitudes about modern art with your partner.
- Think of a creative person you know and describe that person (without naming him or her) to your partner. Your partner may ask you several questions.
- Choose an animal that best describes your role in your organization and tell your partner why you chose that particular animal.
- Share with your partner your reactions about the fact that, thus far, the program schedule has not been circulated to you.
- Imagine that plants and animals have been crossbred to produce planimals. Describe to your triad what life in this world looks like.
- Think of all the processes in an organization that parallel the bodily excretion process. Share with your partner.
- Coin four new words using English and one other language you know. Give each a meaning and share with your partner.
- Decide how you would plant four rose plants so that the distance between any two is the same as that between any other two. Take three minutes to think about it and then share with your partner what processes went on in your mind.
- Describe the various associations the word *arm* arouses in you.
- Use anything in this room to prepare something you would like to give as a present to someone you like. You have ten minutes.
- Assemble in small groups and prepare a nonverbal skit to present your feelings and reactions to this lab.

USES OF A MICROLAB

A microlab can be used in different situations and in different ways. A practitioner can frame his or her own items depending on the kind of program being conducted. There are no rigid rules in using a microlab.

Some innovative trainers use microlabs not only in the beginning of a training program but also in the middle whenever they find the group to be frozen or inhibited, with no movement taking place. It is also possible to use the microlab technique continuously. For example, every day's program could begin and end with a short microlab. If used on a daily basis, the microlab could include items dealing with the previous day's concepts. Thus it could serve the purpose of recapitulating as well as of introducing.

Microlabs can also be used as closing mechanisms for training programs. A variation of the microlab is very commonly used at the end of achievement motivation training programs as a goal-setting exercise. This works as a good closing device and also sets a good climate for post-program activity. Besides presenting a summary of the concepts and skills learned during the program, the items should be aimed at helping participants to transfer their learning to their job settings. The items could help participants to reflect on opportunities for using what they learned, problems they are likely to confront, strategies they could use to overcome these, review mechanisms they would like to try out, external help they might need, and other such dimensions.

REFERENCE

Lewin, K. Group decision and social change. In E. E. Maccoby, T. M. Newcomb, & E. L. Hartley (Eds.), *Readings in social psychology* (3rd ed.). New York: Holt, Rinehart and Winston, 1958.

T. Venkateswara Rao is an associate professor of organizational behavior at the Indian Institute of Management, Ahmedabad, Gujarat, India. He is currently on leave from the Institute and working with Bharat Earth Movers Limited, Bangalore, as an advisor on human resource development.

Udai Pareek, Ph.D., is Larsen & Toubro professor of organizational behavior at the Indian Institute of Management, Ahmedabad, Gujarat, India. Dr. Pareek's background is in organization development, human resource development, organizational designing, and change in persons and systems. He has consulted with industrial and nonindustrial systems in various countries and with many international organizations.

VIDEOTAPE TECHNIQUES FOR SMALL TRAINING GROUPS

Jerry L. Fryrear

Videotape is enjoying increasing use in human relations training and psychotherapy, leading to the development of many innovative approaches. In recent reviews, Davidson (1979), Hung and Rosenthal (1978), Fleshman and Fryrear (in press), and Francis (1979) describe some creative applications of video equipment. Often, however, the videotape recorder is simply turned on during group sessions and later the group members view the tape. Such self-confrontation is no doubt valuable, especially in allowing one to view oneself from an external perspective. A more strategic approach, however, based on a model of group interaction, would be more advantageous and heuristic.

THE SMALL-GROUP ADAPTIVE SPIRAL MODEL

This paper proposes a workable model, the Small-Group Adaptive Spiral model (diagrammed in Figure 1), and describes examples of human relations training that follow from the model. The model is specifically designed to provide a theoretical rationale for the use of videotape with small groups of people who desire to improve their social skills.

The adaptation of an individual to a small group follows the spiral shown. Each individual member enters the group for the first time with a set of social orientations that exercise a basic influence on his or her perceptions of the group. The individual may be generally affiliative, generally suspicious, generally affectionate, etc. These social orientations determine the individual's perceptions of other members in the group, and these perceptions in turn influence his or her personal goals with respect to each other person in the group. For example, the individual may wish to invite one person to dinner later, may want to find out where another buys his shirts, and so forth. In order to carry out his or her goals, the individual plans social strategies involving each of the group members. A person may plan strategically to avoid talking to one member, flirt with another, lie to a third. The individual then puts the strategies into effect, resulting in group interaction and communication. All members, of course, are simultaneously employing personal strategies that automatically produce conflicts and the need for compromise.

As a result of the new information that comes from interaction and communication, the perceptions each person has of the other members will change. Because of the conflict in goals and the need for compromise, goals will also change. Therefore, further interactions will be altered, further perceptions will be altered, further goals will be altered, and so on in a spiral that ends only when the group dissipates. In rare instances, such as might occur in group therapy or human relations training, the individual's basic social orientation may also change. He may become less fearful, more confident, less boastful, more poised, or less suspicious. An important point to consider for the purposes of human relations training is that an individual's perceptions may be more or less accurate, goals may be more or less realistic, strategies may be more or less effective, and communication may be more or less clear. A person will be socially skillful to the extent that he or she perceives others

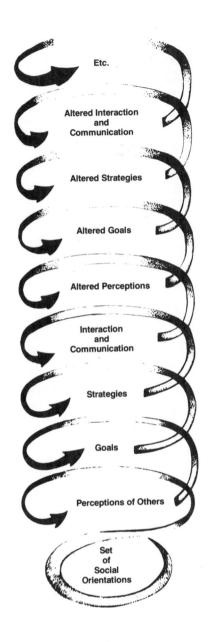

Figure 1. The Small-Group Adaptive Spiral Model

University Associates

accurately, establishes realistic goals with respect to the group, plans effective strategies, and communicates clearly.

VIDEOTAPE TECHNIQUES

Videotape is useful in developing social skills by helping a person develop more accurate perceptions, plan more realistic goals, establish more effective strategies, and communicate more clearly. All of these improvements should result in more adaptive and satisfying social orientations.

Using the Small-Group Adaptive Spiral as a model, several videotape techniques can be suggested for use with human relations training groups of three to seven people. All of the techniques use as a central idea the prescription of incompatible goals. The group interaction, during which each member attempts to realize his or her goal, is then videotaped, and the tapes are used as the stimulus for a group examination of the perceptions, strategies, and communications of each member.

Living Sociograms

In one session, each member is asked to write down on an index card the name of one other member with whom he or she would like to spend the next ten minutes (a standard sociogram). Members are asked not to show the cards to one another. The facilitator collects the cards and then asks the group members to make their choices. Naturally, there is not perfect reciprocity, and the group members soon find that they must adapt to a situation in which their personal goals are at variance with the goals of some other members. The "living sociogram" that unfolds is videotaped and, after a set period of time (usually ten minutes), the action is halted. The group members are then asked to write down the name(s) of the people who they believe had chosen them. This second "perceived sociogram" is a valuable indication of both unclear communication of goals and insensitivity to other people's goals.

The group leader now has three sociograms that will be used as the basis for group discussion. The first is the standard sociogram that is diagrammed on a blackboard for the group members' information. The second is the perceived sociogram, which is diagrammed also. The third is the living sociogram which has been captured by the video recorder. All three sociograms are then used to stimulate a group discussion of the interaction that took place during the taping. The discussions examine what the individual group members wanted to do (standard sociogram used as a reference), what they perceived the others wanted to have happen (perceived sociogram), and the interactions, communications, insensitivities, and strategies that were employed (living sociogram). Ineffective strategies, unclear or conflicting communications, and a wealth of other information are readily obvious on the tape. For example, a member may be so intent on carrying out her own goals that she turns her back on a person who is approaching her. As another example, not a single person may make the simple statement, "I choose you." A direct approach may carry too much risk of rejection, and an ambiguous approach may be seen as safer but may not be, in the long run, more satisfying than a direct approach.

Hidden Agendas

A second technique makes use of hidden agendas. Group members are told they are at a convention in San Francisco and are obligated to present a group symposium the next day. An index card specifying instructions for a particular agenda is given to each member. On the index cards, one member might be instructed to persuade the others to spend the next few minutes going over the program in anticipation of the presentation. Another member is instructed to talk privately with just one other member to discuss a personal problem. A third member is excited about being in San Francisco and wants to get the entire group to go out to dinner and a nightclub. A fourth wants to go shopping, but not alone. A fifth person simply wants to be left alone.

As in the first technique, these incompatible goals give rise to elaborate strategies as each member tries to carry out his or her agenda. Again, the interaction is taped for a few minutes and the tape used as a vehicle for discussion. The situation and agendas can be modified to reflect the interests of the group members. College students, for example, can be asked to imagine that they all live in the same dormitory and one wants to study, one is taking a survey for the school paper, one wants to have a party, and one wants to go to the movies with someone.

At the conclusion of the taping, members are asked to write down their perceptions of each of the others' agendas. Again, these perceptions serve as excellent stimuli for an examination of unclear or conflicting communication (which can be pointed out during the replay) or insensitivity on the part of members to others' goals and needs. Also, in either of these two techniques, there will be many examples of *effective* social strategies and skillful and sensitive social interactions that can be pointed out and reinforced.

Other Techniques

Several other structured activities can be used with this model.

Joining a Club

All but one of the group members are directed to form an imaginary club by standing in a circle with their arms around each other. The one who is left out is to try to join the club. Each member is given a turn as the "extra" member and his or her efforts to join the group are videotaped. Strategies, apparent perceptions, and communications, as captured by the camera, are discussed later.

Bribery, flattery, flirtation, trickery, and appeals to reason or compassion are frequently used strategies. Of special interest in this activity is the person toward whom a particular strategy is directed. Most people seem unaware of the motivations behind the selection of a particular individual to attempt to influence, but the selection process is worthy of discussion. The selected individual may be surprised and even angry at the discovery that someone perceives him as easily influenced by a certain strategy such as flattery.

First in Line

Another activity asks group members to imagine that they all arrive at a movie theater at precisely the same time, and each wants to be first in line. This activity readily identifies people who are unassertive and points out other strategies and communication styles. For a group of shy, unassertive people this is a very difficult and threatening activity. It might be wise to use it only after several group sessions.

CONCLUSION

It is not difficult to invent situations that lend themselves to the Small-Group Adaptive Spiral model (see Pfeiffer & Jones, 1969-1979). The activities outlined here have in common the prescription of goals that lead to interaction and communication and the necessity of adjusting to a group. It is possible, using the Small-Group Adaptive Spiral model as an intervention, to structure human relations training in other ways. A facilitator can, for example, influence members' perceptions of each other by giving them real or imaginary information about each other prior to an activity. The interaction and communication itself can be structured by using a fixed role-play technique or by otherwise specifying interaction and communication patterns. The goal, of course, remains the same—the attainment of more satisfying and effective social skills for each group member.

Whether these videotape exercises are either effective or (perhaps) harmful is an empirical question. The model lends itself well to research, however, and should prove to be heuristic in that respect. Basic social orientations, accuracy of perceptions, clarity of communications, and effectiveness of social strategies are all quantifiable. Social orientation can be measured by instruments such as the FIRO-B and FIRO-F (Schutz, 1976). Accuracy of perceptions and clarity of communication can be assessed by using judges or by asking the opinions of the group members. Before-training and after-training tapes of an activity can be compared in order to measure improvement in social skills. Fryrear and Van Dusen (1978) have carried out one study using this model, and further studies are planned. Now that videotape is coming into widespread use, this approach provides an additional alternative for application in training and research. Its flexibility lends itself to creative applications beyond those envisioned here.

REFERENCES

Davidson, A. R. Selecting an appropriate video system. In J. E. Jones & J. W. Pfeiffer (Eds.), *The 1979 annual handbook for group facilitators.* San Diego, CA: University Associates, 1979.

Fleshman, R., & Fryrear, J. L. *The arts in therapy.* Chicago: Nelson-Hall, in press.

Francis, D. Video feedback in groups and organizations. In J. E. Jones & J. W. Pfeiffer (Eds.), *The 1979 annual handbook for group facilitators.* San Diego, CA: University Associates, 1979.

Fryrear, J. L., & Van Dusen, R. Human relations training through videotaped living sociograms. Unpublished manuscript, 1978.

Hung, J. H. F., & Rosenthal, T. L. Therapeutic videotaped playback: A critical review. *Advances in Behaviour Research and Therapy,* 1978, *1,* 103-135.

Pfeiffer, J. W., & Jones, J. E. (Eds.). *A handbook of structured experiences for human relations training* (Vols. I-VII). San Diego, CA: University Associates, 1969-1979.

Schutz, W. FIRO-B. In J. W. Pfeiffer, R. Heslin, & J. E. Jones, *Instrumentation in human relations training* (2nd ed.). San Diego, CA: University Associates, 1976.

Jerry L. Fryrear, Ph.D., is an associate professor of psychology at the University of Houston at Clear Lake City, Houston, Texas, where he teaches courses in psychopathology and psychotherapy and conducts research on the use of video in counseling and therapy. He received his doctorate in clinical psychology from the University of Missouri at Columbia and was previously on the faculty of Tulane University, New Orleans, Louisiana. He has co-authored a book on the arts in therapy and is currently co-editing a book on videotherapy in mental health.

A STRATEGY FOR MANAGING "CULTURAL" TRANSITIONS: RE-ENTRY FROM TRAINING

Art Freedman

Each person is a *member of* and *lives in* a number of very different social "worlds" or "cultures." People are members of their respective family worlds, community worlds, work worlds, and religious worlds. In the work world, people may be members of some special "subculture" like the hourly workers' union, first-line supervisors, middle management, or the executive group. Some may belong to several work subcultures at once; for example, a manager may also be a member of a professional association.

Usually people live in only one of these social worlds at a time. That is, at work they tend not to be conscious of the fact that they are, simultaneously, citizens of their respective communities and also members of their respective families. Occasionally, however, people do live in two or more worlds simultaneously: for example, when an employee asks the boss for a raise in order to maintain the family's standard of living in the face of spiraling inflation, or when work for his employer begins to conflict with his union contract or with the ethical standards of her professional organization, or, perhaps, when the disposable by-products of the company's manufacturing processes are found to be contaminating the community.

At times like these, people become uncomfortably aware of real conflicts among their own various vested interests. It becomes apparent that what is acceptable to believe and say and do in *one* world is often quite different from (and can be in direct conflict with) the values, attitudes, and standards of *other* worlds. We become conscious that what is O.K. in one setting definitely is not O.K. in another. However, most of the time, people do not spend much time thinking about this paradox, probably because many people have been trained from early childhood to expect (without being consciously aware of it) that life *is* different in the different social settings among which individuals have to move as they engage in the process of living. Because such differences are expected, they are not surprising. When experience in life corresponds to expectations, there is usually little reason *consciously* to think about the paradox.

However, there are times when an unexpected conflict between what is expected and what is actually experienced is jolting. For example, a young man is surprised by just how much he is expected to allow his thinking, behavior, and style of life to be controlled by his superiors when he enters the military. A person put into prison or a mental hospital is shocked by the unusual, strange, and unexpected way in which the staff responds to his or her behavior—usually disconcertingly different from the way any other person has ever responded to that individual. Similarly, the tourist is often shocked by the enormous differences in expectations of behavior between citizens of a *foreign* culture and the citizens of his or her *native* culture.

Participants of a residential workshop often experience "culture shock" when they pass from their predictable, "real-life" worlds of family, work, social relationships, and religion into the temporary, artificial "foreign" workshop world and then back. Since most people who participate in such an experience do so voluntarily, presumably they hope to derive some personal learning from the event that they can use in their respective "back-home" worlds. However, the extent to which such learning is effectively and appropriately *applied* and *maintained* in participants' back-home environments is not clear. It has been demonstrated that, although participants derive a great many personal learnings from their workshop experiences, these learnings do not always hold up over time (Freedman, 1963).

APPLICATIONS

The concept and its related procedure discussed here may enable internal and external consultants, trainers, organizational managers, personnel specialists, and human-service providers to facilitate people's negotiation of a number of different types of life transitions. These could include temporary migrations into and out of such institutions as, for example, mental and general medical-surgical hospitals, prisons, residential rehabilitation centers, companies, foreign assignments, and residential communities, in addition to intense, experiential "cultural island" training experiences or the military.

Some examples of functional work groups might be (a) off-shore oil/gas drilling crews; (b) crews for long-distance ocean-going vessels; or (c) engineering/construction crews working in a third-world nation. Other application possibilities could include such situations as (a) taking a first job with a company after having completed college or a training program (e.g., for the hard-core unemployed); (b) being promoted within the organization; and (c) being transferred from one geographical-cultural location to another (e.g., the headquarters of a multinational company moves from New York City to Houston). Modifications could also be developed for one-time-only migrations such as permanent moves to a foreign country, a nursing home, or a hospice for the terminally ill.

ENTRY: MIGRATION FROM "NATIVE" TO "FOREIGN" CULTURE

Most often, when people find themselves in a "foreign" culture with which they have very little past experience, they generally—quite naturally—behave in ways that are familiar to them. They do what they are already skilled in doing. When they discover that their behaviors—the things they say and do—and their expectations are not acceptable to the residents of the foreign culture, they first experience a sense of disconfirmation *of their expectations or hopes*. Then they are faced with a complex decision that cannot be avoided. They must decide whether to (a) continue to behave in the same ways they are used to, comfortable with, and skilled in (regardless of whether or not these ways are acceptable or tolerated in the foreign culture); (b) leave the uncomfortable foreign culture (either by returning to their native culture or by becoming "psychotic"); or (c) discover and adapt to the expectations of the citizens of the foreign culture—even if that means giving up, suspending, or modifying previous attitudes, values, and behaviors. If they choose the last option, they place themselves in the awkward and uncomfortable position of knowing little, if anything, about the new culture and having to learn *everything* about what it takes to get along there.

Many inexperienced participants in intensive workshops expect that their trainers will function like the leaders of the traditional, goal-oriented work groups with which they are familiar. When they realize that these expectations are not going to be fulfilled and that the trainers will not set agendas or tell them what to do or how to do it, participants tend to become extremely uncomfortable. In an attempt to allay their discomfort, participants frequently attempt to cajole, threaten, or implore the trainers to act according to their expectations. When these attempts fail, participants must assume responsibility for themselves in order to make sense of their experiences.

The "Pioneer" Experience

Those who choose to explore the foreign culture and adapt or accommodate themselves to it soon learn that their experience is analogous to that of the pioneer or explorer. What is not known about the new environment (the "foreign" culture) is much greater than what is known. And most of what *is* known consists of the individual's increasing awareness of his or her own restlessness, uncertainties, fears, hyperactivity, social errors, or misunderstandings.

Nontypical Behaviors

An increasing sense of tension develops, and out of this tension certain nontypical behaviors evolve. *Attention narrows*. Whereas in their familiar and comfortable native culture people may allow themselves to be open to all the sights and sounds and events that occur constantly around them, in the foreign culture their vision becomes selectively constricted (a sort of "tunnel" vision) and focused on only those events that correspond most closely with whatever their preoccupation is. For example, a person may feel unattached to and isolated from the foreign culture and may experience the need for a home base (a "safe" place to "live") from which to venture forth and explore the new environment and to which he or she can withdraw when feeling overwhelmed or overextended. For this person such places as hotels, motels, rooming houses, apartment houses, YWCA's, hostels, etc., will be most prominent, while other aspects of the environment will blend into the background.

Having established a "safe" home base, a person may now get in touch with the tensions that relate to being (or feeling) socially isolated, unattached, and alienated. In response to these feelings, the individual may initiate a search, perhaps by trial-and-error or in a frantic or calculating manner, for candidates who might be able and willing to serve as companions, escorts, guides, behavior models, and/or interpreters. Such people might be friendly citizens of the foreign culture, other caring migrants who are more familiar with the host culture, or simply other uncertain and searching migrants who seem to have similar needs. Schutz (1971) refers to this phase, in the natural evolution of personal-growth groups, as the "inclusion phase." This might also be called a search for a "mentor."

Decrease of Tension

Once one or more supportive persons have been found, the tensions and inner turmoil of the "pioneer" will probably decrease. This release will probably be experienced as joyous and freeing, enabling the individual to expand the limits of his or her vision enough to begin to *see* the way life in the foreign culture unfolds for its natives. This less-restricted vision will, in turn, assist the immigrant to identify and then modify or eliminate those aspects of his or her behavior that conflict with the host culture's norms and standards of acceptable behavior.

At first, attempts to experiment and practice with behaviors that are new will feel (and appear to others to be) awkward. People will probably feel visible, vulnerable, ungainly, and embarrassed. However, with practice, they will become rather proficient at the new behaviors and the new language. Even the new style of thinking will become natural, and they will almost automatically think, feel, and act in a way that is at least acceptable to the host culture's citizens. When this plateau—virtual automatic proficiency—has been achieved, people have adapted or become *socialized* to the foreign culture to which they have migrated.

RE-ENTRY: MIGRATION FROM "FOREIGN" TO "NATIVE" CULTURE

If the migration is permanent, a major cross-cultural hurdle will have been successfully negotiated. However, when people have been temporary, transient residents (more than

University Associates

just tourists) and return from the foreign culture to their native culture, they will soon discover that their cross-cultural problems are far from over.

Conflict

Upon re-entering their native culture without adequate preparation, people are likely to discover, much to their surprise, that they cannot simply pick up where they left off. Their friends, family members, and work associates did not go into hibernation when they were away. Not only that, those who stayed behind have no way of knowing what the migrants went through or how they were affected by their experiences. Friends remember them more or less as they were when they left. In all likelihood, they are expected to be very much the same. However, to the extent that they really did allow themselves to become immersed in the foreign culture, they will *not* be the same people they used to be. They will walk, talk, think, and feel in ways that are strange and perhaps unheard-of to the citizens of their native culture. Thus, a situation with a surprisingly high potential for conflict between "foreigner" and "native" is created.

The conflict results from common human needs: people strive to create their worlds in ways that are comfortable to them. Comfort—relatively speaking—is what we feel when the world and the people in it behave in ways that correspond with our expectations: our world is predictable, and we feel comfortable. When a discrepancy occurs and people act in an unpredictable manner, we become uncomfortable. Thus, as people try to put potential solutions for some of their back-home problems into operation, they are actually creating new problems for other people. The returnees are no longer predictable, and the citizens of the native culture become uncomfortable and attribute the cause of their discomfort to the migrant.

Disconfirmation

Very much like the feelings of the pioneer entering the foreign culture, the hopeful expectations of family, friends, and associates may be disconfirmed. However, the citizens of a person's native culture—to a much greater extent than those of a foreign culture—can be expected to exert a considerable amount of pressure on the returning culture-crossing traveler to give up his or her strange and unpredictable behaviors and to return to the comfortably predictable person they once knew.

It is a simple fact that our family, friends, and co-workers can have power to influence us only if and when we give them this "power" to determine our choices. We care about them, and we are concerned that our behavior might be displeasing to them and that they might withdraw from us. Our own human desires for acceptance and affiliation set us up to be perfect targets for subtle forms of blackmail and bribery. People who are important to us inform us that unless we return to our culture's traditional norms and standards, we risk being excluded and isolated. We may be asked to feel bad or guilty about what our behavior is "doing to" people about whom we care. But if and when (but not until) we "shape up," all kinds of nice things will happen for us.

During this re-entry process, individuals' levels of comfort, effectiveness, and satisfaction dip down almost as far as when they first migrated to the foreign culture. However, after going through the same cycle of cultural-shock impact, recoil, and accommodation, their equilibrium becomes somewhat restored, low levels of effectiveness and satisfaction "bottom-out," and new but increasingly secure relationships begin to be established with the citizens of the native culture.

Renegotiation

To be enduring and meaningful, new relationships have to be based on the creation of new and mutually acceptable expectations: what can both sides legitimately expect of each other? This process becomes an explicit renegotiation of what used to be an implicit contract between people who want or need to live with one another in home, community, or work settings.

It becomes clear that the re-entering, culture-crossing travelers will have to be prepared to modify their recently acquired "foreign" behavior. Most people would prefer that citizens of their native culture not reject, isolate, or expel them. However, in order not to give up the benefits derived from their travels, they will attempt to model their newly acquired behavior for their fellow natives—inviting their native culture's citizens to tolerate, then accept, and then, maybe, experiment with the new behavior themselves. This is the process by which transcendental meditation, Tai Chi, the martial arts, Zen, acupuncture, and other aspects of Eastern cultures were probably introduced to the Western world.

THE W-CURVE HYPOTHESIS

In order to prepare people to leave a foreign culture and return to their native, back-home cultures of family, community, and work, it is helpful to explain the concept of transitions by presenting it in the form of a diagram (see Figure 1).

There are two points that the diagram illustrates that have not been discussed. One is *hope:* without that, few people would bother to try anything new. They might be terribly dissatisfied with the current conditions of their lives, but without the hope that life does not *have* to be that way, people would tend to say something like "Better to live with the devil I know than the devil I don't." And they would sit dead still and endure chronic dissatisfaction or suffering.

The second point is that, in terms of levels of comfort, satisfaction, and effectiveness, the dips tend to be shallower and the peaks higher as people move from their foreign culture back to their native culture. It is this curvature that lends its name to this concept.

This model is especially helpful in providing workshop participants with some conceptual handles that they can use in re-entering their "native" culture. This concept helps absorb a great deal of the tension and anxiety that participants tend to experience toward the end of a workshop when they begin to anticipate the re-entry process. They begin to ask themselves, "How are my people back there *ever* going to understand me now? How can I let them know what I've been through here?" This model allows participants to anticipate the re-entry "dip" and develop a plan that will reduce its depth.

FACILITATING CROSS-CULTURAL MIGRATION: A SKILL-PRACTICE ACTIVITY

The following activity deals with both terminating a workshop experience and planning explicitly for re-entry to participants' native cultures. It is best if participants have been given a thorough understanding of the W-Curve Hypothesis before they are guided through the following procedures.

1. Each participant takes several copies of the sheet "Preparation for Cross-Cultural Migration" (Figure 2). The facilitator works from an enlarged copy drawn on newsprint. In the total group, participants are asked to identify those normative behaviors within their "foreign" workshop community that they observe as (a) acceptable, encouraged, rewarded, or at least tolerated, or (b) discouraged, punished, confronted, or avoided. Those behaviors identified as acceptable and appropriate are listed by the facilitator on the newsprint under the heading of "Foreign Culture—O.K." Some examples might be: "to express my real feelings"; "to ask for feedback about behavior about which I am concerned"; "to accept responsibility for the consequences of my own acts"; "to experiment with new ways of trying to get what I want." Those behaviors that the group agrees are unacceptable and inappropriate are listed under the heading "Foreign Culture—Not O.K." Examples might

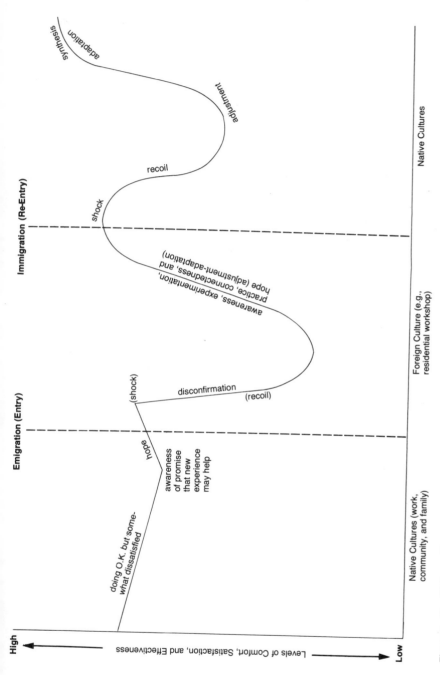

Figure 1. The W-Curve Hypothesis Model

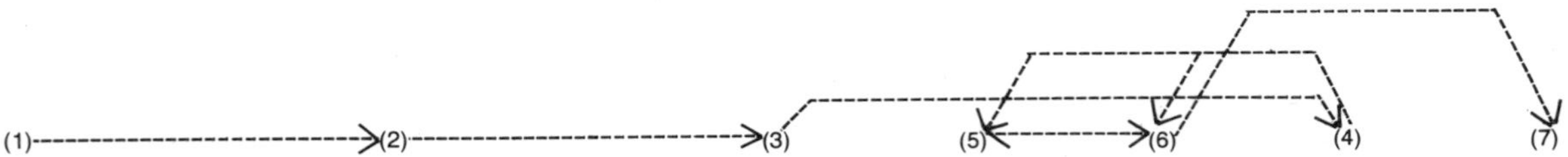

| Foreign Culture | Native Cultures | | | Important Identified Discrepancies | Driving Forces | Restraining Forces | Change Objectives | Action Plans |
	(A) *Family*	(B) *Work*	(C) *Community*					
O.K.	Not O.K.	Not O.K.	Not O.K.					
Not O.K.	O.K.	O.K.	O.K.					

(1) (2) (3) (4) (5) (6) (7)

Figure 2. Preparation for Cross-Cultural Migration

be: "to say 'we' or 'you' when I really mean 'me'"; "to interpret other people's behavior"; "to ask a question when I'm actually trying to make a statement"; "to blame others for the consequences of my own actions." Participants then copy these norms and standards on their own personal forms. (A modification of the "Do's and Don'ts" norms questionnaire by Miles, reported in Schmuck et al., 1977, may be helpful to the facilitator in order to quantify comparisons.)

2. Working as individuals, participants next explicate the similarities and differences between the workshop culture's norms and those that exist in their own, personal, native cultures. They list these under the heading "Native Cultures," working on "family," "work," and/or "community" subcultures, whichever ones seem most meaningful to them. Participants are to indicate on their sheets whether the identified workshop culture's norms are (a) "the same" as those of the native cultures, (b) "different" in some specific way, or (c) "not O.K." in one or more of their native cultures. For example, it might be O.K. to tell another workshop participant and one's spouse (in the native family culture) exactly what one is feeling, but in one's native "community" or "work" subculture this behavior may be thought to be definitely *not* O.K.

3. Still working as individuals, participants next specify in writing (in column 3) *only* those *differences* or *discrepancies* between the norms of the foreign workshop and the native cultures that they believe are really important obstacles likely to interfere with their trying out some new behaviors learned in the workshop and that they would like to eliminate or reduce in power. These should represent the native culture as it currently exists. For example, a participant may see the native norm that it is O.K. to express thoughts but not O.K. to express feelings as being a great obstacle that will interfere with his or her desire to become more personally expressive.

4. At this point, the participants are asked to join one or two other participants from whom they would like some consultation or to whom they would like to provide some consultation. The task for these consultation dyads or triads is to assist each person to formulate (in column 4) in very explicit and descriptive terms exactly how he or she would like the norms of a selected native culture or cultures changed. For example, a participant might say that the native subculture's norms should be that "it is not O.K. for people to impose their beliefs and desires on others"; "it is O.K. for people to strive to achieve their own potential in their own chosen style even if that style is different from the culture's traditions."

5. The next step is to begin to get some answers to the question "How can we get from 'here' (the present nonsatisfying condition) to 'there' (the way we would like it to be)?" Participants (in their consultation groups) are asked to specify in column 5 all those forces operating within the native culture that are driving or pushing the existing norms to change in the direction of the "Change Objectives." For example: "my own desire for the norms to be changed"; "my own dissatisfaction with current conditions in this native culture"; "my own and my family members' (friends', companions', associates') frustration and impatience with our culture's restrictive traditions."

6. At the same time that they are working on the driving forces, participants are also to specify in column 6 all those forces operating within the native subculture that interfere with or restrain movement in the direction of the change objectives. For example: "my own and my family members' (friends', companions', associates') fears that a change in our traditional norms will somehow destroy our culture entirely"; "reluctance to risk investing time and energy in a 'social engineering' project that does not have a guaranteed pay-off"; "unwillingness of one or more key people to go along with the idea."

7. When all major driving and restraining forces have been identified, participants consider what they, personally, have the will and resources to do that might be likely to

help eliminate or reduce the strength of one or more of the restraining forces identified in column 6. Specific actions are written in column 7—in sequence and with a date next to each action step indicating the deadline by which the specific action must be taken. For example: "On my return to my native culture (June 21, 1980), I will begin to *model* what I have learned about expressing my emotions, and I will express those feelings in the form of *words*. I will observe my family members (friends, companions, associates) closely to determine their response to my unusual self-disclosure. If they accept or even tolerate it, I shall express my feelings more frequently and intensively. I shall continue to watch their responses to my behavior, and when I observe someone experimenting with expressing feelings I shall make it a point to be *obviously* approving and accepting."

The writing and consulting phase of the model might be followed and supplemented by role playing or a psychodrama based on specific situations that the participants are anticipating. Situations to be role played should be selected on the basis of their reflection of common group concerns.

A shorter version of this design would consist of working only with columns 1 and 2 and then asking participants to discuss the similarities and differences between the norms of the foreign (workshop) culture and those of their own native (back-home) culture; to identify those differences that are likely to be real obstacles; and to consider what individuals can realistically do in order to eliminate those obstacles to the application of their workshop learnings.

CONCLUSION

In presenting this material, the facilitator might wish to point out that these concepts relate to all of us who find ourselves moving, with increasing frequency and rapidity, from one temporary social system to another (Toffler, 1970; Bennis & Slater, 1968). The unprepared individual can be expected to experience chronic migrational shock. However, through the use of the concepts and procedures presented here, people can learn to cope with and then overcome the impact of constant cultural migration so that the dips flatten out and a rising slope of satisfaction, effectiveness, and comfort gradually replaces the temporary peaks.

REFERENCES

Bennis, W. G., & Slater, P. E. *The temporary society*. New York: Harper & Row, 1968.

Freedman, A. M. Changes in perception of on-the-job problems following human relations laboratory training: II. Unpublished master's thesis, Boston University, 1963.

Hall, E. T. *Beyond culture*. Garden City, NY: Anchor Press/Doubleday, 1976.

Schmuck, R. A., et al. *The second handbook of organization development in schools*. Palo Alto, CA: Mayfield, 1977.

Schutz, W. C. *Here comes everybody*. New York: Harper & Row, 1971.

Toffler, A. *Future shock*. New York: Random House, 1970.

Tryhurst, J. S. The role of transitional states—including disasters—in mental illness. In *Symposium on Social and Preventive Psychiatry*. Washington, DC: Walter Reed Army Hospital Institute of Research, 1957.

Art Freedman, Ph.D., is the director of the Stress Management Institute, Chicago, Illinois, an executive management consulting firm specializing in organization development, human resource development, and career and employee assistance counseling. Dr. Freedman also provides individual, couple, and group psychotherapy services through the Institute. He received his B.S. and M.B.A. from Boston University and his Ph.D. from the University of Chicago. He was formerly assistant regional administrator for training and development and chief psychologist for the Illinois Department of Mental Health in the Chicago area. He is a member of the NTL Institute and is active in traintrainers and consultants.

CONSULTATION TO HUMAN-SERVICE ORGANIZATIONS

Leonard D. Goodstein

Those organizations that attempt to offer services that either promote human welfare or reduce human misery are typically termed human-service organizations. The range and diversity of these organizations are enormous. The more numerous ones include schools, churches, hospitals, and clinics; governmental agencies, including public safety organizations such as police and fire departments; political parties; labor unions; cultural organizations such as museums, symphony orchestras, and zoos; and the entire range of welfare agencies including social service agencies, fund-raising organizations (United Way, March of Dimes), and so on. The scope and complexity of these organizations are so great that any attempt to organize or catalog them is doomed to failure.

SOME CHARACTERISTICS OF HUMAN-SERVICE ORGANIZATIONS

There are certain dimensions along which such agencies or networks may be differentiated from other institutions. They offer services rather than products. They are largely in the nonprofit sector of the economy. They tend to be bureaucratic in their form of organization. Each of these dimensions affects the nature of organizational life within these agencies and may directly lead to a need for consultation help.

Providing Services

Offering services rather than producing products increases the difficulty of evaluating the quality of the organization. When an organization produces a product—a dress to wear, a car to drive, a dinner to eat—there is a tangible end product to evaluate. The dress fits, the car drives well, the dinner tastes good. While there are certainly differences in human tastes and standards, there can be reasonable agreement about the quality of such tangible products, and consumers can make judgments about which of these products they wish to choose.

There is, however, far less agreement about what constitutes, for example, quality education, effective public safety, or good health care. To illustrate just some of the issues involved, does quality education involve teaching children basic skills (the "three R's") or human relations skills; does public safety mean preventing crimes and fires or catching criminals and putting out fires; should a health care agency devote most of its energy to promoting physical well being or curing illness? Not only is there no agreement about such critical issues in the establishing of institutional goals, but there is also little or no open discussion of these issues in most human-service agencies.

One frequent kind of consultation help asked for by human-service systems is assistance in evaluating the services provided. This can be done (and often is done) in a perfunctory fashion by, for example, simply counting units of service so that the consultants offer no real challenge to the underlying value assumptions of the agency. One would question the usefulness of such exercises in the life of agencies.

It should be noted that the consumer of a product typically sees only the end product. There is little interest on the part of most of us to watch the products we consume being produced. But we are typically actively engaged in the delivery systems for our services. We directly experience our schools, churches, museums, orchestras, and police departments, and the processes through which they deliver these services are far more apparent to us than those involved in creating a product. Thus many of our reactions to the service systems that we encounter are based on evaluations of our experience of the process. In contrast, our evaluation of a product will be primarily concerned with the quality of the end product, with little or no attention paid to the processes, either physical or psychological, that may have been involved.

The Nonprofit Sector

A second dimension differentiating most human-service systems is the system's place in the economy. While there are some profit-making human-service organizations—group medical and law practices, for example—most such organizations either are funded by the public, with tax dollars, or are in that peculiar neither-public-nor-private sector that has come to be known in organizational behavior literature as the third sector. All organizations that are neither operated for profit nor funded by tax dollars fall into this sector. Churches, private educational institutions, foundations, and all the organized charities and human-welfare organizations, like Planned Parenthood and the Easter Seal Society, are third-sector organizations. Because profitability is not a criterion and because the human services provided are difficult to assess, these third-sector organizations most often take on the same bureaucratic characteristics of public agencies, even though they were developed to redress social grievances (Levitt, 1973). This development is especially true of the new third-sector agencies—the free clinics, such advocacy groups as Friends of the Earth or Nader's Raiders—all of which were developed in the 1960s during that period of aroused social concern. One of the problems faced by such organizations is how they can impact and perhaps reform the society in which they exist without destroying that society in the process. On the other hand, it is difficult for such organizations to have continual commerce with society and not be co-opted by it. Consultants will frequently be asked to demonstrate their credentials as part of the counterculture movement before they are accepted by such clients.

Part of the public nature of human-service systems is that most persons have little or no choice in deciding which system they will use. If we have children who need education, there typically is only one neighborhood school that will accept them, there is only one postal service to accept our mail, one fire or police department to answer our distress calls, and so on. While the wealthy may have some choice, the majority of society is required to accept those human-service systems that are established for their utilization.

This lack of competition makes many human-service systems rather complacent about the quality of their services, as there is never any feedback in terms of reduced demand. These systems are guaranteed a client base and need do little but provide a minimum level of service in order to maintain themselves—in sharp contrast to organizations in the business and industrial sector where survival requires meeting marketplace demands for quality and effectiveness. Such insulation of human-service systems makes it difficult for any consultant to demonstrate clearly that such a system is failing to fulfill its mission. After all, the patients (students, clients, or whatever) keep coming.

But public-sector organizations are responsive to other pressures, for example, review by those higher in the executive hierarchy; by the legislative bodies that provide the funds; by a variety of special-interest groups, such as the PTA, professional associations of

214

teachers, social workers, physicians; by consumer groups; by regulatory commissions, such as the hospital and clinic accreditation groups. Also, the media see it as part of their job description to monitor and, where necessary, "expose" failures in the public sector. Administrative mistakes that would go unreported in a large private corporation become front-page headlines when public organizations are concerned. This publicity also means, of course, that the work of consultants, including their reimbursement, is conducted in a fishbowl (see Goodstein & Boyer, 1972).

Bureaucracy in Human-Service Organizations

Weber (1947), the best known student of bureaucracy, described it as technically superior to all other forms of organization and thus indispensable for complex organizations. He saw the superiority of bureaucracy stemming from its logical, rational approach and its exclusion of emotional or nonrational considerations. The values and attributes of bureaucracy coincided very well with the then-pervasive scientific management approach that dominated the profit-making sectors of the Western world. It was necessary to modulate this definition of bureaucracy in order to apply it to the business and industrial world because of bureaucracy's failure to require profitability. This characteristic is also present in human-service organizations, which have taken on the formalism and lack of caring that characterizes much of the drab world of government service. Here success is measured, not by task accomplishment, but rather by the degree to which rules and regulations have been followed.

Harrison (1972) characterizes such organizations as *role oriented:* a strong emphasis on hierarchy and status with most, if not all, organizational behavior articulated in agreements, rules, and procedures. Such an approach is in marked contrast to the *task orientation* found in business organizations, where getting the job done in order to produce profit (or prevent bankruptcy) is the paramount value. In role-oriented organizations the cardinal sin is operating outside of one's prescribed role or job description. In sharp contrast, the cardinal sin in task-oriented organizations is failing to get the job done on time. An employee is expected to do what is necessary to get a task accomplished; it would be more or less unthinkable to refuse to help because "it's not in my job description."

Clearly the kind of people who are attracted to and maintain their allegiance to such role-oriented organizations are different from those attracted to the task-oriented organizations in our society. They are typically more comfortable with high structure, reluctant to live with ambiguity, and made anxious by overt conflict. Since bureaucratic organizations are structured to exclude emotions, such as anger, from the work place, it is not surprising that such organizations should be attractive to avoiders of conflict. But conflict stemming from incompatible interests and differences of opinion are normal parts of human interactions, including bureaucratic organizations.

Conflict Management

In bureaucracies, conflicts are typically handled by "smoothing over," by denial, by compromising, by any means other than directly confronting the differences in an open manner, acknowledging them, and focusing on conflict-management processes. Conflict-smothering strategies include keeping conflict latent rather than manifest, "sweeping differences under the rug," voicing harmony that is nonexistent, and pretending agreement when there is none. While there are exceptions, it is clear that there is a great deal more open confrontation about differences in the private sector—plant staff meetings, meetings of corporate planning groups, and so on—than there is in human-service organizations.

IMPLICATIONS FOR CONSULTANTS

The significant differences between essentially bureaucratic human-service organizations and those in the profit-making private sector need to be kept in mind by potential consultants. The strong role orientation in human-service systems will frequently lead workers, even highly trained professionals, into questioning the possibility of producing any system change in the organization. Even when workers themselves are supportive of the change, they frequently will question whether "the others" can be convinced that the change is possible. The most frequent response to any suggested change is an examination of the procedures and policies to determine why the program suggested *cannot* work. The negative mind-set and extreme cautiousness require patience and acceptance by the consultant, coupled with an awareness that there are almost always some ways in which the proposed changes can be implemented.

Consultants also need to be aware of the strong conflict-avoidance norms that characterize human-service systems. Strategies that tend to surface conflict or that attempt to legitimize differences among people, such as encounter group meetings of people from the same work group, are highly likely to be anxiety provoking. Indeed, some human-service organizations report that early experiences with this kind of interventionleft the organizations virtually destroyed as a consequence of some rather unstructured group experiences in which the consultant urged people to "get things off their chests." This violation of the long-term norms of the organization can only have negative effects, especially if there is no carefully designed and widely accepted follow-up in which these hurts can be healed.

Bureaucracy and Size

One frequent criticism of bureaucratic organizations is that there is a greater overlay of administrative control than is found in the private sector. Indeed Parkinson (1957) suggests that the less work done in an organization, the greater the number of bureaucrats. He offers the extreme example of the British navy, which, from 1914 to 1928, showed a 31 percent decline in the total number of men at sea but a 78 percent increase in admiralty personnel. However, during this period there was a technological revolution in sea warfare and a shift from a wartime to a peacetime navy. This law of Parkinson's has many examples, and consultants are frequently asked to help "reform" the bloated bureaucracy.

It is important for the consultant to bureaucratic human-service organizations to recognize that human-service systems are complex, highly differentiated systems that require a large amount of coordination in order to be effective. For example, when a person applies for some kind of welfare program, not only must eligibility be determined and an overall program of support be established, but health and medical programs often also need to be established, child-support services need to be initiated, counseling and other psychological needs may have to be met, and the entire package of programs must be coordinated. While added administrative personnel necessary for coordination add only marginally to the total productive output of the organization, without this kind of coordination, the entire program will be ineffective. A slashing of the personnel budget is probably not the answer to inefficiency and waste in many such systems.

Clearly, however, the sheer size of many human-service systems is part of the problem. Large school systems, massive hospital complexes, and multiversities preclude any sense of community among their members, and a common sense of shared purpose is almost impossible to achieve. Kasarda (1974), in an examination of 178 school systems in Colorado, found that as systems grow in size and complexity communication becomes more and more difficult, and the failure to resolve these difficulties of communication has dramatic negative effects upon the vitality of the organization. Successful organizations require both a

216

clarity of purpose and a commitment to that purpose by virtually all the members of the organization. In large, complex, human-service systems these requirements are not present.

Amorphous Goals

In contrast to the single-minded pursuit of profit found in the profit-making sector, human-service systems have rather amorphous goals of "providing quality education," "promoting human welfare," etc. It should be noted that although there are issues around goal clarity in the profit-making sector (for example, How much pollution can be permitted in the pursuit of profit? Can quality be sacrificed to meet shipping deadlines?), these issues are always in the context of profitability. In human-service organizations, not only is there no "bottom line" as a final parameter, but there is also no forum for the open and frank discussion of goals and purposes. The vague and nonoperationalized goals are accepted, and, within the ambiguity permitted by such statements, each individual or each individual subunit can do what it thinks best without any sense of acting in contradiction to the organization's goals. Thus, one hospital unit can press for more research funds and space while another argues for more patient beds, with each unit feeling that its aims fit the overall goal of providing quality health care. It is toward the clarification of these disparate goals that organizational consultants should devote their energies.

Complex Services

Another issue that affects the high personnel costs of human-service systems is found in the very nature of their services. The provision of such services is far more complex, difficult, and demanding than the typical production of a product. In the case of the human-service organization, there is no passive, compliant set of materials that yields to the stamping machine or the welder's torch; instead, live human beings, with all their fractiousness and independence and their own ideas about what they want done with their lives, must be dealt with. Rendering human services involves higher standards than the production of a product, and there need to be more supervisory checks than one would find in a typical factory. Also, it should be noted that neither the human services themselves nor the supervision of these services can readily be automated, computerized, or otherwise mechanized. Indeed, the efforts to do this cause part of the strong negative reaction to our automated age. We can all resonate with the statement "I am a human being: do not fold, mutilate, or spindle." The consultant to human-service systems needs to help them become more humanistic, not more mechanical.

MODELS FOR CONSULTING WITH HUMAN-SERVICE ORGANIZATIONS

Three different approaches or models of consultation are useful in working with human-service organizations: the educational, the individual process, and the systems models. The preceding discussion, by clearly focusing on systems issues, may suggest that a systems model should be the primary mode of intervention. There are few organizations, however, either in human services or production, that have the sophistication to self-diagnose their systems problems and seek consultation from a systems-oriented consultant. Instead, the organization tends to see that there are some kinds of problems confronting the organization and to seek help from either an educational or an individual-process model.

Educational Model

In this case, the client system conceptualizes the problem as a lack of skill or knowledge. As one director of a mental health agency once suggested, "Our major problem is that our performance appraisal system just isn't working. Maybe the system is not well designed and maybe it's just that mental health professionals won't really engage in performance appraisal, but what we need is an expert in performance appraisal to review our system and then teach our supervisory personnel how to do their jobs effectively." Similarly, a research laboratory director asked a consultant for a series of lectures on organizational behavior so that the supervisors and managers in the lab would have a better understanding of the nature of their roles—at least on some theoretical basis.

In both of these cases, as in thousands more, the client system (or at least one powerful person in that system) has made a diagnostic judgment about the nature of the problem facing the system and also prescribed an intervention strategy. Both of these examples diagnosed a lack of information and proposed a solution to remedy that information gap. As is always true of intervention strategies, the consultant has to start where the client is, but there is usually a serious question about the adequacy of such a self-diagnosis.

The identified concerns may be mere symptoms of more basic and more pervasive problems. For example, rather than a problem in performance appraisal, the mental health agency may have a more generic problem of inadequate leadership, low morale, and a failure of upper management to support those to whom they should have delegated authority. Rather than a lack of understanding of organizational behavior, the research lab staff may be suffering from problems of low cohesion, inadequate direction, and conflicting goal messages from the research director. Thus, the central issue for the consultant emerges: when the client's diagnosis should be accepted as adequate and when it should be questioned.

It needs to be noted that there are any number of consultants who have packaged programs for teaching performance appraisal, organizational behavior, communication skills, or whatever, and these consultants are ready and willing to provide their programs to the marketplace. Their approach is a commercial one; they describe their programs fairly and sell them to whoever is willing to buy them. If there is any caution, it clearly is "caveat emptor." There is no dishonesty or immorality to such a program, but it simply differs from that espoused by a professional consulting model. In such a model, the client and the consultant jointly agree to review the symptoms or causes of concern, to consider the possible causes for these concerns, to develop a series of potential intervention strategies, to consider the potential cost-benefit consequences of these strategies, and then to go ahead with a mutually agreed-upon course of action. Although not all programs of intervention—medical, legal, educational, or psychological—are carried out according to this formula, it does represent the best professional model. The true professional does not insist that "the doctor knows best," but neither is there an assumption that "the consumer is always right," as is true for a commercial model of consultation.

If the consultant begins with this professional educational model as one way of considering the situation, he or she may begin to use his or her awareness of systems issues to open up an additional series of alternatives. The consultant may agree that an educational intervention is one possible strategy but, at the same time, begin to question the client's data base or the processes by which the client determined to use a particular intervention. While, in the final analysis, the client may be right and some educational program may be useful as a first step, the consultant has broadened the client's understanding of the system, of how to go about diagnosing problems in the system, and of what possible interventions may follow from a variety of diagnoses.

There are many examples of educational interventions that have been designed to meet organizational needs following such a diagnosis. For example, a major American airline was experiencing extreme problems with its counter personnel, who had become abusive to passengers whose flights were delayed or cancelled. The consultants called in to help interviewed the personnel and found that they thought the passengers behaved "childishly" when their flights were not on time. It became apparent that the counter personnel then responded "parentally." Training in transactional analysis was suggested to help the agents understand the dynamics of their own behavior and change it accordingly. A training program was initiated with a highly beneficial result in terms of reduced passenger complaints and reduced absenteeism and turnover on the part of agents. Clearly an educational model can be useful in consulting with human-service systems, but consultants need to be wary about uncritically accepting the client's stated needs or desires for particular training programs.

Individual-Process Model

The individual-process model, where the focus is on the psychodynamics of one or more members of the organization, is probably the least widely used model in working with human-service organizations—indeed with any organizations. This does not imply that individual processes are not operating in organizations, but rather that the level of conceptualization and intervention is typically focused on a group or a system. While attitudes are always on the individual level, they become part of the psychological characteristics of an organization, its norms and values, when they are widely shared. Indeed, the process of socialization into an organization (Katz & Kahn, 1978) attempts to make certain that all new members of the organization "buy into" these norms and values.

Nevertheless, there are times when an individual process model should be called into use in organizational consultation. It does happen that a single individual's behavior can have strong negative effects on an organization, especially if that person is in a position of power or influence. In one such case, a young corporation executive requested consultation after his participation in a sensitivity training course for managers. It was clear to the consultant that the executive was operating his family-owned company in an erratic and reckless fashion, expanding faster than the marketplace, and paying little or no attention to the company's cash flow. He would not heed the advice of other corporate officers to move more slowly, and there was a sense of quiet desperation throughout the organization.

While it was initially unclear why this competent and well-educated young man was behaving in such a fashion, clinical interviews indicated that he had taken over the company after his father's death, against the protests of his mother, who felt that he was too young for such responsibilities. He was determined to double the net worth of the company within eighteen months after assuming control to prove to his mother that "I'm as much a man as my father ever was!" When the consultant began to focus on the individual processes of this client and the effects of his behavior on his organization, the client terminated the consulting relationship. Within a year, the bankruptcy of the company was headline news in the local papers. Clearly the client's intrapsychic conflicts, which were accessible only through the use of an individual clinical model, were central to the problems facing the organization, and only by dealing directly with these issues could any change have taken place. Although this particular example is not drawn from human-service organization, it can be assumed that such problems are prevalent in these organizations as well.

Systems Model

Since organizations are systems, it should not be surprising that a systems model for consultation has the widest utility. Since the initial entry of consultants into human-service systems is very often based on an educational model, the utilization of the educational model needs to be understood in systems terms. For example, the introduction of a token economy program in a large mental hospital can be done through an educational model, but, if the system-wide implications of adopting such a model are not worked through, it is unlikely that the program will be successful. There are certain to be issues involving which patients are entered into such a program, how they are to be moved into and out of the program, and who is to manage the program. There is no question that the introduction of any substantial change in an organization will cause a ripple effect through the organization and have profound, long-term implications for the organization. Most of the programmatic changes that fail in organizations do so because the persons responsible for the innovation have failed to conceptualize the organization in systems terms and to plan accordingly.

When most of us are asked to describe an organization with which we are familiar, we tend to draw an organizational chart with hierarchically arranged boxes. But such a static model of an organization is inadequate to describe the important psychological characteristics of any organization, its patterns of communication, power, support, and influence. An open-systems model of organizational life (Katz & Kahn, 1978) is a far more adequate model since it is concerned with the elements of the system, the structure of the system, the interdependency of the elements of the system, and the way the system is embedded in the environment.

Open-systems theory conceptualizes organizations as patterns of recurrent activities in which energy (information, personnel, raw materials, etc.) is imported into the system and transformed in some fashion or another, and the resulting product (or service in the case of human-service systems) is exported back into the environment. In contrast with closed systems, notions of which stem from classical Newtonian physics, open systems maintain themselves through a constant interchange with the host environments, and thus there is a continual exchange of energy between the system and its environment. The analogue of the open-systems model is the living cell, not a static hydraulic system.

Thus an open system involves a recurring cycle of input, transformation, and output. Both the input and output characteristics of the open system keep the system in constant commerce with the environment, while the transformation process is contained within the system. An effective open system requires a balance among the three stages of the cycle, with the input taking into account both environmental demands and the capacity of the transformation cycle, and the transformation process absorbing the flow from the input and moving to the output stage.

Levinson and Astrachan (1976) provided an excellent example of how such an open-systems model helps explain the role of the intake staff in a community mental health center and the problems that such a staff encounters in regulating the organization's boundary conditions. The intake staff held the important and primary responsibility "of regulating the patient-input boundary so as to import an appropriate patient population at a manageable rate" (p. 22). When the intake staff took in more patients than the transformation (or treatment) system could handle, the overflow patients were neglected, transferred or referred elsewhere, or discharged early through the "revolving door."

On the other hand, the intake staff may be highly selective, admitting only a special group of "suitable" patients and turning large numbers away. While this may meet the treatment staff's criteria of suitability, this failure to meet environmental needs leads to a loss of support from the surrounding community. Thus the task of the intake staff is to manage a delicate balance between demand and capability, between environmental need and internal resources, or it will lose credibility in managing its interface between the organization and its environment.

The organizational consultant who can operate from this open-systems model can begin to understand some of the intrinsic issues that will continually emerge in organizations as the cycle of input, transformation, and output is interminably repeated. Such a consultant will understand that the problems involved in the role of the intake staff, for example, are never solvable in any final sense, but rather that there is a dynamic tension that must always exist in those segments of the organization responsible for boundary-condition management, as the attempt is made to balance the conflicting interests of the system and the environment. The solution that worked today will almost certainly not work tomorrow.

AN OPERATIONAL GUIDE

While open-systems theory provides an overview and a theoretical structure by which a systems-oriented consultant can function, it does not provide an operational guide for actual consultation practice. One such operational guide is found in the work of Weisbord (1978), whose model for organizational diagnosis and consultation is based on open-systems theory.

Weisbord provides a semi-standardized series of questions, rating forms, and areas of inquiry that focuses the attention of the consultant on six interrelated organizational processes that are involved in all organizations and that need to be understood by consultants and their clients. The six processes are (1) purposes; (2) structure; (3) relationships; (4) rewards; (5) leadership; and (6) helpful mechanisms.[1]

The *purposes* or goals of the organization involve both the clarity of these goals and the degree of commitment to the goals by members of the organization. Obviously the former is necessary for the latter. But as one of the characteristics of human-service systems is low goal clarity, a problem that systems-oriented consultants may encounter is a need for increasing that clarity. This effort often involves helping members of the client system to surface and accept differences about goals, differences that have remained latent over some time—not a simple task and one that requires time and energy for both client and consultant.

An analysis of *structure* involves both the formal organization chart and, even more importantly, the informal social structure that helps (or hinders) getting the work done. Many tasks in human-service organizations have low interdependency and probably require less need for close teamwork than is commonly assumed. For example, classroom teachers operate quite autonomously, and a typical elementary school can function fairly effectively with rather distant interpersonal relationships. On the other hand, a team in the operating room or a group of fire fighters cannot The organizational consultant needs to consider how important teamwork is for task accomplishment and to strive for it only when necessary. Many consultants operating in the human-service area already have a strong value commitment to teamwork, even when it is not necessary for task performance.

The *relationships* that may be involved in an organization include the interpersonal, the intergroup, and the interactive ones between the employees and the technology. Since typically there is little technology involved in human-service systems, this last kind of interaction tends to have little importance. As we noted earlier, a strong norm in human-service systems says that conflict, both interpersonal and intergroup, but especially the former, is "unprofessional" and that human-service workers, especially those professionally trained, must "get along." While a failure to confront differences might be assumed to have a disastrous effect on human-service organizations, such is not the case. The low interdependence in such organizations permits the typical avoidance of conflict to work reasonably well, except when real collaboration is necessary, as in long-range planning.

---

[1]See R. C. Preziosi, "Organizational Diagnosis Questionnaire," in the Instrumentation section of this *Annual*.

However, the inability of these systems to accept differences among members of the organization may be seen as critical in reducing their effectiveness and provide another entry point for the systems-oriented consultant.

Organizational *rewards* include such things as salary, promotions, and bonuses, and the like and the more informal, personal rewards and support that one person can give another for work well done. In most human-service bureaucracies, supervisors and managers tend to focus their attention on the former and overlook the latter. The former, however, are difficult to use because of the way such rewards are managed bureaucratically; there is also some question about how well such rewards motivate people. In working with these systems, consultants need to concentrate on helping the system use its informal, psychological rewards more effectively.

The role of *leadership* in an organization is to keep the other elements of the system in balance and constantly to monitor the functioning of the system. In most human-service systems, the task of leadership is poorly understood and legitimized. All too often, the assumption is that the workers are highly trained, competent professionals and that the system runs itself. Perhaps the most blatant example of this notion is the university academic department. One frequent need that the consultant may thus encounter is a clearer understanding of the role of the organizational leader and how that role can be adequately filled. There may be a need for both a theory-based input using an educational model and a series of coaching sessions using the individual-process model.

Helpful mechanisms such as budgeting, management information systems, and evaluation research is the last of Weisbord's six processes. Unfortunately, all too often these systems are absent, poorly implemented, or abused in human-service organizations. For example, the typical budgeting procedure in human-service agencies requires that future budgets be pegged at previous levels of client services, making innovation and change very difficult and tending to reduce the interest of the agency in developing cost effectiveness. Consultants need to be aware that such agencies' helpful mechanisms must be integrated into an overall systems approach and that there will be strong resistance to such processes throughout the organization.

SUMMARY AND CONCLUSIONS

Human-service systems touch all our lives, as citizens and consumers. The need to have such systems operate both effectively and humanely should be immediately obvious to even the most casual observer.

For those who are interested in consulting with human-service systems, either externally or internally, the delineation of some of the specific characteristics of these systems should be helpful. Weisbord's model of organizations is one systems-oriented model for working with human-service systems; the educational and individual-process models can complement the systems model. There are other fairly well-developed and tested strategies (see Goodstein, 1978, for a further discussion of these) for consulting with human-service systems. Both those who would work as consultants in such systems and those who would be consumers of such help need to be adequately informed about the research and theory that is now available.

REFERENCES

Goodstein, L. D. *Consulting with human service systems*. Reading, MA: Addison-Wesley, 1978.

Goodstein, L. D., & Boyer, R. K. Crisis intervention in a municipal agency: A conceptual case history. *Journal of Applied Behavioral Science*, 1972, 8, 318-340.

Harrison, R. Understanding your organization's character. *Harvard Business Review*, 1972, 50, 119-128.

Kasarda, J. D. The structural implications of social systems size: A three level analysis. *American Sociological Review*, 1974, 39, 19-28.

Katz, D., & Kahn, R. L. *Social psychology of organization* (2nd ed.). New York: Wiley, 1978.

Levinson, D., & Astrachan, B. Entry into the mental health center: A problem in organizational boundary regulation. In E. J. Miller (Ed.), *Task and organization*. London: Wiley, 1976.

Levitt, T. *The third sector: New tactics for a responsive society*. New York: Amacom Press, 1973.

Parkinson, C. N. *Parkinson's law*. Boston: Houghton-Mifflin, 1957.

Weber, M. *The theory of social and economic organizations* (Translated from the German by A. M. Henderson and T. Parsons). New York: Oxford University Press, 1947.

Weisbord, M. R. Organizational diagnosis: Six places to look for trouble with or without a theory. *Group & Organization Studies*, 1976, 1(4), 430-447.

Weisbord, M. R. *Organizational diagnosis*. Reading, MA: Addison-Wesley, 1978.

Leonard D. Goodstein, Ph.D., is the president of University Associates, Inc., San Diego, California. He was previously professor and chairman of the Department of Psychology, Arizona State University, Phoenix, and was a senior consultant for University Associates. Dr. Goodstein has been the author or editor of several texts, including Organizational Change Sourcebook I *and* II *(1979). Dr. Goodstein served as the editor of* The Journal of Applied Behavioral Science *and has consulted with a variety of organizations.*

EVALUATION OF HUMAN-SERVICE PROGRAMS

Karen Sue Trisko and V. C. League

The word evaluation conjures up fearful images in the minds of many people. But it need not be perceived as a complex evil that only highly credentialed statisticians should be allowed to do. Those responsible for the planning, development, and implementation of human services and educational programs should be the people involved in evaluation.

Workers in all fields constantly seek feedback to reinforce certain behaviors that seem to work well on the job and to modify others that do not seem effective. Administrators and office staff would like to identify the most efficient ways of doing their work, and continual interaction with their working environments yields this feedback. An example of such feedback would be the number of word-of-mouth referrals made to a human-service program or a sudden drop (or rise) in the number of people voluntarily seeking services.

Throughout the implementation of a program, staff members will be asking themselves, "How am *I* doing?" and administrators will ask, "How are *we* doing?" At the end of a fixed period of time, some external person or agency will ask, "How well did it go? Should it be done again? Was it worth the effort?"

In anticipation of these judgmental questions (and evaluation is, by definition, a judgmental process), it makes sense to build in, at the outset of program implementation, the mechanisms needed to answer them. "Self-correcting" mechanisms enable progress to be monitored throughout the life of the program. Monitoring, quite simply, is the process of checking the road map (the program plan) to verify location and getting back on the path or selecting an alternate route for getting to the final destination—achievement of program objectives and goals.

Depending on who is asking evaluation questions, and for what reasons, either "process evaluation" or "outcome evaluation" will be chosen. Process evaluation assesses a program's *means*, and outcome evaluation measures its *end results*. Program staff members are likely to seek "process" or "formative evaluation" to monitor how well day-to-day tasks and activities are carried out. Program administrators and outside people are likely to seek "outcome" or "summative evaluation."

Evaluation activities should take place in the same sequence as the implementation of the program. First (1) *tasks* should be *monitored*; (2) *activities* should be *assessed*; (3) *outcomes* (achievement of objectives) should be *enumerated*; (4) *goal attainment* should be *measured*; and (5) a judgment as to whether the *problem* has been reduced should be made (Figure 1).

LEVELS OF EVALUATION

Each level of evaluation builds on the previous one. Information obtained at level 1 supplies the groundwork for level 2; level-2 information provides the basis for level 3; and so on. Figure 2 illustrates all five levels and the central questions addressed at each level.

Adapted from K. Trisko & V. C. League, *Developing Successful Programs* (Chapter Seven). Oakland, CA: Awareness House, 1978. ©Karen Trisko and V. C. League. Used with permission of the authors.

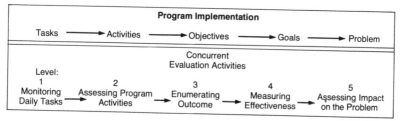

Figure 1. Sequence of Program Implementation and Evaluation Activities

Process/Formative Evaluation		Outcome/Summative Evaluation		
Level 1 Monitoring Daily tasks	**Level 2** Assessing Program Activities	**Level 3** Enumerating Outcomes	**Level 4** Measuring Effectiveness	**Level 5** Assessing Impact on the Problem
Are contractual or service obligations being met? Is activity taking place where and when it should? Are staff members working where and when they should? Is the program administratively sound? Are daily tasks carried out efficiently? Are staff adequately trained for their jobs?	What is done to whom? What activities are taking place? Who is the target of activity (numbers and types of people with what problems/needs, from what areas, etc.)? How well is the activity implemented? How could it be done more efficiently? Were clients satisfied? Does the program have a favorable image?	What is the result of the activities described in level 2? Should different activities be substituted? Have program objectives been achieved? What happened to the target population? How is it different from before? Have unanticipated outcomes also occurred and are they desirable? What activities might be repeated to ensure their future occurrence?	What would have happened to participants in the absence of the program? What are all the factors that may have contributed to the changes documented at level 3? How cost effective is the program, compared to others with the same goals?	What changes are evident in the problem? Has the problem been reduced as a result of the program? What new knowledge has been generated for society about the problem or ways to solve the problem?

Figure 2. Evaluation Levels

Level 1: Monitoring Daily Tasks

The internal workings of a program are under scrutiny at level 1: accounting and financial records and procedures, organizational functioning and staffing patterns, rules, regulations and procedures, timekeeping, staff training and development. An assessment, formal or informal, could be made of the organization's structures and tasks by asking staff members:

"What's right around here? What's wrong around here? What would you change about the day-to-day operations to make it better? What would make it easier for you to do your job?"

For the most part, management problems are uncovered and dealt with at level 1. The depth of evaluation activity depends on the number of problem areas suspected or the seriousness of malfunctioning within the organization. Probing of specific problem areas is undertaken. Work analyses, resource expenditure studies, management audits, procedural overhauls, and audits are considered level-1 evaluation activities.

Level 2: Assessing Program Activities

Before it can be determined how to improve program activities, the characteristics of current activities need to be known. Level 2 assesses numbers and types of program services, the recipients of those services, the timing and appropriateness of activities, and the efficiency with which they are carried out. Client-satisfaction measures and assessment of public image are common level-2 activities. Some determination of what seems to work best with what types of people is made at this level. Obviously, evaluation activity at the first two levels is highly subjective, requiring the heavy involvement of program staff members, to whom the judgments are most valuable. The underlying premise in evaluation is that problems cannot be solved if they are not recognized.

Level 3: Enumerating Outcome

At this level of evaluation, it is possible to determine whether program objectives—the immediate short-term outcomes—have been achieved. To ascertain what resulted from the activities described in level 2, some through-time measures are needed. How is the target population different now from the way it was before participating in the program? Behavior, attitudes, skills, information level, legal or employment status, or other characteristics of the clients need to be documented. Changes that occurred simultaneously with the program's existence cannot, however, be attributed to the program. For example, a repeated juvenile offender might "straighten out," i.e., get a job and manage not to get arrested during the time of participation in a juvenile-services program. But the reason for the change in behavior could be that the young person's family relationships improved and thus offered motivation not to get into trouble. Another example of the cause-effect fallacy would be the academic improvement of students enrolled in a tutoring program during a year when grading policy at the school changed.

If objectives are not being met, then more questions should be raised. For instance, have the wrong activities been selected to achieve this particular objective? Was the objective realistic and measurable in the first place? Conversely, if objectives are being met, level-3 evaluation activities help program staff to reinforce what works.

Level 4: Measuring Effectiveness

Effectiveness measurement tells us whether program goals have been accomplished. The major questions addressed are "What would have happened in the absence of the program? Is it better than no program at all? Does it make a difference?" To answer these questions, a cause-effect relationship must be established, meaning that a "control" group or program is needed for comparison. That control group must match as closely as possible the group participating in the program. It is important to identify and match as many of the other variables that could be influencing a change in conditions or behavior. As close a link as possible needs to be established between cause and effect to measure effectiveness of goal attainment—the long-range, ultimate outcomes desired.

Level 5: Assessing Impact on the Problem

If a program is worthwhile and perfect in every way, an improvement in the problem situation should be evident. The reality is that most programs do not have the necessary resources to carry out evaluation activities at this level. Nor is it possible to make the environment stand still in order to enable us to ascertain whether a program effort caused a reduction in the problem. So many external variables exist that it is virtually impossible to determine real impact on social problems resulting from program intervention. Social value changes, new public policies, changes in economic conditions, and the multitude of factors that influence society and individuals all have an impact on the problems in the world. Nevertheless, program staff members are forced every day to try to answer the ultimate question: "Did the program reduce the problem?" Usually the person asking the question actually needs other information, and it is the program staff's responsibility to cull it out. Usually these information needs are political or economic and can be satisfactorily answered with information gathered at the first four (probably the first two) levels of program evaluation.

Evaluation Needs and Intensity

The time and resources needed to carry out all five levels of evaluation would be phenomenal, even for a small, community-based human service program. To determine how far to pursue evaluation, the guide in Figure 3 can be used.

Circle the number on each continuum that most closely describes your program. This guide can help you determine at what level you actually can or need to evaluate:

Expectations: Who has expectations for evaluation: staff? board? funding source? What questions need to be answered? Is process or outcome evaluation needed?

1	2	3	4	5
NO EXPECTATIONS			HIGH EXPECTATIONS	

Quality of Goals and Objectives: Do those of your program meet these criteria: specific, time limited, measurable/observable, and realistic/attainable statements of end-result?

1	2	3	4	5
MEET NO CRITERIA			MEET ALL CRITERIA	

Availability of Data: Are the data needed to evaluate at each successive level available? (Refer to the questions encompassed at each level.)

1	2	3	4	5
NO DATA AVAILABLE			EXTENSIVE DATA AVAILABLE	

Resources: What technical skills and staff commitment exist? What level of financial resources is available?

1	2	3	4	5
NO RESOURCES			UNLIMITED RESOURCES	

The lowest number you circled on each of the four continuums will dictate at what level you realistically can evaluate:

1	2	3	4	5
Monitoring Daily Tasks	Assessing Activities	Enumerating Outcome	Measuring Effectiveness	Assessing Impact on the Problem

Figure 3. Evaluation Needs and Intensity Guide

QUALITY OF GOALS AND OBJECTIVES

The greatest task in evaluation is to shape goals and objectives so that they can be evaluated. They must be end statements that are (1) concrete and specific, (2) realistic and attainable, (3) measurable, and (4) time bound.

In order to be measurable, goals and objectives must be operationally defined. This means translating them into observable indicators of success. For example:

Goal

To reduce by one-half the number of employment-service clients who are unable to locate jobs because of their lack of job-finding skills.

Objective #1

To increase employment-service clients' ability to complete job-application forms by the end of a four-week training program.

The objective is not operational until "increased ability" is defined.

Operational Definition

Clients' overall scores on four job-application forms as measured against the criteria of completeness, legibility, and accuracy, will reach an average level of 70 percent or better.

Another objective related to the same goal:

Objective #2

To increase participants' skills in using the public transportation system.

Operational Definition

Participants will demonstrate skill in using the public transportation system as evidenced by using public transportation to arrive on time at two pre-arranged interviews.

An operational definition is behavioral, recognizable by anyone, and *not* subject to broad interpretation. It specifies the conditions or events that signal success or failure.

It is important that both evaluator and program implementer agree on operational definitions for their particular program goals and objectives. Otherwise, an evaluator may measure one thing, while a program implementer is striving for something entirely different. This is true for in-house evaluators as well as for external evaluators, although the need for absolute agreement is heightened with external evaluators.

EVALUATION RESEARCH DESIGNS

Once goals and objectives have been operationally defined so that they are measurable, the next step is to select a research design.

Single-Group Postprogram Design
(Program → Measurement)

A group of program participants (either the whole population or a representative subgroup) is measured against predetermined criteria (according to program objectives). This design is probably the one most often utilized in human-service programs for a variety of reasons.

University Associates

For instance, evaluation may have begun after the program started, thereby eliminating the possibility of measuring participant characteristics before the program began. Or the program activities may be such that access to participants is impossible before they become involved in the program.

Single-Group Preprogram/Postprogram Design
(First Measurement→Program→Second Measurement)

Again, a group of participants is measured against predetermined criteria, both before involvement in the program and again after completion of the program. The same kind of measurement must be used, so that evidence of change can be traced. There may be more than one postprogram measurement in order to identify the lasting effects of change upon participants.

Split-Group Preprogram/Postprogram Design
(First Measurement, Group I→Program →Second Measurement, Group II)

Basically the same as the previous design, this design measures one group of participants before, and a different but matching group after, program participation. The groups must be similar. This design is used when the same group of people is not accessible for pre- and postprogram measurement.

Control-Group Postprogram Design
(Program Group→Measurement)
(Control Group→Measurement)

No preprogram measures are taken. Two separate groups of people are measured against the same predetermined criteria. One group consists of program participants, the other of people who have had no exposure to the program but who are characteristically similar. This design would enable testing the hypothesis that one type of program was better than none at all.

Control-Group Preprogram/Postprogram Design
(First Measurement→Program Group →Second Measurement)
(First Measurement→Control Group→Second Measurement)

Two separate but matching groups of people are measured before and after a program. This design makes it possible to track participants' changes through time, as compared to nonparticipants' changes through time. A sound cause-effect relationship can be established by using this design, if proper control of all variables is established. For example, the effects of a program to reduce in-school dropouts could be compared to the situations in like schools with no such programs. This design will work only if all characteristics of the school systems are alike, i.e., suspension and expulsion policies, teacher-student ratios, grading policy, and the multitude of other variables that could affect a student's decision to drop out.

Variation of Control-Group Preprogram/Postprogram Design
(First Measurement→Program I→Second Measurement)
(First Measurement→Program II→ Second Measurement)

This design could be used to compare two different programs with like goals. Such a design would yield information as to which program produces better results, given the same conditions and target populations. It would also tell which type of program is more cost-effective, or which program seems to work best with what types of target populations.

DATA COLLECTION

After selecting an appropriate research design that will yield answers to the questions posed, it is time to determine how to collect the necessary data: What data will be collected? From/by whom? When? In what format?

What Data?

The answer to "what data?" is determined by the operational definitions of objectives. Data could be specific behaviors or events to be observed, items on a paper-and-pencil questionnaire, interview questions, police or hospital statistics, and so on.

Data can be considered "hard" or "soft." Hard data are quantitative: dollar amounts, number of people served, number of days of effort, scores on paper-and-pencil questionnaires, behavior indicators (such as numbers of arrests, days absent from school, grades, hospital admissions, recidivism rates, deaths, overdoses), either/or indicators (such as "drug free," "employed," etc.). Soft data are qualitative: self-perceptions, attitudes, client-satisfaction measures, types of interactions between people, changes in "climate," judgmental observations, etc.

In either case the data must be *valid* (Does it measure what it is intended to measure?) and *reliable* (Does it measure consistently, over time, and with different types of people?). Validity has to do with previously discussed absolute agreement between evaluator and program staff regarding indicators of success. For instance, measuring change in attitudes toward criminals would not be a valid measure for a program for which an objective is to increase participants' usage of local community referral sources.

Reliability has to do with whether several observers, for example, are looking for the same phenomena or whether items on a questionnaire are interpreted alike by everyone reading them. An unreliable measure, for instance, is the I.Q. test because it may not be applicable to all groups because of given language and cultural considerations.

Data from/by Whom?

Whoever is closest to the source should collect data, and usually the closest are program staff members and participants. The phenomenon of bias, then, must be addressed. The mere fact that staff members know why data are being collected is likely to cause them, either subconsciously or consciously, to present only positive data. Self-report data by participants could be biased if they wish to be perceived in a favorable light. For these reasons, outside evaluators are hired to collect data. To eliminate bias, verification by other sources could be used. For instance, self-report by youngsters in school about their learning could be verified by their teachers, or by grades, a source of hard data. The surest way to collect unbiased data is to use several sources that can collaborate.

Data: When and Where?

When and where data collection occurs is largely determined by the research design being implemented. If it is a pre- and postprogram design, then there must be access to participants prior to any involvement with the program, as well as upon completion of that involvement. When to collect data also must be considered with respect to program activities. For example, observations of groups must be made at times that are not disruptive to the process of the activity; otherwise, the occurrences in the group are likely to be

230

different from what they would have been without a disruption. Where to collect data is usually a matter of convenience, but ideally those supplying data should be afforded a comfortable setting that is consistent for all data suppliers.

The "experimenter effect" must also be taken into account. It simply means that the act of collecting data (observing a group, administering a questionnaire, photographing evidence of vandalism with the principal's permission) influences the results.

Common Errors in Data Collection

Many efforts to gather data are sabotaged because of *failure to:*

1. Pretest items on surveys and questionnaires to correct weaknesses in format, directions, grammar, completion time, etc.
2. Select and train data collectors, interviewers, observers.
3. Introduce and explain the study to respondents.
4. Ensure confidentiality or anonymity where appropriate.
5. Establish rapport with data providers, use the language of the respondent.
6. Clarify unclear responses with nonsuggestive probes; avoid "leading" questions.
7. Record data at the time of collection to ensure accurate recall.
8. Review questionnaires for completeness before respondents leave.
9. Describe the reporting procedures that could have affected the data, especially when collecting existing data.
10. Use comparable scales and rates (avoid comparing apples with oranges).
11. Control and standardize analysis procedures.
12. Utilize the findings.

Ideally, evaluation efforts should be characterized by the following conditions:

1. Evaluation should be built in at the start of project planning.
2. There should be honesty between the program staff members and the evaluator.
3. A clear understanding of evaluation purpose should exist.
4. The project's goals and objectives should be clearly understood and stated in measurable terms.
5. Agreement on "success indicators" and "failure indicators" must exist.
6. There must be an understanding of the evaluation design: when data will be collected and by whom, what interventions are likely to interfere with project activities, etc.
7. The evaluation design should be flexible enough so that time lines and data-collection methods can be altered midstream, if necessary.
8. There should be joint consultation regarding study results, and a joint interpretation of results before conclusions are drawn and resulting decisions made.

SUMMARY

Some ethical guidelines and suggestions can be helpful in presenting evaluation findings:

- Delineate the complete program picture (problems, goals, objectives, activities, tasks).
- Outline the entire evaluation design, including what prompted the study and what decisions are likely to result.

- Present the limitations and weaknesses of the design for what they are.
- Present raw data in the final report, allowing audiences to draw their own conclusions.
- Ensure confidentiality when it has been promised.
- Establish authority over the findings.
- Apply the findings to future program development.

It is important to remember that program development and evaluation logic is a circular process (Figure 4) that continually answers four questions in sequence:

1. What outcome is expected? (program plans)
2. What is the actual outcome? (evaluation)
3. What is the discrepancy between the two? (evaluation)
4. How can the discrepancy gap be closed? (revised program plans)

Figure 4. Circular Evaluation Process

If this concept is applied to every level of program plans and evaluation, the success of human-service programs can be greatly increased.

Karen Sue Trisko is the director of professional development, American Dental Hygienists Association, Chicago, Illinois, responsible for developing and managing programs of continuing education and services. Ms.Trisko served as assistant director in a regional prevention training and technical assistance center and directed a national information system for eight such centers. She consults with human services and educational organizations in areas related to assessment, planning, evaluation, and information management. She is a co-founder and a member of the board of directors of the National Association of Prevention Professionals. Her background is in organizational psychology and management.

V. C. League is the director of the Region 8 Training and Development Center, U.S. Office of Education, Oakland, California. He is a co-founder and chairperson of the National Association of Prevention Professionals and the Grantsmanship Center, Los Angeles, California. He has consulted with over two hundred organizations in the United States and abroad. His areas of expertise include management, organization development, negotiations, and community organizing.

MULTIPLE MEASURES TO ASSESS THE IMPACT OF ORGANIZATION DEVELOPMENT INTERVENTIONS

Diane L. Lockwood and Fred Luthans

Inevitably, at some time during the career of every organization development (OD) change agent, he or she confronts the enigmatic question "How is it possible to know if what is being done in this organization is really effective?" Obviously, the answer is to *measure* the impact of interventions. Not so obvious, however, are the criteria used to assess so-called "effectiveness" and the particular methods or tools employed to collect data. All change agents have their "pet" assessment tools such as pre- and post-intervention surveys, formal interviews, informal discussions with managers and others, "hard" data from company records, or systematic observations of organizational behavior. Relying unduly on any one particular assessment tool, however, is behaving somewhat like the child who, given a hammer, proceeds to pound everything with it. In other words, it is no more plausible to rely on one method or only a few methods of assessment than it is to use the same type of OD intervention strategy regardless of the particular needs and constraints of the client organization. Sechrest (1971) suggests that any single data-collection method, to a greater or lesser extent, is fallible in its validity and that proper recognition of the effects of the method on assessment techniques is lacking. Webb, Campbell, Schwartz, and Sechrest (1966) have, therefore, maintained that "it is convergence in the consistency and direction of findings yielded by a combined series of different measures, each with its idiosyncratic weaknesses, which leads to the most fertile search for validity" (p. 174).

Taking the lead of Webb et al. (1966), we are suggesting that OD practitioners and researchers should employ a multiple approach to measuring the nature and extent of organizational change. Specifically, the purposes of this paper are (1) to survey the different methods and techniques currently used to assess the impact of OD interventions; (2) to discuss the strengths and weaknesses that characterize these methods; and, finally, (3) to suggest some alternative but heretofore seldom-used methods of data collection and measurement that could be used in future assessment research.

Measurement of the impact of planned-change programs is greatly dependent on *what* criterion variables are selected to be analyzed and *how* data relevant to these variables are collected. For example, criterion variables used to assess organizational change may include overall performance, productivity, employee satisfaction, and/or profit. These variables, in turn, may be operationalized and measured by utilizing employee and supervisory performance ratings, unit productivity data, self-report satisfaction questionnaires, and/or financial records. Obviously, these examples of criterion variables are not the only ones that may be used to assess change. Furthermore, the above variables may be operationalized and measured in ways different from those previously mentioned. However, it is usually recognized (e.g., Cantalanello & Kirkpatrick, 1968) that four levels of evaluation can best be used to assess the impact of OD interventions:

An earlier version of this paper was presented at the Midwest Academy of Management meeting, Milwaukee, Wisconsin, 1977.

a. *Affective Reactions:* participants' attitudinal responses to the intervention program *per se* (e.g., Did participants *like* the program? Did they find it interesting, useful, or beneficial?);

b. *Learning:* participants' understanding and retention of material covered in the program (e.g., Did participants *learn* anything as evidenced by, for example, pre-post difference scores on multiple-choice tests, follow-up interviews, or open-ended survey responses?);

c. *Behavioral Changes:* participants' actual behavioral changes on the job, as evidenced by, for example, observational response frequency charts;

d. *Performance Changes:* "hard" organizational measures (e.g., productivity and quality rates, sales volume, profit, absenteeism, and turnover), as well as more subjective performance appraisal ratings.

All too often we are tempted to stop at the first level of analysis (affective reactions), or, conversely, we jump to the fourth level (performance changes) without an adequate assessment of learning and behavioral-change correlates of organizational performance changes. Obviously, various assessment techniques are more or less appropriate to these different levels of evaluation.

ASSESSMENT TECHNIQUES FOR OD

Five assessment methods (the questionnaire, the interview, observation, archives, and self-generated measures) are reviewed here with special emphasis given to the strengths and limitations of each (see Table 1). This list of methods is not intended to be exhaustive, but it does include the most common and potentially useful techniques.

The Questionnaire

In the behavioral sciences as a whole, research and resulting field applications are based largely on questionnaire data. In a recent literature review of organization development research, Pate, Nielsen, and Bacon (1976) found that over half the studies did not employ any data-collection methods other than attitude and perception questionnaires. A quick examination of any journal in the field of organization change gives evidence of the reliance on questionnaire instruments.

Advantages

Reasons for the extensive use of questionnaires are obvious. First, there are numerous standard questionnaires that are easily accessible to evaluators. This availability eliminates the tedious rigor and time involved in developing new instruments for each assessment effort. Second, questionnaires are relatively easy to administer. This becomes an especially important consideration when data are collected at multiple points in time for purposes of longitudinal analyses. Third, questionnaires do have certain advantages over other assessment techniques. In general, the positive aspects of questionnaires include the following:

a. ability to generalize is greater in comparison to other more situationally bound methods (e.g., "critical incident" methods);

b. restrictions on content are minimal;

c. high reliability can be obtained by using standardized procedures that are generally known and successfully tested;

d. clarification and depth of responses are possible when open-ended items are included on the instrument.

University Associates

Disadvantages

On the other hand, questionnaires also have some severe limitations. Webb et al. (1966) have emphasized that questionnaires tend to be highly reactive and obtrusive. In other words, when respondents are aware that their behavior is under scrutiny, their behavior changes on this basis alone. Questionnaires also may lack validity. Even though a questionnaire may have reliability (consistency and accuracy), this is not a guarantee of its validity (measurement of what it is supposed to measure). Possible threats to the validity of questionnaires include "social desirability biases" (Golembiewski & Munzenrider, 1975), questionable anonymity, language difficulties, and extreme-response sets. In addition, the concept of individual differences (Guion, 1973) can be particularly problematic. For example, it is difficult to determine whether questionnaire measures of attitudes are more reflective of individual differences in perceptions of different work roles or of the intended properties of the organizational environment. Most importantly, perhaps, questionnaire results should not be regarded as an end in themselves; rather, they should be considered only as a springboard or means to stimulate further discussion and analysis of the issues surfaced.

Questionnaires are obviously needed for a variety of reasons, but they should clearly not be the only measure used and should always be used in combination with other measures. A multiple-measure approach enables the evaluator to examine the extent of convergence among many different findings. Simply, consistency or inconsistency of findings across different measures is very important to the validity of any assessment effort.

The Interview

Interviews rank with questionnaires as a popular way of gathering data for organizational-change research. White and Mitchell (1976), for example, found that twenty-six out of the forty-four studies reviewed relied on subjective reports by participants as their method of measurement. Despite its popularity, there is a tendency to disparage the interview method on the ground that it yields qualitative "anecdotal" or "testimonial" evidence. The advantages are seldom recognized. (See Jones, 1973, for a full consideration.)

Advantages

According to Crano and Brewer (1973), the interview represents one of the most useful methods of data collection in the hypothesis-generation phase of a study or a systematic assessment. Rather than arbitrarily choosing a specific set of hypotheses from the multitude of possibilities, the evaluator can more clearly focus efforts through the use of questioning techniques in an interview. Such interviewing can lead to a concrete, manageable series of propositions. Lofland (1971) provides a useful guide for conducting such interviews.

Interviews also have the advantage of flexibility. There is the possibility of exploiting an unexpected lead or of probing ambiguous responses (Sechrest, 1971). Finally, the interview can be legitimately employed in a field setting to cross-validate obtained relationships. For example, one study of organizational change (Benedict, Calder, Callahan, Hornstein, & Miles, 1967) found that qualitative data and the interviewees' impressions prior to seeing the data agreed that the OD intervention was not successful.

One comparison of questionnaire and interview data that was collected by one of the authors in a consulting project is shown in Figure 1. Using the interview transcripts, frequency counts of specific responses were made by two highly trained interviewers working independently. Items on which the coders agreed were retained for the content analytic summary report. Comparison of the data yielded by the two methods, summarized in Figure 1, illustrates that there is substantial agreement between the two results, although

Questionnaire Item

Which of the following best describes how problems are resolved *between* departments in this organization?

1975 (pre) %	1976 (post) %	
11.7	7.8	(1) Little is done about these problems—they continue to exist.
15.6	8.6	(2) Little is done about these problems—they work themselves out in time.
7.8	11.7	(3) The problems are appealed to a higher level—but are still not resolved.
39.8	40.6	(4) The problems are appealed to a higher level—and are usually resolved.
25.0	31.3	(5) The problems are worked out at the level where they appear through mutual effort and understanding.

Content Analytic Summary of Interview Responses

Q. 13 "How are conflicts *between* departments resolved?"

Time 1. Summary for January 1975

The most frequent response was "by discussion between the department heads involved." In descending order of frequency, other responses included: (1) president has the final say; (2) they are turned over to a higher authority; (3) not sure they ever get resolved, or we work around them; (4) by edict, or people pull rank; (5) arbitration by insurance committee; and (6) "don't know" or "no response."

Time 2. Summary for October 1976

"Personal contact between the department heads involved" was by far the most frequent response. The second most frequent response was "if the conflict is not resolved at the first level, it is sometimes necessary to go up a level." "By using OD process" was also a frequent response. Finally, five respondents mentioned that they "didn't know of any conflict."

Changes from Time 1 to Time 2

Responses in period 2 were more consistent than in period 1. That is, a variety of methods were stated in period 1 as opposed to "resolution primarily at the level where the conflict occurred" in period 2. The application of OD principles was evident in period 2. Finally, comments pertaining to "they never get resolved" appeared less frequently in period 2 than in period 1.

Figure 1. Sample Comparison of Questionnaire and Interview Data

the interview data are relatively more explanatory. Such convergence of results yielded by two different methods increases the validity of the assessment.

Disadvantages

Serious weaknesses to the method of interviewing, however, are that it can be extremely costly and time consuming. In addition, similar reactive threats to validity discussed under questionnaires also apply to interviews.

Observation

Ideally, the evaluation of organizational change should follow three major stages:

1. First, there should be *systematic observation* of the change that occurs in the actual setting. This observation in the naturalistic setting allows the assessor to suggest functional or causal relationships between the change technique and its intended effect.

2. Second, the suggested *relationships should be isolated* and verified under more highly controlled experimental (field or laboratory) settings.
3. Finally, there should be a *re-evaluation* and *verification* of the findings in the second stage through systematic observation in the naturalistic setting.

Traditionally academic researchers have ignored the first and third phase and concentrated on experimental studies; OD practitioners have done a peripheral, nonsystematic job of the first and third steps and ignored the second experimental step. What is called for is *systematic* observational techniques that precede and follow the more scientifically rigorous experimental methods (e.g., control-group designs) of evaluation of organizational-change efforts.

Advantages

Observational techniques have very distinct advantages as a basic data-collection method for the assessment of organizational change. Even relatively unstructured observations can provide initial descriptive information useful in the construction of a category system for investigating previously unexplored phenomena. Bales' (1950) early work with interaction analysis, for example, was originally developed by utilizing a series of relatively unstructured observations of group processes. Later Mintzberg (1973) developed an effective observational method to describe characteristics that typified the nature of managerial work. Another example is the use of observational techniques by Benedict et al. (1967) to provide a detailed content-and-process summary of group meetings within an educational system. Written or tape-recorded "process observations" by participants in OD team skill-training sessions are an example of the way observational analyses can be conducted. Also, Nadler, Jenkin, Miruis, and Macy (1975) have urged the use of structured observations of task characteristics for validating the assessment of job-enrichment interventions. To help the practitioner better understand and use the mechanics of systematic observation and analysis, the work by Lofland (1971) is suggested.

Probably the greatest single advantage of the measurement technique of observation is that it can minimize respondent reactions. The key to this advantage is to use natural participant or "confederate" methods and to conduct the observation unobtrusively. It may not be as difficult as it sounds. Margulies and Wallace (1973) point out that with a little practice managers and secretaries alike can become skillful in the use of structured observations. Furthermore, these employees are a natural part of the organizational environment. An example of an unobtrusive observational approach is the measurement of physical distance between interacting persons (Hall, 1963, 1966). A relatively large physical distance may be indicative of stress in supervisor-subordinate relationships.

Methods for observing and recording nonverbal behaviors are reviewed by Knapp (1972). As previously discussed, instruments are subject to biases about social desirability, particularly with "leadership style" questionnaires. That is, respondents assume that some styles are more socially acceptable than others and thus create an evaluation bias. Every internal psychological dimension, according to Webb et al. (1966), can be expected to manifest itself in a variety of ways, some more or less accessible to observation. The point is that the gathering of observational data appears to be limited only by the creativity and imagination of the evaluator.

Disadvantages

The disadvantages inherent in observational techniques are fairly apparent. First, when the behavior being observed is obtrusively recorded, these techniques are subject to the same response biases as questionnaires and interviews. Although the highest ethical standards must always be maintained, observational methods should be as unobtrusive as possible: hidden, secretive recording is not called for; common sense is.

Second, a primary consideration in any method of assessment is its reliability: "Do the ratings of two or more observers who have witnessed the same event(s) coincide?" Agreement between raters is the major goal, since, without it, little use can be made of the unreliable data. Unless the data are *reliable*, they cannot be *valid*. Paul, Robertson, and Herzberg (1969) were able to obtain reliable data (i.e., data with high rater agreement) from unobtrusive observational techniques in a research and development department of a major chemical firm.

Other potential methodological problems with observational techniques are observer bias, changes in standards of observation over time, and high dross (useless data) rates (Webb et al., 1966). However, used appropriately, observational methods can be a valuable *supplement* to almost any other kind of measurement in OD assessment.

Archives (Organizational Records)

Public and private organizations continuously keep numerous records that reflect various dimensions of organizational performance. Productivity, quality rates, profit, cost, grievances, absenteeism, and turnover are common examples. Nadler et al. (1975) developed some useful behavioral economic measures that include standardized methods of data retrieval from archival records. Longitudinal data on hard measures of organizational performance, however, are notably absent in the OD assessment literature (Nielsen & Kimberly, 1974).

Perhaps a major reason for the under-utilization of hard measures is that the dominant way of thinking about organizational behavior purports that attitudinal changes precede behavioral or performance changes. It follows, then, that change agents will concentrate their assessment efforts on attitudinal rather than on performance changes. However, if a behavioristic instead of a cognitive perspective is taken, the behavioral, not the attitudinal, link to performance is emphasized more. There is as much evidence that behavioral changes lead to attitudinal changes as there is for the reverse. For example, Porter and Lawler (1968) have demonstrated that performance *led to* satisfaction. Furthermore, quantifiable performance data are, from a pragmatic viewpoint, generally preferred by top management to other "soft" attitudinal measures.

Once again, the suggestion is not that assessment of attitudes should be abandoned when determining the impact of OD interventions; rather, attitudinal data should always be used in combination with other quantifiable, archival measures of performance. Such emphasis would enhance the overall credibility of OD as a viable change strategy.

Advantages

Archival data have certain clear advantages when compared to other assessment measures. For example, archival data generally do not prompt reactions since the records constitute a natural part of the organizational environment; they have been compiled for other than current purposes. In addition, archival data are "just lying there" and thus cost little to obtain and are usually readily accessible. Another big advantage of archival data is that they allow evaluation over changing conditions and times and thus are particularly suitable for longitudinal analyses of organizational change.

Disadvantages

Just as with other techniques, caution must be exercised in the interpretation of archival data. First, information contained in organizational records may be selectively edited in order to make the figures "look good." In other words, "the statistical lie" syndrome is often present. Consequently, organizational records should be checked against other reports for validity. Second, archival data are subject to intra-instrument processes (Campbell & Stanley, 1966) in which record-keeping procedures may change over time. This problem is especially acute if a large personnel turnover or absenteeism rate is evident. Therefore, if possible, basic record-keeping procedures for performance assessment should be held constant throughout the period of evaluation. Record-keeping procedures should also be the same across comparison groups.

A third problem encountered in the use of archival data concerns what Meyer (1971) calls "the mushy measurements problem." Clearly, many contaminating variables affect performance measures, and, consequently, the interpretation of organizational change is difficult. Normal fluctuations in business cycles, large wage settlements, and new competitors are only a few examples of contaminating variables that may be beyond the control of the evaluator but that nevertheless affect performance measures. If care is taken to recognize and account for record-keeping errors, however, they need not preclude the use of archives as an effective method for assessing the impact of OD interventions.

Self-Generated Measures

There are some occasions on which dimensions of organizational change can be measured by those directly involved. For instance, organizational participants are often the only ones who can realistically determine which specific behaviors will have the greatest impact on performance. Data relevant to such performance-related behaviors can then be used to assess organizational change. Examples of self-generated measures include action plans, objectives used in management by objectives (MBO), behavioral-frequency charts, self-recorded performance check-off systems, and behaviorally anchored rating scales (BARS).

Action planning is commonly used in OD survey feedback and team-building techniques to identify: (1) *what* has to be done (goals); (2) *how* it is going to be done (processes and procedures); (3) *who* is going to be involved and who is responsible; and (4) *when* it is going to take place (start/finish dates). Once organizational goals or objectives are identified by participants in the planned-change process, means for attaining those goals must be specified in ways that are quantifiable, i.e., measurable. For example, if one objective of an employment agency is to increase job placements by 10 percent by the end of the following year, then the *number* of job placements is quantifiable. Similarly, if one supporting aim of the employment firm is to increase the number of phone calls made by personnel agents to client organizations, then the number of phone calls made in a given time period is quantifiable. In this manner, progress data generated from follow-up studies of action plans could be measured and analyzed to assess changes in organizational performance. Similar data are generated using MBO techniques.

Another method of collecting quantifiable performance-related data is by the use of response-frequency charts generated during organizational behavior-modification interventions (Luthans & Kreitner, 1975). In this approach, performance-related behaviors are first identified and then their occurrences are charted over a specified time period. Data collected from the tally sheets can be analyzed to assess quantifiable performance changes tracked over time.

Specific employee behaviors related to organizational performance can also be measured by the appraisal technique of behaviorally anchored rating scales (BARS). In essence, the BARS instrument is developed by asking supervisors to identify behaviors directly relevant to job performance. Supervisors then rate employee performance on the basis of these behaviors, and items with low interrater reliability are discarded. According to Cummings and Schwab (1973), the BARS technique is still subject to most of the limitations inherent in questionnaires (e.g., reactive effects), but it does appear to have at least two major advantages. First, items are tested on supervisors within the organization to determine the extent of intercoder reliability. Second, the supervisors' participation aids in the development of scales with a high degree of relevant meaning to the users of the instrument.

Advantages and Disadvantages

The fact that self-generated measures represent the respondents' own criteria for effectiveness and that these measures are usually flexible enough to be tailored to the relevant situation are two of their advantages. In addition, because these measures are collected in most organization development interventions and some appraisal programs, they are easily obtained for analysis. However, there is the possibility that the data in self-generated measures will be distorted because the respondent is obviously aware that he or she is being measured. Therefore, the researcher should always check the accuracy of self-reports by cross-validating them with other measures. On the other hand, there is some evidence (Emery Air Freight, 1973) to indicate that valuable data may be obtained by positively reinforcing accurate, not necessarily good, self-recorded behavior. Finally, and perhaps most importantly, self-generated measures are an invaluable mechanism for immediate and ongoing performance feedback to employees.

SUMMARY AND IMPLICATIONS FOR THE FUTURE

The use of multiple assessment measures that compensate one another in strengths and weaknesses adds an important degree of validity to the conclusions concerning the impact of OD interventions. It must be recognized that no single measure is satisfactory by itself; all measures are subject to the effects of the particular method. Recognition of the factors that jeopardize the reliability and validity of measures as well as their consistency of findings is critical to the meaningful assessment of organizational change.

Professional respectability should not be based on the particular methods by which data are collected. Rather, the key should be the validity and appropriateness of the measuring techniques as applied to the specific organizational setting. Recent critical self-appraisals by many organizational practitioners and researchers have resulted in a renewed appreciation for data-collection methods other than questionnaires and interviews. Following the lead of Webb et al. (1966), it is suggested that increased attention be given to the availability of organizational-change assessment methods such as (1) naturalistic observations, (2) participant observations, (3) archival data retrieval, and (4) self-generated measures.

Clearly, a major task confronting future OD change agents is the determination of specific "if-then" contingency relationships (Luthans, 1976) between various types of OD interventions and the most effective assessment methods appropriate to a given client organization. Ideally, a contingent relationship of this nature would take the following form: "*Given* X intervention(s), *then* a combination of A, B, and C methods would be most appropriate to assess organizational impact along specified criteria."

Unfortunately, OD assessment research appears to be lagging far behind the practice of OD. Thus, specification of such verifiable contingency relationships is not yet possible. Moreover, the particular combination of measures that would be most appropriate depends on the idiosyncratic characteristics of a given client organization. Renewed attention is, however, being paid to assessment by both practitioners and academicians. It is hoped that this discussion has made the reader more aware of the methodological options available, as well as of the necessity for using multiple measures, in assessing organization development change efforts.

Table 1. Methods Used to Assess the Impact of OD Interventions

Method	Examples	Type(s) of Data Generated	Strengths	Limitations
Questionnaire/ Survey	• Michigan Organizational Assessment Package (Nadler, 1975) • Quality of work life or climate surveys • Job Diagnostic Survey (Hackman & Oldham, 1974) • Job Orientation Inventory (Blood, 1969) • Study of Values (Allport, Vernon, & Lindzey, 1960) • Managerial Grid (Blake & Mouton, 1964) • Various instruments contained in Pfeiffer & Jones (1972-1980) • Sociometric choice questionnaires • Tests/exams	• Affective reactions: attitudes, satisfaction, personality, preferences, perceptions, motivations, values • Demographic details: age, sex, job position, salary, length of service, education, location • Structural variables: hierarchy, span of control, decentralization, ownership, departmentation, environment • Subjective performance ratings (e.g., employee or supervisory performance appraisal forms) • Learning and understanding of concepts	• Ease of administration, especially for longitudinal purposes • Relatively low cost of processing results • Ease of generalizing results in comparison to more situationally bound methods • Assurances of anonymity of responses • Known reliability with standardized instruments • Few restrictions on content	• Obtrusiveness (e.g., "social desirability" response biases) • Individual differences in interpretation of items and scales • Reactive effects of testing in which a pretest becomes an intervention in itself • Questionable validity • Need to exercise caution when making inferences from attitudinal to behavioral or performance data
Interview	• Individual: one-on-one interchange with internal or external change agent in which responses and questions vary on a continuum from unstructured (open-ended) to structured • Work groups: interviews with intact work units using group-on-group techniques, tape recordings, etc.	• Affective reactions (e.g., attitudes, perceptions, likes/dislikes, desired changes) • Descriptive (e.g., organizational policies and procedures, organizational history, job descriptions, long- and short-range goals) • Processes (e.g., decision making, communication, planning, control, coordination, conflict management)	• Virtually unrestricted content, depending on the nature of the questions asked • Usefulness in hypotheses-generation phase to identify critical variables • Flexibility to probe ambiguous questions and responses	• Cost and time necessary to conduct and process • Reactive effects: interviewee self-selection of information and interviewer perceptual biases • Less amenability to quantitative analysis • Difficulty of generalizing results

Table 1 (continued)

Method	Examples	Type(s) of Data Generated	Strengths	Limitations
Interview *(Continued)*			• Ability to give change agent some indication of clients' willingness to confront issues (i.e., climate of trust) • Increase in the probability that individuals will be involved in subsequent action and follow-up because of specific attention paid them	
Observation	• Unstructured naturalistic observation of ongoing phenomena to develop categorical schemes (Mintzberg, 1973; Bales, 1950) • Content analysis of journal, client log, or calendar entries • Deposit studies (famous content of the "trash can" studies, Webb et al., 1966) • Structured participant observation or "confederate" studies of ongoing phenomena	• Virtually unlimited (e.g., affective reactions; descriptive structural learning: behavioral, performance, process data)	• Provision of insight into previously unexplored phenomena, thus facilitating development of new categorical schemes • Minimal respondent reactivity, depending on the degree to which observers and methods constitute a natural part of the original environment • Reliable results, provided high intercoder agreement achieved • Provision of construct validation for instruments, using comparison of "known groups" methods, enhancing meaningfulness and relevancy of data generated	• Cost and (especially) time needed to record and process • Need for internal "confederates" or access to the client organization over an extended period of time • Requirement of a high level of expertise in the initial stages of development • Ethical issues surrounding unobtrusive data collection • Observer biases, although minimized when intercoder agreement is achieved • Changes in standards of observation when different observers are used at different times

Table 1 (continued)

Method	Examples	Type(s) of Data Generated	Strengths	Limitations
Archives	• Organizational history documents	• Corporate by-laws, stock issuance and transfers, minutes from board of directors' meetings, policies of all types	• Relative inexpensiveness and minimal time necessary to collect, particularly if ongoing in-house MIS records are used	• "Selective editing" of records or "doctored" reports
	• Productivity records	• Quantity, quality, ratio, or percentage data (e.g., productivity, quality, maintenance, scrap, sales, inventory control rates)	• Top management's preference of quantifiable performance data to other more qualitative data	• Susceptibility to changes in record-keeping procedures over time, thus making comparisons across time difficult
	• Financial records	• Fiscal data (e.g., profit/loss, return on investment, labor cost, support system cost, forecasting errors, taxes, reserves, bank notices, stockholders' dividends)	• Particular suitability to longitudinal, forecasting, and quantitative decision-making techniques	• "Mushy measurements" problem, which contributes to the difficulty of data interpretation
	• Personnel records	• Job descriptions, promotion-demotion, transfers, recruitment, exit or debriefing data, attendance, absenteeism, turnover rates, grievances		
	• Time records	• In/out time, overtime, turn-around time, shipping or delivery time, claim processing time		
	• Government regulatory reports	• OSHA safety records, EPA, EEOC/affirmative action, Labor Department, SEC, FDA, Treasury Department, ICC, FAA, FCC, etc.		

Table 1 (continued)

Method	Examples	Type(s) of Data Generated	Strengths	Limitations
Self-Generated	• Action plans • MBO • Behavioral frequency charts • Behaviorally Anchored Rating Scales (BARS) • Performance check-off systems (e.g., number of units completed, customer service calls, pickup and delivery logs) • Employee-completed performance appraisals and career development self-assessments	• Learning and development • Behavioral • Performance	• Relative inexpensiveness when collected as part of ongoing organizational activities • Particular usefulness for follow-up studies that assess progress toward goals and objectives • Ability to determine coder reliability and accuracy of recording through cross-checking of reports • Likelihood of generating meaningful and valid data because of employees' active participation in assessment • A potentially valuable mechanism for immediate and ongoing feedback	• Reactive effects: possible recorder biases in self-assessment strategies • Need to exercise caution when making inferences from behavioral data to affective or psychological states • Possibility of overloading employees with paperwork

REFERENCES

Allport, G. W., Vernon, P. E., & Lindzey, G. *Study of values test booklet.* Boston: Houghton Mifflin, 1960.

Bales, R. F. *Interaction process analysis.* Reading, MA: Addison-Wesley, 1950.

Benedict, B. A., Calder, P. H., Callahan, D. M., Hornstein, H. A., & Miles, M. A. The clinical-experimental approach to assessing change efforts. *Journal of Applied Behavioral Science,* 1967, *2,* 347-380.

Blake, R. R., & Mouton, J. S. *The managerial grid.* Houston, TX: Gulf Publishing, 1964.

Blood, M. R. Work values and job satisfaction. *Journal of Applied Psychology,* 1969, *53,* 456-459.

Campbell, D. T., & Stanley, J. C. *Experimental and quasi-experimental designs for research.* Chicago: Rand McNally, 1966.

Cantalanello, R. F., & Kirkpatrick, D. L. Evaluating training programs. *Training and Development Journal,* May 1968, *22,* 2-9.

Crano, W. D., & Brewer, M. B. *Principles of research in social psychology.* New York: McGraw-Hill, 1973.

Cummings, L. L., & Schwab, D. P. *Performance in organizations.* Glenview, IL: Scott-Foresman, 1973.

Emery Air Freight. Positive reinforcement boosts performance. *Organizational Dynamics,* Winter 1973, pp. 41-50.

Golembiewski, R. T., & Munzenrider, R. Social desirability as an intervening variable in interpreting organization development effects. *Journal of Applied Behavioral Science,* 1975, *11,* 317-332.

Guion, R. M. A note on organization climate. *Organizational Behavior and Human Performance,* 1973, *9,* 120-125.

Hackman, J. R., & Oldham, G. R. The job diagnostic survey and an instrument for diagnosing the motivational potential of jobs. *Technical Report No. 4* (Department of Administrative Sciences), Yale University, 1974.

Hall, E. T. A system for the notation of proxemic behavior. *American Anthropologist,* 1963, *65,* 1003-26.

Hall, E. T. *The hidden dimension.* New York: Doubleday, 1966.

Jones, J. E. The sensing interview. In J. E. Jones & J. W. Pfeiffer (Eds.), *The 1973 annual handbook for group facilitators.* San Diego, CA: University Associates, 1973.

Knapp, M. L. *Nonverbal communication in human interaction.* New York: Holt, Rinehart and Winston, 1972.

Lofland, J. *Analyzing social settings.* Belmont, CA: Wadsworth, 1971.

Luthans, F. *Introduction to management.* New York: McGraw-Hill, 1976.

Luthans, F., & Kreitner, R. *Organizational behavior modification.* Glenview, IL: Scott-Foresman, 1975.

Margulies, N., & Wallace, J. *Organizational change: Techniques and applications.* Glenview, IL: Scott-Foresman, 1973.

Meyer, H. H. Practical problems in implementing field research studies. *Academy of Management Proceedings,* 1971, *31,* 72-80.

Mintzberg, H. *The nature of managerial work.* New York: Harper & Row, 1973.

Nadler, D. A. (Ed.). *Michigan organizational assessment package: Progress report II.* Ann Arbor, MI: Institute for Social Research, University of Michigan, 1975.

Nadler, D. A., Jenkin, G. D., Miruis, P. H., & Macy, B. A. A research design and measurement package for the assessment of quality of work interventions. *Academy of Management Proceedings,* 1975, *35,* 360-362.

Nielsen, W. R., & Kimberly, J. R. The impact of organization development on the quality of organizational output. *Academy of Management Proceedings,* 1974, *34,* 528-529.

Pate, L. E., Nielsen, W. R., & Bacon, P. C. Advances in research on organization development: Toward a beginning. *Academy of Management Proceedings,* 1976, *36,* 389-394.

Paul, W. J., Robertson, K. B., & Herzberg, F. Job enrichment pays off. *Harvard Business Review,* 1969, *47,* 61-78.

Pfeiffer, J. W., & Jones, J. E. (Eds.). *The annual handbook for group facilitators* (1972-1980). San Diego, CA: University Associates, 1972-1980.

Porter, L. W., & Lawler, E. E. *Managerial attitudes and performance.* Homewood, IL: Irwin, 1968.

Sechrest, L. Unobtrusive measures in data collection. *Academy of Management Proceedings,* 1971, *31,* 58-66.

Webb, E. J., Campbell, D. T., Schwartz, R. D., & Sechrest, L. *Unobtrusive measures: Nonreactive research in the social sciences.* Chicago: Rand McNally, 1966.

White, S. E., & Mitchell, T. R. Organization development: A review of research content and research design. *Academy of Management Review,* 1976, *1,* 57-73.

Diane L. Lockwood is a Ph.D. candidate at the University of Nebraska and senior associate at Nielsen & Associates, Lincoln, Nebraska. She has done extensive consulting in organization development and served as an external change agent for various government agencies concerned with the status of women. Her areas of interest include organization behavior, speech communication, individual management development, program evaluation, flexitime, and organization development.

Fred Luthans, Ph.D., is regents professor of management, the University of Nebraska, Lincoln, Nebraska. He has published more than a dozen books and numerous articles and papers. A consulting co-editor for the McGraw-Hill Management Series, Dr. Luthans also is on the editorial boards of a number of journals. He is an active consultant and conducts workshops on behavioral management in this country and abroad.

INTRODUCTION TO THE RESOURCES SECTION

ON THE NATURE OF MAXIMALLY SOFT TOOLS

This section of the *Annual* has always been the most varied and unpredictable. The resources we thought of when we created this section were not of the physical, concrete, or "hard" type but rather were informational or "soft." We thought it might be useful to readers to publish a list of growth centers or a selective annotated bibliography on small groups; we did not think deeply on the nature of information and its use. In the past decade the study of how knowledge—valid information—is translated into use has grown and developed into a field of social science research known to those active in it as "KD & U," or knowledge dissemination and utilization.

Theorists in communication science, most notably Marshall McLuhan, have focused on the new electronic mass media and their effects on our social systems. In examining an earlier medium, print, McLuhan (1969) took a similar approach, showing how print technology altered and affected patterns of perception and of social conduct. Such analyses, useful as they are, seem to neglect the major impact of the social system itself as a medium of communication, a fact long known by scholars—rural sociologists interested in the spread of the use of hybrid corn (Lionberger, 1954), medical sociologists examining the pattern of adoption of new drugs (Menzel & Katz, 1955-1956), or political sociologists investigating how voting choices are made and the impact of political campaigns (Lazarsfeld, Berelson, & Gaudet, 1948).

These scholars identified patterns of interaction that showed how new information—innovation—is disseminated by means of a system of social interaction. They did not, however, do much to apply that knowledge, with the exception of some rural sociologists who showed the Department of Agriculture how to run the U.S. Agricultural Extension System more effectively (so that farms would adopt more of the scientific innovations). Only recently have some social scientists, most notably Rogers (1962) and Havelock (1969), begun to show how it is possible to apply what is known about social systems as a medium of communication to cause (or improve) the adoption of innovations.

At least three important kinds of knowledge are necessary to diffuse and implement innovations effectively, in addition to knowledge about the innovation itself. First, those who would cause innovation to be adopted must have knowledge and skill in the area of *social interaction* or, more commonly, human relations. This, of course, is our stock in trade and the primary occupation of most *Annual* users. It is important, however, to realize that group facilitators are interested in the adoption of interpersonal and group interaction skills as innovations and must therefore also understand the other two knowledge and skill areas if their innovations are to be successfully adopted. Moreover, since the specialized training skills of group facilitators are necessary for effective adoption of any innovations, facilitators should be alert to training needs that are associated with efforts to implement innovations. Interaction skills are needed by Peace Corps volunteers trying to gain adoption of simple technological innovations (such as boiling water), by computer system engineers installing technologically sophisticated innovations (such as a new organizational inventory system), and by school administrators developing new programs (such as "mainstreaming"—the inclusion of children with special needs in regular classrooms).

Second, effective KD & U requires a practical understanding of *social networks*. Conceptually, this is just an extension of sociometry, the mapping of social interaction patterns. Most group facilitators are implicitly, if not explicitly, aware of the sociometric pattern of interaction in a small group. Causing effective adoption of innovations requires taking this perspective and applying it on a larger scale, to an organization, a set of organizations, a community, a city, or even a nation. While not necessarily difficult to conceptualize, it may often be hard to specify concretely the members of a network or draw its precise configuration. Usually one must directly observe and identify network members and measure through interview or questionnaire the pattern or configuration.

Third, successful KD & U depends on *linkage* of two types: *conceptual*—the process of linking knowledge about the innovation from the knowledge producers to the users—and *practical*—finding or developing "linking agents," people who can act as linkers as well as identify the appropriate linkages that must be made (in terms of social networks).

This section of the *Annual* has, in past volumes, touched upon each of these knowledge and skill areas. First, we have organized significant content materials broadly concerned with human relations training. Our intent in this respect has not been comprehensiveness but rather a focus on basic or key content areas: OD terms and concepts (1973); small-group training research (1977, 1979); current work on the nature of the helping process (1975). We have tried, unlike some publications of resources, to be highly selective in determining the content of this section.

Second, we have focused on networks: the "Association for Humanistic Psychology Growth Center List" (1977, 1979); a directory of consulting organizations (1975); graduate programs in applied behavioral science (1978); human relations training in Europe (1973). Networks consist of people and organizations that have been, are, or are likely to be in contact (linked) due to some common interest, and our concern in this section of the *Annual* has been with networks that are of particular relevance to group facilitators and to the field of human relations training.

Third, we have touched upon the issue of linkage, albeit indirectly, by providing a list such as "Alphabet Soup" (1972), consisting of organizations that *might* be linked in certain ways for certain purposes, thus identifying components of potential social interaction networks.

Of course, the Resources section is by no means so perfectly focused as we might wish it to be. We have in the past included—and will probably continue to include—miscellaneous topical items of interest, as well as materials concerning the "hardware" side of human relations training (such as selecting sites, 1978, and purchasing video equipment, 1979). We continue to welcome suggestions for this section of the *Annual*.

This year we include four resource items: a detailed reference glossary of OD terms, to supplement the OD jargon dictionary in the 1973 *Annual;* a listing of professional associations by alphabetical abbreviation, an update of the 1972 list; a directory of consulting organizations, an update of the 1975 list; and an annotated bibliography on career development.

REFERENCES

Havelock, R. G., Guskin, A., Frohman, M. A., Havelock, M., Hill, M., & Huber, J. *Planning for innovation*. Ann Arbor, MI: Institute for Social Research, The University of Michigan, 1969.

Lazarsfeld, P. F., Berelson, B., & Gaudet, H. *The people's choice: How the voter makes up his mind in a presidential campaign* (2nd ed.). New York: Columbia University Press, 1948.

Lionberger, H. F. The relation of informal social groups to the diffusion of farm information in a northeast Missouri farm community. *Rural Sociology*, 1954, *19*, 233-243.

McLuhan, M. *The Gutenberg galaxy: The making of typographic man*. New York: New American Library, 1969.

Menzel, H., & Katz, E. Social relations and innovations in the medical profession: The epidemiology of a new drug. *Public Opinion Quarterly*, 1955-1956, *19*, 337-352.

Rogers, E. M. *Diffusions of innovations*. New York: Free Press, 1962.

A BRIEF GLOSSARY OF FREQUENTLY USED TERMS IN ORGANIZATION DEVELOPMENT AND PLANNED CHANGE

Marshall Sashkin

This glossary is intended to provide clear definitions of the most important concepts and terms in common use by organization development (OD) practitioners and applied behavioral scientists. Each term is referenced with the most basic—not necessarily the most current—discussions. The terms included here overlap to some extent with those listed by Vaill (1973), but where he concentrated on the common jargon of the profession, the focus here is on the basic concepts, with definitions in some depth.

This glossary was started in the early 1970s, has gone through numerous updates and revisions, and has been distributed informally among colleagues. In preparing the present version for publication, the author found himself pleasantly suprised at how few major revisions or additions were needed. Of course, quite a few new jargon terms have developed over the past few years, but these refer for the most part to specific interventions, such as Oshry's "Power Labs," rather than to basic ideas, approaches, or issues. An example of the latter type of addition is the concept of "quality of work life," a notion that has become increasingly important during the late 1970s.

The seeming scarcity of such major new ideas might be due to the author's increasing narrowness of interest within OD. He would prefer, however, to believe that OD is "settling down" as an area of applied behavioral science, that the basic concepts and approaches are increasingly well-defined, and that truly new ideas will appear as developments of these basic concepts rather than as previously unheard-of discoveries. It is hoped that the user will find the present glossary an aid in the professional application of behavioral science. In using this glossary the reader is advised to check for more than one word in a phrase. For example, "entry" is listed under "point of entry" and alphabetized under "p." At the end of each glossary item is a brief list of primary sources that the user can consult for an in-depth treatment of that topic.

Action-Research: Coined by Lewin, this type of activity involves active collaboration between a client and change agent for the purpose of solving client problems through research activity followed by change actions and evaluation of the effects of actions taken. In addition, general scientific research knowledge is often gained through action-research. Bennis et al. (1969) note that

> Lewin . . . was preoccupied with [the] issue of the relationship between the abstract and concrete. He once compared this task to the building of a bridge across the gorge separating theory from full reality [see Maier, 1965, Chapter 1]. "The research worker can achieve this only if, as a result of a constant intense tension, he can keep both theory and reality fully within his field of vision" (Lewin, 1948). (p. 4)

Lewin (1951) also said: "Even experiments which are designed to solve theoretical problems presuppose close cooperation between the research worker and the practitioner . . . and the recognition that any such research on groups is, to a degree, social action" (p. 168).

Corey (1953) provides a well-stated outline of action-research: Studies must be undertaken by those who may have to change the way they do things as a result of the studies . . . [T]hey must . . . identify the practices that must be changed . . . try out those practices that give better promise, and methodically and systematically gather evidence to test their worth. This is the process I call action-research. (p. viii)

Action-research is not the same as OD but can be and has been applied to OD activity. (Primary sources for further study: Bennis, Benne, & Chin, 1969; Clark, 1972; Corey, 1953; Frohman, Sashkin, & Kavanagh, 1976; Lewin, 1948, 1951.)

Authentic-Nonauthentic Relationships: Traditional management values, stressing the impersonal task-oriented nature of organizations, lead to nonauthentic relationships. Such relationships are characterized by the use of coercion, as being unhelpful, closed to change, and basically false. Nonauthentic relationships do not allow feelings that occur in task and organizational contexts to be expressed openly. Nonauthentic relationships lead to decreased interpersonal competence (q.v.), which produces mistrust, conflict, conformity, rigidity, etc., which finally results in negative effects on organizational effectiveness (q.v.). The above line of thought is developed most fully by Argyris (1962) and describes, essentially, Likert's (1967) "System 1" as operating under McGregor's (1960) "Theory X." Etzioni (1969) refers to "inauthentic" relationships as characteristic of the institutions upon which modern society is based. (Primary sources for further study: Argyris, 1962; Schein & Bennis, 1965.)

Change Agent: Person involved in helping to create planned change in an organization, usually not a formal, permanent member of the system, although this is not always the case (see *Inside-Outsider*). Change agents are professionals, often with doctoral degrees in the behavioral or social sciences. They are quite varied in goals, theoretical orientations, and methods used, but are for the most part concerned with human relationships, within and among groups of individuals. Changing relationships is seen as the means for changing organizations. The term change agent is being used less, it seems, in favor of such terms as "OD consultant," "OD practitioner," and "interventionist" (see *Intervention*). This shift may be due to an increased focus on the role of permanent organization members in actually creating and carrying out organizational change. (Primary sources for further study: Bennis, 1966, 1969; Havelock, 1973; Havelock & Havelock, 1973; Lippitt, Watson, & Westley, 1958.)

Change Program: Coordinated series of interventions (q.v.), which are seen as interrelated and building upon one another to produce certain changes in the client system. The program may be tightly planned, as in Blake and Mouton's (1969, 1978a) Grid OD, or modified greatly as it continues (e.g., Seashore & Bowers, 1963; Marrow, Bowers, & Seashore, 1967). The crucial factor is that the specific activities involved are interrelated and interdependent, perhaps synergistic, forming an integrated whole that is designed to produce specific changes. (Primary source for further study: Bennis, 1969.)

Client System: The organization involved in a change program in collaboration with a change agent. The client is the group, organization, community, culture, family, club, etc., being helped in some way by the change agent (q.v.). The client is generally a fairly autonomous organization, complete in itself (see *System*). (Primary source for further study: Beckhard, 1969.)

Consultant: May or may not be a change agent (q.v.) and may or may not be involved in organization development (q.v.). The reference here is to a consultant who is a change agent and is involved in OD activities. The change agent/consultant is not a formal member of the client system and, often, is not as totally involved in a change program as a change agent/researcher. Schein (1969), for example, as a consultant, often contracts to spend a certain number of days per month "on site." The consultant engages in specific interventions to work on specific problems, often with top or middle managers exclusively. (Primary

250

sources for further study: Beckhard, 1969; Kolb & Frohman, 1970; Lippitt & Lippitt, 1978; Schein, 1969.)

Confrontation: In a general sense, a basic element in all OD work is that a major aim in OD is for the client system (q.v.) to develop the ability to identify and effectively deal with (confront) problems. Confrontation may occur with respect to problems of either an interpersonal or a nonpersonal nature. Sometimes interpersonal confrontation is prerequisite to effective collaborative work on nonpersonal problems. Interpersonal confrontation may occur between two parties (Schein, 1969) or two groups (Golembiewski & Blumberg, 1968). Confrontation of nonpersonal problems may involve an entire management staff (Beckhard, 1967). Several specific interventions (q.v.) have been designed by OD practitioners to facilitate confrontation of both types (e.g., see Beckhard, 1967; Fordyce & Weil, 1971; Golembiewski & Blumberg, 1968). It is particularly important to note that confrontation, used in the sense given here, does *not* necessarily involve the expression of emotion. When emotions are involved, confrontation may include the stating of and discussion about feelings. (Primary sources for further study: Beckhard, 1967; Fordyce & Weil, 1971; Golembiewski & Blumberg, 1968.)

Content/Process: See *Process Analysis.*

Contingency Theory: "Contingent" means "it depends." Many recent theories in the behavioral sciences are contingency theories. Fiedler (1967), for example, has developed a contingency model of leadership effectiveness, which states that the most effective leadership style depends on certain characteristics of a particular leader in a particular leadership situation.

Lawrence and Lorsch (1969a, b) developed a contingency theory of organizations that states that the most effective organization structure depends on the tasks or functions of the organization and on the characteristics of the environment within which the organization exists. There are three key concepts in their theory. *Differentiation* refers to the extent to which the various subsystems (of which the organizational system is composed, e.g., departments, groups, etc.) are clearly separated according to their function. Differentiation is a more sophisticated term for "division of labor." *Integration* refers to the process by which the differentiated subsystems are "tied together" within the context of the organization as one system. A more common term would be "coordination." *Environmental uncertainty* refers to the "changingness" of the environment within which the organization operates. Changingness refers, for example, to the rate of change in technological development, the rate of change in product demand, and the degree of organizational mobility of the organization members (turnover).

The degree of environmental uncertainty determines the type of integration processes most appropriate for a given organization, as well as the degree of differentiation required. Differentiation, however, also depends on the organization's tasks and functions and also affects the types of integration processes required. Thus, the theory is quite complex, in terms of interaction among the variables of primary concern. There has been at least one attempt, by Beer and his associates, to apply contingency theory in the context of an OD effort, reported by Bennis (1971). (Primary sources for further study: Bennis, 1971; Lawrence & Lorsch, 1969a, b.)

Experiential Learning: Traditionally learning has been thought of as the transmission of information from a book or teacher to the learner or student. In the early part of this century John Dewey pioneered the approach of "learning by doing," a general idea that has developed in a variety of directions (including, for example, vocational education). One offshoot of Dewey's approach has been the experiential method of learning.

In this method, simulations, games, role playing, or various group activities are designed to provide students with a direct experience that exemplifies, illustrates, or simulates the effects that would be experienced in a real-life situation. Students can then define, elaborate, and abstract the concept from the simulated (but concrete) situation. This is part of a learning process that many educators believe is far more effective than the traditional approach of presenting students with abstract concepts which they are to apply to concrete real situations. (Primary sources for further study: Kolb & Fry, 1975; Pfeiffer & Jones, 1979.)

Entry: See *Point of Entry.*

Family Group: Complete work group, consisting of a manager and all immediate subordinates. This term is often used in referring to laboratory training (q.v.) or survey feedback (q.v.).

Feedback: A thermostat sends "feedback" signals to a furnace: it senses when the furnace has increased the temperature in the building to the desired level and signals the furnace to shut off. When the temperature falls below the desired level the thermostat signals the furnace to start up again. Thus, feedback is information sent by one system (q.v.) or part of a system ("subsystem") to another system or subsystem concerning the performance of the receiver and resulting in some change in the action of the receiver. For human systems the changes are usually voluntary rather than automatic. Thus, person A gives person B feedback when A tells B how A perceived B's actions and how those actions affected A. B may then choose to change his or her behavior so that the effects on A will be more desirable from the point of view of both parties. One OD intervention often required is teaching persons in an organization how to give feedback, positive or negative, in helpful and nonthreatening ways. (Feedback is also a basic concept in the science of cybernetics [Wiener, 1954]. In that context the words "positive" and "negative" have different meanings from the use made here.) (See also *Survey Feedback.*) (Primary sources for further study: Anderson, 1970; Gibb, 1961; Maier, 1976.)

Force-Field Analysis: Model for diagnosing and implementing change originated by Kurt Lewin. "Change is an alteration of an existing field of forces" (Bennis et al., 1969, p. 315). Many psychological and social forces are at work in any situation, "counterpoised in dynamic tension. Changes involve a force field with high tension or low tension . . . [thus] we have choice in change . . . we can control some forces and not others . . . we can increase tension or decrease it" (p. 315).

A specific example is given by Maier (1965, pp. 432-433) concerning the forces at work among a group of workers involved in a discussion of a proposed change in work procedures. Morris and Sashkin (1976) give a detailed description and example of the force-field analysis procedure. Bennis et al. (1969) note that "the effective change agent is one who helps a client to recognize the forces in his field, to understand the consequences of manipulating certain forces, and to provide whatever support is needed to take action" (p. 315). (Primary sources for further study: Bennis, Benne, & Chin, 1969; Coch & French, 1948; Lewin, 1958; Morris & Sashkin, 1976.)

Grid OD (Managerial Grid®): Blake and Mouton (1964, 1968, 1969, 1978a) developed this very popular "packaged" OD program, based on the two concepts of "concern for people" and "concern for production." The program consists of six sequential "phases" designed to maximize both these concerns, as measured on nine-point scales and plotted on a "grid." The methods used are based on the idea of "instrumented laboratory training" (q.v.). That is, the training approach is experience-based but highly structured and uses many questionnaire "instruments" and conceptual inputs (readings, lectures). Blake and Mouton set up a highly successful consulting organization, Scientific Methods, Inc., which continues to offer Grid OD training programs to organizational clients. Many organizations have carried out extensive phase one and phase two training programs, but few results have been reported to document the full application of the six-phase OD program. Blake and Mouton (1978b) have most recently argued strongly against the contingency approaches to leadership and management, asserting that while behavioral tactics may appropriately vary, there is one best basic strategy of leadership, involving high concern for both people and production, the style Blake and Mouton term "9,9." (Primary sources for further study: Blake & Mouton, 1964, 1968, 1969, 1978a, 1978b).

Helping Relationship: Carl Rogers (1961) has developed most extensively the idea of the helping relationship. Such a relationship exists between two parties when "at least one of the parties has the intent of promoting the growth, development, maturity, improved functioning, improved coping with life of the other. The other . . . may be one individual or a group . . . One of the participants intends that there should come about, in one or both parties, more appreciation of, more expression of, more functional use of the latent inner resources of the individual" (pp. 39-40). Research has uncovered several characteristics associated with effective helping relationships. Most generally, it is clear that the attitudes and feelings of the helper are more significant than the theoretical orientation. The most significant aspect of the relationship is the perception of the client about the helper's desire to understand the client's meanings and feelings. Also of great importance is the helper's sensitivity to the attitudes of the client and the degree of interest and involvement shown by the helper. Remoteness is not helpful; neither is oversympathy or emotional overinvolvement. (Primary source for further study: Rogers, 1961.)

Insider-Outsider: Lippitt et al. (1958) define a change agent (q.v.) as a person from outside a system who attempts to effect change within the system. Bennis et al. (1969) regard this as too narrow a view, because the essence of organization development (q.v.) is to provide the client system with internal change resources to facilitate problem solving and adaptation. Cartwright (1951) has stated that the system undergoing change must be the source, target, and agent of change if the change is to be successful—a view that is in line with Lewin's idea of action-research (q.v.). Bavelas (1948) has shown, using Lewinian methods, that change introduced at the periphery of a system (from outside) cannot spread faster, and will usually spread much slower, than change introduced within the system.

Current practice commonly involves an internal or inside change agent who works in collaboration with the outside agent(s) as part of a team. The extensive literature on "gatekeepers" (Lewin, 1958) and opinion leaders and, more generally, on the nature of *linkers* in the knowledge-diffusion process (Havelock, 1968) adds support to the concept of the inside-outside change-agent team. (Primary sources for further study: Bennis, Benne, & Chin, 1969; Havelock, 1968.)

Internal Resource Persons: One basic aim of organization development is to change the system so that fuller use is made of internal resources for change, adaptation, and problem solving. This aim is achieved by identifying, training, and involving people within the system who possess or can develop change-oriented skills. Thus, the system is made less dependent on the environment, generally, and on the change agent, specifically, for solutions to problems.

Interpersonal Competence: A concept developed by Argyris (1962) which refers to the degree of skill an individual possesses in creating and continuing authentic relationships (q.v.). Such relationships are characterized by nonevaluative feedback; honest recognition and "ownership" (conscious experience) of one's attitudes, values, and feelings; helping others to recognize and own their attitudes, values, and feelings; and openness to new attitudes, values, and feelings. (Primary source for further study: Argyris, 1962.)

Intervention: One highly specific action taken by a change agent in order to facilitate the change process. Any specific planned activity that "interferes" with a sequence of events by being interposed between two such events, thus changing the nature of the events that follow, is an intervention. Thus, *any* action taken by an OD practitioner with respect to a client system can be seen as an intervention, although the term usually means some specific action designed to facilitate the OD process. Examples could be laboratory training (q.v.) for a top-management group or a halt called by the change agent in a management meeting in order to analyze certain points of process (see *Process Analysis*). Both these activities are specific interventions.

Fordyce and Weil (1971) describe a variety of specific interventions in great detail with instructions for their use and some examples. French and Bell (1978) provide a useful categorization and listing of OD interventions. In a more general sense, Argyris (1970) prefers the term "interventionist" to that of "change agent" (q.v.), since he believes that organizational change must come about through the actions of organization members, not as a direct result of the activity of an outsider. Argyris defines the work of the interventionist as (a) generating valid information; (b) presenting the data to organization members to serve as a basis for informed decisions; and (c) helping to develop commitment to any decisions that are made. (Primary sources for further study: Fordyce & Weil, 1971; French & Bell, 1978.)

Job Enlargement: A job-design change whereby a particular job is expanded by the addition of more specific job elements. The elements usually do not "fit together" to make a "whole" job, in direct contrast to the job enrichment (q.v.) approach. Although it is fashionable to ridicule job-enlargement approaches as giving workers several poor jobs instead of only one, there are some scholars and consultants who believe that providing a degree of task variety through job enlargement can be useful for both the worker and the organization. It is important to be aware that job enlargement has been used as a synonym for job enrichment but that in current usage these terms are not at all synonymous. (Primary sources for further study: Davis & Taylor, 1979; Suojanen et al., 1975.)

Job Enrichment: A technique used most at lowest organizational levels but also applied with increasing frequency at supervisory and management levels. In essence, job enrichment means redesigning a job (Davis, 1966) so that the worker accomplishes a psychologically meaningful task. Workers are motivated to do a good job because the work itself is intrinsically motivating. For example, instead of repeating one operation over and over, a worker becomes responsible for a complete product or, at least, for a complete subproduct. Instead of sewing cuffs on shirts all day, a worker might produce a complete shirt, or might become responsible for finishing all seamwork on a shirt. Extrinsic rewards such as pay and job security become secondary in importance to such intrinsic rewards as achievement and responsibility.

The basic dimensions of job design have only recently been studied in depth (see Hackman & Oldham, 1975). The basic principles of job enrichment go back to the Gestalt school of psychology (Köhler, 1960), although the widespread implementation of job enrichment, particularly at management levels, owes much to the work of Herzberg and his associates (Herzberg, Mausner, & Snyderman, 1959) and followers (Ford, 1969; Myers, 1970). Herzberg (1977) has trademarked the term "Orthodox Job Enrichment," which differs only in that workers whose jobs are redesigned are explicitly excluded from the design process, a practice with which most OD practitioners and organizational psychologists would disagree. (Primary sources for further study: Davis, 1966; Herzberg, 1968.)

Laboratory Training: Includes all experiential training (see *Experiential Learning*). That is, in any type of lab-training situation, individuals learn by experiencing and examining their own behavior in small groups. Although sometimes used interchangeably with sensitivity training, the term laboratory training does not necessarily involve T-groups. There is a particular aim to the training (e.g., improving managers' "styles"), and conceptual and cognitive inputs are generally included (lectures, films, discussions). Lab training includes structured forms of group training. Often "instruments" such as questionnaires or structured exercises are used. Grid OD, for example, is often referred to as "instrumented laboratory training." Trainers are generally more directive and controlling than in T-groups, but this tendency can vary greatly. (Primary sources for further study: Beckhard, 1969; Benne, Bradford, Gibb, & Lippitt, 1975; Bradford, Gibb, & Benne, 1964; Miles, 1959; Schein & Bennis, 1965.)

Linkers: A fairly new field of inquiry concerns the dissemination and utilization of scientific knowledge (D & U). The linking role has been found to be crucial to the dissemination process. That is, the originator of knowledge communicates to an intermediary, who carries the information to the user. Lazarsfeld, Berelson, and Gaudet (1948) found this model to apply to voting behavior and labeled it the "two-step information flow." Menzel and Katz (1955-56) found a similar process involved in physicians' adoptions of a new drug. Lionberger (1953) noted an analogous process in agriculture, with the federal agricultural service agent serving as linker. Linking roles seem to pervade society and organizations as well. Organization development efforts often involve an inside change agent, who links the knowledge of the external change agent with the organizational users of the knowledge (see *Insider-Outsider*). (Primary sources for further study: Havelock, 1968; Havelock et al., 1969; Havelock & Huberman, 1977.)

Linking-Pin: A key concept in Likert's (1961) "new patterns of management." Likert conceives of an organization run by group discussion and decision making at all levels. Each supervisor and subordinates form a "family group" (q.v.), and the supervisor is a member of another family group consisting of peers and superior. Thus, each manager serves as a linking-pin from one level to the next, all the way up and down the hierarchy. Communication is facilitated, while authority becomes a shared group process. (Primary sources for further study: Likert, 1961, 1967.)

Management by Objectives: Term coined by Peter Drucker (1954) but operationalized primarily by Odiorne (1965, 1979). The idea is that every supervisor and subordinate pair in an organization will meet, develop, and agree upon a set of specific measurable job objectives for the subordinate. When supported organizationally, from the top down, MBO has been demonstrated to be effective in improving and maintaining performance (Ivancevich, 1972). Although MBO is often spoken of as though it is by definition an organization-wide, coordinated, OD effort (Beck & Hillmar, 1972), this assumption is frequently not valid. When MBO is applied without long-term top-level support, without extensive training in the method, or to only some departments or units, there is typically no benefit to individuals or system. When properly applied, MBO can be useful by making jobs more clearly defined (reducing role ambiguity) as well as by involving subordinates in setting their own goals and making an open commitment to achieving those goals. (Primary sources for further study: Beck & Hillmar, 1972; Ivancevich, 1972; Levinson, 1970; Mager, 1962; Odiorne, 1979.)

Norms: Homans (1950) says "a norm . . . is an idea in the minds of the members of a group, an idea that can be put in the form of a statement specifying what the members . . . should do, ought to do, and are expected to do, under given circumstances" (p. 123). There is an important difference between measuring norms, as Homans defines the term, and measuring *normative behavior.* While all workers in a group might, for example, say that no one should loaf on the job, that workers ought to produce a fair day's work, and that each worker is expected to put forth his or her best effort on the job, observation of the actual on-the-job behavior of persons in the group may show that the *behavioral* norms of the group run directly counter to their *stated* norms.

The term "organizational norms" refers to statements of behaviors, as defined above, which are shared by the majority of the organization's members. When interdependent groups have radically different norms, or when a substantial minority of the organization's members hold norms that differ greatly from those of the majority, there is likely to be serious intergroup or organizational conflict present. When stated norms are strongly divergent from behavioral norms, it can be generally concluded that there are serious hidden organizational problems. (Primary source for further study: Homans, 1950.)

NTL: The National Training Laboratories, formerly associated with the National Educational Association, are now incorporated as the NTL Institute of Applied Behavioral Science. Among the founders of NTL were Lippitt, Benne, and Bradford. Kurt Lewin played a major role in the founding of NTL, but died before the first laboratory sessions opened in 1947 at the NTL site in Bethel, Maine. NTL still conducts sensitivity training (q.v.) laboratories at Bethel and other sites around the United States. (Primary sources for further study: Back, 1972; Chin & Benne, 1969.)

Organic Systems: Although it is explicitly affirmed by a few OD practitioners that organizations are to be treated as living systems, this view has been a past, unrecognized problem (Katz & Kahn, 1966). Most practitioners now agree that organizations are *not* alive, although they contain living elements (human members). The term "organic," when used in the context of organizations or OD, generally means that the system is an integral whole, a "gestalt." The subsystems are not discrete independent units but must be effectively interdependent if the organization is to continue to exist. These subsystem relationships are often consciously directed by organization members. Thus, "organic" implies a degree of self-determination not found in an interdependent mechanical system (such as an automobile engine). The term "organic system" is often used as a contrast to earlier "mechanistic" approaches to organizations. (Primary sources for further study: Bennis, 1969; Bennis, Benne, & Chin, 1969; Burns & Stalker, 1961.)

Organizational Climate: One of the most used and least well-defined terms in OD. Climate can mean any number of things to different researchers and practitioners. Perhaps the two most frequent uses are (1) a general pattern of management practices and policies (most clearly defined by Likert, 1961, 1967, as "Systems 1, 2, 3, and 4": System 1 is exploitative-authoritative, 2 is benevolent-paternalistic, 3 consultative, and 4 participative); (2) more specifically in reference to "leadership climate" or the general leadership style that predominates in the organization.

Other popular uses of the term include that of Litwin and Stringer (1968) who use it to refer to the general motivation pattern among organization members, which is supported by organizational reward systems, formal and informal—most generally, achievement climate, power-attainment climate, and affiliation climate (derived from Atkinson's work on motivation theory—see Atkinson & Feather, 1966). Thus, Litwin and Stringer specify that the term organizational climate means "the patterns of expectations and incentive values that impinge on and are created by a group of people who live or work together." Blake and Mouton (1969) use the term to refer to the way an organization fits on their people-concern/production-concern grid, claiming that a "9,9" climate (maximum concern for both people *and* productivity) results in greatest organizational effectiveness (q.v.). (Primary sources for further study: Likert, 1967; Tagiuri & Litwin, 1968.)

Organization Development: A planned effort to improve the effectiveness of an entire organizational system through applications of behavioral science knowledge to the processes and structures of the system. Through the OD process of solving organizational problems, people become better able to solve future problems, and the organization becomes more adaptive and more likely to survive and to prosper. (Primary sources for further study: Beckhard, 1969; Bennis, 1969; French & Bell, 1978.)

Organizational Effectiveness: There are a number of ways of looking at organizational effectiveness. For some, effectiveness is measured in "dollar criteria." Others see effectiveness as best defined by how successfully the system adapts to its environment in its battle for survival. Another view (Yuchtman & Seashore, 1967) suggests that effectiveness can be measured by how well an organization obtains and "exploits" the resources available in its environment. Still other views are given by Bennis (1966, 1969) and Beckhard (1969). They argue that effectiveness is best measured in terms of (1) the health of the organization (seen as the physical and psychological health of the members) and the adequate operation of organizational processes and (2) the degree to which certain, specified goals are attained at reasonable cost (in economic terms and considering the effects upon organizational health). (Primary sources for further study: Beckhard, 1969; Bennis, 1969.)

Planned Change: Much of the change that takes place in the world is not planned; it just happens. Ford's invention of the assembly line produced significant changes in American industry that were certainly not planned and not even imagined. Although Katz and Kahn (1966, 1978) argue that major organizational change is always a result of external forces acting upon the changing system, organizational psychologists recognize that for change to be effective (see *Organizational Effectiveness*), the system must be the source and agent of change.

Thus, planned change involves an external change agent (q.v.) who, in a collaborative relationship with individuals and groups within the system, intervenes (see *Intervention*) in ongoing organizational processes in order to produce certain anticipated changes in these processes and in organizational effectiveness. Planned change means that both the change agent *and* those in the system understand the goals of change and the means available for it and can collaboratively choose among those means. Such means must be in accord with the norms and values of those in the system. Often specific interventions will be spontaneous events, but, even though an OD plan is generally seen as tentative, the overall program, in terms of means and ends, is carefully planned. (Primary sources for further study: Bennis, Benne, & Chin, 1969; Bennis, Benne, Chin, & Corey, 1976; Lippitt, Watson, & Westley, 1958.)

Point of Entry: The level of the organization toward which the change agent directs his initial efforts. To some extent, the choice of entry point will depend on the specific organization and the type of OD effort contemplated. Generally, it seems that entry is best made at top-management levels (Argyris, 1962; Beckhard, 1969). At the very least, top-management support and involvement seem prerequisites for successful change. (Primary sources for further study: Beckhard, 1969; Bennis, 1969; Glidewell, 1959.)

Power Equalization (PE): Leavitt (1965) deals extensively with power equalization as a general, people-oriented approach to applied organizational change. Essentially, this approach implies that power should be distributed as equally and generally as possible throughout the system, basically through group decision making. Decisions should be made by groups of persons who have the relevant information and who will be instrumental in actually carrying out the decisions. In terms of an OD change strategy, PE assumes that the distribution of power in the system must be changed and that the way to go about this is by helping organization members to change the system, starting with the development of a collaborative equal-power relationship between the client and external change agent. One basic tool in such an OD effort is sensitivity training (q.v.), itself a power-equalized method, since trainers generally refuse authority and force the group to set its own agenda and expose and solve problems. Bennis (1969) noted that OD avoids the issue of power, but more recently Oshry (1976) has developed a laboratory training approach to help people confront power issues, researchers such as Salancik and Pfeffer (1977) have examined the basis of power in organizations (control of strategic resources), and OD practitioners have begun to examine the issues of power (e.g., Schein, 1977). (Primary sources for further study: Leavitt, 1965; Oshry, 1976.)

Process Analysis: In a group discussion the focus is generally on some specific content topic or issue—the task of the group. But if a group is to become more expert at solving problems, the participants must understand, be aware of, and be skillful in the *process* of group interaction, that is, *how* the group functions rather than *what* is accomplished. T-groups are devoted almost entirely to training the participants in group process dynamics and skills. Most ordinary task-directed groups could also benefit from occasional attention to issues of group process. A skillful change agent (q.v.) or consultant can help groups do this in the course of normal group interaction by intervening in the group's task discussion and leading the group in an analysis of the process of the discussion. Ideally, the group will ultimately be able to switch back and forth from content to process as needs dictate, without outside assistance. (Primary sources for further study: Morris, 1976; Schein, 1969.)

Quality of Work Life (QWL): A broad label for a variety of organizational change programs that seem to share the characteristics of (1) worker (and union) participation in the change, (2) job or task redesign such that jobs form a coherent "whole," and (3) the introduction of work groups or teams (autonomous or semi-autonomous groups) that often take an unusually high degree of responsibility for their own supervision and quality control. Quality-of-work-life programs often explicitly recognize the sociotechnical (see *Sociotechnical Systems*) nature of organizations and involve the redesign of technology. In Europe, QWL efforts may incorporate "worker democracy," meaning the formal participation of workers on boards of directors, with a voice in determining basic organizational policy. In the United States, QWL projects typically involve formal union cooperation and explicitly deny that the program is intended to increase profits or productivity. Some of the most notable QWL projects in Scandinavia (e.g., Volvo) as well as in the United States (e.g., the General Motors Tarrytown, New York, plant) have been undertaken as a response to extreme organizational problems involving worker alcoholism, absenteeism, tardiness, turnover, and grievances. The commonly stated aims of QWL are increased worker satisfaction and organizational viability. Quality-of-work-life efforts are on the increase in the United States, and this trend seems likely to continue for the foreseeable future. (Primary sources for further study: Davis & Cherns, 1975; Mills, 1978; O'Toole et al., 1973.)

Quasi-Stationary Equilibrium: See *Force-Field Analysis* and *Unfreezing, Moving (Changing), Refreezing.*

Resource Person: Generally, an outsider or change agent (q.v.) who possesses certain knowledge or skills that can be drawn upon as needed by the client system (q.v.). One goal of organization development is the identification and training of internal resource persons (q.v.) so that the system need not rely exclusively on external assistance in solving problems, creating organizational change, or adapting to environmental demands.

Sensitivity Training (T-Groups): Developed at NTL (q.v.) in the late 1940s. Groups of about fifteen strangers would meet at an isolated retreat with a trainer for all-day sessions over a period of about two weeks.

> The idea . . . was that participants, staff, and students would learn about themselves and their back-home problems by collaboratively building a laboratory in which participants would become both experimenters and subjects in the study of their own developing interpersonal and group behavior within the laboratory setting. (Chin & Benne, 1969, p. 45)

The group has no agenda and no specified activities. The task of the trainer is to establish a climate of trust and acceptance. Trainers' behaviors and their specific "interventions" (q.v.) vary greatly but are always aimed toward the goal of establishing a climate wherein the individuals can feel free and safe enough so as to reveal themselves openly. By doing this, they can receive honest and accurate feedback about themselves and their behavior. "The concern of the T-group is with the immediate existential confrontation, the here-and-now experience" (Winn, 1966, p. 175).

T-groups are not therapy groups, but *training* groups ("training" being what the "T" stands for). They are immensely involving and are not intended for individuals with severe personal or emotional problems, but for basically healthy individuals.

A major problem in the use of T-groups in organization development is that the learning that occurs is on an individual level. When the individual returns to the job setting, all the social forces (see *Force-Field Analysis*) that operated to produce and reinforce old behaviors are still in effect, and these forces act against change. Often the effect of training is lost because the individual cannot put learnings into effect. For this reason, modified T-groups were developed, referred to broadly as laboratory training (q.v.).

There are several types of sensitivity training groups.

The "cousin" group consists of a "diagonal slice" across the organizational chart. The people in a specific T-group are not from the same department and are not functionally related. The "family" laboratory involves two or three hierarchical levels of a division, department, or plant. The "interface laboratory" consists of an intergroup set-up like staff-line or head office-plant personnel, functionally related. (Winn, 1966, p. 174)

The idea here is that individuals in the back-home environment will reinforce each other's new learnings, since they have a common, shared experience. But these groups also present a "danger": participants face their associates, superiors, and subordinates in an environment that includes not only current data but also past experiences and anxieties, frustrations, and feelings generated by those experiences. No certain answer exists about the effectiveness of sensitivity training. Much depends on the organization involved; in some cases, T-groups would clearly not be desirable (see Schein & Bennis, 1965). In some cases sensitivity training has been shown to be highly successful in aiding improved organizational (and personal) effectiveness (q.v.). Most research studies indicate that sensitivity training does have some effect in changing values, attitudes, and behavior, but that specific changes are hard to predict and may be negative as well as positive. Perhaps as many as 10 percent of the people attending a sensitivity-group training experience suffer some lasting psychological harm. (Primary sources for further study: Back, 1972; Bradford, Gibb, & Benne, 1964; Campbell & Dunnette, 1968; Cooper, 1977; Lieberman, Yalom, & Miles, 1973; Schein & Bennis, 1965; Winn, 1966.)

Sociotechnical Systems: Von Bertalanffy (1950) has demonstrated the importance of viewing biological systems as open systems (see *System*), that is, open to influence from external sources due to the interchange with the environment. The same can be said of social systems. Perhaps the single most important external system that influences any social system is the technology within which the social system is operating. Trist (1969) has shown that in modern industry the social and technological systems are so interdependent that it is not possible to be concerned with one without showing equal concern for the other. Thus, modern organizations are sociotechnical systems and, moreover, *open* sociotechnical systems—open, that is, to the influence of the social and technical environments.

The social organization of workers is greatly affected by the technology of the work, although for any given technology it is usually possible for the social sysem to be varied and still get tasks accomplished adequately. Trist (1969), describing one investigation, says:

So close was the relationship between these two aspects that the social and the psychological could be understood only in terms of the detailed engineering facts and of the way in which the technological system as a whole behaved in the environment. (pp. 272-273)

The 1980 Annual Handbook for Group Facilitators

Although it is popular among organizational psychologists to acknowledge the importance of regarding systems as social *and* technical, this viewpoint has not really been reflected in research and practice until very recently, especially with respect to quality-of-work-life (q.v.) change projects. (Primary sources for further study: Pasmore & Sherwood, 1978; Trist, 1969; Trist & Bamforth, 1951.)

Source, Target, Agent of Change: In a change effort it is possible to identify the source of change, the target of change, and the agent of change. However, as Cartwright (1951) and Caplan (1967) have stated, change can be successfully attained *only* when the system undergoing change is not just the target but also the source and agent of change. Such a notion fits with the concept of power equalization (q.v.) and accounts for the effort by an external change agent to establish a collaborative relationship with the client, so that the client can act as the source of change and the agent of change. (Primary source for further study: Cartwright, 1951.)

Survey Feedback: A specific type of organization development intervention, developed by Mann (1957) and others at the Survey Research Center of the Institute for Social Research (University of Michigan). Survey data is analyzed and summarized so that individual respondents (and sometimes even small groups) are anonymous. The data are then "fed back" (see *Feedback*) to the originators, typically in family-group (q.v.) meetings. The data serve as a focus for group discussions at all levels of the organization concerning improvements indicated by or derivable from the data. This approach to OD seems most useful when combined with a variety of other interventions as part of a broad OD program. (Primary sources for further study: Bowers, 1973; Bowers & Franklin, 1972; Mann, 1957; Neff, 1965; Taylor & Bowers, 1972.)

System (Open System): Any relatively independent, organized, functioning, autonomous unit is a system—e.g., the solar system, the eco-system, a political system, organizational systems, and the nervous system. All are influenced by one another. Although human beings are barely on the verge of directly influencing the solar system, we obviously affect all the other systems cited.

Organizations were in the past viewed as closed social systems, in which the dynamics of an organization were internally determined, chiefly on the basis of precisely defined roles and role relationships. This view is, however, not generally true. All systems are more or less open to direct or indirect influence from sources outside the system boundaries. More recent conceptions have defined organizations as systems of human social relationships. This definition is also inadequate, for organizations are affected by other than social factors (see *Sociotechnical Systems*). Systems are *differentiated,* composed of numerous parts or subsystems that must then be *integrated* into a smoothly functioning whole. Differentiated subsystems define the organizational structure, while integration is a continuous process. Both factors are open to environmental influences. (Primary sources for further study: Ashby, 1958; Katz & Kahn, 1966, 1978; Von Bertalanffy, 1950, 1956.)

System 4: Catchword for the "participative" management model developed by Likert (1961, 1967; see also Bowers, 1972). "System 1" conforms to McGregor's (1960) "Theory X," involving exploitative authoritarian management; "System 2" is run by a paternalistic, benevolent despot; "System 3" involves some degree of consultation of lower levels, with decision-making authority remaining concentrated at upper levels; and "System 4," much like McGregor's (1960) "Theory Y," involves full participation of all organization members in decisions directly relevant to their work activities.

The two fundamentals of System 4 are the "principle of supportive relationships":

The leadership and other processes of the organization must be such as to ensure a maximum probability that in all interactions and in all relationships within the organization, each member, in the light of his

University Associates

background, values, desires, and expectations, will view the experience as supportive and one which builds and maintains his sense of personal worth and importance" (Likert, 1961, p. 103) and the process of group decision making using the linking-pin (q.v.) concept. (Primary sources for further study: Bowers, 1972; Likert, 1961, 1967.)

Task/Process: See Process Analysis.

Team Development (Team Building): A general category of OD interventions (q.v.) that are designed to help members of a work team or a management group improve the ways they work together as a cohesive team, particularly with regard to interpersonal relationships, but also with respect to specific task-directed activity. Team development generally involves some form of laboratory training (q.v.), with all group members participating as a team. (Primary sources for further study: Fordyce & Weil, 1971; Reilly & Jones, 1974.)

Temporary Systems: A short-term social system designed to accomplish some express purpose, aim, or function. A project work team is a temporary system, for when the project is completed the group disbands. Temporary systems can also be used to create organizational change. For example, a residential laboratory or workshop and a temporary change-planning group are temporary systems used as part of a change strategy. The aim of such devices is the re-education of persons and of role occupants in various social systems. (Primary sources for further study: Bennis & Slater, 1968; Chin & Benne, 1969; Miles, 1964.) 1964.)

Unfreezing, Moving (Changing), Refreezing: The three phases of change as conceived by Lewin (1958). Lewin's use of the terms refers to force-field analysis (q.v.). In any social situation there exists a field of social forces that maintains people's behavior within certain limits. This is a "quasi-stationary equilibrium." To alter the behavior of persons in the situation the equilibrium must be shifted to a new level. *Unfreezing* involves altering the limits of the equilibrium by creating the awareness of a need for change and a desire for change. *Moving* involves actively manipulating certain of the social forces, decreasing those pressing toward a less desirable level of behavior and increasing those pressing toward a more desirable level of behavior. Thus, the equilibrium level is shifted toward the more desirable level of behavior. Finally, in *refreezing*, the equilibrium is stabilized at this level, insuring that the social forces will remain stable and will not revert to the prior state. Lewin (1958) notes that "the unfreezing of the present level may involve quite different problems in different cases" (p. 211).

Most generally, the system involved (person or organization) must be made aware of the forces in the situation and of a need for change. In other words, a "felt need" regarding the undesirability of present behavior must become conscious. Often this involves "pain." Lippitt et al. (1958) provide further detail on these phases of change. Although this process sounds abstract, Lewin (1947, 1958) provides concrete illustrations. Schein (1964) gives an application of Lewin's framework to individual change. (Primary sources for further study: Lewin, 1947, 1958; Schein, 1964.)

REFERENCES

Anderson, J. Giving and receiving feedback. In G. W. Dalton, P. R. Lawrence, & L. E. Greiner (Eds.), *Organizational change and development*. Homewood, IL: Irwin-Dorsey, 1970.

Argyris, C. *Interpersonal competence and organizational effectiveness*. Homewood, IL: Irwin-Dorsey, 1962.

Argyris, C. *Integrating the individual and the organization*. New York: Wiley, 1964.

Argyris, C. *Intervention theory and method*. Reading, MA: Addison-Wesley, 1970.

Ashby, W. R. General systems theory as a new discipline. *General Systems Yearbook*, 1958, 3, 1-6.

Atkinson, J. W., & Feather, N. T. (Eds.). *A theory of achievement motivation*. New York: Wiley, 1966.

Back, K. *Beyond words*. New York: Russel-Sage Foundation, 1972.

Bavelas, A. A mathematical model for group structures. *Applied Anthropology*, 1948, 7, 16-30.

Beck, A. C., Jr., & Hillmar, E. D. *A practical approach to organization development through MBO.* Reading, MA: Addison-Wesley, 1972.

Beckhard, R. The confrontation meeting. *Harvard Business Review*, 1967, 45(2), 149-153.

Beckhard, R. *Organization development: Strategies and models.* Reading, MA: Addison-Wesley, 1969.

Benne, K. D., Bradford, L. P., Gibb, J. R., & Lippitt, R. (Eds.). *The laboratory method of changing and learning.* Palo Alto, CA: Science and Behavior Books, 1975.

Bennis, W. G. *Changing organizations.* New York: McGraw-Hill, 1966.

Bennis, W. G. *Organization development: Its nature, origins, and prospects.* Reading, MA: Addison-Wesley, 1969.

Bennis, W. G. (chairperson) *Improving integration between functional groups: A case in organization change and implications for theory and practice.* Symposium held at the 74th annual convention of the American Psychological Association, Washington, D.C., September 3, 1971. (Participants: Michael Beer, Gerald R. Pieters, Samuel H. Marcus, Alan T. Hundert, and Paul R. Lawrence.)

Bennis, W. G., Benne, K. D., & Chin, R. (Eds.). *The planning of change* (2nd ed.). New York: Holt, Rinehart and Winston, 1969.

Bennis, W. G., Benne, K. D., Chin, R., & Corey, K. *The planning of change* (3rd ed.). New York: Holt, Rinehart and Winston, 1976.

Bennis, W. G., Schein, E. H., Steele, F. I., & Berlew, D. E. (Eds.). *Interpersonal dynamics* (Rev. ed.). Homewood, IL: Dorsey Press, 1968.

Bennis, W. G., & Slater, P. E. *The temporary society.* New York: Harper & Row, 1968.

Blake, R. R., & Mouton, J.S. *The managerial grid.* Houston, TX: Gulf, 1964.

Blake, R. R., & Mouton, J.S. *Achieving corporate excellence through Grid organization development.* Houston, TX: Gulf, 1968.

Blake, R. R., & Mouton, J.S. *Building a dynamic corporation through Grid organization development.* Reading, MA: Addison-Wesley, 1969.

Blake, R. R., & Mouton, J.S. *The new managerial grid.* Houston, TX: Gulf, 1978. (a)

Blake, R. R., & Mouton, J.S. Interview. *Group & Organization Studies*, 1978, 3, 401-426. (b)

Bowers, D. G. *System 4: The ideas of Rensis Likert.* Ann Arbor, MI: University of Michigan Press, 1972.

Bowers, D. G. OD techniques and their results in 23 organizations. *Journal of Applied Behavioral Science*, 1973, 9, 21-43.

Bowers, D. G., & Franklin, J. L. Survey guided development: Using human resources management in organizational change. *Journal of Contemporary Business*, 1972, 1(3), 43-55.

Bradford, L. P., Gibb, J. R., & Benne, K. D. *T-group theory and laboratory method.* New York: Wiley, 1964.

Burns, T., & Stalker, G. M. *The management of innovation.* London: Tavistock, 1961.

Campbell, J. P., & Dunnette, M. D. Effectiveness of T-group experiences in managerial training and development. *Psychological Bulletin*, 1968, 70, 73-104.

Caplan, N. Motivation and behavior change. In Industrial Relations Research Association, *Proceedings*, Winter, 1967.

Cartwright, D. Achieving change in people: Some applications of group dynamics theory. *Human Relations*, 1951, 4, 381-392.

Chin, R., & Benne, K. D. General strategies for effecting changes in human systems. In W. G. Bennis, K. D. Benne, and R. Chin (Eds.), *The planning of change* (2nd ed.). New York: Holt, Rinehart and Winston, 1969.

Clark, P. A. *Action research and organizational change.* London: Harper & Row, 1972.

Coch, L., & French, J. R. P., Jr. Overcoming resistance to change. *Human Relations*, 1948, 1, 512-533.

Cooper, C. L. Adverse and growthful effects of experiential learning groups. *Human Relations*, 1977, 30, 1103-1129.

Corey, S. M. *Action research to improve school practices.* New York: Bureau of Publications, Teachers College, Columbia University, 1953.

Davis, L. E. The design of jobs. *Industrial Relations*, 1966, 6, 21-45.

Davis, L. E., & Cherns, A. B. (Eds.). *The quality of working life* (2 vols.). New York: Free Press, 1975.

Davis, L. E., & Taylor, J. C. *Design of jobs* (2nd ed.). Santa Monica, CA: Goodyear, 1979.

Drucker, P. *The practice of management.* New York: Harper & Row, 1954.

Etzioni, A. Man and society: The inauthentic condition. *Human Relations*, 1969, 22, 325-332.

Fiedler, F. E. *A theory of leadership effectiveness.* New York: McGraw-Hill, 1967.

Ford, R. N. *Motivation through the work itself.* New York: American Management Association, 1969.

Fordyce, J., & Weil, R. *Managing with people.* Reading, MA: Addison-Wesley, 1971.

French, W. L., & Bell, C. H., Jr. *Organization development* (2nd ed.). Englewood Cliffs, NJ: Prentice-Hall, 1978.

Frohman, M. A., Sashkin, M., & Kavanagh, M. J. Action-research applied to organization development. *Organization and Administrative Sciences*, 1976, pp. 129-161.

Gibb, J. R. Defensive communication. *Journal of Communication*, 1961, 11, 141-148.

Glidewell, J. C. The entry problem in consultation. *Journal of Social Issues*, 1959, 15(2), 51-59.

Golembiewski, R. T., & Blumberg, A. The laboratory approach to organization change: "Confrontation design." *Academy of Management Journal*, 1968, *11*, 199-210.

Hackman, J. R., & Oldham, G. Development of the job diagnostic survey. *Journal of Applied Psychology*, 1975, *60*, 159-170.

Havelock, R. G. Dissemination and translation roles. In T. L. Eidell and J. M. Kitchell (Eds.), *Knowledge production and utilization in educational administration*. Eugene, OR: University Council for Educational Administration and Center for the Advanced Study of Educational Administration, University of Oregon, 1968.

Havelock, R. G. *The change agents' guide to innovation in education*. Englewood Cliffs, NJ: Educational Technology Publications, 1973.

Havelock, R. G., & Havelock, M. G. *Training for change agents*. Ann Arbor, MI: Institute for Social Research, The University of Michigan, 1973.

Havelock, R. G., Guskin, A. E., Frohman, M. A., Havelock, M., Hill, M., & Huber, J. *Planning for innovation*. Ann Arbor, MI: Institute for Social Research, The University of Michigan, 1969.

Havelock, R. G., & Huberman, A. M. *Solving educational problems*. Paris, France: UNESCO, 1977.

Herzberg, F. One more time: How do you motivate employees? *Harvard Business Review*, 1968, *46*(1), 53-62.

Herzberg, F. I. Orthodox job enrichment. *Defense Management Journal*, 1977, *13*(2), 21-27.

Herzberg, F., Mausner, B., & Snyderman, B. *The motivation to work* (2nd ed.). New York: Wiley, 1959.

Homans, G. C. *The human group*. New York: Harcourt, Brace, 1950.

Ivancevich, J. M. A longitudinal assessment of management by objectives. *Administrative Science Quarterly*, 1972, *17*, 126-138.

Katz, D., & Kahn, R. L. *The social psychology of organizations*. New York: Wiley, 1966. (2nd ed., 1978)

Köhler, W. *Dynamics in psychology*. New York: Grove Press, 1960. (New York: Liverright, 1940)

Kolb, D. A., & Frohman, A. L. An organization development approach to management consulting. *Sloan Management Review*, 1970, *12*, 51-65.

Kolb, D. A., & Fry, R. Towards an applied theory of experiential learning. In C. L. Cooper (Ed.), *Theories of group processes*. London: Wiley, 1975.

Lawrence, P. R., & Lorsch, J. W. *Organization and environment*. Homewood, IL: Irwin, 1969. (a)

Lawrence, P. R., & Lorsch, J. W. *Developing organizations: Diagnosis and action*. Reading, MA: Addison-Wesley, 1969. (b)

Lazarsfeld, P.F., Berelson, B., & Gaudet, H. *The people's choice* (2nd ed.). New York: Columbia University Press, 1948.

Leavitt, H. J. Applied organizational change in industry: Structural, technological, and humanistic approaches. In J. G. March (Ed.), *Handbook of organizations*. Chicago: Rand-McNally, 1965.

Levinson, H. Management by *whose* objectives? *Harvard Business Review*, 1970, *48*(4), 125-134.

Lewin, K. Frontiers in group dynamics. *Human Relations*, 1947, *1*, 5-42.

Lewin, K. *Resolving social conflicts*. (G. Lewin, Ed.) New York: Harper & Row, 1948.

Lewin, K. *Field theory in social science*. (D. Cartwright, Ed.) New York: Harper, 1951.

Lewin, K. Group decision and social change. In E. E. Maccoby, T. M. Newcomb, & E. L. Hartley (Eds.), *Readings in social psychology* (3rd ed.). New York: Holt, Rinehart and Winston, 1958.

Lieberman, M. A., Yalom, I.D., & Miles, M. B. The impact of encounter groups on participants: Some preliminary findings. *Journal of Applied Behavioral Science*, 1972, *8*, 29-50.

Lieberman, M. A., Yalom, I. D., & Miles, M. B. *Encounter groups: First facts*. New York: Basic Books, 1973.

Likert, R. *New patterns of management*. New York: McGraw-Hill, 1961.

Likert, R. *The human organization*. New York: McGraw-Hill, 1967.

Lionberger, H. F. Some characteristics of farm operators sought as sources of farm information in a Missouri community. *Rural Sociology*, 1953, *18*, 327-338.

Lippitt, R., & Lippitt, G. L. *The consulting process in action*. San Diego, CA: University Associates, 1978.

Lippitt, R., Watson, J., & Westley, B. *The dynamics of planned change*. New York: Harcourt, Brace & World, 1958.

Litwin, G. H., & Stringer, R. A., Jr. *Motivation and organizational climate*. Boston: Division of Research, Graduate School of Business Administration, Harvard University, 1968.

Mager, R. *Preparing instructional objectives*. Belmont, CA: Fearon, 1962.

Maier, N. R. F. *Psychology in industry* (3rd ed.). Boston: Houghton-Mifflin, 1965.

Maier, N. R. F. *The appraisal interview* (Rev. ed.). San Diego, CA: University Associates, 1976.

Mann, F. C. Studying and creating change: A means to understanding social organization. In Industrial Relations Research Association (C. M. Arensberg, Ed.), *Research in industrial human relations*. New York: Harper, 1957. (IRRA publication no. 17)

Marrow, A. J., Bowers, D. G., & Seashore, S. E. *Management by participation*. New York: Harper & Row, 1967.

McGregor, D. M. *The human side of enterprise*. New York: McGraw-Hill, 1960.

Menzel, M., & Katz, E. Social relations and innovation in the medical profession. *Public Opinion Quarterly*, 1955-56, *19*, 337-352.

Miles, M. B. *Learning to work in groups*. New York: Bureau of Publications, Teachers College, Columbia University, 1959.

Miles, M. B. On temporary systems. In M. B. Miles (Ed.), *Innovation in education.* New York: Bureau of Publications, Teachers College, Columbia University, 1964.

Miles, M. B., Hornstein, H. A., Callahan, D. M., Calder, P. H., & Schiavo, R. S. The consequence of survey feedback: Theory and evaluation. In W. G. Bennis, K. D. Benne, and R. Chin (Eds.), *The planning of change* (2nd ed.). New York: Holt, Rinehart and Winston, 1969.

Mills, T. Europe's industrial democracy: An American response. *Harvard Business Review,* 1978, 56(6), 143-152.

Morris, W. C. Combining observation and participation in a problem solving group. In W. C. Morris and M. Sashkin, *Organization behavior in action.* St. Paul, MN: West, 1976.

Morris, W. C., & Sashkin, M. *Organization behavior in action.* St. Paul, MN: West, 1976.

Myers, M.S. *Every employee a manager.* New York: McGraw-Hill, 1970.

Neff, F. W. Survey research: A tool for problem diagnosis and improvement in organizations. In S. M. Miller and A. W. Gouldner (Eds.), *Applied sociology.* New York: Free Press, 1965.

Odiorne, G. *Management by objectives.* New York: Pittman, 1965.

Odiorne, G. *Management by objectives II.* Belmont, CA: Fearon-Pittman, 1979.

Oshry, B. Power and the control of structure. *Social Change,* 1976, 6(3), 1-2ff.

O'Toole, J. (Chairman) and associates. *Work in America.* Cambridge, MA: MIT Press, 1973.

Pasmore, W. K., & Sherwood, J. J. *Sociotechnical systems.* San Diego, CA: University Associates, 1978.

Pfeiffer, J. W., & Jones, J. E. Introduction. In J. W. Pfeiffer & J. E. Jones, *Reference guide to handbooks and annuals* (3rd ed.). San Diego, CA: University Associates, 1979.

Reilly, A. J., & Jones, J. E. Team-building. In J. W. Pfeiffer & J. E. Jones (Eds.), *The 1974 annual handbook for group facilitators.* San Diego: CA: University Associates, 1974.

Rogers, C. R. *On becoming a person.* Boston: Houghton-Mifflin, 1961.

Salancik, G. R., & Pfeffer, J. Who gets power—and how they hold on to it. *Organizational Dynamics,* 1977, 5(3), 3-21.

Schein, E. H. The mechanisms of change. In W. G. Bennis, E. H. Schein, F. I. Steele, and D. E. Berlew (Eds.), *Interpersonal dynamics.* Homewood, IL: Dorsey, 1964.

Schein, E. H. *Process consultation: Its role in organization development.* Reading, MA: Addison-Wesley, 1969.

Schein, E. H., & Bennis, W. G. *Personal and organizational change through group methods.* New York: Wiley, 1965.

Schein, V. E. Political strategies for implementing organizational change. *Group & Organization Studies,* 1977, 2, 42-48.

Seashore, S. E., & Bowers, D. G. *Changing the structure and functioning of an organization.* Ann Arbor, MI: Survey Research Center, Institute for Social Research, The University of Michigan, 1963. (Monograph No. 33)

Seashore, S. E., & Bowers, D. G. The durability of organizational change. *American Psychologist,* 1970, 25, 227-233.

Suojanen, W. W., McDonald, M., Swallow, G. L., & Suojanen, W. W. (Eds.). *Perspectives of job enrichment and productivity.* Atlanta: Publishing Services Division, Georgia State University, 1975.

Tagiuri, R., & Litwin, G. H. (Eds.). *Organization climate: Explorations of a concept.* Boston: Division of Research, Graduate School of Business Administration, Harvard University, 1968.

Taylor, J. C., & Bowers, D. G. *The survey of organizations.* Ann Arbor, MI: Institute for Social Research, 1972.

Trist, E. L. On socio-technical systems. In W. G. Bennis, K. D. Benne, and R. Chin (Eds.), *The planning of change* (2nd ed.). New York: Holt, Rinehart and Winston, 1969.

Trist, E. L., & Bamforth, K. W. Some social and psychological consequences of the longwall method of coal-getting. *Human Relations,* 1951, 4, 3-38.

Vaill, P. B. An informal glossary of terms and phrases in organization development. In J. E. Jones & J. W. Pfeiffer (Eds.), *The 1973 annual handbook for group facilitators.* San Diego, CA: University Associates, 1973.

Von Bertalanffy, L. An outline of general system theory. *British Journal of the Philosophy of Science,* 1950, 1, 139.

Von Bertalanffy, L. General system theory. *General Systems Yearbook,* 1956, 1, 1-10.

Wiener, N. *The human use of human beings.* Garden City, NY: Doubleday, 1954.

Winn, A. Social change in industry: From insight to implementation. *Journal of Applied Behavioral Science,* 1966, 2, 170-183.

Yuchtman, E., & Seashore, S. E. A system resource approach to organizational effectiveness. *American Sociological Review,* 1967, 32, 891-903.

Marshall Sashkin, Ph.D., is a professor of industrial and organizational psychology at the University of Maryland, University College, College Park, Maryland. He is also senior editorial associate with University Associates, San Diego, California. He is a co-author of Organization Behavior in Action *(1976) and* Resourcebook for Planned Change *(1978) and has published numerous articles in scholarly journals. Dr. Sashkin's background is in group dynamics, including leadership and problem solving, human relations training, and organization development consulting with a wide variety of organizations.*

ALPHABET SOUP: 1980 *

Frank Pierce Johnson

The field of applied behavioral science is, like most fields, cluttered with a multitude of initials. Following is an overview of organizations involved to varying degrees in human relations training and related concerns.

AAMC

The *American Association of Marriage Counselors* provides a professional recognition process and a directory of those who are qualified to do marriage counseling. Ray Fowler is the executive director and the address is 225 Yale Avenue, Claremont, CA 91711. Phone: (714) 621-4749.

ACC

The *Association for Creative Change in Religious and Other Systems* was founded in 1968 by a group who shared a mutual concern for applying the tools of social psychology to the life of religious institutions. The original name of the organization was the Association for Religion and Applied Behavioral Science (ARABS). A few years later this was changed to the current title to reflect a broader purpose and membership.

Members of ACC share mutual interests in humanizing organizations and in providing professional standards of competence. The Professional Development Recognition Committee has developed a five-stage process utilizing peer and client evaluation and feedback. ACC keeps an up-to-date list of members who are recognized in the fields of group development, personal growth, organization development, and experiential education. ACC has conferences each year for its membership.

For further information, write Dorothy Brittain, Executive Director, P.O. Box 2212, Syracuse, NY 13220. Phone: (315) 424-1802.

AGPA

The *American Group Psychotherapy Association* includes psychiatrists, psychologists, social workers, and others teaching and practicing in the mental health field. AGPA strongly supports group research and publishes seven journals, including the *International Journal of Group Psychotherapy*. Offices are located at 1995 Broadway, New York, NY 10023. Phone: (212) 787-4900.

AHP

The *Association for Humanistic Psychology* was founded in part as an alternative to the American Psychological Association (APA) (which now has a Division of Humanistic Psychology). The membership is open to all interested in applied behavioral science and the helping professions; a primary value of the organization is humanizing society. The annual meetings often demonstrate the latest experimental approaches within the area of personal awareness and growth. Local chapters provide further opportunity for meetings, and there are annual regional meetings. Dues are $24 annually and include a newsletter and the *Journal of Humanistic Psychology*. For more information, write Elizabeth Campbell, Executive Officer, 325 Ninth Street, San Francisco, CA 94103. Phone: (415) 626-2375.

AMA

The *American Management Association* includes executives in industry, commerce, government, service-oriented and noncommercial organizations, and teachers of management at the college level. Its purpose is clear—to help managers do a better job. AMA provides many educational services to further this goal and has an extensive catalog of courses offered around the United States. Classes and workshops are often presented in cooperation with local business schools. Through its publication division, AMACOM, AMA publishes several practitioner-oriented journals—including *Personnel, Management Review*, and *Organizational Dynamics*—as well as an extensive line of books and tapes, often prepared by the best-known scholars and practitioners. Academic membership dues are around $50 a year; dues for practicing executives are higher. The offices are at 135 W. 50th Street, New York, NY 10020.

AOM

The *Academy of Management* is a research- and teaching-oriented group, composed primarily of full-time college and university faculty members. Members present papers, hold symposia, and sponsor workshops at the annual August meetings. There is a variety of divisions and interest groups. The $26 annual dues include subscriptions to two quarterly journals—the *Academy of Management Journal* and the *Academy of Management Review*—and the *Academy Newsletter*. Membership information is available from Charles R. Kuehl, Director of Membership, School of Business, University of Missouri at St. Louis, St. Louis, MO 63121.

APA

Not to be confused with the "other" APA, the *American Psychiatric Association* is composed of a membership restricted to psychiatrists holding the M.D. degree. An annual convention is held in New York in December. The address is 1700 Eighteenth Street, N.W., Washington, DC 20009.

APA

The *American Psychological Association* was founded in 1892 and has explicit aims: "to advance psychology as a science, as a profession, and as a means of human welfare." Full membership is limited to psychologists or Ph.D.-level people with a primary background in psychology. Associate membership is available for some others. APA is one of the largest organizations of behavioral scientists in the world, publishing numerous research journals and having over thirty special-interest divisions. There are huge annual conventions held over the Labor Day holiday weekend, as well as regional meetings. Dues vary depending on the divisions one belongs to and the journals one subscribes to, but they average over $100. For more information, write the Executive Officer, 1200 Seventeenth Street, N.W., Washington, DC 20036. Phone: (202) 833-7600.

APGA

Not to be confused with the AGPA, the *American Personnel and Guidance Association* is a large organization with broad purposes and a diverse membership. APGA has developed many different divisions in response to the needs of its members, which include guidance personnel in elementary and secondary schools, higher education, community agencies, and organizations of government, business, and industry. Membership means receiving the *APGA Journal*, divisional journals (depending on the divisions one joins), and a newsletter. It also qualifies one for low-cost professional insurance (as does membership in either APA). APGA members meet once a year in a giant convention, within which all the divisions have their own meetings.

For information, write to Charles Lewis, Executive Vice President, 1607 New Hampshire Avenue, N.W., Washington, DC 20009. Phone: (202) 483-4633.

ASA

The *American Sociological Association* is a professional society of sociologists, social scientists, and others interested in research, teaching, and the application of sociology. There are numerous divisions (including a Division of Social Psychology), as well as annual national and regional meetings. For information, write to the Executive Officer, 1772 N. Street, Washington, DC 20036. Phone: (202) 833-3410.

ASTD

The *American Society for Training and Development* is an organization for those who are interested in applying behavioral science to the work environment. ASTD publishes *Training and Development Journal* for its members and a directory, *Who's Who in Training and Development*. Most moderate-sized or large cities have local chapters. The national organization is quite large and has a number of special-interest divisions (including an OD division). Annual dues are around $50. Write Kevin O'Sullivan, Executive Director, P.O. Box 5307, Madison, WI 53705. Phone: (608) 274-3440.

CPA

The *Canadian Psychological Association* is similar to its U.S. counterpart, though smaller. APA and CPA have joint membership provisions. For information, write to the Canadian Psychological Association, 558 King Edward Avenue, Ottawa, Ontario KIN 7N6, Canada. Phone: (613) 238-4409.

IAAP

The *International Association of Applied Psychology* is a true international group, drawing most of its membership from the United States and European countries. A semi-annual journal is published in French and English, and an annual convention is usually held outside the United States. There is a Division of Organizational Psychology. Full membership is open only to Ph.D. psychologists; associate membership is generally open to all. Dues are $15 per year. For information in the United States write to Dr. Harry C. Triandis, 329 Psychology Building, University of Illinois, Champaign, IL 61820. Outside North America, write to the Secretariat, 47 rue César Franck, 4000-Liege, Belgium.

IAASS

The *International Association of Applied Social Scientists* was founded in 1971 to provide a means to accredit professional practitioners in the field of applied behavioral science. IAASS has regional committees that work with people interested in becoming accredited. The organization maintains a current list of those judged to be qualified in laboratory education, organization development, community development, and as internal organization development consultants.

For further information, write: Edwin M. Bartee, Vanderbilt University, Owen Graduate School of Management, 2505 West End Avenue, Nashville, TN 37203. Phone: (615) 322-2534.

ITAA

The *International Transactional Analysis Association* has a variety of membership stages, through which one must pass by taking classes and training seminars. ITAA is an organization of professionals with the primary aim of developing and spreading the quasi-therapeutic approach called transactional analysis (TA) that Eric Berne, a psychiatrist, created based partly on Freudian theory. ITAA is a large organization, publishes a journal and newsletter, and is open (at the introductory level) to anyone seriously interested in TA. For information, write to ITAA, 1772 Vallejo Street, San Francisco, CA 94123.

NTL

National Training Laboratories (NTL) is the pioneer organization in applied behavioral science. It hearkens back to the work of Kurt Lewin, who was the grandfather of us all. It was at Gould Academy in Bethel, Maine, after Lewin's death, that the conference was held in 1947 that led to the organization of National Training Laboratories. The meetings were seen as experimental social interaction laboratories, within which participants could learn about group dynamics. This was the origin of the term "laboratory learning."

NTL began as a nonprofit branch of the National Education Association (NEA), but in 1967 it became a corporation—the NTL Institute for Applied Behavioral Science. NTL publishes a newsletter, *Social Change*, and the *Journal of Applied Behavioral Science*, known to many as *JABS*. NTL as presently constituted is a membership-by-invitation organization. Members conduct laboratories, usually with topical foci (for new women managers, on system power issues, etc.), all over the United States, but the organization remains best known for its summer labs at Bethel. NTL headquarters are at 1501 Wilson Boulevard, Arlington, VA 22209. Inquiries can be directed to Harold L. Hodgkinson, president. Phone: (703) 527-1500.

ODI (IRODP)

The *Organization Development Institute*, also known as the *International Registry of Organization Development Professionals*, was until recently called the Midwest OD Network and was founded in 1968 as the Ohio OD Network. The approximately 250 members are located primarily in the Midwest states, but include people on both coasts as well as a small number of foreign members. ODI sponsors a variety of professional programs throughout the year, including an annual spring "What's New in OD" meeting. Most of the seminars, programs, workshops, etc., are held in the Midwest. There is a monthly newsletter as well as the detailed membership directory, the *IRODP*. The current directory costs $10 and also lists periodicals with OD emphases, local groups or contact persons, other OD associations, academic programs, and OD job-search contacts. There are two primary membership categories: "regular" (no requirements; $30 annual dues) and "professional consultant" (requires academic training, full-time OD experience, and peer and client recommendations; $60 annual dues). Full-time students may join for $20. The monthly newsletters provide very up-to-date information on OD in the United States and Canada.

For more information write to Don Cole, 11234 Walnut Ridge Road, Chesterland, OH 44206.

ODN

One of the primary goals of applied behavioral scientists has been the improvement and humanization of organizational life. The *Organization Development Network* was founded in 1964 to provide affiliation and linkage among people who share such goals and concerns. The ODN is the oldest and largest organization composed solely of OD practitioners.

It was formerly linked with NTL, and its founders and original supporters were NTL staff and associates. In 1975 formal ties with NTL were severed; the ODN is now an independent nonprofit corporation. ODN sponsors semi-annual national meetings in the spring and the fall. There are currently over 1000 members. While the majority of members are OD practitioners who are employed full-time within organizations, a substantial proportion of the membership is academically based. A quarterly newsletter, the *OD Practitioner*, is edited by Larry Porter (P.O. Box 808, L-357, Livermore, CA 94550). The newsletter is distributed free to members; subscriptions are not available. Membership in the ODN is unrestricted and costs $30 a year (corporate memberships are $225 a year). For further information, write: Tony Petrella, 1011 Park Avenue, Plainfield, NJ 27060.

UA

University Associates was founded in Iowa City, Iowa, in 1968 as a collaboration between Bill Pfeiffer and John Jones. In 1973 they moved to San Diego, California. A Canadian office opened in Toronto in 1976, and a European office in Mansfield, England, in 1978. UA is best known as a publisher of human relations training materials, including seven volumes of the *Handbook of Structured Experiences for Human Relations Training;* the *Annual Handbook for Group Facilitators* (1972-1980); a quarterly journal, *Group & Organization Studies;* and a good many books relating to the technology of applied behavioral science. UA staff members conduct training workshops in major cities in the United States and Canada. The UA Graduate School of Human Resource Development was established in 1979 with two learning centers: in Vancouver, Canada, and in San Diego, California. The UA Graduate School offers a Master of Human Resource Management and a Master of Human Resource Development and is authorized by the state of California. For more information, write to University Associates, 8517 Production Avenue, San Diego, CA 92121. Phone: (714) 578-5900.

Here are a few other groups of more specialized interest:

AAPC

American Association of Pastoral Counselors
3 W. 29th Street
New York, NY 10001
Phone: (212) 889-7663

AASECT

American Association of Sex Educators, Counselors, and Therapists
5010 Wisconsin Avenue, N.W.
Washington, DC 20016
Phone: (202) 686-2523

CGSN

Cooperative Goal Structuring Network
162 Windsor Lane
New Brighton, MN 55112

MCCP

Minnesota Couples Communication Program
300 Clifton Avenue
Minneapolis, MN 55403

ODC

O.D. Canada
Robert Lescarbeau, Executive Director
5055 Gatineau
Montreal, Quebec H3V 1E4
Canada

PET/LET/TET/ETW

All of these refer to applications of Thomas Gordon's communication skill training approach (for parents, leaders, teachers, and women).

Effectiveness Training Associates
110 S. Euclid Avenue
Pasadena, CA 91101

RET

Rational Emotive Therapy Institute
45 E. 16th Street
New York, NY 10021

VC (Values Clarification)

National Humanistic Education Center
110 Spring Street
Saratoga Springs, NY 12866

Frank Pierce Johnson is an assistant clinical professor at the Institute of Psychiatry and Human Behavior, Medical School, University of Maryland, College Park, Maryland, and a group counselor at the University's Counseling Center. His background is in Jungian psychology and Gestalt group work, and he has served as a consultant to many industrial, religious, and educational organizations. He is the co-author or author of numerous articles.

APPLIED BEHAVIORAL SCIENCE CONSULTING ORGANIZATIONS: AN UPDATED DIRECTORY

In the 1975 *Annual* we published a directory of applied behavioral science consulting organizations as a resource for both consultants and those seeking consulting services. For this updated version, we contacted the organizations listed in the 1975 directory, as well as those organizations that had asked to be included since that time, and requested that they bring their listings up to date.

Our criteria for inclusion, as before, were the following: the organization had to use an applied behavioral science approach, had to employ at least two full-time professional consultants, had to have billed at least $25,000 worth of services in the past twelve months, and had to have been in existence for at least a year.

Many organizations in the original listing have moved and many requests for an update were not forwardable. Because the listings were obviously incorrect, we deleted them if neither the principals nor the organization was listed in other available directories. Clearly, many eligible organizations have not been included—simply because we did not have information about them. Users of the *Annual* are invited to send corrections, alterations, additions, or suggestions for updated versions of the directory to be published in later issues of the *Annual*.

CANADA

C.I.M., Inc.
(Centre Interdisciplinaire de Montreal, Inc.)
5055 Gatineau Avenue
Montreal, Quebec H3V 1E4
(514) 735-6595
Principals: I. M. Aubry, Director; L. Auger, Director; Y. St. Arnaud, Director.
Founded: 1969
Full-time consultants: 5
Part-time consultants: 10
Major Services: Human relations training; management/leadership development; organization development; community development; psycho-therapy.
Area of Emphasis: Interdisciplinary approach.
Typical Clients: Education; government.

Consultative Educational Services Ltd.
58 Harvard Crescent
Saskatoon, Saskatchewan S7H 3R1
(306) 373-2628
Principals: M. P. Scharfe, President; M. J. Balabuck, Secretary-Treasurer.
Founded: 1970
Full-time consultants: 2
Part-time consultants: 4

Major Services: Human relations training; management/leadership development; organization development.
Areas of Emphasis: Training programs for school trustees; personal growth programs.
Typical Clients: Government agencies; business; hospitals; schools; organizations.

Farren-Smith Associates Ltd.
4850 Cote des Neiges (#A1507)
Montreal, Quebec H3V 1G5
(514) 731-9795
Principals: Charles E. Smith, President; Caela Farren, Vice President.
Founded: 1974
Full-time consultants: 2
Major Services: Management/leadership development; organization development.
Areas of Emphasis: Performance appraisal; managerial style development; applying Gestalt methods to problems of personal and organization development.
Typical Clients: Industry and commerce.

International Communications Institute
Box 8268, Station F
Edmonton, Alberta T6H 4P1
(403) 432-1319
Principals: A. C. Lynn Zelmer, Partner; Amy Elliott Zelmer, Partner.

Founded: 1969
Full-time consultants: 2
Major Services: Human relations training (in-house); management/leadership development; design and production of educational materials (films, television, simulations, training programs, etc.).
Areas of Emphasis: Community use of and access to media services (especially low-budget production); international development education; appropriate or intermediate technology; simulations and games; cross-cultural education.
Typical Clients: Colleges and universities; adult education agencies; government and industry training departments; community groups (voluntary agencies).

Management Renewal Limited
P.O. Box 6071, Station J
Ottawa, Ontario K2A 1T1
(613) 829-2813
Principals: Frank T. Laverty, President; Michael R. Laverty, Vice President; Joy J. Laverty, Business Manager.
Founded: 1970
Full-time consultants: 3
Part-time consultants: 12
Major Services: Human relations training; management/leadership development; organization development.
Areas of Emphasis: Management by objectives; transactional analysis; consulting skills; support staff development; positive action for women.
Typical Clients: Government; industry; education; health care; service industries.

Nativ-ety Consultants Ltd.
7721 110th Street
Edmonton, Alberta T6G 1G3
(403) 436-0279
Principal: Arnold Strynadka, President & General Manager.
Founded: 1974
Full-time consultants: 2
Part-time consultants: 4
Major Services: Human relations training; management/leadership development; organization development; community development.
Areas of Emphasis: Cross-cultural communication and acceptance programs.
Typical Clients: Government and ethnic organizations.

P. S. Ross and Partners
200 University Avenue
Toronto, Ontario M5H 3C8
(416) 363-8281
Principal: A. R. Aird, Managing Partner.
Founded: 1956
Full-time consultants: 95

Major Services: Human relations training; management/leadership development; organization development; community development; computer and information systems.
Areas of Emphasis: Personnel services; marketing; executive search; management information systems.
Typical Clients: All types of public and private groups.

Quetico Centre
Box 1000
Atikokan, Ontario P0T 1C0
(807) 929-3511
Principals: C. M. McIntosh, President; M. Kelly, Chairman of the Board; A. Bartholomew, Vice Chairman; L. E. Wiens, Secretary.
Nonprofit organization
Founded: 1958
Full-time consultants: 3
Part-time consultants: 2
Major Services: Constructive organizational change; management/leadership development; community development; human relations training; creative arts development; youth leadership; health and wellness learning.
Areas of Emphasis: Training materials on system changes; in-house and public activities.
Typical Clients: Business and industry; municipal and provincial government agencies; community agencies; schools and colleges; individuals.

EASTERN and SOUTHERN UNITED STATES

Block Petrella Associates, Inc.
1009 Park Avenue
Plainfield, New Jersey 07060
(201) 754-5100
Principals: Anthony Petrella, President; Peter Block, Director; Marvin R. Weisbord, Vice President.
Founded: 1968
Full-time consultants: 8
Part-time consultants: 4
Major Services: Human relations training; management/leadership development; organization development; community development; training of in-house trainers and organization development specialists.
Areas of Emphasis: Team-building and consultation skills; management training for first-line supervisors; career planning.
Typical Clients: Industry; government; hospitals and medical centers; school systems; volunteer organizations.

The Center for Organizational and Personal Effectiveness, Inc. (C.O.P.E.)
520 Westfield Avenue
Elizabeth, New Jersey 07208
(201) 351-6770
Principals: Harry N. Dubin, President; Morris Liss, Vice President.
Founded: 1967
Full-time consultants: 2
Part-time consultants: 20
Major Services: Management/leadership development; organization development; community development; transactional analysis in organizations; train-the-trainer programs.
Area of Emphasis: Concrete, measurable programs.
Typical Clients: Business; prisons; school systems; community organizations.

Development Consultants, Inc.
2028 Powers Ferry Road, Suite 190
Atlanta, Georgia 30339
(404) 952-0898
Principals: Hyler J. Bracey, President; Aubrey C. Sanford, Vice President; Roy W. Trueblood, Vice President.
Founded: 1973
Full-time consultants: 4
Part-time consultants: 11
Major Services: High-quality, custom-designed management skill building and real live problem-solving events.
Areas of Emphasis: Team work, leadership, and communications skills and organization development.
Typical Clients: Middle- and upper-level executives.

Felix M. Lopez & Associates, Inc.
14 Vanderventer Avenue
Port Washington, New York 11050
(516) 883-4041
Principals: Felix M. Lopez, President; Felix E. Lopez, Secretary-Treasurer.
Founded: 1970
Full-time consultants: 4
Part-time consultants: 4
Major Services: Human relations training; management/leadership development; organization development; management by objectives; performance evaluation.
Areas of Emphasis: Restructuring selection systems for EEOC conformation; individual and corporate accountability programs.
Typical Clients: Business; government agencies; school systems; religious organizations.

The Gemini Group
RD #2, Box 117
Bedford, New York 10506
(914) 764-4938

Principal: Kenneth Finn
Founded: 1977
Full-time consultants: 2
Part-time consultants: 5
Major Services: Large personnel systems; management development; organization development; cost effectiveness; survey feedback; consultation skills development; growth dynamics management.
Areas of Emphasis: Total systems approach; measurement technology; strategy planning; business growth; marketing.
Typical Clients: Small growing companies; high technology companies; large personnel groups; Fortune 500.

Human Dynamics, Inc.
28 Overlook Terrace
Simsbury, Connecticut 06070
(203) 658-2077
Principals: James B. Aiken, President; Paul Mico, Vice President; Rita Ridgway, Secretary.
Founded: 1969
Full-time consultants: 2
Part-time consultants: 4
Major Services: Human relations training; management/leadership development; organization development; community development.
Typical Clients: Education; business and industry; government.

Human Resources Institute (HRI)
(Scientific Resources, Inc.)
Tempe Wick Road
Morristown, New Jersey 07960
(201) 267-1496
Principals: Robert F. Allen, President; Stanley Silverzweig, Vice President; Elaine J. Allen, Secretary-Treasurer.
Founded: 1965
Full-time consultants: 10
Part-time consultants: 20
Major Services: Human relations training; management/leadership development; organization development; community development.
Area of Emphasis: Working with normative systems, which assist organizations in understanding and modifying the organizational cultures of which they are a part.
Typical Clients: Corporations; prisons; government; school systems.

Instituto De Relaciones Humanas, Inc.
G.P.O. Box 1755
San Juan, Puerto Rico 00936
(809) 751-2147
Principals: José E. Viñas, President; Rafael Ramirez, Secretary-Treasurer; Juan A. Rossello, Chief Consultant.
Nonprofit organization

Founded: 1967
Full-time consultants: 3
Part-time consultants: 20

Major Services: Human relations training; management/leadership development; organization development; community development; training of trainers for organization and community development.

Areas of Emphasis: Consultation; professional development for leaders in group dynamics.

Typical Clients: School systems; community mental health projects; government service agencies; universities; hospitals; business and industry; Federal government.

The Institute for Organization Development
3384 Peachtree Road, N.E.
Atlanta, Georgia 30345
(404) 237-8962
Principals: Arthur M. Cohen, President & Treasurer; Lois P. Cohen, Vice President & Secretary.

Founded: 1972
Full-time consultants: 2
Part-time consultants: 2

Major Services: Human relations training; management/leadership development; organization development; community development.

Areas of Emphasis: Individual adjustment problems; performance analysis and career development; conflict management.

Typical Clients: Business and industry; religious systems; professional organizations.

J. Miguel Bernal & Associates, Consultants
8865 Thunderbird Drive
Pensacola, Florida 32504
(904) 477-8926
Principals: J. Miguel Bernal, President; Sergio Hernandez, Director, Consulting Services for Latin America; Guillermo Vega, Operations Manager.

Founded: 1969
Full-time consultants: 2
Part-time consultants: 1

Major Services: Human relations training; management/leadership development; organization development; cross-cultural training.

Area of Emphasis: Process consultation.

Typical Clients: Multinational corporations; international institutions; government agencies; universities.

Management Services Division
Department of Finance and Administration
State of Tennessee
505 State Office Building
Nashville, Tennessee 37219
(615) 741-3881
Principal: Thomas B. Wilson, Director.

Nonprofit organization
Founded: 1971
Full-time consultants: 2

Major Services: Management/leadership development; organization development; financial and systems consulting.

Areas of Emphasis: Management personnel; interagency decision making; problem solving.

Typical Clients: Agencies within the Tennessee state government.

McBer and Company
137 Newbury Street
Boston, Massachusetts 02116
(617) 261-5570
Principals: David C. McClelland, Chairman, Board of Directors; David H. Burnham, President/Chief Executive Officer; Richard E. Boyatzis, Director of Research; George O. Klemp, Director, Competency Testing; David Miron, Director, Entrepreneurial Development; Paul Pottinger, Director, Assessment Services; Lyle M. Spencer, Jr., Director, Organization Development.

Founded: 1963
Full-time consultants: 10
Part-time consultants: 10

Major Services: Management/leadership development; organization development; competency testing and assessment; alcohol treatment; career and life planning; consultant and trainer training; sales training.

Areas of Emphasis: Preparing client personnel to provide internal consulting, training, and development services; empirical research.

Typical Clients: Corporations; government agencies; schools and colleges; nonprofit and volunteer agencies; foreign countries.

Mid-Atlantic Association for Training and Consulting, Inc.
1500 Massachusetts Avenue, N.W. (Suite 325)
Washington, D.C. 20005
(202) 223-0582
Principals: Vera Pierce, Acting Executive Director; Jack Andersen, Chairman; James Henkelman, Vice Chairman; David Caldwell, Secretary.

Nonprofit organization
Founded: 1965
Full-time consultants: 2
Part-time consultants: 140

Major Services: Human relations training; management/leadership development; organization development; personal planning; training of trainers; training of lay ministers.

Areas of Emphasis: Training and consulting for religious and voluntary systems (general consulting skills, etc.); conflict and power utilization; educational design skills.

Typical Clients: Church jurisdictions and organizations; prisons; school systems; voluntary organizations such as drug education centers and charities.

Nicvee, Inc.
15 Floral Drive
Hastings-on-Hudson, New York 10706
(914) 478-1168
Principals: Nic Paster, President & Executive Secretary; Vera Paster, Vice President.
Founded: 1971
Full-time consultants: 2
Major Services: Human relations training; management/leadership development; organization development; community development; group therapy.
Areas of Emphasis: Personal growth; life planning; team building; couples laboratories; conflict management; humanizing education and administration.
Typical Clients: School systems; colleges and universities; public health agencies; professional groups and associations; personnel departments of business and industry; consulting firms.

NTL Institute
1501 Wilson Blvd., Suite 1000
P.O. Box 9155, Rosslyn Station
Arlington, Virginia 22209
(703) 527-1500
Principals: Harold L. Hodgkinson, President; R. E. Gibbons, Vice President, Finance; Lynn DeGroote, Director, Publications; Virginia L. Sprecher, Director, Admissions and Marketing; Lynn Wrigley, Director, Program Management.
Nonprofit organization
Founded: 1947
Full-time consultants: 2
Part-time consultants: 350 professional members
Major Services: Human relations training; management/leadership development; organization development; community development; training of trainers.
Area of Emphasis: Programs for executives, managers, trainers, and consultants.
Typical Clients: Education; hospital and health care agencies; national and international business and industry; social service agencies; police; service academies; Federal and local government agencies.

Personnel Development Corporation
1201 North Calvert Street
Baltimore, Maryland 21202
(301) 547-0909
Principals: Robert B. Sprague, President; Morris E. Sumner, Vice President; Roger M. Windsor, Secretary; Michael Hinkle, Treasurer.
Founded: 1972
Full-time consultants: 2
Part-time consultants: 1
Major Services: Human relations training; management/leadership development; organization development; career guidance; personal assessment; public seminars; sales and sales management training.

Area of Emphasis: Effective selection techniques.
Typical Clients: Hospitals; business and industry; individuals; colleges and universities; religious organizations.

Pollitt and Alban
19 Washington Square North
New York, New York 10011
(212) 228-6370
Principals: Irving Pollitt, Partner; Billie T. Alban, Partner.
Founded: 1968
Full-time consultants: 2
Major Services: Human relations training; management/leadership development; organization development; community development; sociotechnical system work.
Area of Emphasis: Management consultation.
Typical Clients: Industry; banks; insurance companies.

Robert H. Schaffer & Associates
401 Rockrimmon Road
Stamford, Connecticut 06903
(203) 322-1604
(212) 751-7430
Principals: Robert H. Schaffer, President; Richard A. Bobbe, Vice President; Robert A. Neiman, Vice President.
Founded: 1959
Full-time consultants: 6
Major Services: Management/leadership development; organization development; consulting development; planning development.
Areas of Emphasis: Increasing an organization's achievement as well as its basic capacity to sustain higher levels of accomplishment; consultation with key people; programs for executives, staff groups, or technical groups; programmed materials for use by an organization's internal consulting staff.
Typical Clients: Industry; hospitals; education; government; public service agencies; R & D groups; internal consulting groups; training and development departments.

Robert Saunders Associates
Candlewood Isle
New Fairfield, Connecticut 06810
(203) 746-2473
Principals: Robert C. Saunders, President; Henry R. Hein, Associate.
Founded: 1970
Full-time consultants: 2
Part-time consultants: 1
Major Services: Management/leadership development; human relations training; organization development.

Areas of Emphasis: Career and self-development; supervision and consulting skills; sales and sales management; in-house and public training programs.

Typical Clients: Business and industry; government agencies; executives and professionals.

S. M. Scherzer & Associates
11 Poplar Plain Road
Westport, Connecticut 06880
(203) 226-3042

Principals: Saul M. Scherzer, President; Jack Butler, Associate; Richard Lazar, Associate; Alex Oliver, Associate.

Founded: 1972

Full-time consultants: 4
Part-time consultants: 3

Major Services: Human relations training; management/executive/leadership development; organization development; community development.

Areas of Emphasis: Organization development top-down model; management consultation; outplacement counseling.

Typical Clients: Conglomerates; home building industry; service industries; package and food business.

Synectics, Inc.
26 Church Street
Cambridge, Massachusetts 02138
(617) 868-6530

Principals: George M. Prince, Chairman; Cavas M. Gobhai, President; Amarjit Chopra, Senior Vice President; Richard A. Harriman, Vice President; John C. Philipp, Vice President.

Founded: 1960

Full-time consultants: 15
Part-time consultants: 3

Major Service: Management/leadership development.

Areas of Emphasis: Teaching skills for cooperative accomplishment; innovation; meeting structure; creative problem solving with groups.

Typical Clients: Education; business; government; church groups; hospitals; interested individuals.

Trust, Inc.
4905 Radford Avenue (Suite 206)
Richmond, Virginia 23230
(804) 359-9491

Principals: Richard F. Perkins, Executive Director; William D. Cushnie, Senior Associate.

Nonprofit organization
Founded: 1967

Full-time consultants: 3
Part-time consultants: 7

Major Services: Management/leadership development; organization development; community development; management by objectives; career planning and development.

Areas of Emphasis: Utilization and development of human resources; consultation on problem solving, decision making, conflict management, etc.

Typical Clients: Government; educational institutions; prisons; industry; hospitals.

CENTRAL UNITED STATES

Alverna Center for Human and Spiritual Growth
8140 Spring Mill Road
Indianapolis, Indiana 46260
(317) 257-7339

Principals: Maury Smith, Program Director; Mario DiCicco, Associate Director.

Nonprofit organization
Founded: 1970

Full-time consultants: 2
Part-time consultants: 2

Major Services: Human relations training; management/leadership development; organization development; community building for religious communities.

Areas of Emphasis: Value clarification; pastoral counseling; professional development, leadership, and supervisor's workshops.

Typical Clients: Church administrators; religious communities and individuals; schools; lay leaders.

CENCOAD, Inc.
2118 South Summit Avenue
Sioux Falls, South Dakota 57105
(605) 336-5236

Principals: Victor V. Pavlenko, Director; Irma E. Herrboldt, Administrative Assistant.

Founded: 1969

Full-time consultants: 5
Part-time consultants: 1

Major Services: Human relations training; management/leadership development; organization development; community development; clinical pastoral education; environmental conflict resolution.

Areas of Emphasis: Participative management systems; decision making; problem solving; planning processes.

Typical Clients: Rural communities; community agencies; business; religious organizations; local governments.

The Center for Applied Behavioral Sciences
P.O. Box 829
Topeka, Kansas 66601
(913) 234-9566

Principals: Roy W. Menninger, President; Tobias Brocher, Center Director; Jerry W. Johnson, Director of Administration; Glenn Swogger, Director of Consultations.

Nonprofit organization
Founded: 1973

Full-time consultants: 10
Part-time consultants: 15

Major Services: Human relations training; management/leadership development; community development.

Areas of Emphasis: Seminars for executives; personal and organizational consultations.

Typical Clients: Private executives; government.

Communication Consultants, Inc.
8 York Drive
Athens, Ohio 45701
(614) 594-7539

Principals: Sue DeWine, Midwest Associate; Jacqueline Rumley, East Coast Associate; Marie Shafe, Florida Associate; Craig Brubaker, Indiana Associate.

Founded: 1973
Full-time consultants: 4
Part-time consultants: 6

Major Services: Human relations training; management/leadership development; organization development; operations research; future planning; career development; communications, multimedia programs.

Areas of Emphasis: Optimizing human potential in organizations; management science; interpersonal communication; group dynamics.

Typical Clients: School systems; college faculties; business and industry; hospitals; prisons; voluntary organizations.

Community Psychology Institute
University of Cincinnati
336 Dyer
Cincinnati, Ohio 45221
(513) 475-5981

Principals: W. Brendan Reddy, Director; Dan Langmeyer, Coordinator of Research.

Nonprofit organization
Founded: 1966
Full-time consultants: 2
Part-time consultants: 6

Major Services: Human relations training; management/leadership development; organization development; community development; program evaluation; surveys.

Area of Emphasis: Local human and public service organizations.

Typical Clients: Schools; agencies; institutions.

Counseling and Educational Development Services, Inc.
P.O. Box 7158
Missoula, Montana 59807
(406) 543-3550

Principals: Rowan W. Conrad, Administrative and Research Director; Gracia Schall, Counseling Director; Dennis Duncan, Training Director.

Founded: 1976

Full-time consultants: 4
Part-time consultants: 3

Major Services: Counselor skills training; program development and administration; program evaluation; staff training and organization development; women's programs and counseling; personal and marriage counseling; human relations training.

Areas of Emphasis: Skills training for helping service professionals; design of workshops; evaluation of human service programs.

Typical Clients: Government agencies; business; industry; school systems; private individuals.

David L. Ward and Associates, Inc.
360 West Wellington Street
Chicago, Illinois 60657
(312) 929-3993

Principals: David L. Ward, President; Gary Pielemeir, Director.

Founded: 1968
Full-time consultants: 3
Part-time consultants: 4

Major Services: Human relations training; management/leadership development; community development.

Areas of Emphasis: Motivation; behavioral science; transactional analysis; career counseling.

Typical Clients: Business and industry; government.

Educational Administration Development Associates (E/A/D/A)
P.O. Box 1206
Manhattan, Kansas 66502
(913) 537-9151

Principals: Eddy J. Van Meter, Executive Director; Chris Nasbe, Program Coordinator.

Founded: 1973
Full-time consultants: 2
Part-time consultants: 3

Major Services: Management/leadership development; organization development.

Area of Emphasis: Publication of the Educational Organization Development Handbook.

Typical Clients: Elementary school systems; community and junior colleges; four-year and graduate educational institutions.

Growth Associates, a division of Prairie View, Inc.
Box 467
Newton, Kansas 67114
(316) 283-2400

Principals: Merrill F. Raber, Division Director; Colleen Stagner, Director, Seminars and Workshops; Gordon Funk, Director, Organization Consultation; George Lehman, Organization Consultant.

Nonprofit organization
Founded: 1968
Full-time consultants: 3
Part-time consultants: 3

Major Services: Management/leadership development; organization development; community development; personal growth.

Areas of Emphasis: Management training and consultation; personal growth; continuing education.

Typical Clients: Colleges; government agencies; business; industry; social service and mental health agencies; churches.

Hobert-Martin Consulting Psychologists, Inc.
4028 IDS Center
Minneapolis, Minnesota 55402
(612) 338-8461

Principals: James F. Martin, President; Robert D. Hobert, Secretary-Treasurer; Thomas M. Vessey, Vice President; George M. Golden, Vice President; Douglas M. Baker, Director, Center for Organizational Effectiveness.

Founded: 1972
Full-time consultants: 5
Part-time consultants: 3

Major Services: Personnel assessment; career planning; management/leadership development; organization development; management consulting.

Areas of Emphasis: Appraisal and development of human resources; career development; management/leadership development seminars; consultation with managers; organization audits/surveys; personnel research and planning; organization development and planning.

Typical Clients: Corporations; government; law-enforcement agencies; professional organizations; education; hospitals.

Human Resource Associates, Inc.
121 East Second Street
Hastings, Minnesota 55033
(612) 437-3976

Principals: David W. Helmstetter, President; Donald G. May, Vice President.

Founded: 1969
Full-time consultants: 13
Part-time consultants: 30

Major Services: Employee-assistance programs; clinical demonstration programs; dissemination of educational alternatives; inservice training in affective education; management/leadership consulting.

Areas of Emphasis: Leadership and group dynamics; problem solving; human relations skills; designing and implementing nontraditional human service delivery systems.

Typical Clients: Schools; mental health centers; government agencies; private business and industry.

Human Resource Development Associates
of Ann Arbor
1820 Green Road
Ann Arbor, Michigan 48105
(313) 994-4732

Principals: Ronald O. Lippitt, President; Kendall W. Cowing, Director.

Founded: 1973
Full-time consultants: 4
Part-time consultants: 10

Major Services: Human relations training; management/leadership development; organization development; training of volunteer coordinators and trainers.

Typical Clients: Business; education; health care; government.

Human Services Design Laboratory
Case Western Reserve University
School of Applied Social Sciences
Cleveland, Ohio 44106
(216) 368-2330

Principal: Richard E. Isralowitzi, Director.

Nonprofit organization
Founded: 1968
Full-time consultants: 6
Part-time consultants: 12

Major Services: Management/leadership development; organization development; community development; technical assistance in program planning and evaluation.

Area of Emphasis: Applied social science research.

Typical Clients: Human service organizations.

Human Synergistics, Inc.
39819 Plymouth Road
Plymouth, Michigan 48170
(313) 459-1030

Principals: J. Clayton Lafferty, Chief Executive Officer; D. Joseph Fisher, President; Justs Grinvalds, Executive Vice President.

Founded: April 1970
Full-time consultants: 3
Part-time consultants: 3

Major Services: Management consulting; training material and program development; selection system development; leadership, communication, and organization development; safety awareness and training programs.

Areas of Emphasis: Diagnostic evaluation; achievement, motivation, and communication building; group processes; task delegation; human resource utilization.

Typical Clients: Public utilities and communications; automotive, electronic, and industrial equipment manufacturers; food industry; educational and government institutions; finance and banking; retailers; data processors; health care.

Industrial Administration Department
General Motors Institute
1700 West Third Avenue
Flint, Michigan 48502
(313) 766-2641

Principals: Tony Hain, Dept. Head; J. P. Zima, Prof., Org. Comm.; H. O. Patterson, Prof., Org. Psych.; R. Widgery, Prof., Org. Psych.; S. L. Tubbs, Prof., Org. Comm.

278

Nonprofit organization
Founded: 1969
Full-time consultants: 9
Part-time consultants: 20

Major Services: Management/leadership development; organization development; community development.

Areas of Emphasis: Management of change; human resources accounting; communication audits; management information systems; lead indicators of social change.

Typical Clients: Business and industry.

Institute for Research and Training in Higher Education
446 French Hall
University of Cincinnati
Cincinnati, Ohio 45220
(513) 475-2228

Principals: Ronald Boyer, Director; Anthony Grasha, Acting Director.
Founded: 1967
Full-time consultants: 4
Part-time consultants: 4

Major Service: Organization development.

Areas of Emphasis: Faculty and staff development; program/personnel evaluation in higher education.

Typical Clients: Colleges and universities.

Roland S. Larson & Associates, Inc.
2442 Gettysburg Avenue South
Minneapolis, Minnesota 55426
(612) 545-6077

Principals: Roland S. Larson, President; Doris E. Larson, Secretary-Treasurer.
Founded: 1967
Full-time consultants: 2
Part-time consultants: 8

Major Services: Career development; outplacement counseling; staff development; customized training events and workshops.

Areas of Emphasis: Life work planning; stress management; team effectiveness; marriage enrichment; value clarification; communication skills; peer counseling; positive learning programs.

Typical Clients: Schools; colleges; religious institutions; government; community agencies; business and industry.

Lawson Associates
134 Blue Ridge Road
Indianapolis, Indiana 46208
(317) 283-1475

Principals: Peter Lawson, Partner; Mary Helen Lawson, Partner.
Founded: 1972
Full-time consultants: 2
Part-time consultants: 14

Major Services: Human relations training; management/leadership development; organization development; community development.

Areas of Emphasis: Development of human resources within systems; Gordon's Effectiveness Training courses.

Typical Clients: Business; government; education; agencies; families.

Mid-Continent Regional Educational Laboratory (McREL)
3100 McCormick Avenue
Wichita, Kansas 67213
(316) 943-2168

Principals: L. C. Nixon, Jr., Director; James W. Abbott, Director, Staff Development.
Nonprofit organization
Founded: 1966
Full-time consultants: 8
Part-time consultants: 18

Major Services: Human relations training; management/leadership development; organization development; community development.

Areas of Emphasis: Humanizing education; humanizing staffs.

Typical Clients: Education; business; government.

MOLD, Inc.
P.O. Box 8652
Detroit, Michigan 48224
(313) 884-7220

Principals: Robert Rodreick, President; Stella M. Rodreick, Treasurer; William R. D. Martin, Director.
Founded: 1971
Full-time consultants: 2

Major Services: Human relations training; management/leadership development; organization development and consultation.

Areas of Emphasis: Participative management systems; team building.

Typical Clients: Trade associations; business and industry.

PDI Corporation
2071 Lawrence Avenue
Cincinnati, Ohio 45212
(513) 631-6536

Principals: Compton Allyn, Chairman; William L. Holloway, President; Joseph C. Busken, Jr., Secretary.
Founded: 1967
Full-time consultants: 2
Part-time consultants: 10

Major Service: Management/leadership development.

Area of Emphasis: Project management in mental health and criminal justice.

Typical Clients: Government service agencies in mental health and criminal justice; industry; school administrations.

Personnel Decisions, Inc.
821 Marquette Avenue
Foshay Tower
Minneapolis, Minnesota 55402
(612) 339-0927
Principals: Marvin D. Dunnette, Chairman; Lowell W. Hellervik, President; Pierre Meyer, Vice President; Marlys M. Gimble, Secretary-Treasurer
Founded: 1966
Full-time consultants: 10
Part-time consultants: 6
Major Services: Management/leadership development; organization development; personnel research; test validation; interviewing; performance appraisal; counseling training.
Area of Emphasis: Assessment center concept.
Typical Clients: Industry; government; municipalities; education.

Response and Associates
P.O. Box 333
Chicago Heights, Illinois 60411
(312) 758-4600
Principals: Robert T. Wall, President/Principal Consultant; Julie O'Mara, Principal Consultant.
Founded: 1969
Full-time consultants: 2
Part-time consultants: 37
Major Services: Workshops and consultation on women in management; career planning for women; human resource management; human relations training; management/leadership development; organization development.
Areas of Emphasis: Women's issues in various organizations; personal growth; work-group development.
Typical Clients: Business; industry; government agencies; school systems; colleges and universities; professional organizations.

WESTERN UNITED STATES

The Center for Designed Change
215 Cleveland Court
Mill Valley, California 94941
(415) 388-8872
Principals: Marion Stringham Vittitow, President; Natalie Rogers Fuchs, Vice President; Richard L. Vittitow, Secretary-Treasurer.
Nonprofit organization
Founded: 1973
Full-time consultants: 3
Major Services: Human relations training; management/leadership development; organization development; community development; client-centered counseling; training of trainers.
Areas of Emphasis: Developing humanistic organizations; designing and implementing individual and organizational change; personal growth.

Typical Clients: Human service organizations; trainers and counselors in government and industry; school systems; colleges and universities; nonprofit organizations.

Center for Human Resources and Organizational Development
7124 Highway 17
Santa Cruz, California 95066
(408) 354-4041
Principals: Patrick M. Williams, Director; Gay Williams, Partner.
Founded: 1969
Full-time consultants: 2
Part-time consultants: 3-5
Major Services: Organization and management change and development; human relations training; leadership development; quality of working life.
Areas of Emphasis: Team building; training internal organization development consultants; leadership skill building; good management practices.
Typical Clients: Business organizations; school systems; city governments.

Edward Glaser & Associates
10889 Wilshire Boulevard (Suite 1120)
Los Angeles, California 90024
(213) 879-1280
Principals: Edward M. Glaser, Managing Associate.
Founded: 1952
Full-time consultants: 2
Part-time consultants: 14
Major Services: Executive development; individual appraisal; organization planning and development; quality of work life and productivity improvement; communications analysis; leadership training; innovation facilitation.
Areas of Emphasis: Psychological consultation to management; organization development; personnel assessment and development; managerial and supervisory training.
Typical Clients: Private organizations; government or public agencies.

Educational Communications Corporation
1910 Ocean Front
Santa Monica, California 90406
(213) 399-9241
Principals: Charles Carey, President; Gerald Newmark, Vice President; Ralph Melaragno, Vice President; E. Schnitzer, Treasurer; Altina Carey, Secretary.
Nonprofit organization
Founded: 1959
Full-time consultants: 2
Part-time consultants: 1
Major Services: Human relations training; management/leadership development; organization development.

Area of Emphasis: Humanizing education.

Typical Clients: School systems; colleges and universities; hospitals; dental and medical groups.

Effectiveness Resource Group, Inc.
6709 Topaz Drive, S.W.
Tacoma, Washington 98498
(206) 584-0232

Principal: Don Swartz, President.

Founded: 1973

Full-time consultants: 4

Part-time consultants: 8

Major Services: Human relations training; management/leadership development; organization development and training; public seminars; productivity systems design and installation.

Areas of Emphasis: Communications; consulting skills; leadership/motivation; physical fitness for managers; women in management; OSHA and EEOC compliance; work standards and scheduling.

Typical Clients: Education; government; business and industry; organizations.

Herman Associates
25532 Jesmond Dene Road
Escondido, California 92026
(714) 747-0264

Principals: Stanley M. Herman; Georgia L. Herman.

Founded: 1973

Full-time consultants: 2

Part-time consultants: 6

Major Services: Human relations training; management/leadership development; organization development; training of consultants.

Areas of Emphasis: Authentic management; development of individualized approaches for improving personal and organizational performance; personal growth.

Typical Clients: Business and industry; government.

Human Interaction Research Institute
10889 Wilshire Boulevard
Los Angeles, California 90024
(213) 879-1373

Principals: Edward M. Glaser, President; George H. Clement, Vice President & Treasurer; Kathalee N. Garrison, Secretary.

Nonprofit organization

Founded: 1961

Full-time consultants: 3

Part-time consultants: 21

Major Services: Management/leadership development; organization development; community development; program evaluation; human-services research; consultation.

Areas of Emphasis: Knowledge utilization and management of change; problem solving; quality of work life improvement.

Typical Clients: Federal, state, and local government agencies; school systems; hospitals; industrial organizations.

Humetrics
7761 Starlight Drive
La Jolla, California 92037
(714) 453-2239

Principals: Lawrence N. Solomon; Evelyn K. Solomon.

Founded: 1972

Full-time consultants: 2

Major Services: Human relations training; management/leadership development; organization development.

Areas of Emphasis: Personal growth; male-female roles in work world; team building; conflict management; communication.

Typical Clients: School systems; hospitals, municipal government; industry; civil service; military.

Institute for Developmental Organization
20 Anchorage Street
Marina Del Rey, California 90291
(213) 392-9558
and
P.O. Box 42255
Cincinnati, Ohio 45242
(513) 851-9140

Principals: James V. Clark, Partner; Charles G. Krone, Partner; W. H. McWhinney, Partner.

Founded: 1972

Full-time consultants: 3

Part-time consultants: 3

Major Services: Open-systems planning; training and development services; sociotechnical design of facilities.

Area of Emphasis: Designing and regenerating sociotechnical systems.

Typical Clients: Industrial organizations; communities; educational and family systems.

International Training Consultants, Inc.
99 East Magnolia Boulevard (Suite 113)
Burbank, California 91502
(213) 849-4681

Principals: Edmund John Phillips, III, President; Rowena von Dornum, Director, Creative Services; Farhad Fred Ebrahimi, Computer Sciences.

Founded: 1967

Full-time consultants: 15

Part-time consultants: 8

Major Services: Human relations training, management/leadership development; organization development; community development; educational and vocational training; multi-media development.

Areas of Emphasis: Analytical, educational, evaluative, social research, managerial, and related technical services.

Typical Clients: Government agencies and private organizations in the U.S. and abroad.

John A. Hawley Associates/Team Climate Associates
517 First Street
Manhattan Beach, California 90266
(213) 376-5448
Principal: Jack Hawley, President.
Founded: 1970
Full-time consultants: 1
Part-time consultants: 6
Major Services: Human relations training; management/leadership development; organization development.
Areas of Emphasis: Large organization development programs; organization development resources development; multi-discipline approaches to organization improvement; creation of positive work environments using vertical linking; "total" team-building methods.
Typical Clients: Private industry; Federal, state, and local government.

Joint Center for Human Services Development
School of Social Work
School of Social Work
San Jose State University
San Jose, California 95192
(408) 277-2956 or 277-2235
Principals: Armand J. Sanchez, Dean; James M. Kouzes, Program Director; Gary D. Bergthold, Associate Program Director; Paul R. Mico, Senior Consultant.
Nonprofit organization
Founded: 1972
Full-time consultants: 2
Part-time consultants: 5
Major Services: Management/leadership development; organization development; community development; human services research, consultation, and training.
zations to manage relationships with critical domains and to manage change.
Typical Clients: Mental health; public welfare; education; health care; employment; housing and community development; recreation; rehabilitation; family and child welfare organizations.

Leadership Institute of Spokane (LIOS)
P.O. Box 8005
Spokane, Washington 99203
(509) 534-4324
Principals: Bob Crosby, President; John Scherer, Director, Program Designing; Ron Short, Director, Organization Development Services; Barbara Scherer, Director, Career Development.
Nonprofit organization
Founded: 1968
Full-time consultants: 4
Major Services: Human relations training; management/leadership development; organization devel-

opment; community development; life direction and personal skill assessment.
Areas of Emphasis: Training designed for specific needs; an M.A. program in Applied Behavioral Science in association with Whitworth College.
Typical Clients: Community mental health; government; religious organizations.

Management & Organization Development, Inc.
Box 2321
La Jolla, California 92037
(714) 453-2140
Principals: Philip R. Harris, President; Dorothy L. Harris, Vice President; Alfred E. O'Brien, Treasurer; Woodrow H. Sears, Jr., Senior Associate.
Founded: 1971
Full-time consultants: 2
Part-time consultants: 70
Major Services: Human relations training; management/leadership development; organization development and research.
Areas of Emphasis: Management of change; organization shock; communications; motivation; association renewal.
Typical Clients: Corporations; government agencies; associations; education; criminal justice agencies.

National Indian Training and Research Center
2121 South Mill Avenue (Suite 204)
Tempe, Arizona 85282
(602) 967-9484
Principals: Lawrence Hart, President; Cecil Corbett, Vice President; Lucy Covington, Secretary; Alfreda Bergan, Treasurer.
Nonprofit organization
Founded: 1969
Full-time consultants: 2
Part-time consultants: 10
Major Services: Human relations training; management/leadership development; organization development; community development, consultation; workshops.
Area of Emphasis: Minorities, especially American Indians.
Typical Clients: Education; health; government; Indian tribes.

Pacific Organization Development Associates
235 West MacArthur Boulevard (Suite 600)
Oakland, California 94611
(415) 658-1370
Principals: Robert M. Bramson, Senior Partner; Susan J. Bramson, Consulting Partner; Allen F. Harrison, Partner; Raymond E. Miles, Senior Partner; Nicholas Parlette, Senior Partner.
Founded: 1967
Full-time consultants: 3
Part-time consultants: 2

Major Services: Human relations training; management/leadership development; organization development; community development; program evaluation; cassette team building programs; diagnostic studies.

Areas of Emphasis: Action training and research; staff consultation skills; educational consultation; women in management.

Typical Clients: State and local government; health services; insurance companies; school systems; universities; management training institutes; government leagues and associations.

Personnel-Manpower Systems Associates
1184 Meredith Avenue
San Jose, California 95125
(408) 294-3412
Principals: Robert Farnquist; David Armstrong.
Founded: 1971
Full-time consultants: 2
Part-time consultants: 3
Major Services: Management/leadership development; organization development; career development.
Areas of Emphasis: Affirmative action; personnel systems.
Typical Clients: State and local government; community agencies.

Social Actions Associates
(Social Actions Foundations, Inc.)
6655 North Los Leones Drive
Tucson, Arizona 85718
(602) 299-1104
Principals: Robert E. Calmes, Director, Consulting Services; William A. Reese, III, Executive Director; D. Barbara Winder Reese, Chief Administrator, Dr. F. Winder Memorial Fund.
Nonprofit organization
Founded: 1972
Full-time consultants: 3
Part-time consultants: 7
Major Services: Human relations training; management/leadership development; personal development; growth groups.
Areas of Emphasis: Value and moral development; multi-racial encounter; human interaction; goal setting.
Typical Clients: School systems; community colleges; universities; hospitals; government; business and industry; community agency personnel; correctional and human service agencies.

Thoren Consulting Group, Inc.
5410 S. Lakeshore Drive
Tempe, Arizona 85283
(602) 838-7406

Principals: Donald A. Thoren, President; Charles A. Bivenour, Senior Vice President.
Founded: 1969
Full-time consultants: 4
Part-time consultants: 3
Major Services: Human relations training; management/leadership development; organization development; personal growth; motivation seminars; sales training; interpersonal effectiveness.
Areas of Emphasis: Training of supervisors; personnel practices.
Typical Clients: Small- to medium-sized business; government.

TORI Associates, Inc.
8475 La Jolla Scenic Drive North
La Jolla, California 92037
(714) 453-0133
Principals: Jack R. Gibb, President; Maudeline Flemming, Vice President; Lorraine M. Gibb, Secretary.
Nonprofit organization
Founded: 1966
Full-time consultants: 7
Part-time consultants: 55
Major Services: Human relations training; management/leadership development; organization development; community development.
Areas of Emphasis: TORI theory; development of a climate for creativity and personal growth; effectiveness research.
Typical Clients: Large business; school systems; government agencies; mental health facilities.

University Associates Publishers and Consultants
8517 Production Avenue
San Diego, California 92121
(714) 578-5900
Principals: J. William Pfeiffer, Chairman; Leonard D. Goodstein, President; John E. Jones, Vice President for Research and Development.
Founded: 1968
Full-time consultants: 8
Part-time consultants: 1
Major Services: Training of human resource development practitioners; management/leadership development; organization development; community development; publishing of current practical and theoretical materials for human resource development.
Areas of Emphasis: Laboratory education; use of structured experiences; practical applications; widespread distribution of information; public workshops; customized consultation; large system interventions; personal and professional growth.
Typical Clients: Business and industry; religious groups; human service organizations; health care services; educational systems; government agencies.

Western Center Associates
11326 Magnolia Boulevard, Suite 2
North Hollywood, California 91601
(213) 980-7878
Principals: Harold T. Marckwardt, President; Noble
F. McKay, Vice President.
Founded: 1966
Full-time consultants: 2
Part-time consultants: 18
Major Services: Human relations training; management/leadership development; organization development; community development; training of trainers; career development training; publishing materials for self-directed job seeking.
Areas of Emphasis: Custom-designed interracial and inter-disciplinary involvement efforts at organization improvement; large-scale usages of small-group methodology; implementing affirmative action; applied adult learning.
Typical Clients: School systems; Federal government; county trainers; business and industry; national service organizations; universities; CETA prime contractors.

ENGLAND

Dale Loveluck Associates Ltd.
"Little Oaks"
6, Mitchell Walk
Amersham, Bucks, HP6 6NN
England
Amersham 5224 STD Code 024-03
Principals: Alan Dale, Chairman; Anne Dale, Secretary.

Founded: 1968
Part-time consultants: 30
Major Services: Human relations training; management/leadership development; organization development; community development; consultant development; personal development; publications.
Areas of Emphasis: Eclectic frameworks and methods: behavior, structure, tasks, technology, culture.
Typical Clients: Industry; health; education; training boards; new enterprises.

Sheppard Moscow and Associates, Ltd.
6, Eltham Road
London, SE12 8TF
England
(01) 852-5412
Principals: David Moscow, Chairman; Colin Sheppard, Managing Director.
Founded: 1967
Full-time consultants: 7
Part-time consultants: 2
Major Services: Organization development; human relations training; management/leadership development; team development; development and training of internal organization development consultants and specialist advisors.
Areas of Emphasis: Development and implementation of corporate organization development strategies; training and development of internal consulting resources; management training films.
Typical Clients: Multi-national and large national industrial firms.

CAREER DEVELOPMENT: LITERATURE AND RESOURCES

Howard L. Fromkin and James D. McDonald

Career development can be defined as concepts describing stages of human development in relation to work and nonwork challenges that individuals confront. More broadly, career development may be viewed as a person-environment interaction. This perspective assumes that career development is an inseparable part of the process of human resource management as well as an integral part of the process of individual life planning.

Career development presently is both complex and loosely defined. The term *career development* is used many times as an undifferentiated aspect of the traditional, functional areas of personnel. Yet career development is an area important in and of itself, valuable both to the organization and to the individual. For the individual, the process of career development focuses on a systematic examination of life goals and alternative paths to achieve those goals. The value of career development to the organization is that it provides a means to assess "the needs of the organization to recruit, manage, and develop human resources in order to maintain their effectiveness, survive, and grow" (Schein, 1978, p. 1).

Most recently, career development has burgeoned as an area of research. Researchers who are interested in such concepts as life stages and life planning, matching individual and organizational needs, and counseling and guidance have found exciting areas to pursue.

Although the subject of career development has wisely been linked to many of the traditional areas of personnel—selection and placement, training, and performance appraisal, to name but a few—this selected bibliography ignores the large body of research that has centered around these functional areas and concerns itself with only those articles that have clear relevance to both a functional area of personnel and career development. It has been compiled especially for:

- organizational personnel involved in developing and maintaining the human resource planning function;
- individuals attempting to examine and plan their own lives in relation to the work place;
- the researcher who wishes to examine both the needs of the organization and the individual.

The major journals sampled for this bibliography include the following:

Academy of Management Journal

Administrative Science Quarterly

American Vocational Journal

Business Horizons

The Counseling Psychologist

Human Relations

Industrial Relations

Journal of Counseling Psychology

Journal of Vocational Behavior

Measurement of Education and Guidance

Organizational Behavior and Human Performance

Organizational Dynamics

Personnel

Journal of Applied Behavioral
Science
Journal of Applied Psychology

Personnel Journal
Personnel Psychology
Vocational Guidance Quarterly

We have not attempted to be exhaustive, but to selectively sample the journals' articles over the last five years. For gaining a wide spectrum of career development issues, an examination of the *Journal of Vocational Behavior* has been invaluable. *Organizational Behavior and Human Performance* contains articles with conceptual models that are relative to organizational structures and processes. For the area of mid-career and career change, *Vocational Guidance Quarterly* is a primary source. Other journals, specifically the *Journal of Counseling Psychology* and *The Counseling Psychologist*, have been sources for the category of career counseling and training.

To facilitate the use of this bibliography, the articles have been arranged into twelve categories. While the categories are somewhat arbitrary, and many, if not most, articles fit more than one category, these divisions have been helpful in reflecting current interests in the area of career development.

REVIEWS OF CAREER DEVELOPMENT

For a general overview of the area, annual reviews and books spanning a broad range have been included under this heading. The overviews present ideas of theoretical and research importance to help understand the current state of the art.

Betz, E. L. Vocational behavior and career development, 1976: A review. *Journal of Vocational Behavior*, 1977, 2, 129-152.

Dalton, Ç. W. A review of concepts and research on careers. In A. Zaleznik, G. W. Dalton, & L. B. Barnes (Eds.), *Orientation and conflict in career*. Boston, MA: Harvard Business School, Division of Research, 1970.

Glaser, B. G. (Ed.). *Organizational careers: A source book for theory*. Chicago: Aldine, 1968.

Hall, D. T. *Careers in organizations*. Pacific Palisades, CA: Goodyear, 1976.

Osipan, S. H. Vocational behavior and career development, 1975: A review. *Journal of Vocational Behavior*, 1976, 9, 129-145.

Pietrafesa, J., & Splite, H. *Career development: Theory and research*. New York: Grune & Stratton, 1975.

Schein, E. *Career dynamics: Matching individual and organizational needs*. Reading, MA: Addison-Wesley, 1978.

Zytowski, D. G. Vocational behavior and career development, 1977: A review. *Journal of Vocational Behavior*, 1978, 13, 141-162.

CONCEPTUAL SCHEMES

There have been a number of conceptual schemes proposed to organize the vast literature surrounding career development. The following articles help one to understand the relationships between the large number of concepts and findings in this area.

Crites, J. O. A comprehensive model of career development in early adulthood. *Journal of Vocational Behavior*, 1976, 9, 105-118.

Driver, M. Career concepts: A new approach to career research. In J. Paap (Ed.), *New dimensions in human resource management*. Englewood Cliffs, NJ: Prentice Hall, in press.

Hall, D. T. A theoretical model of career sub-identity development in organizational settings. *Organizational Behavior and Human Performance*, 1971, 6, 50-76.

Kapelman, R. E. Psychological stages of careers in engineering: An expectancy theory taxonomy. *Journal of Vocational Behavior*, 1977, 10(3), 270-286.

McKelvey, B., & Sekaran, V. Toward a career-based theory of job involvement: A study of scientists and engineers. *Administrative Science Quarterly*, 1977, *22*, 281-305.

Munley, P. H. Erickson's theory of psychosocial development and career development. *Journal of Vocational Behavior*, 1977, *10*, 261-269.

Osipan, S. H. *Theories of career development* (2nd ed.). New York: Appleton-Century-Crofts, 1973.

Osipan, S. H. The relevance of theories of career development to special groups: Problems, needed data and implications. In S. Picou & R. E. Campbell (Eds.), *Career behavior of special groups*. Columbus, OH: Charles E. Merrill, 1975.

Schein, E. *Career dynamics: Matching individual and organizational needs*. Reading, MA: Addison-Wesley, 1978.

STAGES OF ADULT DEVELOPMENT

This category represents articles that discuss the psychological stages that influence the individual's perceptions and attitudes toward life tasks and work environment. The focus is on descriptions of key events in the developmental stages (such as increasing age, family, children, social value change, etc.).

Heath, D. H. Some possible effects of occupation on the maturing of professional men. *Journal of Vocational Behavior*, 1977, *2*, 263-281.

Sarason, S. B. *Work, aging, and social change: Professionals and the one-life career imperative*. New York: The Free Press, 1977.

Schlossberg, N. K. Career development in adults. *American Vocational Journal*, 1975, *50*, 38-41.

Sheehy, G. *Passages: Predictable crises of adult life*. New York: Dutton, 1976.

CAREER STAGES AND PROFESSIONAL DEVELOPMENT

This area focuses on the key incidents in the stages of adult development and their implications for the work environment. It also takes into account how an individual's experiences with organizations influence his or her attitudes and career immobility.

Dalton, G. W., Thompson, P. H., & Price, R. L. The four stages of professional careers: A new look at performance by professionals. *Organizational Dynamics*, 1977, *6*(1), 19-42.

Dudley, G. A., & Tiedman, D. V. *Career development*. Muncie, IN: Accelerated Development, 1977.

Gould, S., & Hawkins, B. L. Organizational career stage as a moderator of the satisfaction-performance relationship. *Academy of Management Journal*, 1978, *21*(3), 434-450.

Hall, D. T., & Mansfield, R. Relationships of age and seniority with career variables of engineers and scientists. *Journal of Applied Psychology*, 1975, *60*(2), 201-210.

Ronen, S. Personal values: A basis for work motivational set and work attitude, *Organizational Behavior and Human Performance*, 1978, *21*, 80-107.

Schein, E. H. How career anchors hold executives to their career paths. *Personnel*, 1975, *52*(3), 11-24.

OCCUPATIONAL CHOICE

Factors that determine an individual's choice of occupation are explored here; this literature has generated a variety of constructs useful in examining that decision process. For example, although originally a theory of occupational choice, Holland's (1973) model has developed into a theory of matching the individual's needs and abilities to the structure or environment of various types of organizations. The article by Rainds et al. (1978) in the

Journal of Applied Psychology provides an overview of this theoretical development as well as the pertinent background of references to Holland's work.

Harmon, L. W. Review of making vocational choices: A theory of careers. *Measurement and Education in Guidance*, 1974, 7, 198-199.

Holland, J. L. *Making vocational choices: A theory of careers*. Englewood Cliffs, NJ: Prentice-Hall, 1973.

Krumboltz, J. O., Mitchell, A. M., & Jones, G. B. A social learning theory of career selection. *The Counseling Psychologist*, 1976, 6(1), 71-81.

Rainds, J. B., Jr., Shubsachs, A. P. W., Davis, R. W., & Lofquist, L. M. A test of Holland's environment formulations. *Journal of Applied Psychology*, 1978, 63(5), 609-616.

Van Mannen, J., & Katz, R. Individuals and their careers: Some temporal considerations for work satisfaction. *Personnel Psychology*, 1976, 29, 601-616.

Waterman, A. S., & Waterman, C. K. Factors related to vocational identity after extensive work experience. *Journal of Applied Psychology*, 1976, 61(3), 336-340.

NEW EMPLOYEE ORIENTATION AND SOCIALIZATION

Focusing on the initial contact between an individual's needs and the organization's goals, structures, and expectations regarding that individual, this area faces such questions as how one learns the social values and norms of the work environment and how the "psychological contract" between individual and organization develops.

Greenhaus, J. M., Sugalski, T., & Crispan, G. Relationships between perceptions of organizational size and the organizational choice process. *Journal of Vocational Behavior*, 1978, 13, 113-125.

Lubliner, M. Employee orientation. *Personnel Journal*, 1978, 57(4), 207-208.

Wanaus, J. P. Organizational entry: Newcomers moving from outside to inside. *Psychological Bulletin*, 1977, 84(4), 601-618.

ORGANIZATIONAL STRUCTURES AND PROCESSES

Articles that focus on the interaction between relevant organizational processes, such as human resource planning, and the career plans of individual organizational members are included in this category. The difficult task of matching organizational structures and processes with individual goals is addressed.

Argyis, C. *Integrating the individual and the organization*. New York: John Wiley, 1964.

Anundsen, K. An assessment centre at work. *Personnel*, 1975, 52, 29-36.

Brousseau, K. R. Personality & job experience. *Organizational Behavior and Human Performance*, 1978, 22, 235-252.

Dyer, L. *Careers in organizations: Individual planning and organizational development*. Ithaca, NY: New York State School of Industrial and Labor Relations, Cornell University, 1976.

Katz, R. Job enrichment: Some career considerations. In J. van Maanen (Ed.), *Organizational careers*. New York: John Wiley, 1977.

Keen, P. G. W. Cognitive style and career specialization. In J. van Maanen (Ed.), *Organizational careers*. New York: John Wiley, 1977.

Kerr, S., von Glinow, M. A., & Schrieshein, J. Issues in the study of professionals in organizations: The case of scientists and engineers. *Organizational Behavior and Human Performance*, 1977, 18(2), 329-345.

Miller, N. Career choice, job satisfaction, and the truth behind the Peter Principle. *Personnel*, 1976, 53(4), 58-65.

Muller, D. G. A model for human resources development. *Personnel Journal*, 1976, 55(5), 238-243.

O'Reilly, C. A., III. Personality-job fit: Implications for individual attitudes and performance. *Organizational Behavior and Human Performance*, 1977, *18*, 36-46.

Rotardi, T., Jr. Organizational identification: Issues and implications. *Organizational Behavior and Human Performance*, 1975, *13*, 95-109.

Schein, E. H. The individual, the organization and the career: A conceptual scheme. *Journal of Applied Behavioral Science*, 1971, *7*, 401-426.

Van Maanen, J., & Schein, E. H. Improving the quality of work life: Career development. In J. R. Hackman & J. L. Suttle (Eds.), *Improving life at work*. Los Angeles: Goodyear, 1977.

Van Maanen, J., Schein, E. H., & Bailyn, L. The shape of things to come: A new look at organizational careers. In J. R. Hackman, E. E. Lawler, & L. W. Porter (Eds.), *Perspectives on behavior in organizations*. New York: McGraw-Hill, 1977.

Vardi, Y., & Hammer, T. V. Intraorganizational mobility and career perceptions among rank and file employees in different technologies. *Academy of Management Journal*, 1977, *20*(4), 622-634.

Walker, J. W. Individual career planning: Managerial help for subordinates. *Business Horizons*. Graduate School of Business, Indiana University, February, 1973.

Warr, P. (Ed.). *Personal goals and work design*. New York: John Wiley, 1976.

CAREER COUNSELING AND TRAINING

The variety of approaches designed to help individuals examine their life plans in relation to the work place is the subject addressed in this area. Some of the many factors considered are personality and social style, employee development, and training. The process of how and when to counsel employees and what the counseling process should entail are also considered.

Brandt, J. D. Model for the delivery of career development programs by the college counseling center. *Journal of Counseling Psychology*, 1977, *24*, 494-502.

Brewer, J., Hanson, M., van Horn, R., & Moseley, K. A new dimension in employee development: A system for career planning and guidance. *Personnel Journal*, 1975, *54*(4), 228-231.

Buskirk, R. M. *Your career: How to plan it, manage it, change it*. Boston: Cahners Books International, 1976.

Crites, J. O. Career counseling: A comprehensive approach. *Journal of Counseling Psychology*, 1976, *6*(3), 2-12.

Dawis, R. V., & Lofquist, L. H. Personality style and the process of work adjustment. *Journal of Counseling Psychology*, 1976, *23*, 55-59.

Entine, A. D. Counseling for mid-life and beyond. *Vocational Guidance Quarterly*, 1977, *25*(4), 332-336.

Ginzburg, E. A critical look at career guidance. *Manpower*, 1972, *10*.

Hanson, M. C. Career development: Responsibilities of managers. *Personnel Journal*, 1977, *56*(9), 443-445.

Holland, J. L., & Gottfredson, G. C. Using a typology of persons and environments to explain careers: Some extensions and clarifications. *The Counseling Psychologist*, 1976, *6*, 20-29.

Lippitt, G. L. Developing life plans: A new concept and design for training and development. In W. L. French, C. H. Bell, & R. A. Zawacki (Eds.), *Organizational development: Theory, practice and research*. Dallas, TX: Business Publications, 1978.

Lorsh, J. W., & Barnes, L. B. (Eds.). *Managers and their careers: Cases and readings*. Homewood, IL: Richard D. Irwin, 1972.

Peters, H. J., & Hansen, J. C. *Vocational guidance and career development: Selected readings* (3rd ed.). New York: Macmillan, 1977.

Thoresen, C. E., & Ewart, C. K. Behavioral self control and career development. *The Counseling Psychologist*, 1976, *6*(3), 105-111.

Thornton, C. G., III. Differential effects of career planning on internals and externals. *Personnel Psychology*, 1978, *31*, 471-476.

Walter, V. Self-motivated personal career planning: A breakthrough in human resource management (Part I). *Personnel Journal*, 1976, 55(3), 112.

Walter, V. Self-motivated personal career planning: A breakthrough in human resource management (Part II). *Personnel Journal*, 1976, 55(4), 162-167.

Waters, E., & Goodman, J. Career counseling for adults: Why, when, where, how. *Vocational Guidance Quarterly*, 1977, 25(4), 337-343.

Yeager, J. C., & McMahon, J. Adult career planning: A needed solution. *Journal of College Placement*, 1974, 47.

MID-CAREER AND CAREER CHANGE

A large body of the career development literature concerns problems associated with both (a) the midpoint in one's chronological life span and (b) the midpoint in one's work experience. This area addresses life-planning questions: Do individuals attempt to achieve the same goals at different stages of their career? Has my career reached a plateau in terms of climbing the corporate ladder? Individuals at this stage in their careers also begin to question whether a shift in careers would be more rewarding or fruitful. These and other concerns have been placed under this category.

Anderson, S. D. Planning for career growth. *Personnel Journal*, 1973, 53(5), 358.

Bailyn, L. Involvement and accommodation in technical careers: An inquiry into the relation to work at mid-career. In J. Van Maanen (Ed.), *Organizational careers: Some new perspectives*. New York: John Wiley, 1977.

Chew, P. *The inner world of the middle aged man*. New York: Macmillan, 1976.

Cobb, S., Brooks, G. W., Kasl, S. V., & Connelly, W. E. The health of people changing jobs: A description of a longitudinal study. *American Journal of Public Health*, 1966, 59, 1476-1481.

Davitz, J., & Davitz, L. *Making it from 40 to 50*. New York: Random House, 1976.

Gottfredson, G. C. Career stability and redirection in adulthood. *Journal of Applied Psychology*, 1977, 62(4), 436-445.

Heald, J. E. Mid-life career influence. *Vocational Guidance Quarterly*, 1977, 25(4), 309-312.

LeShan, E. *The wonderful crisis of middleage*. New York: David McKay, 1972.

McCaffrey, J. P. Relationships between mid-life self-concept, achievement and career choice. *Dissertation Abstracts International*, 1976, 37(L-B), 1021.

McDaniels, C. Leisure and career development in mid-life: A rationale. *Vocational Guidance Quarterly*, 1977, 25(4), 344-350.

Morrison, R. F. Career adaptivity: The effective adaptation of managers to changing role demands. *Journal of Applied Psychology*, 1977, 62(5), 549-448.

Murphy, D. D., & Burch, M. O. Career development of men at mid-life. *Journal of Vocational Behavior*, 1976, 9, 337-343.

Rapoport, R. N. *Mid-career development*. London: Tavistock, 1970.

Robbins, P. I., Thomas, E. L., Harvey, D. W., & Kandefer, C. Career change and congruence of personality type: An examination of DOT derived work environment designations. *Journal of Vocational Behavior*, 1978, 13,15-25.

Schultz, D. Managing the middle-aged manager. *Personnel*, 1974, 51(6), 8-17.

Sheppard, H. L. The emerging pattern of second careers. *Vocational Guidance Quarterly*, 1971, 89.

Sofer, C. *Men in mid-career*. Cambridge, England: Cambridge University Press, 1970.

Super, D. E. Vocational maturity in mid-career. *Vocational Guidance Quarterly*, 1977, 25(4), 294-302.

Tausky, C., & Dubin, R. Career anchorage: Managerial mobility motivations. *American Sociological Review*, 1965, 30, 725-735.

Thomas, L. E. Mid-career changes: Self-selected or externally mandated? *Vocational Guidance Quarterly*, 1977, *25*(4), 320-328.

Wiener, Y., & Vaitenas, R. Personality correlates of voluntary mid-career change in enterprising occupations. *Journal of Applied Psychology*, 1977, *62*(6), 706-712.

WOMEN AND CAREER DEVELOPMENT

There is a rapidly developing literature that focuses directly on differences between men and women and their career development. In order to recognize this literature, a separate category has been allotted.

Crawford, J. D. Career development and career choice in pioneer and traditional women. *Journal of Vocational Behavior*, 1978, *12*(2), 129.

Douce, L. A. Career aspiration and career development of women in relation to Adventure Scale score of SCII. *Dissertation Abstracts International*, 1978, 38(10-B), 5091.

Osipan, S. H. (Ed.). *Emerging women: Career analysis and outlooks*. Columbus, OH: Charles E. Merrill, 1975.

Sedney, M. A., & Turner, B. E. A test of causal sequences in two models for development of career orientation in women. *Journal of Vocational Behavior*, 1975, *6*, 281-292.

FAMILY INFLUENCE AND THE NONWORK ENVIRONMENT

Far too often the work place is considered in isolation from other important aspects of an individual's life. For instance, the pursuit of a career is often directly related to family and nonwork influences. At times, the values and pursuits of the work place may be perceived as antagonistic to some of the other aspects of an individual's life. These influences and their integration with the work environment are discussed in this category.

Bailyn, L. Life/career considerations as indicators of quality of employment. In A. D. Biderman and T. F. Drury (Eds.),*Measuring work quality for social reporting*. New York: John Wiley (Sage Publications), 1976.

Bailyn, L. Career and family orientations of husbands and wives in relation to marital happiness. *Human Relations*, 1970, *23*, 97-113.

Dubin, R., & Chanpoux, J. E. Central life interests and job satisfaction. *Organizational Behavior and Human Performance*, 1977, *18*(2), 366-377.

Fogarty, M. P., Rapoport, R., & Rapoport, R. N. *Sex, career and family*. Beverly Hills, CA: Sage, 1971.

Fowlkes, M. R. The wives of professional men: A study of the interdependence of family and careers. *Dissertation Abstracts International*, 38(4-A), 2351.

Kanter, R. M. *Work and family in the United States*. New York: Russell Sage, 1977.

Meissner, M. The long arm of the job: A study of work and leisure. *Industrial Relations*, 1971, *10*, 259-260.

Rapoport, R., & Rapoport, R. N. *Dual career families re-examined*. New York: Harper & Row, 1976.

Slaughter, E. A. Family environment, personality and vocational behavior: A test of Holland's theory. *Dissertation Abstracts International*, 1975, 39(5-B), 2524.

LIFE/CAREER PLANNING: INSTRUMENTS AND DIAGNOSTIC KITS

Many methods have been developed to aid the individual in planning where and how to achieve an integration of life and work goals. These instruments help the individual to examine the factors associated with the integration of the work and nonwork environments.

Bolles, R. N. *What color is your parachute*. Berkeley, CA: Ten Speed Press, 1972.

Crystal, J. C., & Bolles, R. N. *Where do I go from there with my life*. New York: Seabury Press, 1974.

Ford, G. A., & Lippitt, G. L. *Planning your future: A workbook for personal goal setting.* San Diego, CA: University Associates, 1976.

Kirn, A. G. *Lifework planning.* Hartford, CN: Arthur G. Kirn & Associates, 1974.

Knowles, M. S. *Self-directed learning.* New York: Association Press, 1975.

Miller, D. B. *Personal vitality workbook.* Reading, MA: Addison Wesley, 1977.

Pearse, R. F., & Palzer, B. P. *Self-directed change for the mid-career manager.* New York: AMACON, 1975.

Shepard, H. S., & Hawley, J. S. *Life planning: Personal and organizational.* Washington, DC: National Training and Development Service, 1974.

Storey, W. D. *Career dimensions.* Crotonville-on-Hudson, NY: General Electric, 1976.

Van Horn, L. F. *Personality and planning: The impact of life planning on personal planning orientations.* Unpublished doctoral dissertation, Case Western Reserve University, 1972.

Howard L. Fromkin, Ph.D. is a professor of psychology at York University and president of Organizational Consultants International Inc., Toronto, Ontario, Canada. Previously professor and chairman of the Department of Administrative Sciences at Purdue University's Krannert School of Management, Dr. Fromkin has co-authored four books and more than forty professional articles. He has consulted internationally with a variety of public and private organizations. His major interests are organizational effectiveness, assessment and diagnosis, consultation processes, and conflict and conflict management.

James D. McDonald is an associate consultant with Youtec Consulting, Toronto, Ontario, Canada. He is currently completing graduate studies at York University, Downsview, Ontario. Mr. McDonald's background is in cognitive processes, organization development, and program evaluation. His consulting interests include management and information systems development, needs assessment and systems and program evaluation.

CONTRIBUTORS

Anthony G. Banet, Jr., Ph.D.
5489 Barkla
San Diego, California 92122
(714) 452-9693

Rosemary A. Bova
Equitable Life Assurance Society
1285 Avenue of the Americas
New York, New York 10019
(212) 554-3836

W. Warner Burke, Ph.D.
Professor of Psychology and Education
Department of Psychology
Teachers College
Columbia University
New York, New York 10027
(212) 678-3249

Tom Carney, Ph.D.
Professor of Organizational Communications
Department of Communication Studies
University of Windsor
Windsor, Ontario N9A 3P4
Canada
(519) 253-4232

David W. Champagne, Ed.D.
Associate Professor of Curriculum
  and Supervision
School of Education
Room 5P 37 F.Q.
University of Pittsburgh
Pittsburgh, Pennsylvania 15260
(412) 624-1390

Phyliss Cooke, Ph.D.
Director of Professional Services
University Associates
8517 Production Avenue
San Diego, California 92121
(714) 578-5900

Jeanne Bosson Driscoll
Independent Consultant
24 Lee Terrace
Williamstown, Massachusetts 02167
(413) 458-9087

Leigh C. Earley
Pastor
First Christian Church
305 N. Fifth Street
Vandalia, Illinois 62471
(618) 283-2001

Art Freedman, Ph.D.
Director
Stress Management Institute
2319 N. Halsted Street
Chicago, Illinois 60614
(312) 525-8283

Howard L. Fromkin, Ph.D.
President
Organizational Consultants International Inc.
70 Shaftesbury Avenue, Suite 6
Toronto, Ontario M4T 1A3
Canada
(416) 960-0801

Jerry L. Fryrear, Ph.D.
Associate Professor of Psychology
Behavioral Sciences Department
School of Human Sciences and Humanities
University of Houston
Clear Lake City
2700 Bay Area Boulevard
Houston, Texas 77058
(713) 488-7170

Beverly Byrum-Gaw, Ph.D.
Associate Professor of Communication
Wright State University
Colonel Glenn Highway
Dayton, Ohio 45431
(513) 873-2145

Leonard D. Goodstein, Ph.D.
President
University Associates
8517 Production Avenue
San Diego, California 92121
(714) 578-5900

Richard L. Greenblatt
Graduate Student
Department of Psychology
University of Illinois at Chicago Circle
Box 4348
Chicago, Illinois 60680
(312) 996-2540

Allen K. Gulezian, Ph.D.
Professor of Business Administration
Department of Business Administration
School of Business and Economics
Central Washington University
Ellensburg, Washington 98926
(509) 963-3560 or
(509) 963-3339

Annette A. Hartenstein
Associate Director
Supervisory and Special Emphasis Programs
U.S. Government Office of
    Personnel Management
2844 Wisconsin Avenue, N.W.
Washington, D.C. 20044
(202) 632-5671

Barron H. Harvey, Ph.D.
Assistant Professor of Organizational
    Behavior and Accounting
School of Business Administration
Georgetown University
36th & N Streets, N.W.
Washington, D.C. 20057
(207) 625-4721

William J. Heisler, Ph.D.
Director, M.B.A. Executive Program/Associate
    Professor of Management
Babcock Graduate School of Management
Wake Forest University
Winston-Salem, North Carolina 27109
(919) 761-5416

R. Craig Hogan, Ph.D.
Assistant Professor/Curriculum Specialist
Department of Health Sciences Education
University of Health Sciences
Chicago Medical School
2020 West Ogden Avenue
Chicago, Illinois 60612
(312) 942-2840

Frank Pierce Johnson
Assistant Clinical Professor
Institute of Psychiatry and Human Behavior
Medical School
University of Maryland
Counseling Center
College Park, Maryland 20742
(301) 454-2931 or
(301) 528-6637

John E. Jones, Ph.D.
Senior Vice President, Research and
    Development
University Associates
8517 Production Avenue
San Diego, California 92121
(714) 578-5900

H. B. Karp, Ph.D.
Associate Professor of Management
Department of Management
Old Dominion University
1441 Magnolia Avenue
Norfolk, Virginia 23508
(804) 489-2586

Colleen Kelley
Human Relations Consultant
2500 Torrey Pines Road
La Jolla, California 92037
(714) 453-8165

Christopher B. Keys, Ph.D.
Associate Professor
Department of Psychology
University of Illinois at Chicago Circle
Box 4348
Chicago, Illinois 60680
(312) 996-3031

V. C. League
Director
Region 8 Training and Development Center
P.O. Box 9997, Mills College Station
Oakland, California 94613
(415) 632-3775

Diane L. Lockwood
Management Consultant/Senior Associate
Nielsen & Associates, Inc.
6310 Meeker Circle
Lincoln, Nebraska 68506
(402) 488-7162 or
(402) 489-3545

Fred Luthans, Ph.D.
Regents Professor of Management
Department of Management
University of Nebraska
Lincoln, Nebraska 68588
(402) 472-2324 or
(402) 472-3915

James D. McDonald
Associate Consultant
Youtec Consulting
20 Spadina Road
Toronto, Ontario M5R 2S7
Canada
(416) 967-9475

Udai Pareek, Ph.D.
Larsen & Toubro Professor of Organizational
  Behavior
Indian Institute of Management
Ahmedabad 380015
Gujarat
India
(307) 450041

Richard Parker
Associate Director
Supervisory and Special Emphasis Programs
U.S. Government Office of
  Personnel Management
2844 Wisconsin Avenue, N.W.
Washington, D.C. 20044
(703) 379-9817

Robert C. Preziosi, D.P.A.
Director of Personnel and Professional
  Development
Catholic Service Bureau, Inc.
4949 N.E. Second Avenue
Miami, Florida 33137
(305) 754-2444

T. Venkateswara Rao
Associate Professor of Organizational Behavior
Indian Institute of Management (IIM)
Vastrapur, Ahmedabad 380015
Gujarat
India

Robert W. Rasberry, Ph.D.
Assistant Professor of Organizational
  Behavior and Administration
Cox School of Business
Southern Methodist University
Dallas, Texas 75275
(214) 692-3000

Pearl B. Rutledge, Ph.D.
Director
R & R Human Resource Development
3232 Cornwall Drive
Lexington, Kentucky 40503
(606) 276-4544

Suresh M. Sant
Faculty Member
State Bank of India
State Bank Staff College
6-3-1188
Begumpet Road
Hyderabad
Andhra Pradesh 500 016
India

Marshall Sashkin, Ph.D.
Professor of Industrial
  and Organizational Psychology
Graduate Program
University College
University of Maryland
College Park, Maryland 20742
(301) 454-4931

John J. Scherer
Associate Director
Graduate Center for Applied Studies
Whitworth College
Spokane, Washington 99251
(509) 466-3283

Karl A. Seger
President
Corporate Consultants
4424 Sutherland
Knoxville, Tennessee 37919
(615) 588-7957

Robert W. Shively, Ph.D.
Associate Professor of Management
Babcock Graduate School of Management
Wake Forest University
Box 7659 Reynolda Station
Winston-Salem, North Carolina 27109
(919) 761-5413

Donald T. Simpson
Senior Educational Specialist
Management and General Education
Corporate Relations
Eastman Kodak Company
343 State Street
Rochester, New York 14650
(716) 724-2662

Julian J. Szucko
Graduate Student
Department of Psychology
University of Illinois at Chicago Circle
Box 4348
Chicago, Illinois 60680
(312) 739-3150

Karen Sue Trisko
Director
Division of Professional Development
American Dental Hygienists' Association
444 N. Michigan Avenue, Suite 3400
Chicago, Illinois 60611
(312) 440-8900

John F. Veiga, D.B.A.
Associate Professor of Organizational Behavior
Management and Administrative Sciences
 Department
School of Business Administration
University of Connecticut
Box U-41 MA
Storrs, Connecticut 06268
 (203) 486-3638

John N. Yanouzas, Ph.D.
Professor and Head
Management and Administrative Sciences
 Department
School of Business Administration
University of Connecticut
Box U-41 MA
Storrs, Connecticut 06268
 (203) 486-3734

University Associates